Resettlers and Survivors

Worlds of Memory

Editors:
Jeffrey Olick, University of Virginia
Aline Sierp, Maastricht University
Jenny Wüstenberg, Nottingham Trent University

Published in collaboration with the Memory Studies Association

This book series publishes innovative and rigorous scholarship in the interdisciplinary and global field of memory studies. Memory studies includes all inquiries into the ways we – both individually and collectively – are shaped by the past. How do we represent the past to ourselves and to others? How do those representations shape our actions and understandings, whether explicitly or unconsciously? The 'memory' we study encompasses the near-infinitude of practices and processes humans use to engage with the past, the incredible variety of representations they produce and the range of individuals and institutions involved in doing so.

Guided by the mandate of the Memory Studies Association to provide a forum for conversations among subfields, regions and research traditions, *Worlds of Memory* focuses on cutting-edge research that pushes the boundaries of the field and can provide insights for memory scholars outside of a particular specialization. In the process, it seeks to make memory studies more accessible, diverse and open to novel approaches.

Volume 3
Resettlers and Survivors
Bukovina and the Politics of Belonging in West Germany and Israel, 1945–1989
Gaëlle Fisher

Volume 2
Velvet Retro
Postsocialist Nostalgia and the Politics of Heroism in Czech Popular Culture
Veronika Pehe

Volume 1
When Will We Talk about Hitler?
German Students and the Nazi Past
Alexandra Oeser

RESETTLERS AND SURVIVORS

Bukovina and the Politics of Belonging in West Germany and Israel, 1945–1989

Gaëlle Fisher

berghahn
NEW YORK • OXFORD
www.berghahnbooks.com

First published in 2020 by
Berghahn Books
www.berghahnbooks.com

© 2020, 2026 Gaëlle Fisher
First paperback edition published in 2026

All rights reserved. Except for the quotation of short passages
for the purposes of criticism and review, no part of this book
may be reproduced in any form or by any means, electronic or
mechanical, including photocopying, recording, or any information
storage and retrieval system now known or to be invented,
without written permission of the publisher.

Library of Congress Cataloging-in-Publication Data
A C.I.P. cataloging record is available from the Library of Congress
Library of Congress Cataloging in Publication Control Number: 2019057668

British Library Cataloguing in Publication Data
A catalogue record for this book is available from the British Library

EU GPSR Authorized Representative
LOGOS EUROPE, 9 rue Nicolas Poussin, 17000, LA ROCHELLE, France
Email: Contact@logoseurope.eu

ISBN 978-1-78920-667-8 hardback
ISBN 978-1-83695-399-9 paperback
ISBN 978-1-80758-484-9 epub
ISBN 978-1-78920-668-5 web pdf

https://doi.org/10.3167/9781789206678

To my family

Contents

Acknowledgements   viii

Introduction   1

Part I. Backgrounds

Chapter 1. Being Bukovinian before 1945: German and Jewish Bukovinians in the Habsburg Empire, Romania and the Second World War   31

Part II. Establishments

Chapter 2. 'Settling in the Motherland': 'Resettlers' from Bukovina in West Germany after the Second World War   61

Chapter 3. 'A Remarkable Branch of the Jewish People': Survivors from Bukovina between Romania and Israel after the Second World War   109

Part III. Entanglements

Chapter 4. 'Lost Home' and 'Area of Expulsion': Compensating for Loss at the Height of the Cold War   155

Chapter 5. 'Sunken Cultural Landscape': Reimagining Bukovina through the Lens of Literature   202

Conclusion   248

Bibliography   263
Index   285

Acknowledgements

As scholars often emphasize, it is impossible to research, write and publish such a book without receiving support, assistance and guidance of many kinds and from many different sides, be it from colleagues, friends, family or institutions. This project is the outcome of a ten-year journey that took me from London to Bavaria, via Israel, Romania and Ukraine. Along the way, I unavoidably and very fortunately became indebted to many people and organizations. It is my great pleasure to now be able to thank them. While any mistakes or misinterpretations within this text remain very much my own, these individuals and institutions have been instrumental in enabling the book's making and in shaping the end result.

I started working on this topic during my time at University College London. This research was generously funded by the Arts and Humanities Research Council as part of the larger collaborative project 'Reverberations of War in Germany and Europe', which ran from 2010 to 2014 at UCL. In this context, I had the honour and fortune of being supervised by two incredibly supportive, insightful and inspirational scholars, Mary Fulbrook and Wendy Bracewell. As those who believed in and accompanied this book from the outset and who, throughout the years, have continued to offer me both challenging comments and unwavering support, I owe them my first and most sincere thank you. I am also grateful for the lively discussions and stimulating teamwork with UCL colleagues on the team, Stephanie Bird, Alexandra Hills, Julia Wagner and Christiane Wienand, and for the expertise of many other exceptional colleagues at UCL's German Department and School of Slavonic and Eastern European Studies. I extend my heartfelt thanks to Michael Berkowitz who introduced me, when I was still a young doctoral student, to the world of Holocaust Studies and Jewish history and conveyed his passion for research. Finally, I am enormously grateful to Bill Niven and François Guesnet, who engaged with my work carefully and critically, and gave me essential feedback and encouragement as I set out to write this book.

Over the years, this book benefited from the exchange of ideas with many other scholars who shared with me their expert knowledge about Bukovina and the wider region. I would like to express my deep appreciation for helpful exchanges and conversations with Mathias Beer, Andrei Corbea-Hoișie, Dennis Deletant, Mariana Hausleitner, Rebecca Haynes and Florence Heymann. I am also thankful for the many opportunities to present and publish aspects of my work at a range of workshops, conferences and summer schools and in books and journals. For the feedback I received in these contexts, I would like to thank, among others, Neil Gregor, Atina Grossmann, Florian Kührer-Wielach, Guy Miron, Miriam Rürup, David Rechter, Hans Werner Retterath, Stefanie Schüler-Springorum, Nick Stargardt, Ruth Wittlinger and Mirjam Zadoff. I am also thankful for having been able, over the years, to discuss aspects of my work and seek advice, intellectual inspiration and motivation from various friends and colleagues. These include Niklas Bernsand, Tul'si Bhambri, Tom Booth, Dan Brett, Raul Cârstocea, Cristian Cercel, Simon Coll, Dana Dolghin, Alex Drace-Francis, Anca Filipovici, Clara Frysztacka, Nathan Friedenberg, James Koranyi, Karolina Koziura, Irina Marin, Dana Mihăilescu, Raluca Mușat, Stefanie Rausch, Tiia Sahrakorpi and Alexandra Urdea.

Additionally, over the course of my research, I was warmly welcomed by a number of institutions and archives and was offered invaluable expert guidance by their staff. I would particularly like to thank Elisabeth Fendl of the Institut für Volkskunde der Deutschen des östlichen Europa in Freiburg; Otto Hallabrin, Sara Klein and Carola Neidhart of the Bukovina-Institute at the University of Augsburg; Gerald Volkmer of the Institut für deutsche Kultur und Geschichte Südosteuropas in Munich; and Olivier Tourny of Le Centre de recherche français à Jérusalem for either funding or facilitating longer visits to their institutions. The staff of the Bundesarchiv in Bayreuth and the Stadtarchiv in Darmstadt were especially helpful, as were Eugenia Oprescu of the National Museum of Romanian Literature in Bucharest and Adrian Cioflânca and Natalia Lazăr of the Centre for the Study of the History of the Jews in Romania in Bucharest. Luzian Geier, editor of *Der Südostdeutsche* in Augsburg, and Bärbel Rabi, editor of *Die Stimme* in Tel Aviv, deserve a special mention for helping me find interview subjects. I am immensely grateful to those who assisted me in my research by welcoming me into their homes, showing me around their areas and sharing with me personal documents and parts of their lives. These included Hedwig Brenner in Haifa, Gaby Coldewey in Berlin, Corina Derla in Suceava, Eduard Mohr in Rădăuți, Paul Pivtorak in Chernivtsi, Arthur Rindner in Tel Aviv, Erhard Wiehn in Konstanz, Edgar Hauster and many more 'Bukovinians' in Romania, Germany, Austria and Israel who agreed to tell me their stories and brought my research to life. I am grateful for the research and travel funding I received from the British Council in Romania in 2011 and on several occasions from the UCL Graduate School between 2012 and 2013.

Completing this research was only the first half of the journey I embarked on with this book project. As a postdoctoral fellow at the University of Augsburg in 2015–16, I was able to fill gaps in my investigation by drawing on the recently reorganized library and archive of the Bukovina-Institute and a few additional archives, not least thanks to a research travel grant from the BAYHOST programme of the University of Regensburg. I am thankful to Marita Krauss for this opportunity and many other people at the University of Augsburg for their insights and friendship as I started rethinking and reworking my dissertation. Oskar Czendze, Martina Egger, Vincent Hoyer, Katarzyna Madalska, Maria Christina Müller, Daniel Norden and Alexander Weidle deserve a special mention. My biggest thanks goes to Maren Röger for her unique collegiality, critical and constructive comments on my work and much-valued friendship both during my time in Augsburg and since then. This book would not look the same without her input. In the final phase of the manuscript's transformation, as a postdoctoral researcher at the Center for Holocaust Studies at the Institute for Contemporary History in Munich, I have benefited from an exceptional intellectual and academic environment for my writing and I am hugely grateful to colleagues there too for their support and friendship. I would especially like to thank Frank Bajohr, Giles Bennett, Konstantin Eder, Andrea Löw, Caroline Mezger, Christian Schmittwilken, Anna-Raphaela Schmitz, Kerstin Schwenke, Anna Ullrich and Kim Wünschmann. Prepublication, I benefited from further essential feedback and advice. I wish to thank Heidi Samuelson for her careful and thoughtful proofreading, the anonymous peer reviewers for their perceptive comments, Chris Chappell and Mykelin Higham at Berghahn Books for taking on and overseeing this project, and the Worlds of Memory series editors for including this book.

Last but by no means least, the last few years would not have been the same without my friends and family. In particular, I wish to thank Angi S., Anna G., Andrada M., Aurelie R., Barbro E., Emilie B., Issy S., Karine F., Lone L., Marie L., Michael R-V., Rhys L., Vanessa B., Vijay P. and Wolfgang M. for both reminding me that there is more to life and showing continued interest in what I was doing. The same and more applies to my family. They have been exceptionally loving, caring and patient and have supported me in innumerable ways. David, Christine, Christopher, Dad and Mum, I cannot thank you enough. Finally, for helping me see this project through to the end with invaluable attention, understanding and humour, Christian, *merci de tout mon cœur*.

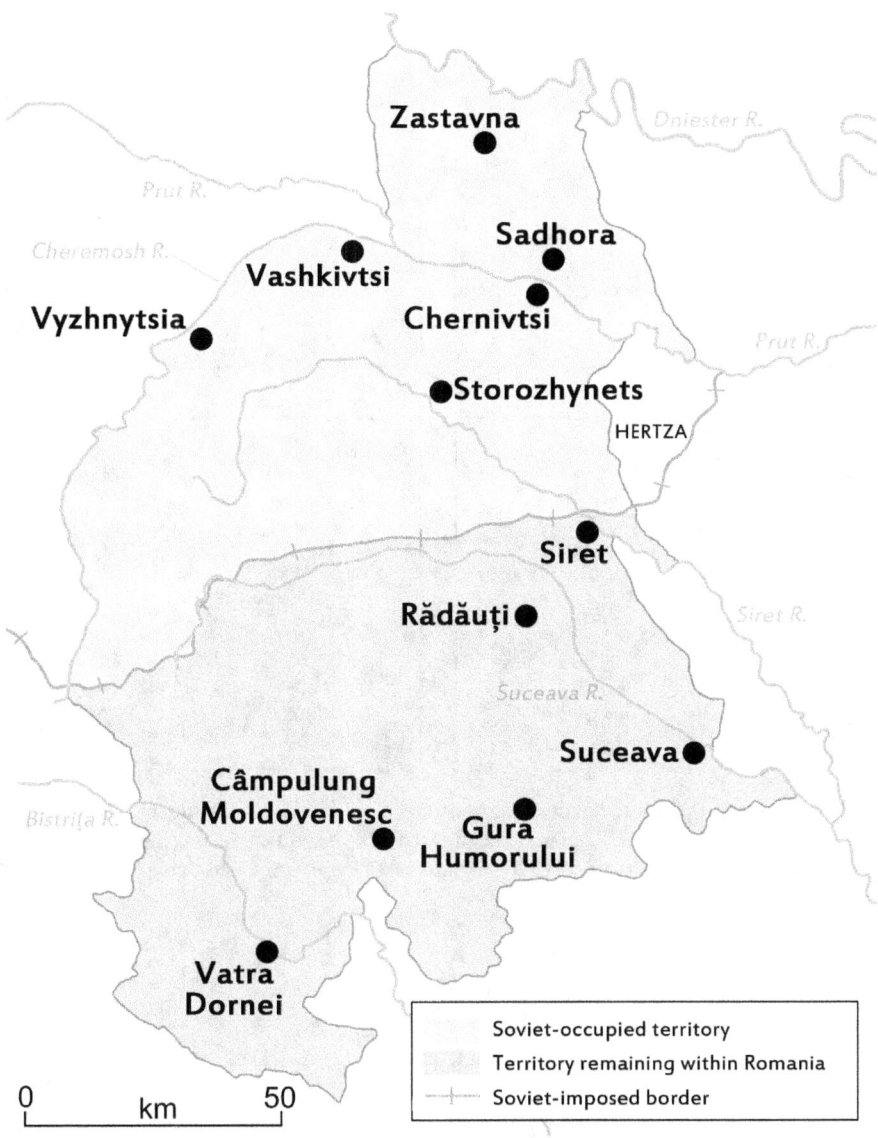

Bukovina in June 1940. Adapted from a public-domain map created by Wikimedia user Andrein.

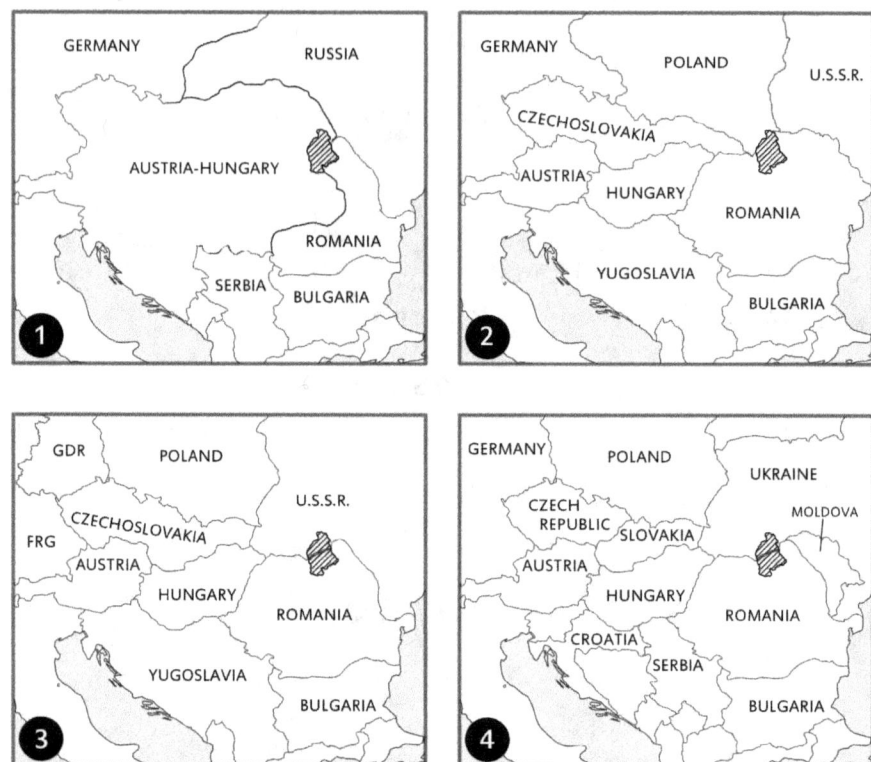

Bukovina (shaded) since the eighteenth century: 1. within Austria-Hungary (1774–1918); 2. as part of Romania (1918–40 and 1941–44); 3. divided between Romania and the Soviet Union (1940–41 and 1944–91); 4. divided between Romania and Ukraine (since 1991).

Introduction

In late 1950, the Israeli historian and politician Manfred Reifer sent a copy of his latest book to the Austrian writer and poet Georg Drozdowski. The volume was a biography of the Zionist politician Mayer Ebner, published in German in Tel Aviv in 1947. At the time, Ebner and Reifer were both living in Israel, whereas Drozdowski was living in Austria. However, all three men had been born in Habsburg Bukovina, once the easternmost province of the Austrian half of the Habsburg Empire. All of them were native Bukovinians.

The thank-you letter Drozdowski sent in response a few days later read as follows:

> I don't quite know how to express my joy. With your letter and your gift, you not only sent me a greeting from our common homeland, you also made clear to me that you include me among the Germans, who can think of themselves as free of any guilt! ... We share something dear despite the distance: our old, beloved Bukovina that lives on in our memory even if we now have a different fatherland.[1]

Reifer, too, was quick to respond. On 27 November 1950, he wrote:

> Your letter was a source of great joy. A voice from the old *Heimat*. A resonant one, similar to the pretty trill of the nightingale. What images this brought to my mind! Towns, villages, mountains, valleys, forests of our Bukovina.

I saw them like in a photograph. And the people! How close we were to them in this El Dorado of the old monarchy. They came closer again, 'these ghostly figures'.[2]

Reifer ended his letter with a reference to life in Israel: 'From the literary perspective, our world here is rather narrow – for writers of German in particular.' He then concluded with a somewhat elusive and philosophical remark: 'everyone would like to live in the free world. But does it exist?'[3]

There is much to unpack in both of these quotes and letters. Reifer's last sentence can seem rather astonishing on behalf of someone who was a well-known Zionist. As for Drozdowski, his self-description as 'a German' and 'free of any guilt' points to both his continued mode of identification as German in the Republic of Austria after the Second World War and the symbolic significance of his Jewish colleague's gesture and gift. However, what is also interesting to know about this exchange is that Drozdowski and Reifer had never even met. Indeed, although they were both born in Austrian Czernowitz and had both lived in what had become Romanian Cernăuți between the two World Wars, the events surrounding the Second World War and the Holocaust had effectively set them on completely different paths. In a way, Drozdowski and Reifer embodied two radically distinct sets of twentieth-century 'Bukovinian' experiences.

Drozdowski, regarded as an 'ethnic German' (*Volksdeutscher*), had been evacuated from the region during the National Socialist mass transfers of Germans abroad known as 'the resettlement home to the Reich' (*die Umsiedlung heim ins Reich*). Drozdowski thus left Bukovina for Germany in the autumn of 1940, as had the vast majority of Bukovina's self-declared ethnic Germans – some 95,000 people – representing, at the time, around 10% of Bukovina's population. Having been granted German citizenship, he was then 'resettled', like many of his fellow German Bukovinians, in newly conquered territories in Eastern Europe. In 1941, he even obtained a job within the German administration in the city of Łódź (then Litzmannstadt). However, declared 'politically unreliable' after the discovery of his earlier marriage to a 'half-Jewish' woman, he was subsequently dismissed and relocated to Vienna. Conscripted into the Wehrmacht in 1943 and deployed in Croatia, he ended up, as the war concluded, in Austrian Carinthia, where he later chose to remain.[4]

Reifer, in turn, identified as a Jew, narrowly survived different waves of anti-Jewish violence and ethnic and political persecution in Bukovina's capital, Cernăuți, during the war. These waves included: the Soviet arrests and deportations to Siberia from northern Bukovina during the Soviet occupation in 1940–41; Romanian and German-instigated pogroms and mass shootings in Cernăuți and the surrounding towns and villages in the summer of

1941; the short-lived German presence in the city following the German attack on the Soviet Union; and, last but not least, the ghettoization and later deportation of the region's Jews to ghettos and camps in Transnistria by the Romanian authorities in 1941 and 1942. These were all events in which thousands of Bukovinian Jews lost their lives; around two-thirds of the 120,000-strong prewar Jewish population of Bukovina did not survive the war and the Holocaust. However, in late 1943, Reifer managed to escape his native region and make his way to Mandatory Palestine, where he arrived in April 1944.[5]

To an extent, Drozdowski's and Reifer's experiences during and in the immediate aftermath of the Second World War mirrored those of their respective postwar communities of 'Bukovinians' – those who, in the ensuing decades, came to think of themselves and be known as 'Bukovina Germans' and 'Bukovina Jews'.[6] But their trajectories are also representative of the experiences of millions of other displaced non-Jewish Germans and Jewish survivors after the Second World War. The estimated 80,000 Bukovinian 'resettlers' who ended up as refugees on the reduced territory of what would become West Germany, East Germany and the Republic of Austria joined the ranks of approximately twelve million Germans who lost their homelands as a result of the Second World War. In turn, unwilling or unable to return to their homes, most of the 50,000 Jewish survivors from Bukovina left the area and went to Israel as soon as they could, as did an estimated one million other survivors of the Holocaust in the first decade after the war.

Reifer and Drozdowski's exchange in 1950 was therefore symptomatic of the broader postwar situation. Their interaction captures key aspects of the relationship between German and Jewish Bukovinians – as well as among many non-Jewish Germans and Jews in general – after the war and the Holocaust. These aspects include both numerous parallels and undeniable commonalities but also a fundamental kind of distance and associated tensions and inhibitions. Bukovinian Germans' experiences and identification as 'resettlers' and Bukovinian Jews' as 'survivors' reinforced the sense that these were two completely separate groups. During the war, the fact that Germans and Jews from Bukovina had once shared a homeland and a language had meant very little. In hindsight, it seemed that what held them apart, and not what united them, was what had mattered. This distinction had been paramount in determining their diverging options and treatment, often even signifying the difference between life and death. This was why, within just a few years, and from the perspective of their new postwar homes – in what Drozdowski called their 'different fatherlands' – this link to the region and to each other seemed extremely special. Not only had Bukovinian Germans and Bukovinian Jews belonged to two different communities of experience during the Second World War, but, as a result, they belonged to two very different postwar communities of identification too.

Though such an instance of direct and friendly contact between a Bukovinian German and a Bukovinian Jew during the early Cold War was quite rare, focusing in on the protagonists of this encounter and considering its wider circumstances can shed important light on the nexus between Bukovina and German and Jewish politics of belonging after the Second World War. First, both Reifer and Drozdowski were prominent postwar Bukovinian figures in their respective countries and leading members of their respective Bukovinian 'homeland societies', the so-called Bukovinian Landsmannschaften, established after the war in West Germany and Israel. These men and these institutions, founded with the official aims of keeping the memory of the region and its inhabitants alive in the postwar period, helped the members grapple with and overcome their experiences of loss, suffering and displacement. Their exchange thus testifies to the fact that although Bukovina no longer featured as a geopolitical entity on the map of Europe, it remained an important point of reference for the identities of many displaced Bukovinians in their new, putatively national homes.

Second, this episode shows that while Bukovina Germans and Bukovina Jews commemorated their specific group experiences and primarily defended their distinctive rights and versions of the past in distinct national arenas and ethnic terms, they were always aware of each other and always defining themselves with other stakeholders of the region's history and identity in mind. This was especially true as German and Jewish Bukovinians shared not only a homeland but also a language, German, and a connection to many of the same people, places, events and even institutions.

Finally, yet importantly, as this example shows, identifying with Bukovina as a *Heimat* – as a home or a homeland – after the Second World War was not merely about the past, or even in spite of the past; it was very much about the present and thereby a source of something new. After 1945, particularly from the perspective of 'the West', the region was perceived as 'lost', 'sunken', 'submerged' or having 'vanished'. In hindsight, after the war and the Holocaust, the relatively peaceful multiethnic society of prewar Romanian Bukovina, and its earlier Habsburg incarnation, seemed all the more exceptional. As a result, Bukovina became a privileged screen for the projection of different, changing and idealized conceptions of Germanness, Jewishness and even Europeanness.

With this in mind, the exchange raises a range of further questions. What did it mean to identify as Bukovinian after the Second World War from the perspective of different postwar contexts? Bukovinians like Drozdowski and Reifer did not simply become Israelis, Austrians or West Germans; they also identified or came to be recognized as 'refugees', 'newcomers' and 'new migrants', as well as 'expellees of the homeland' (*Heimatvertriebene*) and 'survivors of the Holocaust' (first as *She'erit Hapletah*, 'the surviving remnant' and later as 'Holocaust survivors'). How did these different labels and their diverse connotations function and fit together? How did they relate to their specific backgrounds and experiences as Germans, as Jews and as Bukovinians? In other words, how did Bukovinians, as 'coethnics' and 'national refugees', negotiate between notions of similarity and difference; prewar, wartime and postwar modes of identification; experiences of displacement and violence and claims to emplacement and belonging, and ultimately contribute to shaping postwar societies in which they lived?

(Re)Framing the 'Bukovina Myth'

The historical region of Bukovina and especially its capital – Austrian Czernowitz, Romanian Cernăuți, Soviet Chernovtsy and Ukrainian Chernivtsi – are often said to have been the object of mythification and myth.[7] This has been captured in the use of different names and spellings of the region and the city, reflecting both different uses of language and the – often anachronistic but also intentional – emphasis placed on specific periods in their history. What is more, the phenomenon has also been reflected in the use of a series of comparisons, nicknames and metaphors, all offering different takes on the region's exceptional character. Indeed, the associations with Bukovina as a historical space and the region's associated mental maps have been not only remarkably numerous and diverse but also often competing and even conflicting.

Once the easternmost area of the Austrian half of the Dual Monarchy, the Habsburg region, has, for instance, often been compared to 'a small Austria', with the capital city accordingly dubbed as 'little Vienna' (*klein Wien*) and its inhabitants, following a German play on words, as 'Buko-Viennese' (*Buko-Wiener*). However, as the most ethnically diverse and also the 'most Jewish' of the empire's regions, Habsburg Bukovina has also been described as 'a miniature Switzerland', Czernowitz as 'Jerusalem on the Prut River' and the region's inhabitants as a 'motley group'. Indeed, many memoirists have suggested that Habsburg Bukovina was cosmopolitan and profoundly European – 'the West in the East'. Yet, for many contemporaries, it was, rather, 'the East in the West' – an exotic crossroads and meeting point of religions, peoples and cultures, 'an Austrian backwater' or even a Habsburg 'penal colony', home to a 'sanguine bunch'.[8] Similarly, while some have construed it as primarily part of a formerly German-dominated *Mitteleuropa* (Central Europe) and others see it as part of a lost Yiddishland, for most Ukrainians and Romanians, Bukovina, as the home to eminently national monuments, rulers or heroes, belongs decisively and more or less exclusively to the cradle of *their* nation.[9]

Famous literary and artistic portrayals of Bukovina have been equally contentious and fraught. The region has, for instance, often – though mistakenly – been included in the wider area that the native Galician writer Karl Emil Franzos designated as 'semi-Asia' (*Halb-Asien*).[10] By caricaturing it as 'Maghrebinia' (*Maghrebinien*), the writer Gregor von Rezzori also emphasized supposed 'oriental' traits and features, implying that the region was backward and chaotic.[11] In contrast, the region's two most prominent postwar figures, Rose Ausländer and Paul Celan, nostalgically depicted Czernowitz and Bukovina retrospectively as 'a submerged cultural metropolis' (*untergegangene Kulturmetropole*) and a region 'once populated by people and books' (*wo Menschen und Bücher lebten*).[12] They therefore brought forth an idealized vision of harmony and framed the area in the interwar period as a centre of European and German high culture. This vision resonated with many displaced Bukovinians long after the end of the Second World War but largely overlooked Romanian or Ukrainian presence, influence and even sovereignty in the region. Today, such exclusive and romanticized stereotypes and timeless images are subject to scepticism. Bukovina has been cast as the 'archetypal borderland' belonging to the 'shatterzones of empires' or even to the 'bloodlands'; for many, it represents an ultimate example of multiethnic or 'intermixed' Central Europe, which was 'pulverised' by the events of the first half of the twentieth century – the epitome of a ruthlessly destroyed Central European 'vanished world'.[13]

Upon closer consideration, it appears that the 'Bukovina myth' has many different strands and two main dimensions. On the one hand, the region is associated with harmonious ethnic diversity and the notion of peaceful coexistence, linked to Austrian rule and the German-Jewish symbiosis especially. From this perspective, the Bukovina myth might be understood as a regional variation on the nostalgic 'Habsburg myth' identified by the Italian scholar Claudio Magris.[14] Yet, on the other hand, the different understandings of Bukovina suggest that what is exceptional in this case is not so much the memory of harmony – 'unity in diversity' – as the degree of dispute over the place. What is striking is the number of claims made on the region and its people, and the consecutive and brutal political shifts and upheavals the territory and its inhabitants experienced as a consequence. Indeed, flourishing retrospectively after the Second World War, the Bukovina myth draws as much attention to the region's former diversity as it does to its disappearance and destruction. This is all the clearer as the region's unlikely yet remarkable 'afterlife' during and after the Cold War was mainly thanks to German-speaking Jews, who were also survivors of the Holocaust. In a sense, then, the Bukovina myth is characterized by a tension between the paradigm of ethnic diversity and that of 'ethnic unmixing' – plurality and its violent dissolution through war, genocide and policies of ethnic homogenization. From this perspective, rather than resembling the Habsburg myth, the Bukovina myth appears to have more in common with the ambivalent 'myth of Central Europe' (*Mitteleuropa*), which has been discussed by Jacques Le Rider, among others.[15]

The issue of how to explain, disentangle and eventually reconcile these two constitutive yet seemingly incompatible aspects of the Bukovina myth has been the central intellectual problem driving the study of the region. In recent years, the first dimension of the myth in particular – the conception of prewar Bukovinian society as plural, 'multicultural' and peaceful – has been subject to considerable qualification and scrutiny. In line with contemporary concerns for the meaning of multiculturalism and hybridity, many scholars have called for caution and qualification of these terms and claims. They have highlighted the fact that plurality does not equate to pluralism, that concepts of hybridity and diversity may still obey essentialist logics, and that there is a distinction between 'tolerance', 'coexistence' and actual 'togetherness'.[16] Moreover, many scholars have explored in detail and critically re-evaluated the history of Bukovina and the character of social and ethnic categories, and interethnic relations during the Habsburg, interwar and wartime periods. They have thereby sought to explain the specificities of Bukovinian society as well as the causes for the disintegration of social relations against the backdrop of broader political settings and developments and in light of new research on the wider region.[17] Finally, reflecting a growing interest in the politics of memory and the phenomenon of imperial nostalgia in postsocialist Eastern Europe as a whole, a great deal of attention has been paid to the mechanics of the revival of regional identity and history both abroad and on the ground, and the resurrection of the Bukovina myth of peaceful coexistence after 1989–91, particularly in Romania and Ukraine.[18]

The period of the Cold War, in turn, is almost a blind spot in the research on Bukovina.[19] When I started working on this project, I often heard that there was no topic: the region itself no longer existed as such and many of its original inhabitants had been forced to leave. Due to Europe's division and policies of ethnic homogenization, genocide and Sovietization, what was once Bukovina no longer had any of its defining features; especially in Romania and the Soviet Ukraine, but elsewhere too, the region had been forcibly forgotten. However, as I pursued my search, there was much evidence to suggest that the opposite was true. The evidence ranged from the existence of hundreds of books and articles about the region published during the Cold War to the establishment and existence of still-active homeland societies of Bukovina Germans and Bukovina Jews in West Germany and Israel, both still issuing, as I started my research, monthly newspapers, *Der Südostdeutsche* and *Die Stimme*, respectively. In this period, self-identifying Bukovinians had met and corresponded, built memorials and housing settlements, founded cultural institutions and even achieved considerable renown as individuals and as groups. This was the period during which Paul Celan, who was born in 1920 and died in 1970, came to be regarded as one of the most influential German poets, and other Bukovinian writers such as Rose Ausländer, Gregor von Rezzori and Edgar Hilsenrath made their names and careers by writing and speaking, sometimes directly, about their native province. Bukovina may no longer have mattered much as an actual location, but the idea of it had not disappeared.

Therefore, perhaps the emphasis on myth and the attempts to disprove it have been somewhat misleading. How else, if not through myth, are places constituted? Is myth not inherent to any constructed historical narrative or a useful reminder of the constructed nature of any such story? It is the claims made on 'space' that shape the space-time notion of 'place'.[20] As Doreen Massey has argued: 'The identity of places is very much bound up with the histories which are told of them, how those histories are told, and which history turns out to be dominant.'[21] Besides, as Roland Barthes has pointed out, myth is by definition 'falsely obvious'.[22] It is therefore not the myth in itself, but the competition over this narrative that deserves our attention. The Bukovina myth, especially in the aftermath of the Second World War, testifies to the range of ways in which people have interpreted, contested and thereby created the region for the purposes of the present. From this perspective, the region's idealization and the celebration of the region's former diversity is quite compatible with a preoccupation with different (national) projects and their contradictory permutations. Indeed, the Bukovina myth has its own dynamics and history, by virtue of which it is at once local, national and transnational.[23] Its diverse elements are a result of its authors' curious mixture of personal and collective traumas, regional and imperial nostalgias and local, national and global agendas and encounters. Ultimately, therefore, this phenomenon says more about the importance of situating oneself spatially and historically than it does about this space's history.[24]

Bukovina as a Prism

Thus, the period from 1945 to 1989, a period that has been largely ignored but during which the myth thrived, deserves much closer attention. While building on existing insights regarding prewar realities and wartime experiences, the Bukovina myth needs to be analysed as such and placed in the context of its emergence and development. This involves viewing it against the backdrop of the different, and changing political, social, cultural and historiographical settings and questions that informed, animated and restricted its creators and its various manifestations. Such an undertaking therefore involves tracing the activities of the main stakeholders of Bukovinian identity after the Second World War – first, though not exclusively, the homeland societies in West Germany and Israel – and making sense of the evolving political situation in which they found themselves. Bukovina might then function and be conceived of as a prism thanks to which it is possible to cast new light on these two countries' postwar politics, culture and societies.

Broadly speaking, the postwar period might be divided into two halves. In both West Germany and Israel, though for quite different reasons, many initially regarded the loss of prewar homelands in Central and Eastern Europe and the experiences of the inhabitants of these regions as highly political and sensitive matters. In West Germany, after a first postwar decade of considerably politicized activities and research concerning the estimated twelve million 'expellees of the homeland' (eight million of whom were in the Federal Republic where they represented around 16.5% of the population), the subject started falling out of favour.[25] For one thing, the relatively rapid social integration of these 'ethnic refugees' and the growing acceptance of the Cold War status quo defused the urgency of discussing the issue of 'the expulsions' as both a domestic and foreign policy matter.[26] For another, by the 1960s, focusing on the victimhood of non-Jewish Germans and German legacies in Eastern Europe came to seem increasingly contentious.[27] Indeed, the radicalization of the discourse of what came to be known as 'expellee organizations' over the course of the 1950s and 1960s alienated a younger and more liberal generation of students, scholars and even putative members of these groups. Yet, at the same time, explorations of what these groups had been part of 'in the East' and the experiences of the Germans' victims from these same regions were not welcome either. As a result, over time, 'expellee' discourse became increasingly marginalized and insular. But since their activities nevertheless continued to be institutionally supported and were not critically discussed, for several decades, this discourse was neither replaced nor did it disappear entirely.[28]

In Israel, in turn, survivors of the Holocaust did a great deal to rehabilitate themselves and contributed significantly to the creation of the state and the country's early political life. Yet the Zionist agenda with its notorious 'rejection' of both narratives of victimhood and the Diaspora largely sidelined these people's experiences and their organizations.[29] In effect, the Zionist stance discouraged a critical discussion of the experiences of displacement and 'absorption': the immigrants' choice of Israel was presented as self-evident and the Yishuv's stance as beyond question. For a long time, studying survivors was therefore relatively unpopular too. The language requirements for such research as well as the geopolitics of the Cold War constituted major impediments to exploring these topics. In general, as many scholars have shown, it took time for the Holocaust, not to mention its Romanian chapter, to become the subject of broad public debate in Israel.[30] For decades, the immigrants' homeland organizations were regarded as parochial, curious and short-lived phenomena – relics – that were tolerated but best ignored. Therefore, here too, the position of the newcomers was both insular and marginal, but their activities were nevertheless unchallenged and relatively unhindered.[31]

A gradual shift occurred in both countries over the course of the 1960s, 1970s and 1980s under the influence of both domestic and international political developments. Significant turning points include the Eichmann trial in 1961 in Jerusalem, the Auschwitz trials in 1963 in Frankfurt, the establishment of diplomatic relations between Germany and Israel in 1965 and Germany and Romania in 1967, Israel's strengthened international position after 1967, and the political shift to the left in West Germany in the midst of 1968, aligning with generational dynamics. All of these developments spurred on discussions about Jewish suffering and German crimes, as did regular debates and scandals surrounding the issue of financial compensation (*Wiedergutmachung*) for the victims of National Socialist persecution and questions of appropriate historical representation and visibility.[32] Historians even coined the notion of the 'era of the witness' to describe this period when Holocaust survivors came to the fore as ultimate victims, as individuals and even as icons.[33] Though this constituted a truly transnational process, it contributed to a change in public historical and political consciousness in and in relation to West Germany and Israel especially. By the late 1970s, in both countries, interest in the history of Jews in Germany and Europe and what slowly came to be known and understood as 'the Holocaust' had grown significantly. This altered the situation of Jews in Germany and elsewhere, attitudes towards Israel and Israelis, and non-Jewish Germans' perception of Jews in general. It therefore also affected conceptions of recent history, of Europe and 'the East', as well as conceptions of Germanness, Jewishness, community and belonging. Together with the policy of détente and the rapprochement with states in the Communist Bloc, these trends all led to the retreat of traditional stakeholders of German, Jewish and Israeli identity into the background. These actors thereby gradually lost their prerogative over representations of the region and the past – a slow process that would only be fully recognized after the end of the Cold War.

In the meantime, work on 'expellees' and what has come to be known as the issue of 'flight and expulsion' has become a sophisticated field and area of research, which connects in meaningful ways the history of displacement, memory and wartime violence, both in terms of German suffering and questions of perpetration. A vast body of literature deals with policies relating to refugees and citizenship in postwar Germany, the experiences of different groups of expellees, their (memory) politics and even their material culture.[34] A museum on the topic of 'flight and expulsion', taking the experiences of German expellees as a starting point, is now even under construction in Berlin.³⁵ A growing amount of work also discusses German minorities broadly defined, beyond Germany's borders, in an increasingly differentiated manner – their experiences in their homelands or their relations to Germany and the states of Eastern Europe over the course of centuries.³⁶ Dealt with more or less theoretically, the subject has rightly come to be seen as offering a new perspective on crucial and interrelated aspects of modern German, European and migration history.

If more discreetly and gradually, the diversity of Israeli society and the experiences of the one million Holocaust survivors who immigrated to Israel from Europe, specifically, have also become the object of increasing interest and scrutiny. Not only has the phenomenon of immigration itself attracted ever more scholarly attention, but so too have immigrants' everyday lives, experiences, practices and beliefs before and after they arrived in Israel.³⁷ The impact of their arrival on the country's origins, political identity, society and culture have also been better accounted for as Israeli national master narratives have been submitted to more critical examination.³⁸ In recent years, Israel's German-speakers in particular have been 'discovered' and, in general, the interest of Israelis in their European roots has grown exponentially together with a rising recognition of Jews' diverse contributions to the culture and history of European countries.³⁹ An increasing number of scholars have provided a sustained investigation into the experiences of Jews who stayed in Europe or who did not immigrate to Israel after the war and the Holocaust. This includes the case of Germany's 'other Germans', pointing to the diverse meanings of Jewishness and Germanness, as well as the combined legacies of National Socialism and Soviet communism on these populations.⁴⁰ In general, Jewish, German, European and Israeli histories have been the object of ever-greater integration.

However, until now, attention has quite naturally been paid to the leading organizations of immigrants and newcomers – larger groups of 'expellees', Jewish survivors and displaced persons (DPs) and a handful of regions or states in Eastern Europe – as well as to the more practical consequences of displacement and wartime violence on society and political life in general. Moreover, although comparative lines of enquiry and integrated approaches have sometimes been pursued, with regard to the histories of 'expellees' or ethnic Germans in general and Jewish immigrants or Holocaust survivors, such a methodology still tends to be regarded as bold and delicate. Given how closely tied these groups and their representative organizations were to the development of Israel and West Germany, as both states and nations, and how their histories relate to the problematic notions of ethnicity, nationality or even race, these subjects are often thought to preclude comparison. However, the few attempts at comparative or integrated histories have been remarkably thought-provoking and insightful.⁴¹ These studies have shown that this reticence has overshadowed some clear parallels and important convergences regarding the spaces and institutions, but also the policies, processes, rationales, challenges and solutions at stake. Finally, in the last few decades, under the effect of what some scholars have called 'hegemonic Holocaust memory' and the focus on Czernowitz, the history of Bukovina and Bukovinians after 1945 has often been viewed and studied through the lens of its comparatively large, emancipated and educated Jewish minority and thereby primarily construed as a former 'Jewish space'.[42] Yet, even just a quick glimpse at the discourse about Bukovina during the Cold War reveals that this identification of Bukovina as a 'Jewish' – and, by implication, multicultural – space is a recent development that deserves to be explained.

Focusing on the yet underexplored activities and discourses of German and Jewish Bukovinians during the Cold War, and thereby juxtaposing relatively small and separate, yet connected, cases of German 'resettlers' and 'Jewish survivors' thus challenges existing assumptions and throws new light on a range of issues. As separate case studies, German and Jewish Bukovinians offer new insights into the changing politics of identity, memory and belonging in their respective countries, with relevance extending beyond the groups at hand. In combination, these cases open up a new way of thinking about the history of 'expellees' and 'Holocaust survivors' after the Second World War by showcasing their entangled perspectives and practices. Bukovina, conceived of as a prism, can serve to trace both the development of West German and Israeli modes of identification, and the development and intersections of different cultural, historical and ethnic imaginaries after the Second World War.

First, then, this book enriches our understanding of the social and political history of postwar West Germany and Israel. Both countries were new, ethnonational states that welcomed millions of people in the aftermath of the Second World War. While a great deal has been written on this topic, this study looks at what it meant in practice by offering detailed analyses of different aspects of Bukovinians' process of social, political and cultural integration. It thereby highlights where some of these newcomers came from and who they became in the reciprocal process of constructing a sense of belonging and an identity as West Germans and Israelis in the aftermath of the war and the Holocaust. Second, with their diverging yet connected experiences of violence, looking at these two groups gives insight into how different communities of experience wrestled with the legacies of the violent past – how they compensated for loss, for suffering and for guilt. In this sense, it contributes to our understanding of the so-called process of reckoning with the past among a group of self-defining ethnic Germans and another of self-defining Jews after the Second World War and tells us about West Germany and Israel as sociocultural spaces with specific moral and emotional regimes and horizons. Finally, tracing Bukovina tells us not just how different communities of experience transmitted the past, but also *which* history became dominant and why – what images circulated and how and why they changed across space and over time. In this sense, this study contributes to research on the spatial, temporal and generational dynamics of the memory of the war and the Holocaust.

Looking at these two groups together thus opens up new perspectives on how to write the history of the reverberations of the Second World War and the history of the postwar period in general. Indeed, this is not a parallel or a comparative narrative, but a genuinely entangled story in the sense of the French *histoire croisée*.[43] German and Jewish Bukovinians not only engaged with the same space but also interacted and reacted to each other and created Bukovina as a place and as a transnational object of memory in the process. This account is therefore not just one possible way of telling their story, but one that proves that the stories of either group need to be told together, creating parallels to other similar intertwined histories, and challenging the national and ethnic paradigms we often take for granted and work within unconsciously.

Therefore, this book shows that, while the Bukovina myth has been widely noted and discussed, its diverse manifestations and ideological uses and meanings have rarely been the object of systematic analysis.[44] There is a vast amount of literature and research on the region. However, on the one hand, most scholars have failed to account for the fact that Cold War publications were authored, edited and published by Bukovinian Germans in Germany and Bukovinian Jews in Israel, and funded by their respective organizations. On the other hand, the works of literary figures have often been dismissed outright as romanticized without accounting for the fact that these were, in the absence of anyone else, major spokespeople for the region. This study expounds on these issues by seeking to embed the narratives and practices relating to Bukovina in the postwar period. The aim is to provide a new framework for understanding the idealized depictions, which were also efforts to make sense of wartime experiences by displaced Bukovinians. This idealization was an intrinsic part of their postwar lives and therefore relates to the postwar societies in which they lived. This study therefore turns the classic question of 'what makes Bukovina or Bukovinians special?' around and asks, instead, how the Second World War and its aftermath affected Bukovinians' sense of postwar belonging, and elucidates why postwar Bukovinian 'diasporas' developed at all.

Beyond Memory: The Politics of Belonging

This study forms part of a collaborative attempt to rethink the widely used but also widely critiqued concept of 'collective memory' to make sense of the reverberations of the Second World War in Germany and Europe.⁴⁵ The shortcomings and limitations of the term 'collective memory' have been discussed extensively elsewhere and do not need to be repeated here.⁴⁶ Suffice it to say that, having moved away from its Halbwachsian roots, which emphasized the social character of the production of remembrance, studies of 'collective memory' or 'memory' more generally have often analysed top-down, frequently national and mostly monolithic narratives about the past. Pierre Nora's seminal and highly influential work *Les lieux de mémoire* is a case in point.⁴⁷ While Nora usefully drew attention to the abstract, contingent, diversely embodied and always highly political character of practices relating to the past, he concentrated on memory's national manifestations – often state-led initiatives with an integrative function. Such a conception does not fully do justice to the fluid, concurrent, competing and diverse character of the past's effects on society and especially memory's relationship to experience. While some scholars have since qualified the notion of *lieux de mémoire* (places of memory) to account for the contest over them, Bukovina is conceived of here as more than just a repository – even a contested one – of different images and ideas.⁴⁸ Rather, it is a means of enacting social and political choices, identities and even values in an ever-changing present; it is an instrument of the politics of belonging.

The aim of this collaborative research was to concentrate on a broad range of legacies of the past and thereby identify diverse, more or less visible, practices and discourses and different types of continuities and breaks. This involved working with a new and alternative theoretical framework involving the analytical categories of 'community of experience', 'community of connection' and 'community of identification', and seeking to explain the relationship between them.⁴⁹ Central and guiding questions included: how can one conceptualize the relationship between the experiences of an individual or a group (remembering agents) with the later, changing and diverse interpretations of an event's effects and traces? How does the meaning of experience change over time, across space and among individuals, groups and generations? Specifically, what were the mechanics and dynamics of this process in relation to the experience of violence, genocide and displacement in Europe after the Second World War?

Therefore, rather than a mere 'history of memory', this book is conceived of as a 'history of the aftermath', analysing in a relatively *longue-durée* perspective the 'meaning-making processes' at work in the wake of the conflict.⁵⁰ It deals with what others have called 'the war after the war', 'life after death' or what Tony Judt powerfully but simply called the 'post-war'.⁵¹ Writing such a history involves considering a whole range of legacies and consequences of the experience of the war and the Holocaust that cannot be reduced to mere narratives about the past. The notion of reverberations implies that something resonates and persists and thereby shapes the present, but that, at the same time, new circumstances and beliefs arise in the process. This study thus aims to contribute to a growing body of research on the diverse ways in which the postwar world was moulded by the events of the Second World War. These issues range from human rights principles to the system of states; from decolonization to Cold War confrontations; and from notions of refugee-ness to conceptions of nationhood, historical responsibility and belonging.[52] These manifold legacies – human and institutional, social and political, as well as cultural, emotional and physical – still resound today. The war and the Holocaust were instrumental not only for the lives of the millions of people directly affected but also for the character of the societies in which these people and the next generations later lived. In many ways, these events and their appraisal determine what many people nowadays believe and cherish, and how they approach the future.

At first sight, this might seem to fit with Paul Ricœur's description of memory as 'the temporal dimension of identity' or identity through time.[53] However, this definition, which blurs the distinction between the two terms, confers to memory identity's notorious ambiguity and slipperiness – a combination of malleability and fixity, individuality and unlimited diffusion – and renders it quite meaningless. As Ricœur points out, memory, understood as memorization, commemoration or ritual, may have more in common with identity, ideology and justice.[54] Many other scholars have noted that memory, depending on how one defines it, might easily and alternately be equated with subjectivity, destiny, culture, history or heritage.[55] Not only does this reveal the term's imprecision, but, in each case, the question this poses is 'whose memory' or 'memory for whom'. From this perspective, the use of an analytical concept of 'communities' and the search for more precise or less loaded alternatives to the word 'memory', as in this study, seems justified and helpful. In particular, such an approach draws attention to the fact that, after the war, references to Bukovina were primarily a matter of belonging, defined as both a proactive dimension of identity and a pattern of interpretation.[56] The word 'belonging' highlights the collective but also the purposeful, political (inclusive and exclusive), constructed and therefore inevitably unstable character of references to the past. As Nira Yuval-Davis has argued, studying belonging means studying 'social locations; identifications and emotional attachments; ethical and political values'. The politics of belonging thus 'relates to the participatory politics of citizenship as well as to that of entitlement and status'.[57] As she specifies elsewhere: 'The politics of belonging comprise specific political projects aimed at constructing belonging to particular collectivity/ies which are themselves being constructed in these projects in very specific ways and in very specific boundaries.'[58] This, then, also resonates with existing research on the German concept of *Heimat* (lit.: home or homeland), accurately defined in a recent publication as 'at the intersection of memory and space'.[59] As a malleable and supposedly politically uncharged projection of home and region, *Heimat* usually implicitly points to 'longing and belonging', 'Germanness' and even 'the nation', carrying with it all of the historical problems and tensions these terms also imply and entail.[60] This study does not define *Heimat* anew, but draws attention to its manifold uses to highlight the convergences and divergences of German and Jewish Bukovinian discourses and their entangled politics of identity, history and belonging.

The increasingly complex field of 'memory studies' has nevertheless been an essential source of inspiration and insight for the approach adopted here, both empirically and theoretically. Based on the concept of 'memory work', for example, this study seeks to emphasize what people *do* with their memories (as processed experiences) and draws attention to different forms and expressions – namely when, where and how the past was mobilized and for what purpose.[61] Many memory scholars have also stressed the importance of a differentiated understanding of the actors and their aims, as well as how these relate to one another.[62] This is an especially helpful impulse to make a distinction between the elite spokespersons of Bukovinian communities, the members of the communities and the surrounding society, and to highlight who benefited from having a voice and visibility at different times. The increasingly complex conceptualizations of 'Holocaust memory' – its forms, features and conjunctures – is also a case in point.[63] In this connection, analyses of 'Holocaust memory' in relation to 'German memories' and German national identity, and of the ever more intense and entangled engagement with the legacies of the history of National Socialism and the Holocaust in different communities have been especially insightful.[64] Not only have these insights aided the identification, interpretation and contextualization of specific sources, but they ultimately also informed the organization and structure of this book's argument and material.

Part I, titled 'Backgrounds', delves briefly into the period before 1945. Chapter 1 offers a broad historical sketch focusing on the experiences of German and Jewish Bukovinians in the Habsburg and interwar periods and during the Second World War. This chapter emphasizes the conditions for the emergence of German and Jewish Bukovinians as two distinct social groups by describing aspects of the region's changing social and political structure and situation. In particular, it deals with members of these two groups' relationship to each other, to the changing political leadership and to the region's other inhabitants and outlines briefly their respective experiences of violence and displacement during the war.

Part II, under the heading 'Establishments', then deals with how many of these people came to terms with displacement and constructed belonging in their respective new national homelands after the Second World War. This part thus explores how postwar host societies reacted to the new arrivals and what meanings those nations were endowed with in the process. Chapter 2 focuses on the situation of ethnic Germans from Bukovina in the first decade after the war in West Germany – the country where most of them chose to settle after 1945. Contextualizing their experiences against the backdrop of those of millions of other displaced persons and refugees in West Germany at this time, as well as with respect to the views of the local population, it highlights the role of German Bukovinians' identification as 'Bukovinian' or even as 'Bukovina German' but also as 'resettlers' (*Umsiedler*), 'refugees' (*Flüchtlinge*) and eventually 'expellees' (*Vertriebene*) for their so-called integration in the first decade after the war. In particular, it traces German Bukovinians' establishment of institutions such as the 'Homeland Society of German Resettlers from Bukovina' (later the 'Homeland Society of Bukovina Germans') (Landsmannschaft der deutschen Umsiedler aus der Bukowina; Landsmannschaft der Buchenlanddeutschen), founded in 1949, and the concomitant development of narratives framing Germany as both a 'new' and an 'ancestral home', and Bukovina Germans as both victims and 'better Germans'. This chapter thus offers a case study of the activities of ethnic German refugees in West Germany after 1945 and a reflection on the political culture of West Germany in the first decade after the war.

Chapter 3 then turns to the situation of Bukovinian Jews in the first decade after the Second World War. This was a period during which most of the Jewish survivors from Bukovina emigrated from Romania to Mandatory Palestine and later Israel. Starting with a depiction of the situation of refugees repatriated from Transnistria and northern Bukovina to Romania in the immediate aftermath of the Second World War, this chapter traces Jewish Bukovinians' struggle for recognition, citizenship and bare survival in postwar Romania. It discusses the gradual development and promotion of a conception of *Eretz Israel*, the Land of Israel, as an 'ancestral home' and a 'solution and salvation' for Bukovina Jews in particular and Jews in general. Here too, the focus is on the creation, activities and narratives of the Bukovinian homeland society, the 'Association of Immigrants from Bukovina' (Chug Olej Bukowina) and the later 'World Organization of Bukovina Jews' in Israel from 1944 to the early 1950s. This chapter deals with the tension between the leaders' efforts to protect their heritage and culture, to record and commemorate a past of suffering and persecution and to promote 'absorption' into a new Zionist society. This chapter thereby not only sheds new light on the immediate aftermath of the Holocaust in Romania, but also on Jewish and Israeli politics of identity, history and belonging after the Holocaust and on the situation of Holocaust survivors before they were identified as such.

Part III, entitled 'Entanglements' considers the divergent, convergent and conflicting ways in which German and Jewish Bukovinians sought to compensate for loss, for displacement and for the violent past as the Cold War advanced. Chapter 4 explores the relationship between nostalgia, guilt and Germanness by analysing, juxtaposing and comparing the different representations of the region that developed and prevailed among Germans and Jews from the region in the 1960s. Starting by considering the memorial publications of these respective groups, it highlights their idiosyncrasy and dissonance and the irreconcilability of the images of the region conveyed. This is interpreted as evidence of both prewar ethnic understandings of community and the hardening of ethnonational categories during the war and immediately afterwards. This chapter then links these discourses to the conflict that broke out between representatives of the two communities surrounding the issue of West German reparations for Jewish Bukovinians. Indeed, until the early 1960s, Jewish Bukovinians were not able to claim financial compensation for their suffering and persecution and, even then, the regulations did not foresee compensation for their material losses. When many Jewish Bukovinians started placing claims as though they were ethnic Bukovinian Germans – something the rules developed by the West German state theoretically permitted – a dispute erupted among members of the two groups and beyond about the meaning the Germanness. This chapter shows that the struggle over indemnification arose out of the fundamental opposition between different conceptions of Germanness and related conceptions of historical responsibility. However, it also demonstrates how understandings of the past could change and thus illuminates the major societal shift taking place in West Germany twenty years after the end of the war.

The final chapter, Chapter 5, reconstructs the trajectories of different, mostly Jewish, German-speaking Bukovinian writers and traces the international reception of their work up until the end of the Cold War. Focusing on the figure of Alfred Margul-Sperber and the writers who gravitated around him, the analysis first gives insight into the origins of a concept of a German-language 'literary landscape' in the region during the interwar period. It then draws attention to the growing traction of this 'landscape' idea under the influence of the works of relatively famous German-speaking Jewish writers from the region around the world and their growing popularity during the second half of the Cold War. Emphasizing the transnational character and dynamics of this Bukovinian literary trend, and focusing on the particular self-understanding of the members of this loose association of writers from the region, this chapter sheds light on the development of an alternative concept of 'Bukovinian' to that previously promoted by the established communities of Bukovinians. Indeed, in the context of changing East–West relations and generational change and against the backdrop of changing conceptions of identity, history and community in West Germany, Israel and elsewhere during the 1970s and 1980s, literature and literary figures challenged and ultimately shaped both the wider image of the region and even the activities and discourses of the existing Bukovinian organizations (*Landsmannschaften*) themselves. This chapter thus traces the transformation of conceptions of Bukovina from a German or Jewish *Heimat* to an ethnically neutral 'sunken cultural landscape' and explains how and why, by 1989, the region had come to be reimagined as the site of a unique German-Jewish symbiosis.

A Note on Sources, Terminology and Translation

Setting out to understand the significance of the past in the present and how different individuals and groups dealt with their experiences of displacement and violence, this study is guided by anthropologists' concern with the gap between what people say and what people do. It therefore necessarily draws on an eclectic body of sources, some of a bureaucratic and institutional, and others of a highly personal and individual nature. This range reflects an attempt to be as multiperspectival and multiscalar – from the bottom-up and the top-down – as possible. The archival material includes documents from local, regional and national archives, as well as specialist and private archival collections. I have also drawn on a wide array of published sources, including pamphlets, newspapers, testimonies and memoirs. The main archives used for this study include: the German Federal Archives in Koblenz and Bayreuth, the Central Zionist Archives in Jerusalem, the Romanian National Archives, the Center for the Study of the History of Romanian Jews (CSIER) in Bucharest, the state and city regional archives of Stuttgart, Darmstadt and Suceava, the Yad Vashem Archives, the USC Shoah Foundation Archive, the Archive of the National Museum of Romanian Literature and the archive of the Institut für Volkskunde der Deutschen im östlichen Europa (IVDE) in Freiburg. Last but by no means least, I drew from the library and archive of the Bukovina-Institute at the University of Augsburg, with the records of the German Bukovinian Landsmannschaft, which I was fortunate to be able to view while reworking the manuscript for publication. The newspapers of the Bukovinian homeland societies, *Der Südostdeutsche* and its precursors published since 1949 and *Die Stimme* published from 1944 to 2017, held by the IVDE in Freiburg and the Bukovina-Institute in Augsburg, constituted a key source, which I was able to draw on consistently and throughout. In addition to this, over the course of my research, I carried out over thirty oral history interviews with people originating from the region, as well as people involved in activities relating to Bukovina. Though these are not extensively or systematically quoted and analysed in this book, they enabled me to fill in many significant gaps in the material and informed my arguments while substantially enhancing my understanding of the subject as a whole.

Finally, this study posits a distinction between Germans and Jews, which may seem problematic to some readers, especially as 'Jewish' may be both a religious and an ethnic label and many Jews may have identified as Germans or even as both. Yet, as Rogers Brubaker has argued, while ethnicity may merely be 'a perspective on the world', it is a very powerful one, which influences the character of social reality in significant ways.[65] In the case of Bukovina, it is typical to treat Jews, a religious minority, as a separate group. Besides, these terms are present in the sources and are used by the actors themselves, as indicated by the names of their organizations. Since self-identifying Germans and Jews are the focus of this study, it seems legitimate to use these categories and would be quite challenging to do without. Nonetheless, throughout this book, attempts are made to question and ultimately deconstruct the meaning of these terms by looking critically at the discourse they were mobilized to serve. To an extent, the problem of ascription also applies to the term 'Bukovinian'. As with any study of identity or identification, there is a risk of reinforcing or even creating a category by searching for it and writing about it. However, here too, I repeatedly refer to the fact that all potential Bukovinians (namely anyone born in that region), or even all of those persons the Bukovinian organizations claimed to represent, by no means necessarily identify or identified as such. Yet, ultimately, this study is not about numbers, but rather about the narratives that were developed and disseminated in their name, and their impact on and refraction of a wider historical epoch and sociocultural environment.

Finally, such a study requires a note on translation and the use of place names. This matter constitutes a notable problem when writing about regions such as Bukovina, where sovereignty changed several times over a short period. In general, I have tried to use place names in line with the period discussed, i.e. Czernowitz for Austrian, Cernăuți for Romanian, Chernovtsy for Russian and Chernivtsi for Ukrainian times. However, one cannot ignore that these practices are highly political and that the use of names constitutes an expression of power – not simply a reference to a certain time, but also a statement about who is in power and whose experience is being taken into account.[66] These terms therefore cannot be regarded as mere translations. In this context, German-language names such as Czernowitz pose a particular problem, as they are both the German and the Habsburg names of these locations. A German transcription of the current Ukrainian name of the city, Chernivtsi (Tscherniwzi), does exist, but is rarely used. With this in mind, I decided to maintain the use of Czernowitz in English when quoting German sources that use this spelling in order to indicate that this is perhaps not just a reference to the city *in German*, but also a certain characterization of the place.

Notes

1. Georg Drozdowski to Manfred Reifer, 8 November 1950. Letters published in: M. Reifer, *Menschen und Ideen* (Tel Aviv: Edition Olympia, 1952), 364–67, here 364–65. Unless stated otherwise, all translations from French, German and Romanian are my own.
2. Manfred Reifer to Georg Drozdowski, 27 November 1950; Reifer, *Menschen und Ideen*, 366–67.
3. Reifer to Drozdowski, 27 November 1950.
4. For more on Drozdowski and his biography in these years, see G. Guggenberger, *Georg Drozdowski in literarischen Feldern zwischen Czernowitz und Berlin (1920–1945)* (Berlin: Frank & Timme, 2015), 213–15.
5. For Reifer's full biography, see Reifer, *Menschen und Ideen*.
6. These expressions are literal translations of the German collective self-descriptions of German Bukovinians as *'Bukowina Deutsche'* or *'Buchenlanddeutsche'*, and Jewish Bukovinians as *'Bukowina Juden'* or *'Bukowiner'*, respectively. While this combination of nouns may seem unusual in English, it captures the exclusive and distinctive character of this self-identification (the assumption that 'Germans', 'Jews' and members of other ethnicities constituted separate groups), which is what those who used the German terms implied and meant to suggest. This is why they are occasionally used in this book too.
7. S. Marten-Finnis and M. Winkler, 'Quelle und Diskurs: Czernowitzer Pressefeld 1918–1940: Ein Werkstattbericht des Arbeitskreises Czernowitzer Presse zur Digitalisierung von Czernowitzer Zeitungen 1918–40', in S. Marten-Finnis and W. Schmitz (eds), *'… zwischen dem Osten und dem Westen Europas': Deutschsprachige Presse in Czernowitz bis zum Zweiten Weltkrieg* (Dresden: Thelem, 2005), 49–64, especially 52; A. Corbea-Hoișie, 'Zum mystizierten Erinnerungsraum Bukowina', in E. Lappin and A. Lichtblau (eds), *Die 'Wahrheit' der Erinnerung: Jüdische Lebensgeschichten* (Innsbruck: Studienverlag, 2008), 132–41.
8. For more on these diverse images and expressions, see J. van Drunen, *'A Sanguine Bunch': Regional Identification in Habsburg Bukovina, 1774–1919* (Amsterdam: Uitgeverij Pegasus, 2015).
9. On this see S. Frunchak, 'Studying the Land, Contesting the Land: A Select Historiographic Guide to Modern Bukovina', *The Carl Beck Papers in Russian and East European Studies* 2108, vol. 1 (Essay) and 2 (Notes) (2011); G. Fisher and M. Röger, 'Bukovina: A Borderland Region in (Trans-)national Historiographies after 1945 and 1989–1991', *East European Politics and Societies* 33(1) (2019), special issue, 176–195.
10. K.E. Franzos, *Vom Don zur Donau: Neue Kulturbilder aus 'Halb-Asien'* (Leipzig: Duncker und Humblot, 1877). Though he wrote this about Galicia and the region beyond Czernowitz, this label has nevertheless stuck. See A. Corbea-Hoișie, 'Halb-Asien', in J. Feichtinger and H. Uhl (eds), *Habsburg neu denken: Vielfalt und Ambivalenz in Zentraleuropa. 30 kulturwissenschaftliche Stichworte* (Vienna: Böhlau Verlag, 2016), 73–81.
11. See e.g. G. von Rezzori, *Maghrebinische Geschichten* (Hamburg: Rowohlt, 1953); A. Corbea-Hoișie, 'Gedächtnisort Maghrebinien: Eine Lesehypothese', in M. Csáki and P. Stachel (eds), *Die Verortung von Gedächtnis* (Vienna: Passagen Verlag, 2001), 151–62.

12. R. Ausländer, 'Erinnerungen an eine Stadt', in H. Braun (ed.), *Rose Ausländer: Materialen zu Leben und Werk* (Frankfurt am Main: Fischer, 1991), 10. Extract from the speech delivered upon receipt of the Georg-Büchner Prize in Bremen in 1960: P. Celan, *Der Meridian: Endfassung, Entwürfe, Materialen*, edited by B. Böschenstein and H. Schmull (Frankfurt am Main: Suhrkamp, 1999).
13. 'Archetypal borderland': D. Rechter, 'Habsburg Bukowina: Juden am Rande des Reiches', *Grenzen: Jüdischer Almanach der Leo Baeck Institute* (2015), 84–94, here 85; 'shatterzones of empires': O. Bartov and E. Weitz (eds), *Shatterzones of Empires: Coexistence and Violence in the German, Habsburg, Russian, and Ottoman Borderlands* (Bloomington, IN: Indiana University Press, 2013); 'bloodlands': T. Snyder, *Bloodlands: Europe between Hitler and Stalin* (New York: Basic Books, 2010); 'intermixed': T. Judt, *Postwar: A History of Europe since 1945* (London: Heinemann, 2005), loc. 800; 'pulverised': R. Evans, 'Central Europe: The History of an Idea', in *Austria, Hungary, and the Habsburgs: Essays on Central Europe, c. 1683–1867* (Oxford: Oxford University Press, 2006), 304. For 'vanished world', see e.g. the blog by Christian Herrmann: https://vanishedworld.blog/author/cyberorange (retrieved 6 September 2019).
14. According to Magris, this myth, which was linked to the self-created and self-legitimizing myth of a benevolent Habsburg presence, developed in Europe's postimperial spaces after the First World War and was prevalent among these regions' Jewish intellectuals especially. See C. Magris, *Danube* (New York: Farrar, Straus & Giroux, 1989).
15. J. Le Rider, '*Mitteleuropa* as a *lieu de mémoire*', in A. Erll, A. Nünning and S. Young (eds), *Cultural Memory Studies: An International and Interdisciplinary Handbook* (Berlin: Walter de Gruyter, 2008), 37–46, here 42. The literary scholar A. Corbea-Hoişie has also done a great deal to debunk the myth by studying the region's Jewish minority and its writers in particular. See e.g. A. Corbea-Hoişie, *Czernowitzer Geschichten: Über eine städtische Kultur in Mittelosteuropa* (Vienna: Böhlau, 2003); A. Corbea-Hoişie, *La Bucovine: Eléments d'Histoire Politique et Culturelle* (Paris: Institut d'études slaves, 2004).
16. See K. Werner, 'Euphorie und Skepsis: waren die Bukowina und Galizien 'inter'kulturell? Anmerkung zu einer Debatte', in K. Werner (ed.), *Erfahrungsgeschichte und Zeugenschaft: Studien zur deutsch-jüdischen Literatur aus Galizien und der Bukowina* (Munich: IKGS Verlag, 2003), 11–22; M. Csáky, A. Kury and U. Tragatschnig (eds), *Kultur – Identität – Differenz: Wien und Zentraleuropa in der Moderne* (Innsbruck: StudienVerlag, 2004); J. Le Rider, 'Mitteleuropa, Zentraleuropa, Mittelosteuropa: A Mental Map of Central Europe', *European Journal of Social Theory* 11(2) (2008), 155–69; D. Bechtel and X. Balmiche 'Introduction', in D. Bechtel and X. Balmiche (eds), *Les Villes Multiculturelles en Europe Centrale* (Paris: Belin, 2008), 7–14; and, most recently, J. Feichtinger and G.B. Cohen (eds), *Understanding Multiculturalism: The Habsburg Central European Experience* (New York: Berghahn Books, 2014). On the broader debate, see e.g. C. Taylor et al., *Multiculturalism: Examining the Politics of Recognition* (Princeton: Princeton University Press, 1994).
17. For a comprehensive and critical overview of research on the region, see K. Scharr, *'Die Landschaft Bukowina': Das Werden einer Region an der Peripherie 1774–1918* (Vienna: Böhlau Verlag, 2008), 45–78; and K. Scharr, 'Bukowina als historische Region im Überblick', in O.J. Schmitt and M. Metzeltin (eds), *Das Südosteuropa der Regionen* (Vienna: Verlag der österreichischen Akademie der Wissenschaften, 2015), 411–37. See also Chapter 1 in this book.
18. There is a large amount of literature on this subject. For recent analyses and further references on the case of Bukovina, see the special cluster of articles of G. Fisher and M. Röger (eds), 'Bukovina and Bukovinians after the Second World War: (Re)shaping and (Re)

thinking a Region after Genocide and "Ethnic Unmixing"', *East European Politics and Societies* 33(1) (2019), special issue, 176–256. See also S. Frunchak, 'Commemorating the Future in Post-War Chernivtsi', *East European Politics and Societies* 24(3) (2010), 435–63; U. Blacker, 'Living among the Ghosts of Others: Urban Postmemory in Eastern Europe', in U. Blacker and A. Etkind (eds), *Memory and Theory in Eastern Europe* (New York: Palgrave Macmillan, 2013), 173–93; C. Wanner, 'The Return of Czernowitz: Urban Affect, Nostalgia, and the Politics of Place-Making in a European Borderland City', *City and Society* 28(2) (2016), 198–221. On other areas and the wider region, see e.g. P. Ballinger, 'Imperial Nostalgia: Mythologizing Habsburg Trieste', *Journal of Modern Italian Studies* 97 (2003), 84–101; C. Hann and P. R. Magocsi (eds), *Galicia: A Multicultured Land* (Toronto: University of Toronto Press, 2005); T. Richardson, *Kaleidoscopic Odessa: History and Place in Contemporary Ukraine* (Toronto: University of Toronto Press, 2008); E. Narvselius, 'Tragic Past, Agreeable Heritage: Post-Soviet Intellectual Discussions on the Polish Legacy in Western Ukraine', *The Carl Beck Papers in Russian and East European Studies* 2403 (2015); and B. von Hirschhausen et al. (eds), *Phantomgrenzen: Räume und Akteure in der Zeit neu denken* (Göttingen: Wallstein Verlag, 2015).

19. Exceptions include two unpublished doctoral dissertations: P. Weber, 'Regime Changes, Public Memory and the Pursuit of Justice: The Case of German-Speaking Jews in Bukovina, 1920–1960' (D.Phil. thesis, University of Sussex, 2006); and S. Frunchak, 'The Making of Soviet Chernivtsi: National "Re-unification", World War II, and the Fate of Jewish Czernowitz in Post-war Ukraine' (D.Phil. thesis, University of Toronto, 2010).
20. On the distinction between space and place, see D. Massey, *For Space* (Los Angeles: Sage, 2005), especially 130. As Massey argues, places are 'constantly shifting articulations of social relations through time' and further that: 'The identity of places, and indeed the very identification of places *as* particular places, is always in that sense temporary, uncertain, and in process.' D. Massey, 'Places and Their Pasts', *History Workshop Journal* 39 (1995), 182–92, here 188, 190.
21. See Massey, 'Places and Their Pasts', 186.
22. R. Barthes, *Mythologies* (Paris: Seuil, 1957).
23. Cf. V. Glajar and J. Teodorescu (eds), *Local History, Transnational Memory in the Romanian Holocaust* (New York: Palgrave Macmillan, 2011).
24. This relates to the notion of a 'spatial turn'. On this, see Y.F. Tuan, *Space and Place: The Perspective of Experience* (Minneapolis: University of Minnesota Press, 2001); B. Warf and S. Arias (eds), *The Spatial Turn: Interdisciplinary Perspectives* (London: Routledge, 2009).
25. Many scholars have noted that this shift and most studies of expellee organizations focus on the 1950s and 1960s, and end in the early 1970s for precisely this reason.
26. The issue of 'integration' of expellees is subject to debate, but scholars generally agree that, by the 1960s, political and economic integration had been largely achieved. On this, see R. Schulze with R. Rohde and R. Voß (eds), *Zwischen Heimat und Zuhause: Deutsche Flüchtlinge und Vertriebene in (West)Deutschland 1945–2000* (Osnabrück: Secolo Verlag, 2001); I. Connor, *Refugees and Expellees in Post-war Germany* (Manchester: Manchester University Press, 2007); M. Krauss (ed.), *Integrationen: Vertriebene in den deutschen Ländern nach 1945* (Göttingen: Vandenhoeck & Ruprecht, 2008).
27. On this, see R.G. Moeller, *War Stories: The Search for a Usable Past in the Federal Republic of Germany* (Berkeley: University of California Press, 2001), 51–87; P. Ahonen, 'The Impact of Distorted Memory', in R. Ohliger, K. Schönwalder and T. Triadafilopoulos (eds), *European Encounters: Migrants, Migration and European Societies* (Aldershot: Ashgate,

2003), 238–56; and G. Margalit, *Guilt, Suffering, and Memory: Germany Remembers Its Dead of World War II*, translated from Hebrew by H. Watzman (Bloomington: Indiana University Press, 2010), especially 186–220.

28. For a comprehensive and critical overview of the debates surrounding the memory of the expulsions after the Second World War and expellee politics in general, see E. Hahn und H.H. Hahn, *Die Vertreibung im deutschen Erinnern: Legenden, Mythos, Geschichte* (Paderborn: Ferdinand Schöningh, 2010).

29. On the rejection of the Diaspora and silence surrounding the Holocaust, see e.g. T. Segev, *The Seventh Million: The Israelis and the Holocaust*, translated from Hebrew by H. Watzman (New York: Hill and Wang, 1994); I. Zertal, *From Catastrophe to Power: Holocaust Survivors and the Emergence of Israel* (Berkeley: University of California Press, 1998).

30. On this, see B. Cohen, *Israeli Holocaust Research: Birth and Evolution* (New York: Routledge, 2013).

31. On this, see e.g. D. Cesarani and E. Sundquist (eds), *After the Holocaust: Challenging the Myth of Silence* (London: Routledge, 2012); and, most recently, L. Halperin, *Babel in Zion: Jews, Nationalism, and Language Diversity in Palestine, 1920–1948* (New Haven: Yale University Press, 2015).

32. On this, see e.g. M. Fulbrook, *German National Identity after the Holocaust* (Cambridge: Polity Press, 1999); M. Brenner (ed.), *Geschichte der Juden in Deutschland von 1945 bis zur Gegenwart: Politik, Kultur und Gesellschaft* (Munich: C.H. Beck, 2012).

33. A. Wieviorka, *The Era of the Witness*, translated from French by J. Stark (Ithaca, NY: Cornell University Press, 2006). For more literature on this topic, see Chapters 4 and 5 in this book.

34. Many of these works are cited throughout, especially in Chapter 2. Key studies in English include: P. Ahonen, *After the Expulsion: West Germany and Eastern Europe 1945–1990* (Oxford: Oxford University Press, 2003); and A. Demshuk, *The Lost German East: Forced Migration and the Politics of Memory 1945–1970* (New York: Cambridge University Press, 2012). For a concise overview of the events and discourses, see M. Beer, *Flucht Vertreibung der Deutschen: Voraussetzung, Verlauf, Folgen* (Munich: C.H. Beck, 2011). For a recent and comprehensive insight into different aspects of 'expellee' discourse and culture, see S. Scholz, M. Röger and B. Niven (eds), *Die Erinnerung an Flucht und Vertreibung: Ein Handbuch der Medien und Praktiken* (Paderborn: Ferdinand Schöningh, 2015).

35. See https://www.sfvv.de/de (retrieved 6 September 2019).

36. See e.g. D. Rock and S. Wolff (eds), *Coming Home to Germany? The Integration of Ethnic Germans from Central and Eastern Europe in the Federal Republic* (New York: Berghahn Books, 2002); C. Ingrao and F. Szabo (eds), *The Germans and the East* (West Lafayette, IN: Purdue University Press, 2008). On Romania specifically, see J. Koranyi, 'Between East and West: Romanian German Identities since 1945' (D.Phil. thesis, University of Exeter, 2008); C. Cercel, *Romania and the Quest for European Identity: Philo-Germanism without Germans* (New York: Routledge, 2019).

37. Much of this literature is cited and drawn on in Chapter 3. See H. Yablonka, *Holocaust Survivors: Israel after the War* (New York: New York University Press, 1999); D. Hacohen, *Immigrants in Turmoil: Mass Immigration to Israel and its Repercussions in the 1950s and after* (New York: Syracuse University Press, 2003); D. Porat, *Israeli Society, the Holocaust and its Survivors* (London: Vallentine Mitchell, 2008). Most recently, see D. Ofer, F.S. Ouzan and J. Tydor Baumel-Schwartz (eds), *Holocaust Survivors: Resettlement, Memories, Identities* (New York: Berghahn Books, 2012). In recent years, there has been

significant new research on the experiences of Jewish DPs especially. See e.g. A. Patt, *Finding Home and Homeland: Jewish Youth and Homeland in the Aftermath of the Holocaust* (Detroit: Wayne State University Press, 2009).

38. See e.g. R. Wistrich and D. Ohana (eds), *The Shaping of Israeli Identity, Myth, Memory and Trauma* (London: Frank Cass, 1995); I. Zertal, *Israel's Holocaust and the Politics of Nationhood* (Cambridge: Cambridge University Press, 2005). For a recent, concise overview, see M. Brenner, *Israel: Traum und Wirklichkeit des jüdischen Staates: von Theodor Herzl bis heute* (Munich: C.H. Beck, 2016).
39. For a thought-provoking essay on Israelis' relations to Europe more generally, see D. Pinto, *Israel Has Moved* (Cambridge, MA: Harvard University Press, 2013).
40. See e.g. J. Bornemann and J. Peck, *Sojourners: The Return of German Jews and the Question of Identity* (Lincoln, NE: University of Nebraska Press, 1995); M. Bodemann, *Jews, Germans, Memory: Reconstructions of Jewish Life in Germany* (Ann Arbor: University of Michigan Press, 1996); more recently, see J. Schoeps and O. Glockner (eds), *A Road to Nowhere? Jewish Experiences in a Unifying Europe* (Leiden: Brill, 2011).
41. Most recently, on the case of expellees, see M. Borutta and J.C. Jansen (eds), *Vertriebene and Pieds-Noirs in Postwar Germany and France: Comparative Perspectives* (Basingstoke: Palgrave Macmillan, 2016). A number of studies in the last three decades have compared the cases of the migration and displacement of ethnic Germans and Jews and, with this, Germany and Israel. Most recently and systematically, see J. Panagiotidis, 'Laws of Return? Co-ethnic Immigration to West Germany and Israel (1948–1992)' (D.Phil. thesis, European University Institute, 2012). Others working on the cases of expellees or ethnic Germans have also sporadically explored entanglements. See e.g. A.Demshuk, '"Wehmut und Trauer": Jewish Travelers in Polish Silesia and the Foreignness of Heimat', *Jahrbuch des Simon-Dubnow-Instituts* (December 2007), 311–35. For a remarkable example of an integrated history, see A. Grossmann, *Jews, Germans, and Allies: Close Encounters in Occupied Germany* (Princeton: Princeton University Press, 2007).
42. The two most important studies of postwar Bukovina in recent years deal with the history of Jewish memory: F. Heymann, *Le Crépuscule des Lieux: Identités Juives de Czernowitz* (Paris: Stock, 2003); and M. Hirsch and L. Spitzer, *Ghosts of Home: The Afterlife of Czernowitz in Jewish Memory* (Berkeley: University of California Press, 2010). The focus on Jewish history constitutes a wider cultural phenomenon in the region. On this, see e.g. R.E. Gruber, *Virtually Jewish: Reinventing Jewish Culture in Europe* (Berkeley: University of California Press, 2002); E. Lehrer (ed.), *Jewish Space in Contemporary Poland* (Bloomington, IN: Indiana University Press, 2015). The 'discovery' of both Jewish survivors and traces of Jewish life on the ground in Romania and Ukraine after 1989–91 has played an instrumental role and continues to capture a great deal of attention. For recent analyses of the case of Bukovina, see N. Bernsand, 'Returning Chernivtsi to the Cultural Map of Europe', *East European Politics and Societies* 33(1) (2019), 238–56; G. Fisher, 'Looking Forwards through the Past: Bukovina's "Return to Europe" after 1989–1991', *East European Politics and Societies* 33(1) (2019), 196–217; and K. Koziura, 'The Spaces of Nostalgia(s) and the Politics of Belonging in Contemporary Chernivtsi Western Ukraine', *East European Politics and Societies* 33(1) (2019), 218–37. See also F. Heymann, 'Voyage à Chernivtsi ou Retour à Czernowitz? Les Paradoxes de la Mémoire et de la Nostalgie', *Teoros* 29(1) (2010), 17–30; M. Hirsch and L. Spitzer, 'The Web and the Reunion: http://czernowitz.ehpes.com', in M. Hirsch and N.K. Miller (eds), *Rites of Return: Diaspora Poetics and the Politics of Memory* (New York: Columbia University Press, 2011), 59–71.

43. M. Werner and B. Zimmermann, 'Beyond Comparison: *Histoire Croisée* and the Challenge of Reflexivity', *History and Theory* 45(1) (2006), 30–50.
44. On this, see S. Marten-Finnis and M. Winkler, 'Location of Memory versus Space of Communication: Presses, Languages, and Education among Czernovitz Jews, 1918–1941', *Central Europe* 7(1) (May 2009), 30–55.
45. For more on the context of this research project, see S. Bird, M. Fulbrook, J. Wagner and C. Wienand (eds), *Reverberations of Nazi Violence in Germany and Beyond: Disturbing Pasts* (London: Bloomsbury Academic, 2016); see also https://www.ucl.ac.uk/multidisciplinary-and-intercultural-inquiry/research/research-projects/reverberations-of-war (retrieved 6 September 2019). Further studies resulting from this project include S. Bird, *Comedy and Trauma in Germany and Austria after 1945: The Inner Side of Mourning* (Cambridge: Legenda, 2016); and M. Fulbrook, *Reckonings: Legacies of Nazi Persecution and the Quest for Justice* (Oxford: Oxford University Press, 2018).
46. On the original concept, see M. Halbwachs, *On Collective Memory*, translated from French by L.A. Coser (Chicago: University of Chicago Press, 1992). For a critique of the term, see A. Confino, 'Collective Memory and Cultural History: Problems of Method', *American Historical Review* 102 (1997), 1386–403; W. Kansteiner, 'Finding Meaning in Memory: A Methodological Critique of Collective Memory Studies', *History and Theory* 41 (2002), 179–97; Bill Niven, 'On the Use of "Collective Memory"', *German History* 26(3) (2008), 427–36; M. Fulbrook, 'History Writing and "Collective Memory"', in S. Berger and B. Niven (eds), *Writing the History of Memory* (London: Bloomsbury, 2014), 65–87.
47. Pierre Nora (ed.), *Les Lieux de Mémoire*, 7 vols (Paris: Gallimard, 1984–92).
48. See e.g. M. Csáki and P. Stachel (eds), *Die Verortung von Gedächtnis* (Vienna: Passagen Verlag, 2001).
49. For more on these concepts, see Fulbrook, 'History Writing and "Collective Memory"'.
50. See e.g. F. Biess and R.G. Moeller (eds), *Histories of the Aftermath: The Legacies of the Second World War in Europe* (New York: Berghahn Books, 2010), 5.
51. See D. Cesarani, 'Introduction', in D. Cesarani et al. (eds), *Survivors of Nazi Persecution in Europe after the Second World War* (Portland: Vallentine Mitchell, 2010), 1; R. Bessel (ed.), *Life after Death: Approaches to a Cultural and Social History* (Cambridge: Cambridge University Press, 2003); Judt, *Postwar*.
52. See e.g. P. Ther and A. Siljak (eds), *Redrawing Nations: Ethnic Cleansing in East Central Europe 1944–1948* (Lanham, MD: Rowman & Littlefield, 2001); M. Mazower (ed.), *Postwar Reconstruction in Europe: International Perspectives, 1945–1949* (Oxford: Oxford University Press, 2011); J. Reinisch and E. White (eds), *The Disentanglement of Populations: Migration, Expulsion and Displacement in Postwar Europe, 1944–1949* (Basingstoke: Palgrave Macmillan, 2011); G.D. Cohen, *In War's Wake: Europe's Displaced Persons in the Postwar Order* (Oxford: Oxford University Press, 2011). For studies with similarly *longue-durée* perspectives, see P. Ballinger, *History in Exile: Memory and Identity at the Borders of the Balkans* (Princeton: Princeton University Press, 2003); D. Stone, *Goodbye to All That?: The Story of Europe since 1945* (Oxford: Oxford University Press, 2014).
53. P. Ricœur, *Memory, History, Forgetting*, translated from French by K. Blamey and D. Pellauer (Chicago: University of Chicago Press, 2004), 81.
54. Ricœur, *Memory, History, Forgetting*.
55. Much has been written on the relationship between these terms. Jan and Aleida Assmann have famously established a distinction between 'cultural memory' and 'communicative memory': J. Assmann, *Das kulturelle Gedächtnis: Schrift, Erinnerung und politische*

Identität in frühen Hochkulturen (Munich: C.H. Beck, 1992). On history, memory and (popular) culture, see W. Kansteiner, *In Pursuit of German Memory: History, Television, and Politics after Auschwitz* (Athens, OH: Ohio University Press, 2006); A. Erll, *Memory in Culture*, translated from German by S.B. Young (Basingstoke: Palgrave Macmillan, 2011). On history, historical consciousness and memory, see P. Burke, *Varieties of Cultural History* (Ithaca, NY: Cornell University Press, 1997); H. Welzer (ed.), *Das soziale Gedächtnis: Geschichte, Erinnerung, Tradierung* (Hamburg: Hamburger Edition, 2001). On the politics of memory, see K. Hodgkin and S. Radstone (eds), *Contested Pasts: The Politics of Memory* (London: Routledge, 2003). On memory and heritage, see S. Macdonald, *Memorylands: Heritage and Identity in Europe Today* (London: Routledge, 2013). On collective memory and individual subjectivity, see D. Schacter (ed.), *Memory Distortion: How Minds, Brains and Societies Reconstruct the Past* (Cambridge, MA: Harvard University Press, 1995). For a synthetic insight into many of these issues and how they relate to one another, see I. Irwin-Zarecka, *Frames of Remembrance: The Dynamics of Collective Memory* (New Brunswick, NJ: Transaction, 1994); and, more recently, Berger and Niven, *Writing the History of Memory*.

56. G. Rosenthal and A. Bogner, 'Introduction', in G. Rosenthal and A. Bogner (eds), *Ethnicity, Belonging and Biography: Ethnographical and Biographical Perspectives* (Berlin: Lit Verlag, 2009).
57. N. Yuval-Davis, 'Belonging and the Politics of Belonging', *Patterns of Prejudice* 40(3) (2006), 197–214, here 199.
58. N. Yuval-Davis, *The Politics of Belonging: Intersectional Contestations* (London: Sage, 2011), 10.
59. F. Eigler and J. Kugele (eds), *Heimat: At the Intersection of Memory and Space* (Berlin: De Gruyter Oldenbourg, 2012).
60. On the concept of *Heimat*, see C. Applegate, *A Nation of Provincials: The German Idea of Heimat* (Berkeley: University of California Press, 1990); A. Confino, *The Nation as a Local Metaphor: Württemberg, Imperial Germany, and National Memory 1871–1918* (Chapel Hill: University of North Carolina Press, 1997); C. Wickham, *Constructing Heimat in Postwar Germany: Longing and Belonging* (Lewiston: Mellen, 1999); P. Bickle, *Heimat: A Critical Theory of the German Idea of Homeland* (Rochester, NY: Camden House, 2002). In relation to expellees, see also J. von Moltke, *No Place Like Home: Locations of Heimat in German Cinema* (Berkeley: University of California Press, 2005); P. Maeder, *Forging a New Heimat: Expellees in Post-war West Germany and Canada* (Göttingen: Vandenhoeck & Ruprecht Unipress, 2011); and Demshuk, *The Lost German East*.
61. A. Confino and P. Fritzsche (eds), *The Work of Memory: New Directions in the Study of German Society and Culture* (Urbana: University of Illinois Press, 2002).
62. B. Niven and S. Berger, 'Introduction', in Niven and Berger, *Writing the History of Memory*, 1–24. Kansteiner emphasizes the importance of interest and power groups, and the distinction between object, maker and consumer of memory: Kansteiner, *In Pursuit of German Memory*. The concepts of 'prosthetic', 'multidirectional' and 'post-memory' also give a more differentiated, qualified view of the actors. See A. Landsberg, *Prosthetic Memory: The Transformation of American Remembrance in the Age of Mass Culture* (New York: Columbia University Press, 2004); M. Rothberg, *Multidirectional Memory: Remembering the Holocaust in the Age of Decolonization* (Stanford: Stanford University Press, 2009); M. Hirsch, *The Generation of Postmemory: Writing and Visual Culture after the Holocaust* (New York: Columbia University Press, 2012); see also E. Kneightly and D. Pickering, *The Mnemonic Imagination: Remembering as a Creative Practice* (Basingstoke: Palgrave Macmillan, 2012).

63. See e.g. S. Friedländer, 'Trauma, Memory, and Transference', in G. Hartman (ed.), *Holocaust Remembrance: The Shapes of Memory* (Oxford: Blackwell, 1994), 252–65. There has been a considerable amount of work on survivor and Holocaust memory. Seminal works include L. Langer, *Holocaust Testimonies: The Ruins of Memory* (New Haven: Yale University Press, 1991); James E. Young, *The Texture of Memory: Holocaust Memorials and Meanings* (New Haven: Yale University Press, 1993).
64. This constitutes a huge body of literature. Key publications include D. Diner, 'Negative Symbiose: Deutsche und Juden nach Auschwitz', *Babylon* 1 (1986), 9–20; C. Maier, *The Unmasterable Past: History, Holocaust, and German National Identity* (Cambridge, MA: Harvard University Press, 1988); D. Diner: 'On Guilt Discourse and Other Narratives', *History and Memory* 9(1–2) (1997), 301–20; Fulbrook, *German National Identity after the Holocaust*; P. Novick, *The Holocaust and Collective Memory: The American Experience* (London: Bloomsbury, 2001); B. Niven, *Facing the Nazi Past: United Germany and the Legacy of the Third Reich* (London: Routledge, 2002); D. Michman (ed.), *Remembering the Holocaust in Germany, 1945–2000: German Strategies and Jewish Responses* (New York: Peter Lang, 2002); R.G. Moeller, 'Germans as Victims?: Thoughts on a Post-Cold War History of World War II's Legacies', *History and Memory* 17(1–2) (2005), 145–94; B. Niven (ed.), *Germans as Victims: Remembering the Past in Contemporary Germany* (Basingstoke: Palgrave Macmillan, 2006); A. Assmann, *Der lange Schatten der Vergangenheit: Erinnerungskultur und Geschichtspolitik* (Munich: C.H. Beck, 2006); M. Zehfuss, *Wounds of Memory: The Politics of War in Germany* (Cambridge: Cambridge University Press, 2007); R. Wittlinger, *German National Identity in the Twenty-First Century: A Different Republic after All?* (Basingstoke: Palgrave Macmillan, 2010); B. Niven and C. Paver (eds), *Memorialization in Germany since 1945* (Basingstoke: Palgrave Macmillan, 2011); J.K. Olick, *The Sins of the Fathers: Germany, Memory, Method* (Chicago: University of Chicago Press, 2016).
65. R. Brubaker, *Ethnicity without Groups* (Cambridge, MA: Harvard University Press, 2004).
66. On this, see K. Schlögel, *In Räume lesen wir die Zeit: über Zivilisationsgeschichte und Geopolitik* (Munich: Hanser, 2003).

Part I
BACKGROUNDS

Chapter 1

BEING BUKOVINIAN BEFORE 1945

German and Jewish Bukovinians in the Habsburg Empire, Romania and the Second World War

The concept of 'Bukovinian' or, in German, *Bukowiner* is often associated with the figure of the *homo bucoviniensis* – a local version of the *homo austriacus* – a non-national individual and a hybrid, who transcends national differences. This term is therefore closely linked to the myth of peaceful coexistence among different peoples and ethnic groups, often said to have characterized the historical region and especially its capital city, Czernowitz. Yet, another classic Bukovinian trope is what can be described as 'the story of nationalities' – a narrative invoking the region's different ethnic groups (varying in number from five to twelve) and emphasizing the significance of reified ethnic, religious and cultural differences among them. As this shows and many others have also noted, the question of Bukovinian regional identity is necessarily ambivalent.[1]

In this study, the meaning of 'Bukovinian' derives primarily from a nostalgic relationship to the region after its disappearance from the geopolitical map of Europe and following the experience of ethnic, political and interpersonal violence specifically during the Second World War; thus, the meaning is obviously quite different from what it meant to 'be Bukovinian' before the war, displacement and the Holocaust. The members of the Bukovinian 'diasporas' analysed in the following chapters – for the most part West Germans and Israelis, but also East Germans, Austrians, Romanians, Americans and others by citizenship – had strong allegiances to their respective states and often salient ethnic identities as 'Germans' and 'Jews' after 1945 as well.

Nonetheless, if one wants to understand the idealization of the region and permutations of the 'Bukovina myth' after 1945, it is not only necessary to understand the purpose of 'Bukovinian' as a mode of identification in the postwar period, it is also important to consider the earlier experiences, ideas and sociopolitical contexts in which the notion of a Bukovinian identity first appeared and to which its later invocations referred.

Hence, this chapter deals with the mixtures of 'tolerance and intolerance' and 'respect and hatred', which were central to the experience of 'being Bukovinian' before 1945.[2] Indeed, as the historian and cultural theorist Moritz Csáky and others have argued, while processes of modernization starting in the nineteenth century led to Central and Eastern Europe's growing international integration, they also heightened social tensions and fragmentation, introducing a range of new anxieties and challenges. In this area of Europe in particular, social differences developed along different axes, both vertically and horizontally: social (including urban/rural) and cultural (including ethnic) differences reinforced each other to produce a society characterized by a unique kind of heterogeneity, but also recurrent and deep crises.[3] This was a duality with lasting consequences for the people of the region.

Creating Bukovinians: Social Diversity, Imperial Loyalty and Regionalism

Understood both as a place and an idea, Bukovina, like Galicia, can be described as a Habsburg creation.[4] The region was mentioned in medieval texts, and to this day the Bukovinian monasteries and the fortress in Suceava bear witness to its significance during the late Middle Ages when, from 1388 to 1564, Suceava was Moldavia's capital. But by the eighteenth century, and in the aftermath of the Russo-Turkish wars, it was a sparsely populated crossroads of different zones of influence rather than a coherent region. The territory that became Habsburg Bukovina was carved out after the division of Poland in 1772 and offered to the Empress of Austria-Hungary, Maria Theresa, by the Russian Tsar in 1774–75 as a reward for her support. Though Bukovina was poor and remote, for the Habsburgs, the region was strategically important in linking two of the empire's other provinces, Galicia and Transylvania. First placed under military administration, Bukovina was later joined with Galicia in a protectorate in 1786. Then, in 1849, following the 1848 revolutions, it was declared an independent duchy, before becoming part of Cisleithania, the Austrian half of the Dual Monarchy, in 1867.[5]

Throughout their rule, the Habsburgs promoted immigration to the region, Germanization and economic development in a manner resembling 'internal colonialism'.[6] Within the space of a century and a half, they had transformed a hilly region with no natural borders into a relatively integrated province of the monarchy. Over time, the inhabitants came to identify strongly with this new *Kronland* (crownland). In his study of the Bukovinian Jewry, David Rechter traces the development of regional consciousness and an awareness of the particular character of Habsburg society in the region back to the early nineteenth century:

> As the idea and reality of the novel construct of Bukovina assumed a mantle of permanence for its inhabitants, a sense of regional consciousness took shape and a form of local patriotism – a Bukovina 'identity' – emerged. It coalesced early around the myth already alluded to: the vision of Bukovina's ethnic harmony enabled by benevolent Habsburg rule. As early as 1808, one observer expressed surprise at the 'almost unlimited toleration' that prevailed among the various peoples who 'with rare exceptions live here ... peacefully side by side'.[7]

As this shows, the concepts of 'Bukovinian' and the 'Bukovinian myth of peaceful coexistence' were both inseparable from each other and from the Habsburg conception of the state. In other words, there was an intimate link between efforts to promote regional identification and efforts to legitimize an Austrian presence and political ideology, which sought to unite diverse populations through loyalty to a dynasty and an emperor.[8]

Yet if Bukovinian referred to identification with the political space of the Habsburg Empire, it was also about being a part of the social space of 'Central Europe', and therefore concurrently defined by the experience of plurality, heterogeneity and 'difference'.[9] Bukovina was the most diverse region of the Habsburg monarchy, both linguistically and religiously. As Rechter writes, it was a 'unique multinational, multifaith society'.[10] Like in other similar imperial borderlands, the multiplicity of religions, customs and tongues was part of the social fabric and shaped the rhythm of everyday life. The main ethnic groups, according to the classic – albeit notoriously problematic – mode of ethnonational classification, were Ruthenians (Ukrainians), Romanians, Jews, Germans, Russians, Poles, Hungarians, Armenians and Romani people, belonging to the Christian Orthodox, Greek Orthodox, Catholic, Protestant and Jewish faiths, among others. According to the numbers provided for the year 1850, the population of Bukovina consisted of 25,000 Germans, 14,500 Jews, 4,000 Poles, 185,000 Romanians and 145,000 Ruthenians.[11] Some of these inhabitants were autochthonous, but following a colonial logic, the diverse members of the administration came from other parts of the empire. In general, the region's exceptional ethnic and cultural diversity was a result of immigration.[12] Indeed, the acquisition of Bukovina coincided with the high point of Habsburg population and colonization policies.[13] Starting in the late 1770s and continuing under Joseph

II, farmers from the south German lands, as well as Transylvania, Bohemia, Moravia, Moldavia and Galicia, settled the area. By 1779, an estimated seventy German-speaking families, who had been offered land, housing and cattle, had established themselves in the region.[14] In most cases, they joined existing settlements and, though they came from different areas and at various times, these German-speaking colonists came to be known generically as 'Swabians' (*Schwaben*).

If the rulers favoured the immigration of German-speakers, they nevertheless pursued pragmatically liberal immigration policies towards members of other groups. Russian farmers, known as Lipovan 'Old Believers', Armenian, Turkish and Greek traders, as well as craftsmen and miners of various backgrounds soon followed in the 1780s. Over the following decades, especially after 1812, it was Jews who constituted the largest group of newcomers. Many Jews fleeing the harsher circumstances of life further east were drawn to Bukovina because of its famed tolerance.[15] This openness resulted in a strong sense of allegiance to the rulers. The Austrians, in turn, came to regard Jews as their best assets due to both their loyalty and cultural and economic contributions.[16]

By 1910, the population of Bukovina had grown to around 800,000. Overall, this remained a predominantly agricultural area well into the twentieth century. Yet, the region included several small urban centres such as Suczawa, Radautz, Sereth, Kimpolung and Dorna Vatra, and the growth of Czernowitz – from 6,000 inhabitants and a few wooden houses in 1805 to 20,000 in 1838 and 80,000 in 1900 – was especially impressive.[17] On the eve of the First World War, Czernowitz was considered a modern city and regional cultural centre. Architecturally and in terms of its infrastructure, it was a Vienna look-alike, with electric street lighting, good railway connections, a theatre, a large town hall (*Rathaus*), a railway station and even a university – often referred to as 'the easternmost German-language university' – which was opened in 1875 to mark the centenary of Austrian rule. The Jews contributed significantly to urban growth and modernization: by 1914, they represented 13% of the region's overall population, but over 30% of the population of Czernowitz and 40% of students, and they occupied key positions in the liberal professions, commerce and industry. By this point, Bukovina was not only the most diverse but also the most 'Jewish' region of the Habsburg monarchy.

The region's so-called 'German' character was therefore largely a product of its distinct social structure. According to the census of 1910, Germans numbered 70,000, Jews 103,000, Poles 36,000, Romanians 273,000 and Ruthenians 305,000.[18] The number of people who declared German as their native language never exceeded 20% of the population. However, since Ruthenians outnumbered Romanians in the north and the number of Romanians exceeded the number of Ruthenians in the south, no group ever benefited from an absolute majority and 'no social or ethnic group [in Habsburg Bukovina] assumed permanent or dominant control'.[19] Bukovinian society was therefore forced to function by compromise across ethnic groups and the German language was a default common denominator.[20] Besides, as the language of the bureaucracy, the law and the *lingua franca* of commerce and industry, knowing German was also the key to upward mobility.

Having been the main targets of more or less forced Germanization, the Jews soon became the main agents of German culture in the region.[21] In 1787, Jews who immigrated to the region were forced to adopt German names. The introduction of compulsory schooling undercut Jewish institutions and encouraged the use of German among the Jewish population. By the turn of the nineteenth century, an increasing number of Jews declared that their native language was German. As a consequence, some German nationalists started distinguishing between the concepts of *sprachdeutsch* (linguistically or culturally German) and *volksdeutsch* (ethnically German).[22] Yet, by then already, in practice, for many of the region's Jews, functional adjustment had become acculturation.[23] Many historians have described the period after 1867 as a 'Golden Age' for the Jews of Bukovina, whose aspirations of emancipation and assimilation on the Viennese model aligned with those of the Austrian rulers who sought Jews' acculturation to German culture so as to strengthen their hold on power.[24] In 1867, Jews were granted full political and legal rights and could work as state employees.[25] These were all reasons why Emperor Franz Joseph, who ruled from 1848 to 1916, was so highly regarded among Bukovina's Jews.

In effect, then, this was social and ethnic diversity under German cultural domination. The Austrian Habsburg accommodation of minorities was mainly pragmatic and hinged on more or less implicit – though not entirely unchallenged – assumptions of superiority and backwardness, respectively.[26] Over time, the heterogeneity of the population even heightened the salience of group identities and differences and the significance of both ethnic and other types of divisions and hierarchies.[27] As Rechter has argued: 'On Austria's eastern border, collective ascription and self-identification were prevalent.'[28] This tendency manifested itself in the creation of increasingly nationalistic political parties, the growing politicization of student associations (*Studentenverbindungen*) and fraternities (*Burschenschaften*), the building of 'national houses' and the setting up of expressly *national* cultural organizations.[29] As Mariana Hausleitner argues, until the mid nineteenth century, Bukovinian society was still significantly stratified along urban/rural and ethnic lines.[30] But by the 1890s, nationalism had gained ground among the respective elites of different groups. According to Hausleitner, the opening of the university in 1875 was a decisive moment, as competition and tensions developed between Ukrainian and Romanian students regarding the language of instruction of theology, and between Romanian and Jewish students over university spaces.[31]

In 1892, Iancu Flondor founded the Romanian National Party, which had contacts among nationalists across the border in Romania. In 1891, the Romanian nationalist historian and politician Nicolae Iorga created the 'Cultural League for the Liberation of Bukovinian Romanians'.[32] Meanwhile, the self-awareness and extent of self-organization of other groups grew too: self-identifying Ukrainians and Poles established their own associations. Until the 1890s, the Jews had supported the German liberals, but, bolstered by their growing numbers and in the face of rising antisemitism, they soon started forming their own parties. The chief representative of Jewish Bukovinians was Benno Straucher of the Jewish National Party, who adopted a stance described as 'Diaspora nationalism'.[33] At that time, Zionism began to take root in the region too. In 1891, Mayer Ebner founded the student organization Hasmonaea and focused on opening Hebrew and Yiddish schools. Three years later, in 1894, the first issue of the Jewish national weekly *Das jüdische Echo* (*The Jewish Voice*) appeared.[34] Understandably, the last to organize politically were the Germans, who were split between liberal and 'German national' tendencies. Yet, in 1896–97, some of them, including a handful of university professors, founded the 'Association of Christian Germans' (Verein christlicher Deutscher) cementing in the name a clear distinction between non-Jewish and Jewish German-speakers.

In Bukovina, the Habsburgs undoubtedly achieved a certain balance and maintained relative peace between the state and the numerous minorities until the turn of the twentieth century. Celebrated as a 'miniature Austria', the crownland's heterogeneity was not perceived as a liability.[35] Yet, as others have noted, this was an 'uneasy equilibrium'.[36] In particular, the notion of a 'German-Jewish symbiosis' in Bukovina deserves qualification. As Robert Wistrich has shown, unlike in other parts of the empire, in Bukovina there was no 'structural assimilation' of the Jews.[37] For the Bukovinian Jewry, there was no perceived incompatibility between allegiance to the Austrian monarchy, identification with Germanness and a strong sense of Jewish group identity based on an array of Jewish institutions and, significantly, the German-Jewish press.[38] In the words of Andrei Corbea-Hoişie, 'Jews [in Bukovina] did not constitute a nation in the traditional sense'.[39] They combined public supranationality and private Jewish nationality, which involved feeling loyalty towards the Kaiser rather than the German nation and aspiring to belong to a German 'cultural sphere' (*Kulturnation*) rather than achieving full assimilation.[40]

The Habsburgs' attitudes towards the Jews, in turn, were also highly ambivalent. They consisted of a mixture of authoritarianism and tolerance, and were characterized by both pragmatism and (occasionally antisemitic) reluctance.[41] Indicative of this is the work of the Austrian, pan-German historian and ethnographer Raimund Friedrich Kaindl, who despite writing both grand and comprehensive studies of the region's folklore and different inhabitants (emphasizing, notably, the German colonists' 'civilizing' contribution) avoided discussing the regions' Jews or treating them as a separate entity.[42] Yet, most telling in this respect is perhaps the situation that emerged out of the Bukovinian electoral compromise (*Ausgleich*) of 1909–10, when representatives of five different nationality groups (Poles, Ukrainians, Romanians, Jews and Germans) were selected, but Vienna refused to recognize Jews as a distinct nationality and vetoed separate German and Jewish political representation.[43] While in practice the Jews had members and a voice, the conflation benefited the rulers and denied their existence as a group with specific demands and concerns.

It is also worth noting that for a long time, Jewish acculturation to the German language was an essentially bourgeois phenomenon, which affected the urban elite and only started spreading to the assimilating Jewish middle and working classes later on. In the late nineteenth century, a majority of Jews in the region still spoke Yiddish at home. Florence Heymann's study of Jews from Bukovina born at the start of the twentieth century reveals that they often belonged to the first generation to step away from *Yiddishkeit* and the shtetl.[44] The region was also a famous centre of Orthodox and, in particular, Hasidic Judaism.[45] In effect, the Jewish community within itself was highly eclectic. Even if by the turn of the century, the Jews came to be seen as the 'real Bukovinians', they by no means unreservedly embraced regional identity, as the rise of Jewish nationalism, socialism (Bundism), Zionism and transatlantic migration reveals.[46] The lively disputes surrounding the question of language use and the organization of the famous 'Czernowitz Language Conference' in Bukovina in 1908, the first ever conference on the Yiddish language, are cases in point.[47]

Non-Jewish German-speakers were not a cohesive group either. As Pieter Judson has argued, speaking of a German national Diaspora in Bukovina before 1918 would be anachronistic.[48] At the time, those who would later come to be known and designated as 'Bukovina Germans' identified primarily in terms of religion – Protestant or Catholic – and, to some extent, according to one of the three waves of colonization that brought them to Bukovina in the first place.[49] For the ethnic German elite like for others, before the First World War, the political reference point was Vienna and not Berlin.[50] But here too, it is essential to distinguish between this small, politically conscious and active leadership and the rest of the group. As Sergij Osatschuk has argued, well into the interwar period, no middle class had been able to develop among the region's non-Jewish German-speakers, and social relations and community life still very much revolved around relatively homogeneous occupational groups.[51] While occupation undoubtedly often overlapped with ethnicity, these relationships were not comparable to national allegiances in the contemporary sense, and society relied heavily on interethnic cooperation to function.

The same kind of prenational structure and fluidity applies to those identified as Romanians and Ukrainians. By the 1860s, the Habsburgs had added Ukrainian and Romanian as 'external service languages' (*äußere Amtssprachen*), but among the speakers of these languages, analphabetism remained high. Overall, in 1890, the illiteracy rate in Bukovina was around 80%, as compared to 30% in other parts of Cisleithania.[52] By the end of the nineteenth century, some Romanian intellectuals claimed Bukovina as theirs and denounced any foreign presence as illegitimate, but Romanians still only represented 15% of the population of the cities, and their elite consisted, for the most part, of teachers and priests.[53] Ukrainians, weaker and more divided in Bukovina than in Galicia, were a predominantly rural and agrarian population, with an even smaller intellectual class than the Romanians and lower rates of land tenure. They also lagged behind in terms of national and political consciousness, despite having achieved political (though not proportional) representation; indeed, by 1880, they constituted the largest and fastest-growing group among the population. As Bálint Varga argues, although there were three 'Ukrainian' chairs at the University of Czernowitz, a Ukrainian master narrative about Bukovina did not develop until 1914.[54] A key reason for this was that most Ukrainians and Romanians both belonged to the locally powerful Greek Orthodox Church – the region's largest landowner – and Romanians dominated the higher echelons of the clergy.

As several scholars have recently shown, it is easy to overstate retrospectively the power of national identification by drawing on specific sources and discourses.[55] It is equally easy to overlook that the Bukovinian synthesis of regional, national and ethnic identities was primarily a feature and product of a pre-modern, pre-national and patriarchal social structure and environment. Such a system has been described as a 'consociational' arrangement whereby 'the elites of diverse ethnic or social groups succeed in establishing a viable pluralistic society through mutual forbearance and accommodation'.[56] In Bukovina, a predominantly rural society, the gaps and contrasts between the cities and towns and the countryside, rich and poor, gentry and peasantry were lastingly significant. Traditional lifestyles and their sense of normalcy thus survived for longer here than elsewhere, alongside elements of modernization and 'a mature intellectual culture'.[57] But Bukovina was not a democracy in the modern sense and it was not spared from the processes of liberalization, nationalization and democratization that swept across the Habsburg lands in the late nineteenth century. In the midst of military and economic collapse at the end of the First World War, the pressures on the Bukovinian status quo were no less severe than elsewhere, despite the fact that a number of Bukovinians – most notably Jews, but also a number of Ukrainians – clung to the monarchy for lack of real alternatives.

Bukovinians without Bukovina: 'Romanization' and Radicalization

The breakup of the Habsburg Empire at the end of the First World War resulted in the integration of Bukovina into Romania and marked the end of Bukovina's existence as a self-standing political entity. While the region's Romanians and Germans were united in the 'people's council' (*Volksrat*), formed in 1918 to represent them, and supported the annexation, the Jews were more wary and cautious. The Ukrainians, who according to the census of 1910 had been more numerous than Romanians, openly opposed the move. This situation led to a short conflict with the Ukrainians and ongoing tensions between Romanians and Ukrainians later on.[58] But the Romanians stood their ground, and the acquisition was eventually ratified at the 1919–20 Paris Peace Conference.

In general, Romania was one of the big winners of the First World War. Becoming what was known as 'Greater Romania', the country's territory doubled in size and its population increased by a third with the acquisition of several new provinces: Bukovina from Austria, Bessarabia from Russia and Transylvania from Hungary. However, these new territories also brought with them new challenges. Bukovina and Transylvania in particular were more developed than the rest of the country, and all three new regions were much more ethnically diverse than the Romanian 'Old Kingdom'. In the new areas, so-called 'national minorities' constituted nearly a third of the population. Not only were their native languages Russian, German or Hungarian, but their members also often occupied key positions in the administration, held the strings of the economy and were proportionally overrepresented in the liberal professions and higher education. Most of these groups also lived in towns and cities and constituted the urban elite. A traditionally antisemitic and nationalizing state thus suddenly had to reckon with some 800,000 Jews, 800,000 Germans and more than 1.5 million Hungarians, mostly living in the same or concentrated areas.

Bukovina, with 55.5% of its population 'non-Romanian', was the most ethnically diverse and 'least Romanian' area of the country.[59] In this former province, therefore, the political backlash was immediate and very tangible. The Paris Peace Treaties had included guarantees for the protection of minority rights, and Romania's gains had even been made conditional on the emancipation of its Jewish population, which had increased from around 1% to around 6% of the overall population. But the Allies lacked the political leverage to ensure the enforcement of these measures, and the Romanian authorities exploited loopholes to bypass the regulations.[60] By 1924, in Bukovina, Romanian had become the only official language within government and schooling, and a large portion of the former German-speaking elite had been demoted or replaced. In the first years after the end of the First World War, many German-speakers in high positions left for Vienna. Czernowitz, now Cernăuți, had been deprived of many of its administrative functions. Indeed, the breakup of the monarchy triggered an economic crisis not only because the region's former economic ties with the rest of the Empire and traditional trading partners were severed, but also because it marked the onset of a series of policies of centralization and so-called Romanization.[61] These measures of so-called 'national integration' were directed against the region's 'foreigners' and impacted education, the administration and the economy.[62] If Bukovina had sometimes been described as an imperial backwater in the past, its integration into Romania only increased its isolation and peripheral position.

The more numerous Ukrainians were a key target of Romanization. Many of their schools, for example, were immediately closed.[63] However, the Germans, making up around 9% (75,000), and Jews, constituting nearly 11% (93,000) of Bukovina's population, were also severely affected by the transfer of sovereignty and its consequences. Proportionally overrepresented in commerce and industry, the cities and higher education, policies of nationalization and changes to the political, administrative and economic order were especially disruptive and disquieting for the region's Jews.[64] While the 1923 Constitution was supposed to grant all Romanian Jews citizenship, those from the newly-acquired provinces were required to provide evidence of former residence in the region. Yet, after the chaos of war, papers were not always obtainable and thousands of Jewish Bukovinians were rendered stateless. At the universities, advocates of a *numerus clausus* for Jewish students were vocal throughout the interwar period and, over time, as antisemitic ideas gained currency, Romanization increasingly turned into an attack on the Jews specifically.[65] In Bukovina, one of the consequences was ongoing Jewish defiance to Romanian rule. This stance found expression in a form of 'resistant nostalgia' that was enacted, among other things, in the continued use of German – especially in private. Many Jews retreated from the real world, displaying a strong attachment to a nostalgic and an illusory mental construction – an 'imagined image of [Bukovinian] society' – mediated by the works of Goethe, Schiller and others.[66] On the one hand, this attitude was a vital source of the region's uniquely diverse, creative and dynamic cultural life and public sphere.[67] However, on the other hand, this behaviour was inseparable from widespread feelings of vulnerability and anxiety among Jews and a deep sense of the situation's unsustainability. By the 1930s, many young Jews were leaving the region to study, looking for opportunities abroad or turning to radical political alternatives.[68]

Romanization also had a negative impact on members of the predominantly rural German communities. As Sergij Osatschuk has shown, relegated overnight to the status of a minority, Bukovina's Germans faced considerable difficulties during the interwar period.[69] Although the majority were small landowners, they also often worked as artisans or had small businesses. The new situation led to unemployment or underemployment, and the general lack of prospects affected the young in particular. As a result, many looked for work outside Bukovina. In the face of mounting pressure on their institutions, community leaders sought a rapprochement with Germans elsewhere. The 'Association of Germans in Greater Romania' (Verband der Deutschen Großrumäniens), which connected German Bukovinians with the larger groups of ethnic Germans in the rest of the country, most notably the more numerous Transylvanian Saxons and Banat Swabians, was founded in 1919. In the following years, an increasing number of visitors from Germany fostered a sense of ethnic identity and the development of a distinct ethnic consciousness among members of this group.[70] Nevertheless, according to Sergij Osatschuk, under the circumstances – Romanian schooling, mixed settlements and work opportunities in the 'Old Kingdom' – Bukovinian German communities were effectively being forced to assimilate to Romanian culture.[71]

Although the tone had been set since its incorporation into Romania, the situation of minorities in Bukovina and their relationships among each other undoubtedly worsened over the course of the interwar years. This degeneration unfolded against the backdrop of Romania's ongoing struggle to establish a stable and functional parliamentary and democratic political system and the rise of popular and state-led antisemitism.[72] Therefore, the period between the wars was not monolithic, and it is possible to distinguish different phases. According to Hildrun Glass, for a time, the German–Jewish relationship oscillated between hostility and pragmatic collaboration as 'German sister minorities'.[73] Hence, she sees the turning point as occurring in 1932. As Florence Heymann argues, many point to the 1926 murder of David Fallik, a Jewish student at the University of Cernăuți,[74] by a follower of Alexandru C. Cuza, the antisemitic leader of the National Christian Defence League, as a critical moment.[75] Yet, others see this as an isolated event, and Heymann herself dates the disintegration of Christian–Jewish relations to the mid 1930s.[76] Mariana Hausleitner identifies a first shift occurring in 1928 insofar as, until then, the Liberal Party with its moderate agenda had dominated politics, and, to some degree, minority structures and institutions – and cooperation among different minority groups – had continued unhindered.[77] Not until the late 1920s did the lack of unity among the Jews – not only nationalists versus Zionists, but also 'Romanian' versus regional organizations and personalities – prove quasi-insurmountable.[78] While support for the liberal Union of Romanian Jews (UER) led by Wilhelm Filderman, who entered into an alliance with the Liberals, mainly came from the Jews in the 'Old Kingdom', Mayer Ebner's Zionist Jewish National Party had a strong following in Bukovina, and the Jewish Party of Romania was leading in the Banat and Transylvania.[79] As Ezra Mendelsohn argues, there were seven different Jewries in Romania during the interwar period and, despite mounting antisemitism, the country's Jews struggled to form a unified bloc.[80]

Most historians agree that the radicalization the region's Germans was not fully discernible until the early 1930s. Glass argues that National Socialism made inroads in Bukovina later than elsewhere in Romania and that the Germans' orientation towards the Reich, Hitler and identification as *Auslandsdeutsche* (Germans abroad) or *Volksdeutsche* (ethnic Germans), rather than as a 'German minority in Bukovina', was not explicit until after 1933.[81] It was not until then that the ethnic German newspaper the *Czernowitzer Deutsche Tagespost*, which had existed since 1926, encouraged a boycott of Jewish shops.[82] But the antisemitism of the German Christian Social Party pre-dated this, and, with the exception of Social Democrats, the opportunities for German-Jewish political alliances and cultural collaboration had significantly diminished since 1918. In the early 1930s, the combined effects of National Socialist propaganda and economic hardship following the Great Depression spurred on political radicalization. With the growth of support among Germans for the Romanian antisemitic National Christian Defence League, internal resistance was soon sidelined.[83] The Nazi-inspired 'Movement of National Renewal' (*Erneuerungsbewegung*), in turn, with a base among the more numerous Germans in Transylvania, rapidly made progress in Bukovina too, especially among the members of the younger generation. This was reflected in the Nazification of the *Tagespost* and the increasing number of young ethnic Germans from Bukovina going to Germany for their studies.[84] By the late 1930s, Germans in Bukovina explicitly relied on Germany for support. At this time, a handful of ethnic German intellectuals from the region, with the physicist Herbert Mayer at the forefront, started publishing genealogical, sociological and biopolitical studies of Germans from Bukovina from an increasingly *völkisch* and racist standpoint.[85] A collection of regional German poetry published in 1939 deliberately did not include any Jewish poets.[86] With the onset of the Second World War, 350 young German Bukovinians volunteered covertly to join the Waffen-SS.[87]

The effects of the deterioration of Romania's domestic political situation in the late 1930s were especially drastic for Jews. This period was marked by the growth of the homegrown fascist and staunchly antisemitic movement, the Legion of the Archangel Michael – also known as simply 'the Legion' or 'the Iron Guard' – and an increasing rapprochement with Germany rather than the Entente Powers, Romania's traditional allies. In this period, it became clear to many Jews that they might 'Romanize', but they would never be treated as equals. The first regime to put through substantive anti-Jewish legislation in Romania was the short-lived Goga-Cuza government in 1937–38. Since the economic effects were dire, King Carol II dissolved the government after only four months. Yet, under pressure to undermine support for the Iron Guard, in February 1938, Carol himself established a 'royal dictatorship' and put through further antisemitic legislation. By September 1939, around 270,000 Romanian Jews had had their citizenship confiscated.[88] The majority of them were Jews from the new provinces who were deemed 'foreign'. In 1940, a series of laws against Jewish interests followed. As Mendelsohn explains, 'Jews were prohibited from owning land in villages, forbidden to publish newspapers, ousted from the army, and denied any role in public life'.[89] Under the influence of Nazi Germany and fascist-inspired movements throughout Europe, Romanians had taken the stance that Jews were a race rather than a religious group and that their presence in the country was undesirable.

In this context, it is hardly surprising that many Jews in northern Bukovina welcomed the annexation of the region by the Soviet Union in June 1940. But this then served the propaganda regarding an alleged 'Judeo-Bolshevik' threat or conspiracy and the claim that 'Jewish betrayal' had caused the territorial losses. Romania's deepening political crisis in 1940 thus contributed to a sharp surge in antisemitic sentiment across the country, as well as growing disillusionment with the king. This crisis proved decisive for the future of Bukovina, Bukovinians and the country in its entirety. Indeed, though Bukovina had ceased to exist as a meaningful political unit in 1918, the region's real dismantling and transformation began on 26 June 1940, when the Soviet Union issued an ultimatum to Romania to evacuate the northern half of the region. Northern Bukovina was annexed despite the fact that Bukovina had not explicitly been named in the secret protocol of the Molotov-Ribbentrop Pact of 1939, which served to justify this move.[90] With the invasion of Soviet troops, many Romanians tried to flee the northern part of the region for the south. Overnight, the capital Cernăuți became Soviet Chernovtsy and thus began what many have described as the 'Russian year' (*das Russenjahr*). This period was marked by the introduction of Russian as the official language, the restructuring of the economy following the Soviet model and the allocation of new jobs and responsibilities based on class and political affiliations and allegiances. In the following months, thousands of Bukovinian so-called 'anti-communists', including a disproportionate number of Jews, were deported by the Soviets farther into the Soviet Union, mainly to Siberia.

For Romania, which, until then, despite ever-closer economic ties to Germany, had remained neutral, the loss of both Bessarabia and northern Bukovina was a considerable blow. However, in the end, the loss of Transylvania to Hungary in August after the Second Vienna Award proved even more fateful. In early September 1940, a coup led by General Ion Antonescu forced King Carol to abdicate in favour of his son Michael and installed a military dictatorship in an alliance with the fascist Iron Guard. In November 1940, Romania entered into a military pact with the Axis Powers, planning what came to be known as a 'war of reintegration' of the lost provinces and resulting, eight months later, in the German-Romanian joint attack on the Soviet Union.

Bukovinians outside Bukovina: War, 'Ethnic Unmixing' and Genocide

The war not only redrew borders but also radically transformed the region's demographic structure. Aside from those deported by the Soviets and the Romanians, who fled to Romania upon hearing about the Soviet ultimatum, in the autumn of 1940, the Nazis evacuated around 96,000 'ethnic Germans' in the context of what has come to be known as the National Socialist 'resettlement home to the Reich' (*die Umsiedlung heim ins Reich*).[91] Officially, the aim was to put an end to 'the dispersion' (*die Zerstreuung*) of ethnic Germans and 'rescue' them from the trials of life in a multiethnic area, by enabling them to live 'as Germans among Germans'.[92] The propaganda notoriously promised that they would be 'losing the homeland [*Heimat*] but gaining the fatherland'.[93] Since many of them had come under Soviet rule as a result of the Molotov-Ribbentrop Pact, they were also being 'saved' from communism, and the operation was therefore described as 'humanitarian' on two counts. Here too, Bukovina's German minority was included in the programme despite the region not being officially named in the pact's secret protocol. But from the perspective of the Nazis, the Germans' removal only constituted a temporary setback anyway. The plan involved relocating them to newly conquered areas of Europe – mainly in Poland, but later also in parts of what had been Slovenia and France – which they were to help 'Germanize'. This move ultimately served the broader Nazi vision for the reorganization of Europe under German domination and along racial lines.

Officially, resettlement was described as optional or 'voluntary' (*freiwillig*) for any German over the age of fourteen. But genuine fear of the Soviets, effective Nazi propaganda regarding their rosy future in an expanded Germany and the social pressure to join meant that the response was overwhelmingly positive.[94] The vast majority of Germans from southern Bukovina, despite not even being under Soviet rule, chose to join as well and, for this, Nazi Germany and the Romanian state had to reach a separate agreement regarding the transfer of the Germans' properties and possessions in this area.[95] In both the northern and southern parts of Bukovina in the weeks before departure, a commission made up of the representatives of the different stakeholders, including many community leaders, appraised people's belongings and organized the transfer.[96] Then, from September to November 1940, trains were sent to fetch the 'resettlers' and take them to Germany or, as the propaganda read, 'bring them home to their motherland'.[97] The total number of people 'resettled' from Bukovina vastly exceeded the 75,533 Germans believed to have lived in the area according to the census of 1930.[98] One reason for this was the high rates of intermarriage in the region and that foreign spouses were also resettled, but many members of other ethnicities, so-called 'Friday Germans' (*Freitagsdeutsche*), are believed to have joined too.[99] Later on, the Nazi assessors regarded Bukovinian Germans, especially those from Czernowitz/Cernăuți, 'the Paris of the East', as one of the groups of Germans of the 'lowest quality' in racial terms.[100] In general, only around half of them were categorized as O-cases, standing for 'the East' (*der Osten*), namely, considered suitable for Germanization and resettlement among ethnic others.[101] The other half, designated as A-cases, standing for *Altreich* (lit.: 'Old Kingdom'), were regarded as 'politically unreliable' or 'Germans with reservations' (*Deutsche unter Vorbehalt*) and were made to stay within the borders of Germany as of 1937 or within Austria, pending reassessment. Some 8,000 'resettlers' were immediately sent back to Romania and a further 6,000, categorized as S-cases (*Sonderfälle* – special cases), were evacuated into the *Generalgouvernement* or were still in camps as stateless people in 1944.[102]

The resettlement *heim ins Reich* is an infamous episode in the history and memory of the Second World War and the Holocaust.[103] Although potential 'resettlers' might at first have been seduced by the straightforwardness of the slogan and attractiveness of German propaganda images, after arriving in Germany, they soon realized that the honeymoon was over. Not only were the 'resettlers' taken to a country waging war, but once 'resettled', they were housed in camps, politically, ideologically and racially screened, and eventually deployed wherever they were needed most from the perspective of the Nazi authorities. For most Bukovinian Germans, this involved being sent to occupied and annexed territories (for the most part Reichsgau Wartheland and East Upper Silesia, but later also Alsace-Lorraine and Styria), where they were compensated with the goods and properties of the Jewish, Polish, French and Slovene residents who had been either murdered or expelled. The implementation of these policies was not only criminal but also chaotic, corrupt, unfair and demeaning.[104] Besides, since Bukovinian Germans were one of the last of the groups of 'resettlers' to arrive in Germany, they were often some of the last to receive houses, accommodated in temporary housing for months or even years, and were often disappointed with their lot.[105] In many cases, men were called up to serve soon after having obtained a farm, leaving their families alone in what many perceived to be a hostile and foreign environment. Thousands of Bukovinians, the A-cases – many of whom had previously been artisans or small landowners – were sent to industrial areas to work in mines or other industries that supported the war, such as the Hermann-Göring-Werke near Linz or Salzgitter. Bukovinian Germans ended up scattered across German and German-occupied territory, with resettlement policies splitting, unlike they had been promised, both communities and families.[106]

The situation of ethnic German resettlers thus consisted of an ambiguous mixture of discrimination and privilege. On the one hand, they were 'human material', pawns of the Nazis, instrumentalized, often humiliated and even victimized by them; on the other hand, they were perhaps more clearly than any other group the 'beneficiaries of genocide', insofar as their experiences were directly linked to the Nazis' policies of theft, expulsion and extermination.[107] In addition, not only were they embroiled in the mechanics of occupation, wartime violence and the Holocaust, but, as Doris Bergen has argued, they also often had even more of a stake in demonstrating Germanness than other Germans, and this ultimately led to a hardening of identities and radicalization.[108] The degree of actual complicity and involvement of Bukovinians specifically in the National Socialist regime requires further research.[109] Another open question pertains to whether resettlement 'destroyed' or 'created' the group that came to be known as 'Bukovina Germans'. The attitude of the Nazis towards regional identity was undoubtedly ambivalent.[110] Yet, some scholars have argued that the propaganda was self-fulfilling, making a cohesive group of Germans out of previously isolated German settlers.[111] While the collective experience of resettlement and the war may have broken some bonds, it also created new ones.

The circumstances under which Bukovinian Jews were 'displaced' from Bukovina were radically different. Antonescu's fascist-style dictatorship brought with it an intensification of existing discriminatory and spoliatory measures in the context of what has come to be known as the process of 'Romanianization' (Romanian policies of Aryanization).[112] However, the regime change also marked the onset of larger, state-sanctioned, state-led and repeated episodes of direct physical violence against Jews in Romania, of which the declared aim was to rid the country definitively of its Jewish inhabitants.[113] In January 1941, a pogrom broke out in Bucharest, leaving dozens dead.[114] On 22 June 1941, Romania joined the war on the side of the Axis Powers intending to recover the territory it had lost to the Soviet Union. With this came the ambition to 'clean up the field' by ridding the country of 'foreigners', 'communist agents and sympathizers' and 'Soviet warmongers', largely equated with Jews.[115] One of the first major brutal consequences of this was the Iași Pogrom, which was launched in Romania's second-largest city in late June 1941. Under the pretext of evacuating Jews from the front, thousands of men and some women and children were beaten to death, shot or left to suffocate in locked and often stationary train wagons.[116] Over 13,000 Jews are believed to have been murdered in this way, at the hands of the Romanian police, army and civilians, with limited German assistance.

However, this sporadic and localized violence was only the second of three phases of the Holocaust in Romania, the first having been legal restrictions and persecution.[117] Romanian anti-Jewish violence culminated in the series of further massacres committed in the summer and autumn of 1941 in the areas the Romanian army reannexed or conquered with German support. The deportation of the Jews of the borderland provinces of Bukovina and Bessarabia across the Dniester River, to the formerly Ukrainian but by then Romanian-administered region of Transnistria soon followed in late 1941 and early 1942.[118] Although southern Bukovina had not even been occupied by the Soviet Union in 1940–41, the Jews in this area were nevertheless also accused of having supported the Soviets and deported too.[119] The third phase of the Holocaust in Romania thus involved the systematic destruction of Bukovinian, Bessarabian and Ukrainian Jews.

The attempt to exterminate the Jews of Bukovina coincided with the invasion of the German army following Hitler's attack on the Soviet Union in June 1941. In the first few days, some 400 members of the Jewish community of Cernăuți were shot on the banks of the Prut River, and murderous pogroms were encouraged in neighbouring villages.[120] The Germans only remained in the city for two weeks. It was the Romanians who, having regained control of the entire region with German help, were the main perpetrators of the Holocaust in Bukovina. In the autumn of 1941, the 50,000 Jews of Cernăuți and the 39,000 living in the southern Bukovinian towns of Suceava, Rădăuți, Vatra Dornei and Câmpulung, and surrounding smaller towns and villages such as Solca, Burdujeni, Ițcani, Gura-Humorului, Vama and Siret were first expropriated and forced into ghettos and then deported.[121] Some of the men were enlisted as forced labourers to support the Romanian army; others were sent to labour camps in Romania. In Cernăuți, the ethnic Romanian mayor Traian Popovici argued that without the Jews, the city's economy would collapse and issued permits enabling some 20,000 Jews to remain in the town after the first phase of deportations ended and the ghetto was dissolved in November 1941. However, by then, some 30,000 Jews had already been deported, and Popovici was unable to prevent a second wave of deportations in the spring of 1942. In Transnistria, deportees were often left to their own devices in devastated towns and villages that were then turned into hundreds of makeshift camps and ghettos. Devoid of adequate or sufficient food, clothing and housing, most of them died of illness, hunger, cold and exhaustion. Some died on marches or were shot by Romanians; many others, especially those who were transferred by the Romanians into German-occupied territory beyond the Bug River, were killed or worked to death by the Germans.[122]

The fate of Bukovinian Jews was both exceptional in Romania and in Europe. The persecution they experienced was part of the European Holocaust, but it was also the result of indigenous policies and local dynamics and circumstances.[123] Though the abuse that Bukovinian Jews suffered was inspired and influenced by the Germans' actions and the Nazi regime's policies, in this region, genocidal measures were more chaotically and less consistently implemented and ultimately – though quite unintendedly from the perspective of the perpetrators – somewhat less lethal. First, some 17,000 Jews were able to survive in Cernăuți during the war. Second, in Transnistria, the lack of organization meant that it was easier to bribe the victimizers or trade with non-Jewish locals. Besides, Jews from Bukovina, who tended to be wealthier than Bessarabian and local Ukrainian Jews and remained closer to the Romanian border, had higher chances of survival. Indeed, the situation in the different Transnistrian ghettos and camps was extremely variable. As Radu Ioanid argues, the lesser the German involvement, the more Jews survived.[124] While in Mogilev-Podolsk, for example, it was possible to open a foundry and set up some form of Jewish self-administration, farther east, in ghettos such as Shargorod, Tulcin or Bershad, chances of survival were incomparably lower. Finally, the Romanian zeal decreased after the summer of 1942 and after the Battle of Stalingrad in particular.[125] Selective repatriations from Transnistria began at the end of 1943 and the Red Army liberated the territory completely in March 1944.

Whether out of pride or caution, Antonescu continuously refused to hand over 'his' Jews to the Germans. Some scholars argue that while deeply felt, his antisemitism was also opportunistic.[126] Certainly, he appears to have made a distinction between Jews from the new provinces and Jews from the 'Old Kingdom': the vast majority of the estimated 280,000 to 380,000 Jews who perished under Romanian jurisdiction during the war were from Ukraine, Bukovina and Bessarabia.[127] Most of the 280,000 Jews who survived in the country, in turn, were from the provinces of Wallachia and Moldavia and Romanian-speakers. Romania's wartime leaders' main concern was 'Romania for the Romanians' and, as primarily German, Yiddish and Russian-speakers, Bukovinian and Bessarabian Jews were considered 'foreign'.[128] Such racist and discriminatory principles and related policies appear to have been met with indifference or even approval by large sections of the non-Jewish Romanian population.[129] Under these circumstances, and despite the fact that around a third of Bukovinian Jews are believed to have survived the war and the Holocaust, it is clear why most survivors could see no future for themselves in the country, even after Antonescu's arrest and Romania joined the Allies in the war on 23 August 1944.

Conclusion

As scholars working on the subject have argued, whatever fluidity that ethnicity in Bukovina might have possessed before the war, it was conclusively eliminated by the conflict. The same applies to the broad spectrum of prewar Bukovinian cultural, political and ideological modes of identification, which were reduced to a small number of reified and oversimplified oppositions and labels. But these same labels were nonetheless then deployed to make sense of the past, wrestle with the present and tackle the future. During the war, being Bukovinian and either a German or a Jew had been a matter of life or death; when the war ended, retaliatory measures followed the same logic. Ethnic Germans were often the targets of such actions.[130] Yet, due to feelings of guilt, resentment and fear in post-Holocaust societies, Jewish survivors' postwar experiences were not free from violence either.[131] Therefore, in the aftermath of the Second World War, the distinction between Bukovinian German and Bukovinian Jew was associated with specific wartime experiences, which had been and would continue to be framed in ethnic terms.

For Bukovinian Germans, the key experience was 'the resettlement' (*die Umsiedlung*). With this, they saw themselves as the victims of the Soviets, of the Allies and even of Hitler. However, the events had nevertheless strengthened their determination to live 'as Germans among Germans' (*als Deutsche unter Deutschen*). For the 50,000 Bukovinian Jews who survived the war, the crucial experiences were the combined terror and suffering under fascism and communism, as well as the ongoing threat of antisemitism. What they went through stood for the failure of the promise of acculturation and assimilation to German culture and ruled out, for many, a future in Europe. Far from the ideal of a multicultural Bukovina, the war seemed to have confirmed the necessity for the convergence of peoples and borders.

Notes

1. This tension, for instance, comes across in: H. Heppner (ed.), *Czernowitz: Die Geschichte einer ungewöhnlichen Stadt* (Cologne: Böhlau Verlag, 2000). For a critical discussion of the notion of a *homo bucoviniensis*, see A. Corbea-Hoişie, *La Bucovine: Eléments d'Histoire Politique et Culturelle* (Paris: Institut d'études slaves, 2004), 32. For a detailed and comprehensive study of 'Bukovinism' and its many paradoxes and stereotypes, see J. van Drunen, *'A Sanguine Bunch': Regional Identification in Habsburg Bukovina, 1774–1919* (Amsterdam: Uitgeverij Pegasus, 2015). On the reverberations of this phenomenon, see J. Le Rider, 'Mitteleuropa as a *lieu de mémoire*', in A.

Erll, A. Nünning and S. Young (eds), *Cultural Memory Studies: An International and Interdisciplinary Handbook* (Berlin: Walter de Gruyter, 2008), 37–46.
2. A. Colin and P. Rychlo, 'Czernowitz, Cernăuți, Chernovtsy, Chernivtsi, Czerniowce', in M. Cornis-Pope and J. Neubauer (eds), *History of the Literary Cultures of East-Central Europe: Junctures and Disjunctures in the 19th and 20th Centuries*, vol. 1 (Amsterdam: John Benjamins Pub., 2004), 70.
3. On this, see e.g. M. Csáky, J. Feichtinger, P. Karoshi and V. Munz, 'Pluralitäten, Heterogenitäten, Differenzen. Zentraleuropas Paradigmen für die Moderne', in M. Csáky, A. Kury and U. Tragatschnig (eds), *Kultur – Identität – Differenz: Wien und Zentraleuropa in der Moderne* (Innsbruck: StudienVerlag, 2004), 13–44.
4. See J. Le Rider, *La Mitteleuropa* (Paris: PUF, 1994), 90. See also L. Wolff, *The Idea of Galicia: History and Fantasy in Habsburg Political Culture* (Stanford: Stanford University Press, 2010). See also Kurt Scharr, for whom Bukovina is a 'Habsburg landscape': K. Scharr, *'Die Landschaft Bukowina': Das Werden einer Region an der Peripherie 1774–1918* (Vienna: Böhlau, 2010).
5. For more on Bukovina's institutional development, see Scharr, *'Die Landschaft Bukowina'*, 143–78.
6. The term was coined by Michael Hechter to discuss British imperial practices. However, it has been perceived as applicable to the case of Habsburgs: V. Glajar, *The German Legacy in Central Europe as Recorded in Recent German Literature* (Rochester, NY: Camden House, 2004), 6.
7. D. Rechter, *Becoming Habsburg: The Jews of Austrian Bukovina, 1774–1918* (Portland, OR: Littman Library of Jewish Civilization, 2013), 91.
8. On this, see B. Varga, 'Rise and Fall of an Austrian Identity in the Provincial Historiography of Bukovina', *Austrian History Yearbook* 46 (2015), 183–202.
9. M. Csáky, 'Introduction', in M. Csáky and E. Mannová (eds), *Collective Identities in Central Europe in Modern Times*, translated from Czech by M. Styan (Bratislava: Academic Electronic Press, 1999), 7–22.
10. Rechter, *Becoming Habsburg*, 5.
11. Ibid., 113. For similar statistics and a concise overview of the history of the region in this period, see M. Hausleitner, 'Eine wechselvolle Geschichte: die Bukowina und die Stadt Czernowitz vom 18. bis zum 20. Jahrhundert', in H. Braun (ed.), *Czernowitz: Die Geschichte einer untergegangenen Kulturmetropole* (Berlin: Links Verlag, 2005), 31–81.
12. There is no certainty about who lived in Bukovina before 1774–75, but presumably these were mainly Ruthenian and Romanian peasants. The majority religion was recorded as Greek Orthodox, but reference is also made to 500 Jewish families. On this, see G. Stourzh, 'Der nationale Ausgleich in der Bukowina', in I. Slawinski and J.P. Strelka (eds), *Die Bukowina, Vergangenheit und Gegenwart* (Bern: Lang, 1995), 24.
13. R. Bartlett and B. Mitschell, 'State-Sponsored Immigration into Eastern Europe in the Eighteenth and Nineteenth Centuries', in R. Bartlett and K. Schönwälder (eds), *The German Lands and Eastern Europe* (Basingstoke: St Martin's Press, 1999), 96. For more on immigration in the case of Bukovina specifically, see Scharr, *'Die Landschaft Bukowina'*, 179–212.
14. E. Turczynski, 'Die Bukowina', in I. Röskau-Rydel (ed.), *Deutsche Geschichte im Osten Europas: Galizien, Bukowina, Moldau* (Berlin: Siedler, 2002), 233.
15. The 1781 Tolerance Edict implemented in 1789 allowed Jews to work in a range of professions and removed restrictions on owning land common elsewhere.

16. For a concise overview of the situation of Jews in Bukovina over time, see A. Corbea-Hoişie, 'Czernowitz', in A. Corbea-Hoişie (ed.), *Czernowitz: Jüdisches Städtebild* (Frankfurt am Main: Jüdischer Verlag, 1998), 7–26.
17. E. Turczynski, *Geschichte der Bukowina in der Neuzeit: zur sozial- und Kulturgeschichte einer mitteleuropäisch geprägten Landschaft* (Wiesbaden: Harrassowitz, 1993), 64–65.
18. Rechter, *Becoming Habsburg*, 113.
19. T. Ciuciura, 'Provincial Politics in the Habsburg Empire: The Case of Galicia and Bukovina', *Nationalities Papers: The Journal of Nationalism and Ethnicity* 13(2) (1985), 247–73, here 265–66.
20. Rechter, *Becoming Habsburg*, 5.
21. See e.g. A. Corbea-Hoişie, 'Der Beitrag der Juden zur deutschen Kultur in Czernowitz', in B. Rill (ed.), *Deutschland und seine Partner im Osten: Gemeinsame Kulturarbeit im erweiterten Europa* (Munich: Hans Seidel Stiftung, 2004), 137–45. On the forced character of this process, see A. Palimariu, 'Der Raum Bukowina in Wilhelm Reichs autobiographischem Kontext', in E. Dácz (ed.), *Räumliche Semantisierungen: Raumkonstruktionen in den deutschsprachigen Literaturen aus Zentral- und Südosteuropa im 20.–21. Jahrhundert* (Regensburg: Verlag Friedrich Pustet, 2018), 197–209, here 198.
22. Van Drunen, 'A Sanguine Bunch', 243. The census results of 1910 are discussed in more detail in M. Broszat, 'Von der Kulturnation zur Volksgruppe: Die nationale Stellung der Juden in der Bukowina im 19. und 20. Jahrhundert', *Historische Zeitschrift* 200(3) (1965), 572–605.
23. Van Drunen, 'A Sanguine Bunch', 263.
24. On the expression and its history, see D. Schaary, 'The Realpolitik of the Jewish National Leadership in Bukovina', in L. Rotman and R. Vago (eds), *The History of the Jews in Romania Vol. 3: Between the Two World Wars* (Tel-Aviv: Tel-Aviv University Press, 2005), 267–315, here 269. See also F. Stambrook, 'The Golden Age of the Jews of Bukovina, 1880-1914', *Department of History University of Manitoba Working Paper* 3(2) (October 2003).
25. On the eve of the First World War, Czernowitz even had a Jewish mayor for the second time, Salo Weisselberger (1912–14).
26. See J. Le Rider, 'Der österreichische Begriff von Zentraleuropa: Habsburgischer Mythos oder Realität?', *Ingeborg Bachmann Centre Lecture 2007* (London: Institute of Germanic & Romance Studies, School of Advanced Study, University of London, 2008).
27. M. Csáky et al., in Csáky, Kury and Tragatschnig, 'Pluralitäten, Heterogenitäten, Differenzen', 15–17.
28. Rechter, *Becoming Habsburg*, 7.
29. In Czernowity, a 'Jewish House' opened in 1908 and a 'German House' in 1910.
30. M. Hausleitner, *Die Rumänisierung der Bukowina: die Durchsetzung des nationalstaatlichen Anspruchs Grossrumäniens 1918 – 1944* (Munich: Oldenbourg, 2001), 50.
31. Ibid., 53.
32. Ibid., 58.
33. Nationalism is not necessarily state-seeking. See J. Shanes, *Diaspora Nationalism and Jewish Identity in Habsburg Galicia* (Cambridge: Cambridge University Press, 2012), 6.
34. Hausleitner, *Die Rumänisierung der Bukowina*, 74. Later, in 1919, Ebner would found the Zionist biweekly *Ostjüdische Zeitung*.
35. Varga, 'Rise and Fall of an Austrian Identity', 189–90.
36. D. Rechter, 'Nationalism at the Edge: The *Jüdische Volksrat* of Habsburg Bukovina', *ASCHKENAS – Zeitschrift für Geschichte und Kultur der Juden* 18/19(1) (2008/2009), 59–89, here 89.

37. Quoted in F. Heymann, 'Aspects of Jewish Life in Bukovina before the Holocaust', *Holocaust and Modernity* 8(2) (2010), 37–46, here 42.
38. See M. Winkler, *Presselandschaft in der Bukowina und den Nachbarregionen: Akteure – Inhalte – Ereignisse (1900–1945)* (Munich: IKGS Verlag, 2011).
39. A. Corbea-Hoişie in Corbea-Hoişie, 'Czernowitz', 13.
40. This is comparable to the case of Moravia and the concept of Jews' tripartite identity. See M. Rozenblit, *Reconstructing a National Identity: The Jews of Habsburg Austria during World War I* (Oxford: Oxford University Press, 2001), 4; see also M. Rozenblit, 'Jews, German Culture, and the Dilemma of National Identity: The Case of Moravia, 1848–1938', *Jewish Social Studies: History, Culture, Society* 20(1) (2013), 77–120.
41. Rechter, *Becoming Habsburg*. On this, see also A. Corbea-Hoişie in Corbea-Hoişie, 'Czernowitz'.
42. See e.g. R.F. Kaindl, *Geschichte der Bukowina von den ältesten Zeiten bis zur Gegenwart unter besonderer Berücksichtung der Kulturverhältnisse* (Czernowitz: Verlag der k. k. Universitätsbuchhandlung H. Pardini 1895). On Kaindl's work in general, see Varga, 'Rise and Fall of an Austrian Identity', 190–93.
43. M. Winkler, *Jüdische Identitäten im kommunikativen Raum: Presse, Sprache und Theater in Czernowitz bis 1923* (Bremen: Ed. Lumiere, 2007), 26. See also Stourzh, 'Der nationale Ausgleich in der Bukowina'.
44. F. Heymann, *Le Crépuscule des Lieux: Identités Juives de Czernowitz* (Paris: Stock, 2003).
45. In particular, the towns of Wischnitz/Wizhnitz/Vyzhnytsia and Sadagora/Sadagura/Sadhora were centres of Hasidic culture.
46. See Rechter, 'Nationalism at the Edge'.
47. On the debates surrounding language use and politics, see S. Marten-Finnis and M. Bauer, 'Jüdische Konfliktkultur und urbane Öffentlichkeit in Czernowitz, 1908–1922', *Internationales Archiv für Sozialgeschichte der deutschen Literatur* 32(2) (2007), 116–27.
48. P. Judson, 'When is a Diaspora not a Diaspora? Rethinking Nation-Centered Narratives about Germans in Habsburg East Central Europe', in K. O'Donnell, R. Bridenthal and N. Reagin (eds), *The Heimat Abroad: The Boundaries of Germanness* (Ann Arbor: University of Michigan Press, 2005), 219–47, especially 236.
49. By the interwar period, 20,000 German Bukovinians were Protestants and 50,000 were Catholics. See H. Glass, *Zerbrochene Nachbarschaft: das deutsch-jüdische Verhältnis in Rumänien (1918–1938)* (Munich: Oldenbourg, 1996), 103. Villages were known as *Zipser* from Hungary, *Schwaben* from what today would be southern Germany or *Böhmer* from Bohemia. Hausleitner, 'Eine wechselvolle Geschichte', 31.
50. S. Osatschuk, 'Die soziale Dynamik und die politischen Orientierungen der Deutschen der Bukowina-Deutschen', in V. Popovici, W. Dahmen and J. Kramer (eds), *Gelebte Multikulturalität: Czernowitz und die Bukowina* (Frankfurt am Main: Peter Lang, 2010), 39–54, here 47.
51. Osatschuk, 'Die soziale Dynamik und die politischen Orientierungen der Deutschen', 48.
52. M. Röger and G. Fisher, 'Bukowina', Online-Lexikon zur Kultur und Geschichte der Deutschen im östlichen Europa, 2017. Retrieved 12 September 2019 from http://ome-lexikon.uni-oldenburg.de/p32554. See also H. Weczerka, 'Ethnien und öffentliches Leben in der Bukowina 1848–1914', *Südostdeutsches Archiv* 42 & 43 (1999–2000), 23–40, here 32.
53. Hausleitner, *Die Rumänisierung der Bukowina*, 48.
54. On this, see Varga, 'Rise and Fall of an Austrian Identity', 198–200. See also S. Frunchak, 'Studying the Land, Contesting the Land: A Select Historiographic Guide

to Modern Bukovina', *The Carl Beck Papers in Russian and East European Studies* 2108, vol. 1 (Essay) and 2 (Notes) (2011).
55. On this, see e.g. P. Judson, 'Nationalism and Indifference', in J. Feichtinger and H. Uhl (eds), *Habsburg neu denken: Vielfalt und Ambivalenz in Zentraleurope: 30 kulturwissenschaftliche Stichworte* (Vienna: Böhlau Verlag, 2016), 148–55.
56. Ciuciura, 'Provincial Politics in the Habsburg Empire', 266. See also B. Kuzmany, 'Habsburg Austria: Experiments in Non-territorial Autonomy', *Ethnopolitics* 15(1) (2016), 43–65.
57. S. Marten-Finnis and M. Winkler, 'Quelle und Diskurs: Czernowitzer Pressefeld 1918–1940: Ein Werkstattbericht des Arbeitskreises Czernowitzer Presse zur Digitalisierung von Czernowitzer Zeitungen 1918–40', in S. Marten-Finnis and W. Schmitz (eds), '… *zwischen dem Osten und dem Westen Europas': Deutschsprachige Presse in Czernowitz bis zum Zweiten Weltkrieg* (Dresden: Thelem, 2005), 49–64.
58. On this, see M. Hausleitner, 'Konfliktfeldern zwischen Rumänen und Ukrainern in der Bukowina zwischen 1910 und 1920', in F. Kührer-Wielach and K. Gündisch (eds), *Mutter: Land – Vater Staat: Loyalitätskonflikte, politische Neuorientierung im österreichisch-russländischen Grenzraum* (Regensburg: Verlag Friedrich Pustet, 2017), 97–118.
59. M. Hausleitner, *'Viel Mischmasch mitgenommen': Die Umsiedlungen aus der Bukowina 1940* (Berlin: Verlag Walter de Gruyter, 2018), 13. According to the 1930 census, 44.5% of people considered themselves Romanian, 29.1% Ukrainian and Russian, 10.8% Jews, 8.9% Germans, 3.6% Polish and 3.1% other smaller nationalities.
60. In December 1919, Romania signed a regulation not to discriminate against citizens on the basis of race, language or religion and to help with employment, language facilities and schools. See E. Mendelsohn, *The Jews of East Central Europe between the World Wars* (Bloomington: Indiana University Press, 1983), 184.
61. On this, see Hausleitner, *Die Rumänisierung der Bukowina*. See also I. Livezeanu, *Cultural Politics in Greater Romania: Regionalism, Nation Building and Ethnic Struggle, 1918–1930* (Ithaca: Cornell University Press, 1995), especially 49–87.
62. The German university moved to Sibiu (Hermannstadt) in Transylvania.
63. M. Hausleitner, 'Die Deutschen in der Bukowina', *Jahrbuch der Deutschen aus Bessarabien* 64 (2013), 93–101, here 96.
64. Livezeanu, *Cultural Politics in Greater Romania*, 78.
65. On this, see C. Iancu, *Les Juifs en Roumanie (1919–1938): De l'Emancipation à la Marginalisation* (Paris-Louvain : E. Peeters, 1996).
66. On the use of German, see M. Hausleitner, 'Rolul intelectualilor evrei în Europa est-centrală pornind de la exemplul Bucoviniei', *Studia et Acta Historiae Iudaeorum Romaniae IX* (Bucharest: Editura Hasefer, 2005), 263–81. On the notion of 'resistant nostalgia', see M. Hirsch and L. Spitzer, *Ghosts of Home: The Afterlife of Czernowitz in Jewish Memory* (Berkeley: University of California Press, 2010), especially xv. On the general phenomenon of Jewish psychological evasion, see Palimariu, 'Der Raum Bukowina', 198, 200.
67. On this, see e.g. S. Marten-Finnis and M. Winkler, 'Location of Memory versus Space of Communication: Presses, Languages, and Education among Czernovitz Jews, 1918–1941', *Central Europe* 7(1) (2009), 30–55.
68. See e.g. Hirsch and Spitzer, *Ghosts of Home*; or G. Ranner, et al. (eds), '… *und das Herz wird mir schwer dabei' Czernowitzer Juden erinnern sich*, 3rd edn (Berlin: Kulturforum östliches Europa, 2009).
69. Osatschuk, 'Die soziale Dynamik und die politischen Orientierungen der Deutschen', 39.

70. Ibid., 43, 48–49.
71. S. Osatschuk, 'Dokumente zur wirtschaftlichen Geschichte der deutschen Volksgruppe in der Bukowina in der Zwischenkriegszeit', *Kaindl-Archiv* 27(19) (1996),196–204, here 204.
72. On this, see H.C. Maner, *Parlamentarismus in Rumänien (1930–1940): Demokratie im autoritären Umfeld* (Munich: Oldenbourg, 1997).
73. Glass, *Zerbrochene Nachbarschaft*, 195.
74. As mentioned in the introduction, I use the name of the city contemporary to the era discussed, hence Romanian Cernăuți here.
75. See e.g. Livezeanu, *Cultural Politics in Greater Romania*, 79–87.
76. Heymann, *Le Crépuscule des Lieux*, 84.
77. Hausleitner, *Die Rumänisierung der Bukowina*, 91. See also M. Hausleitner, 'Transformations in the Relationship between Jews and Germans in the Bukovina 1910-1940', in Tobias Grill (ed.), *Jews and Germans in Eastern Europe: Shared and Comparative Histories* (Berlin: De Gruyter Oldenbourg, 2018), 199–214.
78. For more on this, see Schaary, 'The Realpolitik of the Jewish National Leadership', 284–315.
79. Hausleitner, *Die Rumänisierung der Bukowina*, 296–98.
80. Mendelsohn, *The Jews of Central Europe*, 191.
81. See Glass, *Zerbrochene Nachbarschaft*, 370. See also Hausleitner, 'Transformations in the Relationship'. On the National Socialist colouring of these terms, see R. Münz und R. Ohliger, 'Auslandsdeutsche', in E. François and H. Schulze (eds), *Deutsche Erinnerungsorte*, vol. 1 (Munich: Beck, 2001), 370–88.
82. In response, Meier Teich, the head of the Jewish community of Suceava, is said to have declared: 'we do not want to be German bearers of culture any longer'. Quoted in Glass, *Zerbrochene Nachbarschaft*, 381.
83. This concerns traditional conservative figures such as Alois Lebouton. See Hausleitner, 'Transformations in the Relationship', 210–11; and M. Hausleitner, 'Die Deutschen in der Bukowina', *Jahrbuch der Deutschen aus Bessarabien* 64 (2013), 93–101, here 99.
84. On the radicalization of the German community in Romania, the wider *Verband der Deutschen in Rumänien*, see O. Trașcă, 'Doppelte Loyalität: die deutsche Minderheit Rumäniens 1933–1940', in M. Beer und S. Dyroff (eds), *Politische Strategien nationaler Minderheiten in der Zwischenkriegszeit* (Munich: Oldenbourg Verlag, 2013), 211–39; and A. Komjathy and R. Stockwell, *German Minorities and the Third Reich: Ethnic Germans of East Central Europe* (New York: Holmes and Meier, 1980). The movement originally known as *Selbsthilfe* (self-help) was later renamed Nationale Erneuerungsbewegung der Deutschen in Rumänien (NEDR) (National Movement of Renewal of the Germans in Romania). See also Hausleitner, *'Viel Mischmasch mitgenommen'*, especially 19–29.
85. Hausleitner, *'Viel Mischmasch mitgenommen'*, 51–60.
86. A. Klug (ed.), *Bukowiner deutsches Dichterbuch* (Stuttgart: E. Wahl, Stuttgarter Volksdeutsche Bücherei, 1939).
87. E. Massier, J. Talsky and B.C. Grigorowicz (eds), *Bukowina: Heimat von gestern* (Karlsruhe: Selbstverlag 'Arbeitskreis Bukowina Heimatbuch, 1956), 263.
88. Mendelsohn, *Jews of Central Europe*, 207.
89. Ibid., 208.
90. The Soviets annexed Bukovina at the same time as Bessarabia, which the secret protocol of the agreement placed within the Soviet sphere of influence. See 'Nazi-Soviet Pact'

and 'Bukovina', in I. Dear and M.R.D. Foot (eds), *The Oxford Companion to World War II* (Oxford: Oxford University Press, 2005).

91. From 1939 to 1943, this policy affected some 629,000 people. On this, see D. Jachomowski, *Die Umsiedlung der Bessarabien-, Bukowina- und Dobrudschadeutschen: Von der Volksgruppe in Rumänien zur 'Siedlungsbrücke' an der Reichsgrenze'* (Munich: R. Oldenbourg, 1984); V.O. Lumans, *Himmler's Auxiliaries: The Volksdeutsche Mittelstelle and the German National Minorities of Europe, 1933–1945* (Chapel Hill: University of North Carolina Press, 1993); O. Kotzian, *Die Umsiedler: Die Deutschen aus West-Wolhynien, Galizien, der Bukowina, Bessarabien, der Dobrudscha und in der Karpatenukraine* (Munich: Langen Müller, 2005); and most recently, Hausleitner, 'Viel Mischmasch mitgenommen'.

92. On this discourse, see E. Harvey, 'Homelands on the Move: Gender, Space and Dislocation in the Nazi Resettlement of German Minorities from Eastern and Southeastern Europe', in M. Röger and R. Leiserowitz (eds), *Women and Men at War: A Gender Perspective on World War II and its Aftermath in Central and Eastern Europe* (Osnabrück: Fibre Verlag, 2012), 35–58, here 48. See also I. Heinemann, *Rasse, Siedlung und deutsches Blut: Das Rasse- und Siedlungshauptamt der SS und die rassenpolitische Neuordnung Europas* (Göttingen: Wallstein, 2003); M. Leniger, *Nationalsozialistische 'Volkstumsarbeit' und Umsiedlungspolitik 1939–1945: Von der Minderheitenbetreuung zur Siedlerauslese* (Berlin: Frank und Timme, 2006).

93. See E. Hahn und H.H. Hahn, *Die Vertreibung im deutschen Erinnern: Legenden, Mythos, Geschichte* (Paderborn: Ferdinand Schöningh, 2010), 168.

94. Only 3,446 stayed behind in North Bukovina and 7,000 in southern Bukovina, where 90% were in favour. See Hausleitner, 'Viel Mischmasch mitgenommen', 100, 107, 110. On the general enthusiasm concerning Nazi resettlement from Romania, see the contemporary account: R.G. Waldeck, *Athene Palace, Bucharest: Hitler's 'New Order' Comes to Romania* (London: Constable, 1943), 239 ff.

95. On this, see Jachomowski, *Die Umsiedlung*, 88–95; Hausleitner, 'Viel Mischmasch mitgenommen', 101–13.

96. This included Franz Kopecki, the German deputy for the Romanian mayor of Cernăuți. On the exact unfolding of the events and the profiles of the diverse German leaders involved, see Hausleitner, 'Viel Mischmasch mitgenommen', 81–113.

97. North Bukovinians were mostly sent to western Poland and South Bukovinians to Austria (*Ostmark*). See Hausleitner, 'Viel Mischmasch mitgenommen', 111.

98. Ibid., 6.

99. For this expression, see Turczynski, 'Die Bukowina', 322. This was especially the case in northern Bukovina, where 20% more people than had declared German as their ethnicity in 1939 left. On this, see Hausleitner, 'Viel Mischmasch mitgenommen', especially 81–101, here 95.

100. Heinemann, *Rasse, Siedlung und deutsches Blut*, 246. See also Hausleitner, 'Viel Mischmasch mitgenommen', 135.

101. Hausleitner, 'Viel Mischmasch mitgenommen', 5.

102. Original statistics concerning resettlement have been published online based on archival data: 'Die Umsiedlung Stand 1. Juli 1942'. Retrieved 12 September 2019 from http://homepages.uni-tuebingen.de/gerd.simon/umsiedlung-statistik.pdf. See also Hausleitner, 'Viel Mischmasch mitgenommen', 95 (North Bukovina), 115.

103. On this, see Hahn and Hahn, *Die Vertreibung im deutschen Erinnern*, especially 168–209, here 180.

104. This as the case of other ethnic German groups too. See e.g. C. Dieckmann, 'Plan und Praxis: deutsche Siedlungspolitik im besetzten Litauen 1941–1944', in I. Heinemann and P. Wagner (eds), *Wissenschaft, Planung, Vertreibung: Neuordnungskonzepte und Umsiedlungspolitik im 20. Jahrhundert* (Stuttgart: Steiner, 2006), 93–118, here 101. Although he emphasizes that it is incomparable to what the Jews and the Poles experienced, Pertti Ahonen also makes this point; see P. Ahonen, *People on the Move: Forced Population Movements in Europe in the Second World War and its Aftermath* (Oxford: Berg, 2008), 114.

105. There is ample evidence of resettlers' dissatisfaction with their situation. See e.g. E. Harvey, 'Management and Manipulation: Nazi Settlement Planners and Ethnic German Settlers in Occupied Poland', in C. Elkins and S. Pedersen (eds), *Settler Colonialism in the Twentieth Century: Projects, Practices, Legacies* (New York: Routledge, 2005), 95–112. As Hausleitner points out, a large number of resettlers from Bukovina sought to return to Romania. Until 1943, 9,000 did, but many more wanted to; see Hausleitner, 'Viel Mischmasch mitgenommen', 6.

106. This might have been the aim of the policy. See Hausleitner, 'Viel Mischmasch mitgenommen', 250.

107. Harvey, 'Management and Manipulation'; R. Schulze, 'Forgotten Victims or Beneficiaries of Plunder and Genocide? The Mass Resettlement of Ethnic Germans "heim ins Reich"', *Annali dell'Instituto storico-germano in Trento* XXVII (2001), 533–64; Isabel Heinemann, 'Towards and "Ethnic Reconstruction of Occupied Europe": SS Plans and Racial Policies', *Annali dell'Instituto storico-germano in Trento* XXVII (2001), 493–517. Resettlement has controversially been described as the prerequisite for genocide. See e.g. G. Aly, *Endlösung: Völkerverschiebung und der Mord an den europäischen Juden* (Frankfurt am Main: Fischer, 1995). For a response, see V.O. Lumans, 'A Reassessment of Volksdeutsche and Jews in the Volhynia-Galicia-Narew Resettlement', in A. Steinweis and D. Rogers (eds), *The Impact of Nazism: New Perspectives on the Third Reich and its Legacy* (Lincoln, NE: University of Nebraska Press, 2003).

108. See D.L. Bergen, 'The Nazi Concept of "Volksdeutsche" and the Exacerbation of Anti-Semitism in Eastern Europe, 1939–45', *Journal of Contemporary History* 29(4) (1994), 569–82; and D.L. Bergen, 'Tenuousness and Tenacity: The "Volksdeutschen" of Eastern Europe, World War II, and the Holocaust', in O'Donnell et al. (eds), *Heimat Abroad*, 267–86.

109. Mariana Hausleitner's recent book is the first to address this question systematically by focusing on specific individuals and their political stances and activities; Hausleitner, 'Viel Mischmasch mitgenommen'. The areas in which many Bukovinians were resettled were often close to key sites of the Holocaust, raising questions about the degree of their knowledge and involvement. On this, see G. Fisher, 'Schweigen, Störung und Stimmigkeit: Erinnerungen an die Umsiedlung "Heim ins Reich" unter den Buchenlanddeutschen', in H.W. Retterath (ed.), *Germanisierung im besetzten Ostoberschlesien während des Zweiten Weltkriegs* (Münster: Waxmann, 2018), 273–304. More research is needed on the everyday lives of Bukovinian Germans specifically during the war.

110. On this, see A. Strippel, 'Race, Regional Identity and *Volksgemeinschaft*: Naturalization of Ethnic German Resettlers in the Second World War by the Einwandererzentralstelle/Central Immigration Office of the SS', in C.W. Szejnmann and M. Umbach (eds), *Heimat, Region, and Empire Spatial Identities under National Socialism* (Basingstoke: Palgrave Macmillan, 2012), 185–98.

111. Leniger, *Nationalsozialistische 'Volkstumsarbeit' und Umsiedlungspolitik*.

112. Romanianization included policies of exclusion, extortion and exploitation; the expropriation of property and assets; the expulsion of individual Jews from their homes; and the wider spoliation of Jewish communities. On Romanianization, see S.C. Ionescu, *Jewish Resistance to 'Romanianization', 1940–44* (Basingstoke: Palgrave Macmillan, 2015).
113. For an overview of these events, see M. Carp, *Cartea Neagră: Suferinţele Evreilor din România, 1940–1944*, 3 vols (Bucharest: Editura Diogene, 1996 [first published 1945–1948]); R. Ioanid, *The Holocaust in Romania: The Destruction of Jews and Gypsies under the Antonescu Regime, 1940–1944* (Chicago: Dee, 2000); T. Friling, R. Ioanid and M. Ionescu (eds), *Final Report of the International Commission on the Holocaust in Romania* (Iaşi: Polirom, 2004); and J. Ancel, *The History of the Holocaust in Romania*, translated from Hebrew by Y. Murciano and edited by L. Volovici with the assistance of M. Caloianu (Lincoln, NE: University of Nebraska Press, 2011). See also S. Geissbühler, *Romania and the Holocaust: Events, Contexts, Aftermath* (Stuttgart: Ibidem, 2016).
114. See C. Guşu, 'Analyse d'une Tragédie: La Représentation du Pogrom de Bucarest dans la Presse de l'Epoque', in G. Bensoussan (ed.), *L'Horreur Oubliée : la Shoah Roumaine* (Paris: Mémorial de la Shoah, 2011), 75–98.
115. See J. Ancel, 'Le Pogrom de Iasi : Sur la Responsabilité des Autorités de l'Etat Roumain dans la Mise en Scène, la Préparation et l'Exécution du Pogrom de Iasi et sur l'Etablissement du Nombre de Victimes', in Bensoussan, *L'Horreur Oubliée*, 143–71.
116. See Ioanid, *Holocaust*, 70. On this, see also J. Ancel, *Prelude to Mass Murder: The Pogrom in Iaşi, Romania, June 29, 1941 and Thereafter*, translated from Hebrew by Fern Seckbach (Jerusalem: Yad Vashem, 2013).
117. Heymann, 'Introduction', in Bensoussan, *L'Horreur Oubliée*, 17–26, here 21. On the phases, see A. Heinen, *Rumänien, der Holocaust und die Logik der Gewalt* (Munich: Oldenbourg, 2007); H. Glass, *Deutschland und die Verfolgung der Juden im rumänischen Machtbereich, 1940–1944* (Munich: Oldenbourg, 2014).
118. On the massacres, see S. Geissbühler, *Blutiger Juli: Rumäniens Vernichtungskrieg und der vergessene Massenmord an den Juden 1941* (Paderborn: Schöningh, 2013). On Transnistria, see J. Ancel, *Transnistria: The Romanian Mass Murder Campaigns*, 3 vols (Tel-Aviv: Goldstein Goren Diaspora Research Center, 2003).
119. This was also the case of Jews from the Dorohoi region.
120. On this, see A. Angrick, *Besatzungspolitik und Massenmord: die Einsatzgruppe D in der südlichen Sowjetunion 1941–1943* (Hamburg: Hamburger Edition, 2003).
121. The order to force the 50,000 Jews of Cernăuţi into a ghetto consisting of just a few streets was implemented on 11 October 1941. The Jews from the south were deported between 9 and 14 October. See Ioanid, *The Holocaust in Romania*, 159–60.
122. Ioanid argues that 'between June 1941 and June 1942, Einsatzgruppe D liquidated about ninety thousand people'; ibid., 187. On *Sonderkommando R*, see E. Steinhart, *The Holocaust and the Germanization of Ukraine* (New York: Cambridge University Press, 2015).
123. On this, see D. Dumitru, *The State, Antisemitism, and Collaboration in the Holocaust: The Borderlands of Romania and the Soviet Union* (New York: Cambridge University Press, 2016).
124. Ioanid, *The Holocaust in Romania*, 200.
125. Ibid., 193.
126. D. Deletant, *Hitler's Forgotten Ally: Ion Antonescu and his Regime, Romania 1940–1944* (Basingstoke: Palgrave Macmillan: 2006), 271–88.
127. This is the range quoted by experts. See Friling, Ioanid and Ionescu, *Final Report*, 179.

128. See V. Solonari, *Purifying the Nation: Population Exchange and Ethnic Cleansing in Nazi-Allied Romania* (Baltimore: Johns Hopkins University Press, 2010).
129. On this, see Ionescu, *Resistance to 'Romanianization'*.
130. The postwar 'expulsions' of Germans are a case in point. See R.M. Douglas, *Orderly and Humane: The Expulsions of the Germans after the Second World War* (New Haven: Yale University Press, 2012). In addition, across Europe, an estimated 380,000 Germans were deported to the Soviet Union for forced labour at the end of the war, including a few hundred Germans from Bukovina. See Ahonen, *People on the Move*, 117.
131. The most notorious case is that of the pogrom in Kielce in Poland in 1946. See J.T. Gross, *Fear: Anti-Semitism in Poland after Auschwitz; an Essay in Historical Interpretation* (New York: Random House, 2006).

Part II
ESTABLISHMENTS

Chapter 2

'SETTLING IN THE MOTHERLAND'

'Resettlers' from Bukovina in West Germany after the Second World War

In 1957, on the twenty-fifth anniversary of the founding of the Heimstättensiedlung, a housing settlement on the outskirts of West German city of Darmstadt, the residents published a small brochure about the area's and its inhabitants' history. The booklet included a contribution about the nearly 1,000 Bukovinian Germans who had settled in this area over the previous decade. A section of the text read as follows:

> After resettlement [in 1940], we long felt depressed and disadvantaged because of our otherness. We spoke differently, and people therefore often looked down on us. Like a tree in new earth, we first needed time to get used to the surroundings. Today [in 1957], most of us have learned to master the new environment. We have lost our misplaced reverence for the way things appear and see things as they are. Now awakes in us, especially among the young, our former efficiency and our will to settle once again, this time in the motherland, and here, as once before in the East, to do our best to be a model of Germanness to others.[1]

At this point, nearly ten years had passed since the first Bukovinian Germans had arrived and started building houses in the area, and some seventeen since their resettlement 'home to the Reich' by the Nazis. By then, as the quote indicates, many had found peace and comfort in what they framed as their 'old-new home'. Indeed, in their own understanding, the war and the end of the war had displaced 'Bukovina Germans' back to their ancestral homeland. However, this 'return', starting with the National Socialist resettlement itself, had been an ambivalent experience. The arguments used in this brochure capture the complexity of Bukovinian Germans' wartime and postwar experiences – experiences marked by a constant oscillation and negotiation between similarity and difference, ethnic pride and German victimhood, tradition and new beginnings. Yet, at the same time, the arguments also suggest how 'being Bukovinian' could and did remain a source of identification and identity in West Germany more than ten years after the end of the Second World War.

As the war came to an end, an estimated 60,000–80,000 Germans from Bukovina, who had survived the Second World War, were scattered across Europe and the territory of what would become the Federal Republic of Germany (FRG), the German Democratic Republic (GDR) and the Republic of Austria. The dominant sentiment was one of confusion. According to postwar accounts, most Bukovinian Germans did not want to return to Bukovina, but they did not know what the future held for them in their 'new homelands' either, or even what these new homelands themselves would look like. Bukovinian Germans were just a fraction of the total number of refugees on what had once been German territory. At the end of the war, millions of foreigners, primarily enslaved, forced and foreign workers, were living in what remained of the German Reich. Many of these so-called Displaced Persons (DPs) were repatriated straight away, but others, most notably Eastern and Central European Jews, did not want to return to their prewar homes. In turn, millions of German prisoners of war were living in foreign custody awaiting repatriation, and millions of Germans who had lost their homes in the bombings were homeless. Last but not least, an estimated twelve million Germans fled or were expelled from their ancestral homelands in Central and Eastern Europe between 1944 and 1952 in what has come to be known as the events of 'flight and expulsion' (*Flucht und Vertreibung*).[2]

Approximately four million of these German refugees ended up in the Soviet zone, which would later become the GDR, and eight million in the Western zones, which would become the FRG. There, in some areas, these 'expellees of the homeland' (*Heimatvertriebene* or, simply, *Vertriebene*), as they soon came to be known represented up to 20% of the population.[3] Most of these people, stemming from the lost territories behind the Oder-Neisse line, had been German citizens before the war. But many others, like the Bukovinian Germans, were so-called ethnic Germans (*Volksdeutsche* or *Auslandsdeutsche* – Germans living abroad) and had not. Fearing the radicalization of this large, uprooted, impoverished and disenfranchised population, the Allies in the Western zones, where most of the Bukovinian Germans ended up, drew up a distinction between refugees who were held to be foreigners and those regarded as coethnics, who were to be granted German citizenship, ethnically coded material benefits and political representation.[4]

Not only did this heighten the significance of being identified as 'German', but it also produced, as Rogers Brubaker has argued, a legal myth based on an ethnonational definition of the state that made it possible to frame 'displacement as return'.[5] As a result, although the violent and forced character of this episode of displacement is unquestionable, the movement of Germans to Germany after the war also bears some similarity to other cases of ethnic or even 'privileged migration'.[6] Still today, how to characterize this movement of population and the circumstances of the so-called postwar 'integration' of expellees remains the subject of contention.[7]

In any event, these circumstances led to a complex politics of belonging by which the definition of Germanness was both considerably stretched and intimately tied to notions of victimhood and these people's prewar and wartime experiences.[8] This, in turn, raises intriguing and important questions about the continuities from Nazism and the significance of war experiences for the character of West German society after the Second World War. As the passage quoted above indicates, there were, for example, inevitable parallels between the postwar events and situations and the Nazis' own attempts to define Germanness, as well as their attempts to 'bring Germans home' to live 'as Germans among Germans'. The reference to the tree in the opening passage certainly resonates with the biological metaphors of 'transplantation' used in the Nazi period. However, the circumstances were nevertheless quite different. While a great deal has been written about experiences of 'expellees' in postwar West Germany, the case of German Bukovinians thus raises a range of new, more specific and intriguing questions.[9] How did they deal with the legacy of their experience of National Socialist resettlement? How did they relate to and contribute to the broader discourse on 'expellees' and 'the expulsion'? How did they conceive of their victimhood as Germans and mobilize it after the Second World War? What means did they have at their disposal and who were the main actors? Finally, as a highly heterogeneous group, stemming from a region known for both its remoteness and diversity, what historical narrative did they hold on to? In other words, how did they conceive of their Germanness or why and in what way did 'Bukovinian' remain a source of identification?

This chapter explores how German Bukovinians constructed belonging in West Germany after the Second World War. It thereby offers a case study of expellee experiences and the politics of identity and integration in the country, while at the same time highlighting the particularities of the history of this group. Within a few years of the end of the war, most Bukovinian Germans had established themselves materially and socially, acquired full civil rights, secured benefits and even obtained an officially sanctioned representational body in the form of their own 'homeland society' (Landsmannschaft) in the Federal Republic.[10] In particular, this chapter examines the triangular relationship developed between the Bukovinian Germans' representative organization and its leaders, their putative members and society at large, and the evolution of this relationship during the first decade after the end of the war. Although expellees' representative organizations were notoriously not representative, they nevertheless controlled the narrative and shaped the political landscape of the early postwar period in Germany. This example thus sheds new light on both the symbolic politics of ethnic German refugees and the character of the political-cultural space of the early Federal Republic. In so doing, this chapter also gives privileged insight into how wider conceptions of Germanness developed after the Second World War.

Displaced Back Home:
West Germany as Both Old and New Homeland

The end of the war was a dramatic and confusing time for many Bukovinian Germans. Those who had been resettled in the West in Alsace and Lorraine, some 5,000 people, fled eastwards in late 1944 as the western Allies liberated the area from the west. A few months later, with the Red Army advancing from the east, most of the up to 58,000 people who had been resettled in German-occupied territories in Poland, Czechoslovakia and Slovenia fled too.[11] Having arrived most recently in these areas, Bukovinian Germans were often among some of the first to leave, before the war was even over, in the cold winter of 1944–45. Many joined treks organized in haste by the National Socialists back to the reduced territory of the *Reich* or to locations behind the front lines. Mothers with young children could sometimes take trains, but the rest had to walk; men were mostly absent, having fallen, been conscripted – some more recently than others – or been taken prisoner. At the time, an estimated 17,000 Bukovinian Germans are believed to have been living in the *Altreich* – namely within the borders of Germany as of 1937 – or Austria. Some of them had not yet left the 'resettler camps'; others had been recruited to work in the war industry or obtained administrative postings in these areas. Yet, having been separated from their communities and relatives, and due to the circumstances of the war itself, mostly their situation had felt temporary, and the future was uncertain for them too. At the end of the war, therefore, most Bukovinian Germans ended up, once again, as refugees in camps or makeshift accommodation and did not know where to go or where they belonged. Until December 1945, a few thousand were repatriated back to Bukovina by the Soviets from Poland, Czechoslovakia and even the Soviet zone.[12]

The pattern of settlement of Bukovinian Germans after the war can be traced back to what had happened in the final weeks and months of the conflict and its immediate aftermath. These circumstances resulted in the dispersion of members of this group across what was once German territory and beyond. A number of those who had been working for the Hermann-Göring-Werke in Salzgitter-Lebenstedt, for example, and others who found themselves in industrial centres, remained where they were. Similarly, among those who had been resettled abroad, many stopped where the treks, organized by the Germans at the end of the war, took them, especially if they found work, housing or relatives already there. This was the case in Bitterfeld in East Germany, where some Bukovinians had been working during the war and where newcomers found work in local industry, as well as in Austrian Linz, where there was both industrial work and a large refugee community. Geographical proximity was often a determining factor. Those who had been resettled in Alsace-Lorraine, for example, were evacuated into the Saarland and often settled there or in western Germany. For this same reason, initially, many who had been living in the eastern territories ended up in the Soviet zone, as this was their first point of arrival. Yet, many Bukovinian Germans, like other members of refugee groups, soon moved on from there, crossing the so-called 'green border' illegally. Not knowing where to go, some returned to the areas they had first been sent to in 1940, as these were familiar places, or tried to join friends and relatives.[13] Others sought out the alleged 'ancestral home' (*Urheimat*) of their ancestors.[14] In the early 1950s, some Bukovinian Germans also left for North and South America, as they could see no future for themselves in postwar Europe or in a reduced Germany, especially if they wished to work in agriculture and own land.[15]

Despite the theoretical difficulty of moving across regions and zones, in the early postwar years, there was a high degree of fluidity and movement across borders as families reunited and people tried to make sense of the new geopolitical situation. According to the numbers provided by the Landsmannschaft to the Ministry of the Interior for the years 1952–53, an estimated 59,000 Bukovinian Germans were living in the West Germany, 3,000 in their native homeland, 9,000 abroad (mostly Austria) and 10,000 in the GDR. One thousand were in custody and 15,000 were dead or missing since 1939. At this time, the regional breakdown for the FRG was the following: 33,200 in Bavaria, 7,200 in the Southwest, 6,500 in Lower Saxony, 6,300 in Hesse, 5,000 in Rhineland Palatinate, 480 in North Rhine-Westphalia, 150 in Berlin, 120 in Schleswig Holstein, 25 in Hamburg and 15 in Bremen.[16]

The situation of Bukovinian Germans was somewhat distinct from that of other German refugees. For one thing, this was their second displacement from their homes in the space of just a few years. In the first case, although they had been told they were merely 'returning to Germany', they had ended up as instruments in the hands of the Nazis, exploited for the sake of conquest and the 'Germanization' of occupied territories.[17] In this situation, many had felt, as the quote at the start of this chapter suggests, betrayed and out of place – treated like second-class citizens. However, their second displacement presented new challenges: not only was it more violent, but they were also joining a society that had just experienced a brutal war, defeat and unprecedented physical destruction. Besides, they were a small group among millions, and their situation was especially insecure since they did not know whether their acquisition of citizenship under the National Socialists, their so-called *Einbürgerung* during the war, would be recognized by the new rulers. In this sense, their circumstances were different from those of the millions of Germans from the so-called 'lost territories', the occupants of which had been German citizens already before the war. Their situation was also different from that of the 'ethnic Germans' (*Volksdeutsche*) who, despite not being German citizens, had fled their native homelands, such as Czechoslovakia, Yugoslavia, Poland or Hungary, under the threat of persecution *because* they were regarded as German and could not stay or return home. After the end of the war, Romania, in contrast to other states, had not evicted its German minority population.

In general, there was considerable confusion concerning the status of different kinds of refugees, and 'resettlers' (*Umsiedler*) were at the mercy of the occupying powers and their definition of who was German. Moreover, even by comparison to other 'resettled' Germans, such as the Bessarabian or the Baltic Germans, Bukovinians were a disunited and heterogeneous group. Not only had they experienced a higher degree of dispersion due to their late resettlement and their comparatively worse treatment by the Nazis, but they had been a sociologically diverse group before the war too. While there was an educated elite, it was small; the majority had been small farmers, farmhands and craftspeople, and many had lived in rural, remote and mixed settlements. This lack of cohesion and homogeneity in terms of their background, social structure and experiences posed a challenged to coordination and collective action. In contrast, Baltic Germans, with their century-old, established upper class and having long constituted the educated elite in their homeland, had rapidly become politically active and, for instance, soon contested their designation as stateless DPs vehemently.[18] As for Bessarabian Germans, not only did they have a more recent history of migration (they had left the German lands in the late nineteenth century) and a more homogeneous experience of 'resettlement' during the war, but due to their experience of living in closed settlements before the war, they also had a stronger sense of their German identity, community and origins. Most of them settled in what would become Baden-Württemberg in and around Stuttgart, in the region of Swabia (*Schwabenland*), which they believed was their 'ancestral home' (*Urheimat*). According to their own account, local politicians also encouraged them to come there.[19]

However, it may have been precisely the precariousness of Bukovinian Germans' situation that led some members of the group to be particularly proactive in organizing mutual assistance. Since early 1945, the desperate situation of many refugees had resulted in a general 'appeal to self-help' (*Aufruf zur Selbsthilfe*) and a number of self-help organizations had developed.[20] Yet, Bukovinian Germans were among the first, in June 1945, to set up a 'Search Bureau' under the aegis of the Relief and Advice Office for Southeastern Europe (Hilfs- und Beratungsstelle für Südosteuropa) within the Bavarian Red Cross and a *Heimatkartei*, namely a register with names of people from the region.[21] Like other groups, they then organized under the umbrella of the churches – a way of sidestepping the occupation authorities' ban on political organizations known as the *Koalitionsverbot*. A Catholic helpdesk (*Hilfstelle*) was first created within the Catholic Caritas; then, in December 1946, a Relief Committee for German Resettlers from Bukovina (Hilfskomitee für die deutschen Umsiedler aus der Bukowina), financed by the Protestant Church (Hilfswerk der Evangelischen Kirche in Deutschland), was also founded.[22] While these two organizations were separate, they served both Catholics and Protestants, and constituted, as others have argued, an 'early embodiment' of the later Landsmannschaft, which brought together all Bukovinian Germans regardless of their confession.[23] The Protestant pastor Edgar Müller and the Catholic priest Kurt Bensch adopted leading roles within these organizations, but so did a handful of others who would become the backbone of the later Bukovinian German Landsmannschaft. These included: Rudolf Wagner (born 1911), a historian by training and former member of the SS, who was the head of the Relief and Advice Office for Southeastern Europe from 1947 to 1953 and the later 'deputy chair' (*2. Vorsitzender*) and then the long-time speaker of the Landsmannschaft;[24] Max Zelgin (born 1911), a lawyer by profession, who had been a youth leader in Bukovina before 1939 and was later a member of the Landsmannschaft's board and then the national leader of the Landsmannschaft (1974–84); Hans Uhrich, who had helped organize resettlement from southern Bukovina in 1940; and Hans Prelitsch (born 1901), a banker in Romania who returned from Soviet custody in 1947 and was later responsible for the Landsmannschaft's 'cultural affairs' (*Kulturreferent*) and, from 1950, the editor of its newspaper.[25]

The early organizations offered pastoral care and aimed to resolve the most urgent social and humanitarian problems the group faced. They assisted the authorities and the Red Cross with regional knowledge and informed Bukovinian Germans about their rights and duties. For instance, they helped with finding and identifying missing persons and replacing lost documents by attesting to people's identity, and helped Bukovinians secure loans and pensions, housing and jobs, as well as achieve family reunification, emigration and zonal transfers. In addition, they lobbied the authorities for the return of prisoners of war, *Heimkehrer* or *Spätheimkehrer* or Bukovinians who were repatriated to Romania by the Soviets and campaigned for financial compensation for lost property and goods. By their own admission, they also helped people manage (e.g. evade) denazification procedures.[26] In their view, integration meant rehabilitation; for instance, they considered the requirement to justify their participation in the SS – 'a criminal organization' – unfair.[27] In this period, the top priority remained to defend Bukovinians' claim to citizenship and Germanness. In effect, they fought for recognition both as refugees and as German citizens.[28] It is no coincidence that they continued to use the National Socialist term *Umsiedler* in their correspondence and, most notably, in the name of their institutions. Other groups of 'resettlers' did this too.[29] This word not only stood for their particular experience of displacement, but also for their obtaining citizenship four years earlier under the Nazis, and as far as they were concerned, there could hardly be a better proof of Germanness.

Few sources from this period have survived. Yet looking at what happened on what was to become two of the main housing settlements (*Siedlungen*) of Bukovinian Germans in West Germany gives an interesting insight into the activities and situation of Bukovinian Germans in the immediate aftermath of the war. These are the 'Bukovina settlement' (*Buchenlandsiedlung*) of the Heimstättensiedlung near Darmstadt in the region of Hesse and the settlement of Büsnau in the area of Vaihingen near Stuttgart in Baden-Württemberg. Both settlements have interesting histories that reflect wider national trends as well as local dynamics and offer a privileged insight into both local contexts and the situation of Bukovinian Germans in this period.[30] The idea for the settlement near Stuttgart, for example, developed because a few Bukovinian Germans were living as refugees in army barracks near an unfinished so-called 'SA settlement' – a settlement initially intended for members of the Nazi Stormtroopers (Sturmabteilung (SA)) – dating from the 1930s. A few houses already stood, but some had been bombed and the rest were empty plots. In early 1946, Adolf Engster, a Bukovinian German from Rădăuți living in the barracks, had approached Arnulf Klett, the Mayor of Stuttgart, with the idea of building more houses in the area for members of his group and had managed to secure Klett's approval. The deal established that the city would provide the land and the materials needed for construction as well as interest-free loans and temporary accommodation. In exchange, the Bukovinian Germans would not only build their own houses, but would also help rebuild the city of Stuttgart, which had been severely damaged by bombings during the war, at no cost over the following three years. The refugees were also to self-administer the process of construction by founding and running their own housing association – the 'Bukovinians' Housing Association' (Buchenländer Siedlungsgemeinschaft e.G.m.b.h.).

Each member's starting contribution was 300 Deutschmarks, with a monthly fee of 10 Deutschmarks and a commitment of at least two years.[31]

The case of Darmstadt is astonishingly similar. There, as the story goes, Mayor Ludwig Metzger had met a few Bukovinian Germans living as refugees in derelict barracks in the city when he was on one of his rounds in 1946.[32] As he later explained, he had been impressed by these people's character – the way they were living in such an orderly manner and getting by with so little.[33] At first, Metzger helped them by providing electricity in their temporary housing. But he then decided to go a step further by offering them land on the edge of an existing settlement on the outskirts of the city known as the Heimstättensiedlung. As in the case of Stuttgart, the city was to provide the refugees with land and materials, and they were to both build their own houses and help rebuild the rest of the town. In Darmstadt too, Bukovinians founded a housing association, the 'Buchenland Housing Association' (Genossenschaft Bauhütte Buchenland), and managed it themselves. Here too, members had to pay a deposit and a monthly fee. As Metzger proudly proclaimed decades later, echoing the discourse of humanitarian work and development aid of the 1980s, this had been 'help to self-help' (*Hilfe zur Selbsthilfe*).[34]

In and of themselves, the settlements were relatively common. Due to the severe shortage of housing in Germany in this period, settlement building and house building, especially among refugees, was a widespread practice.[35] Yet, the examples of Büsnau and Darmstadt are nevertheless revealing with respect to the particularities of this group and its perception and self-understanding after the Second World War. The very fact that Bukovinian Germans started building or planning to build houses so soon after the end of the war, before the FRG had even come into being, for example, is quite remarkable. While it may say something about the importance of house ownership (*Eigenheim*) for people who had been homeowners and farmers abroad, it also clearly demonstrates that they did not intend to return to their native homeland – their determination to stay put. Having been displaced several times, they did not want to leave again. Effectively, living in their own houses in peace among Germans was what the Nazis had promised them and they were determined to make this return to Germany the ultimate one: *heim ins Reich* – but this time for real and for good. Last but not least, by building houses, namely doing what 'settlers' do, this example also shows how their background was mobilized and reinvented as a relevant mode of identification in the present, thereby strengthening or even creating the sense of their existence and identity as a homogenous group in West Germany after the Second World War.

Indeed, what happened in Stuttgart and Darmstadt gives us an insight into how ethnic German refugees and, in this case, a rather small group of

Volksdeutsche or *Auslandsdeutsche* negotiated their position amid the wider refugee crisis and postwar situation. It shows how the rest of the population viewed them and how they presented themselves to them. It is worth noting that, in theory, the Allies were not in favour of closed settlements of refugees, let alone settlements of people from one single area of origin, for fear of radicalization and segregation. However, sources also show that beliefs about the character, experiences and origins of these people as a group nevertheless played an essential role in helping them do just that. The contract signed between the town of Stuttgart and the Bukovinian housing association in September 1946, for instance, read: 'The town of Stuttgart plans to settle, to begin with, 200, and later up to 1,000 resettlers, refugees and expellees from Bukovina. Most of them are families of craftspeople, and some of them have Swabian origins.'[36] The fact that a few years later, in 1961, when Arnulf Klett told this story in a speech, he explained that Adolf Engster had come to him suggesting to settle '1,000 Bukovinian construction workers of *Swabian origin* [emphasis added]' indicates the tenacity and lasting attractiveness of this kind of argument to a local German audience.[37] Not only does this challenge Engster's original claim that the project had been open to all, but it also shows how powerful the idea of the Bukovinians' mere return still was over a decade after the end of the war.

In terms of historical continuities, the case of Darmstadt is perhaps even more interesting. First, Ludwig Metzger, the Mayor of Darmstadt, had worked for the agency responsible for 'resettlers' during the war, the Deutsche Umsiedler Treuhand (DUT), and, as he himself admitted, this made him particularly sensitive to the fate of these people.[38] Beyond this, in his attempt to convince the regional authorities that creating a Bukovinian German settlement (and even transferring people over from the Soviet zone for this purpose) was a good idea, he argued forcefully and repeatedly that these people were not only all qualified builders, but also that they originated from around Darmstadt:

> They are descendants of the construction workers from Hesse who immigrated to Bukovina over 150 years ago and continued to carry out their trade there [after emigration]. In the context of the large resettlement programme organized by the National Socialist regime, they were transferred against their will to the Warthegau. After the end of the war, the Poles expelled them from there to the heart of Germany. There, they were dispersed across different zones of occupation. They live there, in some cases separated from their families, mostly doing temporary work, which does not match their skills and does not guarantee a secure income. It is therefore understandable, after years of being moved around, that they are putting all their energy into settling down and finding the possibility to practise the trade of construction, which has been theirs for generations.[39]

This narrative portrayed Bukovinian Germans not only as settlers by nature and by profession, but also as people who were merely returning home after a few generations. In other words, beyond bare need and hardship, which was a widespread condition, their support and inclusion was justified based on beliefs about both their competence and ethnicity, or even ethnic continuity. In view of the notoriously ethnicized discourse on German work ethic, the two aspects were mutually reinforcing.

As Metzger's efforts also show, the authorities did need to be convinced. Similarly, in Stuttgart, some members of the local government initially met the arrival of large numbers of Bukovinian Germans in Büsnau with scepticism and disapproval. By 1948, some 600 people were living there, most of them in makeshift accommodation. In a report from March 1948, representatives of the Social Democratic Party (SPD) faction compared the situation to the 'Wild West' and derided the plan of the settlement as an unrealistic 'experiment'. They were concerned about the overcrowded and insalubrious – what they called 'primitive' – living conditions, along with the deterioration of social relations in the area, and fundamentally disapproved of the lack of social diversity.[40] In both Stuttgart and Darmstadt, there were indeed difficulties with the local population who were resentful about the help provided to these newcomers and the arrival of the people in and of itself. The problems faced by refugees in Germany and the ambivalent attitudes of the population towards them are well known, and Darmstadt and Stuttgart were no exceptions.[41] At the time, as people competed over scarce resources, there is widespread evidence that 'locals' (*Einheimischen*) felt disadvantaged. In turn, many newcomers reported being derided as foreigners or even 'gypsies' whose unusual customs, accents, dress and cooking were a source of hostility and discrimination. In Darmstadt in particular, the fact that the 'new settlers' often lived together with 'old settlers' – *Altsiedler* as the original inhabitants of the settlement from the 1930s were known – while their houses were being built, only exacerbated the antagonism.[42]

Again, however, it is interesting to see how these difficulties were dealt with and overcome. Following the SPD's claims in Stuttgart, the local authorities launched a debate and carried out some checks on site. In their conclusions after the visit, they admitted that there were problems, but emphasized that 'not everyone was prepared to build their own *Heimat* with their own hands' and even argued that, in view of the housing crisis in Germany, locals should follow suit and start building too.[43] Within a year, Bukovinians were being praised in the local press for their perseverance and initiative, which not only put a roof above their heads but would soon also make them rich.[44] Around the same time, at a local council meeting in Vaihingen, Büsnau was put forward as a model for solving the housing shortage in the entire region.[45] By the end of 1953, some members of the Bukovinian housing association were still living in barracks, but most already had a house or an apartment.⁴⁶ Within a couple of years, the settlement also had a school and a church. By 1954, Bukovinians in Büsnau themselves were complaining about new arrivals and were regarded by the city authorities as 'old settlers'.⁴⁷ Similarly, in Darmstadt, a year after the Bukovinians started building their houses, Hungarian Germans from the Bačka region, known as Danube Swabians (*Donauschwaben*) founded a housing association on the same model and started building their own, even larger settlement alongside the Bukovinians'. Later on, both 'old' and 'new' settlers joined forces to build the Heimstättensiedlung's school and two churches. In 1957, 'expellees' and 'locals' celebrated the settlement's twenty-fifth anniversary together.⁴⁸

In the brochure published on this anniversary, a distinction was made between the sections of the Heimstättensiedlung informally known as the *Buchenlandsiedlung, Donausiedlung* and *Altsiedlung* ('Bukovina settlement', 'Danuble settlement' and 'old settlement'), and each group was given a chance to describe its own distinctive history and experiences. As the passage quoted at the start of this chapter shows, Bukovinians emphasized both their specific experiences during the war and reasserted their Germanness. This opportunity was all the more important for a group like the Bukovinians, where the link to Germanness was quite tenuous. As the quote suggested, and as they had learned during the war, demonstrating Germannesss was what was expected of them. These housing projects' success thus provided Bukovinians not only with a home, but also a platform for their particular – and at times even particularistic – identity politics. Indeed, in the 1950s in both locations, streets were named after Bukovinian towns, cities, rivers and personalities in recognition for their presence in the area and their achievements.⁴⁹ In the local press, Büsnau was described as both a 'living memorial' (*lebendiges Denkmal*)⁵⁰ and a 'model settlement' (*mustergültige Siedlung*).⁵¹ With this, Bukovinians felt they had not only been given land and a new home (*eine neue Heimat*) in postwar Germany, but that they had been able to bring the old *Heimat* back with them.⁵²

In an article about the development of the settlement of Büsnau, published in 1961, the state building officer, Stefan Scribiac, a Bukovinian and Büsnau resident, argued that with their 'clean houses' and 'neat gardens', Bukovinians had shaped Büsnau architecturally (*das Gepräge gaben ihr die Buchenländer*).⁵³ For him, this project was evidence not of 'individualism', but of 'rational community thinking'. As he concluded: 'Here, Swabian-Palatine hard work [*Fleiß*] coming from Bukovina has been preserved!'⁵⁴ However, as Scribiac's last sentence shows, most importantly perhaps, neither the new *Heimat* nor their practices were truly foreign. Indeed, by giving them the opportunity to build houses and name the roads after Bukovinian towns, villages and individuals, the settlements of Büsnau and the Heimstättensiedlung served to demonstrate both their Germanness and the Germanness of their former home. This new home was both the new (*neue Heimat*) and ancestral home (*Urheimat*) and their habits were authentic German ones – even if, in the meantime, they looked quite different. In effect, then, this cycle collapsed the differences between the three distinct spaces and periods: the prenational German lands, Germanized, Austrian Bukovina and contemporary West Germany. The result was 'Bukovinian', local and national all at the same time.

The argument that Germany was the 'old-new homeland' seduced everyone. From this perspective, the time away from Germany had only been a temporary episode – a mission abroad – before returning to the unchanged 'motherland' (*Mutterland*). It therefore provided Bukovinians with a sense of purpose and belonging. However, importantly, it also linked back to a positive German tradition. This imagery was all the more potent as ethnic German refugees, and expellees in general, constituted a mobile and flexible labour force whose contribution to Germany's so-called economic miracle was genuine. As others have shown, in this period, the experience of modernization rapidly evened out visible differences between classes, as well as differences between locals and newcomers.[55] In this context, reactionary politics helped deal with the rapid pace of change. Following an ethnic logic was a source of stability, continuity and consensus. At times, the notion of different 'tribes' (*Stämme*) of the German 'people' (*Volk*) coming together was also celebrated.[56] On the occasion of the national meeting of Bukovinian Germans in Darmstadt in 1951, Metzger, who was by then Hesse's Minister of Education, welcomed the Bukovinian and Hungarian Germans as 'brothers and sisters' and praised them for their 'service to the nation and community' (*Dienst an Volk und Gemeinschaft*). He wished that they would soon feel as though they were 'locals' (*Einheimische*).[57]

Framing this in terms of heredity, kindred and *Volk* made it possible to establish a direct link between refugees and the locals. The Bukovinian poet Heinrich Kipper, for example, was said to have returned to his father's native region. A biography of his published in the paper *Buchenland* in 1950 read:

> This therefore proves that living as settlers among other peoples at the foot of the Carpathians for over a century and a half did not water down anything of the original core of the Palatine migrant of yore. How else could have Heinrich Kipper depicted things so clearly, how else could he have remained a *Palatine* writer?[58]

In a rather extreme case, the Bukovinian Johann Christian Dressler explained how he had come across a distant cousin in the town of Lauterecken, and his wife argued that their sons resembled each other, despite the gap of several generations.[59] In many ways, this was reminiscent of the Nazi belief that the 'pieces of the *Volk*' (*Volkssplitter*) would become part of the 'body of the people' (*Volkskörper*) and other biopolitical arguments and stereotypes of Germanness they had drawn on to justify resettlement in the first place.[60] Even if drawing a direct line of continuity from Nazism to the postwar era is exaggerated, the parallels in terms of vocabulary are notable. Ultimately, such reasoning relied on a conception of the German people as a reified, heterogeneous and stable community, and reflected the legacy of so-called *Stammesdenken* (tribal thinking) with *völkisch* elements.

Although it is not clear how effective and widely accepted these arguments were, the case of Bukovinians shows that, at least in theory, feelings of postwar belonging were grounded in ethnonational arguments and supported by both local politicians and policies. The official endorsement of this narrative and its institutionalization was further embodied in the agreements between different groups of ethnic Germans and regions or cities called *Patenschaften* – a term that refers to a relationship of 'godparenthood' – which were established in the following years.[61] Initially, many Bukovinian Germans had hoped Ludwig Metzger and the region of Hesse would offer their support. But in 1955, the Bavarian district of Swabia (*Bezirk Schwaben*) offered to take on the *Patenschaft* of 'Bukovina Germans'. The word *Patenschaft* does not suggest an equal relationship, as the word *Pate* (godparent) stands for sponsorship and care. Nonetheless, these agreements were not only the result of significant numbers of a group settling in an area of West Germany after the war, but were also connected to the history of the East's settlement by ethnic Germans from southern German lands two centuries earlier. As Mathias Beer has argued, the *Patenschaft* principle relied on an imaginatively supported, organic and circular understanding of history according to which ethnic Germans were returning to their ancestral land and merely rejoining members of their 'tribe' (*Stammesverwandschaft*). It effectively evoked a homogeneous group of Germans, who endured through time and whose integration would not be a problem.[62] However, here too, the benefits were mutual. This political construction was one of a range of ways of framing the displacement of ethnic Germans as 'homecoming' with a quasi-religious and redemptive dimension for all Germans.

The particularity of the situation in West Germany emerges especially sharply in comparison with East Germany and Austria. In Austria, refugees from Southeastern Europe were not described as 'expellees' but, rather, continued to be referred to with the Nazi term of *Volksdeutsche* (ethnic Germans). Besides, although implicitly, as Tara Zahra has shown, ethnicity continued to play an important role, legally they were considered foreigners until the early 1950s.[63] The historical connection to Austria-Hungary highlighted by many Bukovinians never obtained full official endorsement. In general, German refugees were regarded by the authorities as less important than their economic potential, and very little was done specifically for their 'integration'.[64] In the GDR, in turn, refugees were encouraged to 'make themselves a new home' (*sich eine neue Heimat schaffen*) and the authorities declared that they were 'determined to make the way into the new *Heimat* as smooth as possible'.[65] The government was openly assimilationist and rapidly passed legislation to support the newcomers.[66] Yet, as Michael Schwartz has argued, the integration of those generically and indiscriminately known as 'resettlers' (*Umsiedler*) was characterized by an absence of alternatives.[67] If there was certainly no doubt that all ethnic German refugees were regarded as German, they were also discouraged from identifying with their areas of origin or in ethnic terms. The emphasis was on developing a new antifascist, political identity. By 1950 already, the GDR government had declared 'integration' a finished matter; *Umsiedler* had become *Neubürger* (new citizens) and would soon be considered as regular *Staatsbürger* (citizens).[68] The GDR and Austria were therefore new, but not old, homelands for their Bukovinians.

A Community of Fate: Bukovinian Germans as 'Expellees of the Homeland'

'The Homeland Society of German Resettlers from Bukovina' (Landsmannschaft der deutschen Umsiedler aus der Bukowina) was officially founded in October 1949, just under five months after the FRG was established and soon after the Allies' ban on political organizations was lifted. Structured in the same way as other West German homeland societies or so-called 'expellee organizations', it was to have representation in the capital, Bonn, and regional branches across the country. However, since its national office was in Munich, the inauguration took place there in one of the city's large beer houses, the Augustinerkeller in the Arnulfstraße, on 9 October 1949.

This event was reported on extensively in the first issue of the organization's monthly newsletter entitled *Bukovina: Newsletter of the Homeland Society of German Resettlers from Bukovina in Germany* (*Buchenland: Mitteilungsblatt der Landsmannschaft der deutschen Umsiedler aus der Bukowina in Deutschland*). Although only around 1,200 Bukovinian Germans – and only people living in the western zones – were able to attend, the Landsmannschaft's leaders claimed to represent some 80,000 Bukovinian Germans living in the FRG and beyond, and the mood was festive.[69] In the foreground stood the newly elected leader of the Landsmannschaft, the engineer Jakob Jelinek (born 1910) and the speaker Rudolf Wagner, who, together with Christian Armbrüster, was the deputy leader of the Landsmannschaft and by far the most active person among Bukovinians behind the scenes in the previous few years. But also important were the two main representatives of the churches in Bukovina previously mentioned, the Catholic priest Kurt Bensch and the Protestant pastor Edgar Müller, the official heads of the existing religious aid committees. As their speeches published on the front cover of the first issue of *Buchenland* demonstrated, they fully endorsed the creation of the new organization. Bensch addressed Bukovinians as 'My dear sisters and brothers from Bukovina', suggesting they were all members of one big family. He called on them to embrace the initiative and join the Landsmannschaft as a solution to their 'dispersion' (*Zerstreutheit*) and 'uprootedness' (lit.: homelessness, *Heimatlosigkeit*).[70] Müller also called on Bukovinians to become members and described its creation as 'the will of the people', 'the order of the day' and even 'a duty'. According to him, the Landsmannschaft was a manifestation not only of their desire to continue to exist as a community but also for their 'common fate' (*gemeinsames Geschick*).[71]

The endorsement of religious leaders determined and reflected the spiritual level on which the discourse of ethnic German refugees was developing in this period. Indeed, as others have noted, the use of religious narratives, imagery and terminology to make sense of the experiences of these people was a widespread phenomenon.[72] Expressions commonly used such as 'path of suffering' (*Leidensweg*), 'expulsion' (*Vertreibung*), 'wandering' (*Wanderung*) and even '*Heimat*', with its implicit reference to 'the eternal home' (*die ewige Heimat*), heaven, had strong biblical connotations. This narrative also reflected an increasing self-perception and self-representation of refugees as victims. In the case of Bukovinians, for example, one could read that there were two reasons for creating the Landsmannschaft: the first was the 'love of the *Heimat*' (*Heimatliebe*), namely the memory of the Carpathians; the second was helping the 80,000 Bukovinians who had been 'on the road' (*auf steter Wanderung*) since 1940.[73] The latter constituted a continuation of the social and humanitarian work of the existing Hilfskomitee, but this work was no longer framed in the positive sense of 'integration' or helping people 'establish themselves' (*Seßhaftmachung*); instead, it was about alleviating their immaterial problems. Even the first purpose was described as being of a 'spiritual and emotional nature' (*geistigseelischer Natur*) and implied a deficit and a need of a psychological kind.[74] Indeed, the emphasis was now more explicitly on the specific character of Bukovinian Germans' suffering: on their particular experiences such as the duration of their displacement and their social and cultural differences such as their specific cultural identity. As such, the Landsmannschaft did not reject the cyclical understanding of history described above – the notion of a return home to the *Urheimat*. But the emphasis was now less on return than it was on the nature of their loss.

As others have noted, a few years after the end of the war, a transcoding occurred from 'refugee' (*Flüchtling*) to 'expellee' (*Vertriebener*) among ethnic German refugees in West Germany in general.⁷⁵ The case of Bukovinians illustrates this very clearly. It is especially evident if one looks at the Bukovinian Germans' newsletter, where the word *Heimatvertriebene* became ubiquitous and soon replaced not only the term of *Flüchtling* but also that of *Umsiedler*.⁷⁶ Of course, this also has to do with the legal meaning and political significance of the term 'expellee'. This word was a tool in the battle between different groups of victims of displacement in this period in West Germany. An article published in *Buchenland* in the May–June 1950 issue, for instance, posited that the problem of expellees was much bigger than that of DPs.⁷⁷ Besides, expellee as a status was associated with a range of legal and political rights including citizenship, political representation and financial assistance. These were the rights that the Landsmannschaft as an organization had set out to defend for its members. Indeed, aside from providing the *Landsleute* (people from the region) with news from the community – regarding the activities of the various branches as well as who had married, died or was still missing – the newsletter discussed at great length the laws and regulations affecting German refugees, on issues ranging from where they could live to what loans they were entitled to.⁷⁸ They also took an active part in political lobbying on the issue of indemnification for their losses – the legislation that would ultimately become known as the Lastenausgleichsgesetz (LAG), the Equalization of Burdens Act and which, although it was only voted for in 1952, had been discussed since 1948.

This shift from 'resettlers' to 'expellees' is also captured by the fact that Rudolf Wagner was one of the signatories, in Stuttgart on 5 August 1950, of the 'Charter of Expellees from the Homeland' (Charta der deutschen Heimatvertriebenen). Wagner's move was primarily an act of semantic politics. This document contained not only a statement regarding the renunciation of 'revenge and retaliation', but also emphasized a hereditary so-called 'right to the homeland' (*Recht auf die Heimat*), which many associated with the revisionist claim of the 'right to return'. In this context, the fact that Bukovinian Germans had chosen to leave their homeland and that, as some historians have argued, Hitler's widely publicized resettlement of ethnic Germans 'home to the Reich' may even have constituted a precedent for the expulsions carried out at the end of the war, was conveniently ignored.⁷⁹ Besides, in theory, as Matthias Stickler points out, there was an intrinsic contradiction between the 'right to the *Heimat*' and the imperative of integration.⁸⁰ However, *Heimat* was a malleable term that conjured up symbolic spiritual, emotional and religious images, and buttressed a range of political claims. This 'right' was never a legal category and its impotence explains why this call had the nominal support of nearly all political factions.⁸¹ As such, it was at least as much an appeal to West Germany and West Germans for integration as it was a condemnation of communism for the expulsions.[82] In effect, it was a metaphor that helped expellees face the challenge of negotiating between loss and assimilation.

The symbolic nature of the act was symptomatic of expellee politics in the period more generally. Indeed, in quantitative terms, the policies of integration were imperfect: in the first decade after the war, disparities between expellees and the rest of the population remained considerable and, in practice, the help provided by the LAG was quite modest. The electoral successes of the expellee party, the Bund der Heimatvertriebenen und Entrechteten (BHE), founded in 1950, for example, were notoriously short-lived. However, it is worth thinking about the implications of policies, as well as the language used, for perceptions of social reality in other ways. Indeed, words not only describe reality but also create it. The concept of 'expellee', for example, both created a sense of German refugees' homogeneity as a group while simultaneously making them a crucial issue and constituency. A number of historians have argued that the transitory character of the expellee party had more to do with the endorsement of expellee issues by mainstream parties than the issue's irrelevance or disappearance.[83] Some historians even argue that Hitler's 'community of the people' (*Volksgemeinschaft*) appeared to have been replaced by a postwar 'community of fate' (*Schicksalsgemeinschaft*) typified by German prisoners of war, victims of the bombings and victims of the expulsions.[84] In this sense, the concept of 'expellee' contributed to the broader narrative of German victimhood prevalent in the first decade after the war.

Postwar policies and institutions also oriented the engagement with the past in this specific direction. The process of applying for compensation for their losses, for example, led many Germans to think of themselves primarily as victims. As Michael Hughes has argued, it encouraged them to portray themselves as both innocent victims and agency-less.[85] Looking at the case of the Bukovinian German Landsmannschaft and the first preserved files dating from the early 1950s, suggests that, especially in the early years, it was the possibility of compensation that drew many to the organization in the first place; people joined because of the material benefit in doing so. From this perspective, the process of applying for compensation not only shaped the meaning of Bukovinian but also implied that it did indeed mean something. Here again, a glance at Austria, where there were no such compensation rights to secure and where no homeland organization achieved much traction, is very revealing. As Ewald Burian, who lived in Austria until 1953, confidentially wrote to leading members of the West German Landsmannschaft after his arrival in Germany, in the absence of a political goal, there was also a complete lack of 'regional community spirit' (*Landsmannschaftlicher Zusammenhalt*).[86] Bukovinian Germans in Austria were seeking representation in existing organizations and parties.⁸⁷ Since 'ethnic German victim' was not a relevant contemporary social identity, neither was 'Bukovina German'.

This is not to say that these people did not have a genuine sense of victimhood linked to their specific experiences. In the hundreds of letters received by the Landsmannschaft, many Bukovinian Germans described their hardship in great detail.⁸⁸ However, the possibility of their suffering being officially recognized and compensated also provided a platform for the rhetorics of victimization and fostered a real sense of entitlement. People made all sorts of requests, from pensions and hardship remediation to housing or the reimbursement of insurance payments from Romania. In the process, they also took their victimhood for granted. As one man wrote, for instance: 'Of course I was the victim [*der Leidtragende*] because I am an ethnic German [*weil ich ein Volksdeutscher bin*].'⁸⁹ This statement resonates with Michael Hughes' argument that compensation was less about the nature of the wrongdoing than about community.⁹⁰ It also shows the direct connection established by many between suffering and ethnicity.

This focus on suffering also prevented many Bukovinian Germans from reflecting on the wider framework of their experiences. In 1954, for example, one woman sought compensation for the furniture she had obtained via the National Socialist People's Welfare (NSV) organization during the war. When her request was rejected, she wrote to the Landsmannschaft to seek advice on how to appeal. She explained:

> I furnished my bedroom by saving money from my earnings. At the time, I was still single and lived with my parents, who, as resettlers from Bukovina, had been resettled in 1942 to Roskohof in the region of Krenau, Upper Silesia. Since at the time there was no other way to get furniture than through the NSV, I bought my bedroom [furniture] there and can prove that I paid for it. From my point of view, to whom I paid this money should not matter.⁹¹

As Robert Moeller has argued, Germans 'identified themselves as victims of a war that Hitler had started but everyone had lost'.⁹²

Interestingly, this woman also emphasized how long she had been a member of the Landsmannschaft, namely, since 14 September 1952. This specification suggests she indeed saw her membership as a practical tool – like the payment for a service. The Landsmannschaft's main task in this moment was effectively to mediate between its members and the authorities. In turn, the organization used its political leverage to gain members and establish itself more firmly. At this time, members of the Landsmannschaft only represented a small fraction of Bukovinian Germans in West Germany. The numbers provided to the Ministry of the Interior in 1952–53 indicate membership rate of 5–10% on average.⁹³ The head of the Landsmannschaft at the time, Christian Armbrüster, mentioned there was still a need for 'consolidation'.[94] In practice, this meant that they refused to help those who had not paid their annual fee of four Deutschmarks or asked to them to join before they considered their problem. This approach was their business model. In 1953, the creation of the Heimatauskunftstelle Rumänien (Homeland Information Bureau for Romania (HASt)) to provide information about claimants' ownership and nationality to the authorities for the purposes of compensation, officialized this kind of work.[95] These offices were meant to bring together regional experts, so-called *Wissensträger*, to help the authorities evaluate applications in terms of both the property being claimed and the claimants' identity and ethnic belonging. Yet for the most part, these experts were also people from the Landsmannschaft and the HASt relied heavily on the Landsmannschaft's existing human networks.[96]

As searching for voices via the organization or via the requests it received produces quite a biased sample, the interviews carried out in the early 1950s by the Freiburg ethnologist Johannes Künzig with self-identifying 'resettlers' from Bukovina among others constitute a useful and one of the few alternative sources from this period available for the purposes of comparison.[97] On the one hand, as others have noted, Künzig's work illustrates in an exemplary manner with what ease *Ostforschung* (the study of the East) was able to morph into *Vertriebenenforschung* (the study of expellees) after the war.[98] Indeed, continuing the work he had started by travelling in Central and Eastern Europe in the interwar period, Künzig visited ethnic Germans in refugee camps to interview them and primarily set out to record these people's accents and traditions. From this perspective, his research subjects had merely moved closer to home. However, his interview partners were often eager to share their interpretation of their recent experiences and current situation with him – a *Reichsdeutscher* (a German from the Reich) and an academic. And although Künzig himself had a strong opinion about what these people had experienced and what sense should be made of it, these conversations and encounters are nevertheless highly revealing. In particular, they provide a unique insight into the feelings and beliefs of both older and less educated Bukovinians, who may not have left any written trace in the first decade after the war.

These interviews highlight the paradoxes of many Bukovinian Germans' experiences. For one thing, they testify to the authentic sense of loss and vulnerability. Many recalled leaving the *Heimat* as painful and difficult; most of them blamed 'the Russians' for resettlement and recounted this event in passive terms, conveying their perceived lack of agency and options: 'we were resettled', 'we had to resettle', 'we had to leave'. Many then described veritable odysseys from one place to the next over more than ten years.[99] Finally, these interviews capture the difficulties faced by many Bukovinian Germans in West Germany after the war. If some regarded Germany as the 'ancestral homeland' (*Urheimat*), many still depicted the 'new beginning' as an integral part of their suffering and struggle. Nearly ten years after the end of the war, most of them were still living in temporary housing. For many, resettlement under the Nazis, running from the Soviets and life in cramped conditions in West Germany were on one same continuum of hardship. The interviewees spoke of different 'disasters' and 'strikes of fate' (*Unglück und Schicksalsschläge*) in an undifferentiated manner. They had felt equally powerless in all of these situations. Members of the older generations especially felt lonely and isolated, and missed their village and their community (*Gemeinschaft*) now dispersed across the country.[100] As one man emotionally concluded the account of his multiple wartime displacements: 'And now we are here with nothing!'[101]

Yet while they saw themselves as victims, they also had a strong sense of belonging as Germans in Germany. Indeed, the victimhood discourse intermingled with one of ethnic pride and even superiority. This was inherent in the nature of the interview – the focus on German folklore and the specificity of the interview situation, which included the desire to impress the eminent professor. Künzig often encouraged such statements, not least because he himself thought of his interview partners as repositories of authentic Germanness and commented to this effect. Some interviewees dismissed historical analogies, such as the link established by Künzig between accounts of the 'eternal wandering' of refugees in Germany during and after the war, and that of their ancestors centuries before.[102] To them, this was hardly any consolation. Künzig's attempt to make one man speak of Germans' superiority over Romanians failed remarkably.[103] Yet others willingly concurred. One man, for instance, claimed that 'until resettlement, Romanian administrators and others were grateful for the Germans, who were always more culturally advanced and, let's just say it openly, more reliable'.[104] The fact that Romanians had benefited from the Germans' presence was a recurrent trope. Ethnic superiority was also the framework for making sense of their 'settlement' (*Ansiedlung*) in the occupied territories: the Germans had brought Polish farms back up to standard and had shown the Poles how to work the land.[105] However, in the end, no one wanted to go back to Bukovina where many remembered being treated like 'second-class citizens'[106] and having had to live among ethnic 'others'.[107] Moreover, as the recent rumours had it, the situation there was disastrous.[108] Therefore, despite apparent differences of background, education and class, a positively connoted conception of Germanness united interviewee and interviewer.

These accounts offer a mixture of lived experience and official discourse – self-pity and exculpation. Indeed, the combination of victimhood with a positive conception of Germanness produced an unquestioned sense of innocence. Most intriguingly perhaps, they also show that no one was blamed or made responsible for what had happened; there were no culprits or perpetrators. No one, for instance, questioned the rationale for resettlement or even its legitimacy. Many of the narratives also presented notable gaps and silences concerning the time spent in the resettlement camps, military activities and duties or social relationships during the war in Poland especially. The few interviewees who did voice reservations about their treatment by the Nazis, did so in a remarkably muted and hesitant manner.[109] As Doris Bergen has suggested, many ethnic German 'resettlers' may have felt uneasy about attributing their suffering to 'Germans' after the war, both for fear of appearing ungrateful and due to their own identification as German.[110] This situation also reflected the equivalence established between West Germans and National Socialists, and their respective institutions.[111] A discussion between two of Künzig's interviewees captured this perceived continuity between the war and the postwar and undefined sense of grievance. As one of them pointed out: 'Yes, ten years after the flight you're still sitting in a camp without a place to live … They valued our things back then in 1940, the German state was meant to … well until today we have not received anything.' This same speaker then added: 'I heard on the radio that the Jews from whom the Nazis took everything, they are being compensated. But when it comes to us! Not one of us has been compensated even today, nothing.' As this suggests, not only did they equate their experiences with that of other victims of National Socialism, but they also felt that as members of the community, as Germans, they were more deserving.

The concomitant emphasis on victimhood and reluctance to attribute responsibility made it challenging to discuss the history of Bukovinian Germans and their intrinsically ambivalent experiences of displacement under the Nazi regime. A series of controversies show that this was even a sensitive subject for those at the top of the Landsmannschaft's hierarchy. In May 1953, for example, Rudolf Russ-Schindelar, the director of the regional branch of the Landsmannschaft in Baden-Württemberg, made a statement in his opening address at a meeting in Büsnau to the effect that 'our aim is not to regain our old home, and our presence in Germany is not provisional'.[112] Other members then accused him of 'abuse of trust' (*Vertrauensmissbrauch*). However, in response, he pointed out that from the perspective of international law, they had no right to return to Bukovina and that their people deserved clarity.[113] A similar debate broke out when Hans Ludwar declared in an article published in the Romanian newspaper *Patria* that not a single Bukovinian German had been resettled voluntarily (*freiwillig*). This time, Russ-Schindelar himself called for Ludwar's exclusion from the organization. In both cases, at stake was what is known as the issue of *Verzicht auf Rückkehr*, namely, whether to abandon the claim to return and the associated denunciation of the expulsions as a grave injustice or not. Most homeland societies notoriously adopted a hardline approach to *Ostpolitik* and vocally advocated revisionism.[114] The question was what position Bukovinian Germans, who both claimed to belong in Germany and the status of *Heimatvertriebene*, should adopt.

The crisis resulted in the organization of a consultation by the directorate of the Landsmannschaft. Different regional offices were asked to take a written position in preparation for a meeting, and a lively exchange of views ensued. Karl Dressler, who headed the Rhineland Palatinate regional office, for example, pleaded for the freedom of opinions and a balanced stance. According to him, neither had all Bukovinian Germans been in favour of resettlement, nor were they all against it. However, they (by which he meant the leadership) also could not allow for their people (*Landsleute*), as he wrote, 'to sit on packed suitcases' expecting to go home.[115] Another figure, Konrad Gross, argued that while, for him, it was clear that they would not be able to return, the same could not be said of Silesians, Sudeten Germans and East Prussians.[116] Hence, he called on Ludwar to make a declaration in which he pledged to drop the 'yes or no' approach to the issue of 'return' (*Rückkehr*) and asked the leaders of the group to turn their attention to more pressing matters.[117] Adopting a somewhat different approach, the head of the Landsmannschaft in North Rhine-Westphalia, Oskar Beck, pointed out that they would not want to return to the circumstances under which they had lived before the war or even current ones.[118] He argued that by relinquishing their Romanian citizenship, they had effectively given up their *Heimat*. However, he emphasized the need to justify 'renunciation' (*Verzicht*), which, in his view, had consequences both for the feelings of the *Landsleute* and for the Germans who remained in Romania in the present. He concluded by posing the philosophical question as to whether it was at all possible to surrender one's homeland and what this would mean for the work of the organization.[119] While there was no consensual position, all three of them felt that this issue had highlighted their responsibility when speaking as leaders and representatives towards those they saw as 'their people'.

Indeed, these debates highlighted the gap between what could be thought and discussed privately and what could be written or said publicly. In other words, it shed light on the mechanics of the organization's politics of memory. In particular, it reflected the challenge of adopting a position on the issue of resettlement, a policy most of the leaders had either supported or helped implement.[120] Throughout the 1950s, Rudolf Wagner, a historian by training, developed an official version of the past.[121] In short, this version was that although Bukovinian Germans had suffered a great deal, their resettlement had been the result of an irreversible, contractual agreement and was ultimately for the best. First, he argued that although the Nazi resettlement had been described as 'voluntary' (*freiwillig*), this had not been the case in practice.[122] According to him, northern Bukovinians had essentially been forced out by the presence of the Soviets. As for the southern Bukovinians, thereby robbed of their cultural 'epicentre', Cernăuți, and now living so close to Soviet border, they had been compelled to follow. Second, with the Soviet invasion, Bukovina had become 'foreign' and 'insecure' overnight, and 'ceased to be the *Heimat*'.[123] Therefore, as he wrote, one 'was by no means a "Nazi" simply because one aspired to go to Germany, to the land of the Germans, in search of safety'.[124] Bukovinian Germans in both parts of the region had merely and legitimately sought freedom.

Such a justification of the policy of resettlement – its tenets and its outcome – in the early postwar period in a staunchly anti-communist West Germany was not especially unusual.[125] Yet the tone and style of Wagner's text was nevertheless remarkably similar to that of earlier Nazi propaganda publications:

> No one wanted to be the last. Everyone was prepared to sacrifice their house and farm, to go to camps in Germany so long as they could remain free. Bukovina only became the *Heimat* – the 'old' *Heimat* – once more for north Bukovinians when everyone had left and when, from a distance, those terrible days had been forgotten and they could evoke pleasant memories once again.[126]

Since the Soviets were still there, Wagner even dismissed any present longing as nostalgic and delusional. He therefore concluded that not only were Bukovinian Germans 'expellees', they were in fact 'the first expellees of the Second World War'.[127] The anti-Bolshevism that had justified resettlement in 1940 conveniently aligned with postwar West German anticommunism to justify the policy up until the present. With this, resettlement could even be framed as a rescue operation – something that, incidentally, the Nazi propaganda had also done.[128]

This interpretation was full of gaps and silences. Most notably, no connection was established between resettlement and Nazi ideology, let alone the Nazis' policies of Germanization, occupation and genocide.[129] In effect, this narrative even contradicted many aspects of Wagner's own biography and experience. Indeed, Wagner had left Bukovina for Germany to study in the early 1930s. He had then remained there, joining the National Socialist Security Service (SD) in 1938 and the paramilitary Schutzstaffel (SS) in March 1940 after becoming a German citizen. He only returned to his native homeland in the second half of 1940, when he was given the task of facilitating the transfer operation and identifying supposed Soviet spies as a 'staff director' (*Stabsleiter*) of the SS Resettlement Commission.[130] After the war, he not only concealed his personal past, but made a habit of writing selective, apological and exculpatory texts not just for himself, but also for Bukovinian Germans as a group.[131] He even shaped the version of events recorded in the so-called Ost-Dokumentation – the multivolume, state-funded project to collect firsthand accounts of German expellees from Central and Eastern Europe.[132] In the early 1950s, Theodor Schieder, the historian responsible for coordinating the project, had contacted Wagner to ask him for the names of potential Bukovinian contributors, but the latter had said that he did not know anyone.[133] In the end, two texts about the experiences of Bukovinian Germans appeared in the collection. One was an anonymous account by someone from Cernăuți that focused on resettlement from northern Bukovina and ended with Bukovinians' arrival in the Reich in 1940–41.[134] Towards the end, it mentioned briefly that some of the Bukovinians had been mistreated by the SS when living in resettlement camps, but this was qualified by the comment that the author's experiences were not necessarily representative.[135] The only other contribution was a reworked version of a text Wagner had published elsewhere.[136] The author was simply described as originating from the southern Bukovinian town of Gura Humora (Gura-Humorului). As this shows, by this point, the history of the *Umsiedlung* was narrated within precise confines and by a select group of people.[137] In this way, neither could there be any doubt about Bukovinian Germans' Germanness, nor about their status as victims of the Soviets and not the Germans.

Bukovinian Germans as 'the First Europeans'

The extent to which Bukovinian Germans continued to identify as 'Bukovinians' after 1945 and what this meant to them is contested. From the sources, it appears that the newspaper never had more than 10,000 subscribers, and this provides quite a good indication of the number of people belonging to the organization itself. The Landsmannschaft also tended to inflate the numbers. In a letter from the Landsmannschaft's leader, Christian Armbrüster, to Oskar Beck in March 1953, for example, Armbrüster explained that of the 1,256 Bukovinian Germans living in North Rhine-Westphalia, only about 100 were members, but they claimed that 217 were.[138] Having fewer than 10% belong to the organization corresponds to estimates regarding other similar organizations and so did the tendency to inflate numbers to increase their political significance.[139] The reasons for not being a member are difficult to determine. From the Landsmannschaft's sources, it appears that lack of money for membership – or unwillingness to spend money on this – was a key factor for not joining or for leaving the organization.[140] For obvious reasons, other motives such as disapproval with the aims or indifference are more difficult to trace, though undoubtedly widespread. In the end, however, the Landsmannschaft *was* the public voice of Bukovinian Germans and the organization to which both individuals and public offices turned if they wanted information about the region. Besides, by claiming to represent this group, the organization established the sense that there was such a group. In other words, they determined not only what it meant to be Bukovinian, but also *that* it would mean something.

From the outset, the Landsmannschaft pursued not merely social but also so-called 'cultural work' (*Kulturarbeit*). As the major social issues of hunger, housing and work subsided and the responsibility for these matters was transferred to official agencies, the cultural aspect of the organization's work became increasingly important. Beginning in the early 1950s, the leaders of the Landsmannschaft started organizing events including 'cultural meetings' (*Kulturtagungen*) and bringing together so-called *Heimatforscher* – people interested in researching the *Heimat*. Some had been representatives of the German minority in Bukovina before the war and continued the kind of work they had been doing or planning for years.[141] But younger members of the Landsmannschaft, such as Emanuel Turczynski (born 1919), Erich Beck (born 1929), Hugo Weczerka (born 1930) and Kurt Rein (born 1931), who were still students in the 1950s, were also encouraged (and even funded) to do research on Bukovina and became involved in the Landsmannschaft's cultural activities as well.[142] Many of the older members of the intellectual elite were also active in a range of other projects as representatives of Germans from Central, Eastern and Southeastern Europe.[143] In January 1952, the Bukovinians' newspaper was renamed *Südostecho* (later *Der Südostdeutsche*) and became, for a few years at least, a common publication for Germans from Bukovina, Transylvania and Hungary.[144] While emphasizing, as other groups did too, the specificities of their own prewar history, Bukovinians joined forces with others to promote knowledge and research about German groups in Central and Eastern Europe in general.

This focus on culture reflected the growing confidence and establishment of Bukovinian Germans in West Germany. They had reached the point where they wanted to look back on their history. However, this was also the result of political developments and pragmatism. According to §96 of the Bundesvertriebenengesetz, 'cultural work' was the only activity for which the Landsmannschaft (and, for that matter, any expellee organizations and institutions in general) could be funded.[145] In the early 1950s, when a 'Working Group of Bukovinian Academics' (Arbeitsgemeinschaft Bukowiner Akademiker) was created, Turczynski, for instance, said that he believed this was the only way in which the organization would last or prove sustainable.[146] This development reflected the intellectual leadership's embracing of cultural work as a way of doing politics – so-called 'homeland politics' (*heimatpolitische Arbeit*). As Jeffrey Luppes has pointed out, such activities may have been 'commemorative in tone,' but they were 'political in intent'.[147]

The Raimund-Kaindl-Association (Raimund-Kaindl-Bund), founded by Hans Prelitsch in 1950, constitutes a typical example of such a 'homeland political' instrument. The organization was named after the famous Austro-Hungarian historian Raimund Friedrich Kaindl (1866–1930) who had taught at the University of Czernowitz under the Habsburgs and written extensively about Bukovina and its different peoples. Officially, the association aimed to bring together people who worked on Bukovina academically, artistically or culturally, and its main output was the publication of an annual booklet. The first issue, published in 1950, was dedicated to Kaindl himself.[148] It consisted almost entirely of a reprint of extracts from Kaindl's autobiography exposing his both pan-German and ethnoparticularistic ideas. Not only did the reprinting reflected an identification with Kaindl's views, but the issue also included excerpts from the association's 'mission statement' (*Satzung*), and this too largely echoed Kaindl's thinking: the association was to contribute to the Landsmannschaft's mission by 'fostering the ethnic specificity, traditions, customs and history of the region'. However, it was also to promote 'the deepening of the attachment to the new *Heimat* and the awakening of reciprocal understanding [between Bukovinian Germans and other Germans]'.[149] In short, the aim was to promote Bukovinian Germans' integration by emphasizing both the importance of the Bukovinian background and heritage, and the shared Germanness. It stated that 'Non-Bukovinians who, in their spiritual outlook, do not consider that Europe "only" begins or "already" ends somewhere in the Carpathians, on the Drava or the Vistula' were welcome to join.[150] As this indicates, therefore, integration was understood as a two-way process. The association's focus was supposedly as much on helping Bukovinians be more *German* as on making Germans become more *Bukovinian*. The implication was that Bukovinian Germans were indeed 'better' Germans.

The concept of Bukovinians as 'better Germans' did not displace previous modes of identification, but built on them strategically. This can be shown by looking at the speeches and lectures given at the 'national gathering' (*Bundestreffen*) of Bukovinians in Darmstadt in 1951, which were published in full in the second issue of the Raimund-Kaindl-Bund publication as well as in the May 1951 issue of *Buchenland*. This event was described as 'the first big appraisal of Bukovina German culture since resettlement' and was meant to showcase 'the unity and achievements of its community'.[151] It was no coincidence that it took place in Darmstadt, which was in the process of becoming, together with Büsnau, one of the largest settlements of Bukovinian Germans in West Germany. The programme included, as was often the case at such meetings, church services, a commemoration of the dead and fallen, a slideshow with images of the 'old *Heimat*', as well as singing and dancing. However, on this occasion, the leaders used the chance to outline what they believed should be the cornerstones of German Bukovinian identity in the present and the future. Indeed, this was not simply about heritage, remembrance or even reiterating what Bukovinian Germans had just been through, but rather to teach them how to make sense of their experiences and derive from it the right kind of self- and historical awareness – a sense of self-worth and belonging.

The opening address consisted of the reading out of a letter by a prominent Bukovinian figure, Franz Lang (born 1884), who had not been able to come. In Bukovina, Lang, a Professor of Linguistics at the university of Cernăuți, had also been the President of the 'Association of Christian Germans' (Verein christlicher Deutscher), an organization renamed the 'German Cultural Association' (Deutscher Kulturverein) in 1931. The letter began by reminding Bukovinians that if life was hard in the present, it had been hard in Bukovina too. Moreover, as he explained, they had returned to 'the womb of the old faithful mother, [who] holds [her] children on her knees and is one with you in language and heart [*Herzensbildung*]'. And as he claimed, '[this] was worth a great deal of hardship'.[152] Drawing on religious imagery and the idea of the nation as a family, Lang thus emphasized the notion of displacement as return and return as redemption. He then turned to the issue of victimhood – 'the suffering and disaster' (*Leid und Unglück*). Yet, he pointed out that Bukovinian Germans had not merely been victims, but 'martyrs for the new, developing *Europe*' (*Opfer für das neue werdende Europa*) . The experience was therefore a terrible but not a futile sacrifice – it was something they could now be proud of.[153] This speech reflected Lang's belief that the group's intellectuals were responsible for raising Bukovinians' self-awareness as a group and for giving them self-confidence, just as they had in earlier times in the 'old homeland'.[154]

The main speech by Hans Prelitsch, entitled 'Sacred Things and Their Transformation', did the same, yet on a more abstract level and not just with regard to the recent past, but with respect to a timeless notion of German Bukovinian-ness.[155] In particular, it opposed the pure and authentic Germanness of Bukovinians (and, indeed, 'ethnic Germans' (*Volksdeutsche*) in general) with its distorted modern forms. This text stressed in bold print that Bukovinians were 'Christians', for whom 'ethnic culture (*Volkstum*) was sacred', but that while they were proud of their culture, they were 'foreign to Chauvinism'.[156] Moreover, they were said to be 'traditional' but not 'particularistic', respectful of institutions but not of 'red tape' (*Bürokratismus*) and, last but not least, had been unwittingly confronted with 'militarism' (they had been tricked into recruitment to the Waffen-SS).[157] Prelitsch described Bukovinians as defenders of 'humanity' (*Menschentum*) who rejected 'the ills of Socialism and Marxism' and had always constituted a 'state-supporting element' (*staatserhaltendes Element*).[158] The last section of this text, entitled 'the Bukovinian as European', drew attention to the fact that in Czernowitz, 'a European city' and 'Bukovina's metropolis', streets had been named after 'the Germans *Goethe* and *Schiller*, the Romanian *Eminescu*, the Ukrainian *Schewczenko*, the Pole *Sienkewicz* [*sic*], the Jew *Heine*'.[159] With this, the text pointed to Bukovinian Germans' superior cultural and political capital, and even their moral high ground: erudition, tolerance and innocence. Bukovinian Germans were therefore at once the same as and different from the German 'locals' (*die Einheimischen*), who, as many of these contributions suggested, were more tainted by Nazism and had suffered less.

Indeed, the aim of these speeches was not only to counteract any assumption of foreignness among West Germans, but also to rehabilitate and valorize the history of Bukovinian Germans. However, in the process, their history was not so much rehabilitated as reinvented and rewritten. This phenomenon was particularly obvious in two other contributions. The first, written by the then young historian Emanuel Turczynski, dealt with 'The Economic and Cultural Achievements of Bukovina Germans in the New and the Old *Heimat*' and expounded how the Germans had come to dominate the region without oppressing their neighbours.[160] He mentioned significant figures such as the historian Kaindl and the surgeon Johannes von Mikulicz. In the print version, pictured alongside Kipper 'the poet' and Karl Ewald Olszewski 'the painter', they created a German Bukovinian hall of fame. In particular, Turczynski emphasized the importance of the university in Czernowitz, 'the easternmost German-language university', which had opened in 1875. He concluded that the year 1940 was a caesura, which seemed to have affected the 'abilities' of Bukovinian Germans negatively. However, as he argued, this was 'only an impression' and, 'like a tree in new earth', they simply needed time.[161] Not only did this account misleadingly equate Austrian culture in Bukovina with that of Bukovinian Germans, but it also reflected the kind of reified and organic thinking about the group and its survival through time, reminiscent not only of Kaindl, but also of National Socialist thought. No mention was made of the Jewish contribution to the region's German culture.

The second historical account, written by Rudolf Wagner, focused on the 'fateful' year of 1940 and posed the question of 'who should be held responsible' (*Wer ist schuld*), thus borrowing from the terminology used to speak about the past in liberal circles.[162] Wagner did not name the cause of the blame (presumably the war, suffering or the loss of the *Heimat*) explicitly, but the main answer was 'imperialism', something largely equated to Bolshevism. The author explained that Bukovinians had left 'voluntarily' because as 'Westerners' (*Abendländer*) they quite naturally felt closer to Germany than to the Soviet Union: 'We would *not* have left if the general geopolitical situation had not pointed in this direction and if one had not known that staying behind meant resettlement to Siberia. One was a German after all!'[163] In conclusion, therefore, the *Heimat* had been lost for good and 'a return' was 'out of the question'. However, as he explained, all was not lost:

> An old German cultural heritage in the last corner of Central Europe seems to have been lost for good. But it will only be lost when it is no longer alive in our hearts and if it is no longer possible to make use of the most important European achievements among the German people and to place them in the interest of the European idea. It would be a shame if this does not succeed and if such an achievement of the German people was lost. As no other, the German people accomplished a Western mission in Europe and this not least through its colonists to whom we Bukovinians belong … We want to tell mainland Germans [*Binnendeutsche*] about our way of getting on with foreign peoples and make the most of our experiences.[164]

By reiterating and summing up the conclusions of others, the main message was that nothing was in vain. They were German, but being from Bukovina was evidence of their truly European heritage and nature. Bukovinians were model Germans because they were model Europeans.

The appropriation of the discourse on Europe by expellees and their representatives was by no means unique to Bukovinian Germans. As Sabine Vosskamp has argued, after the war, Europe was perceived as the only possible political orientation and the source of a 'basic consensus' (*Grundkonsens*) in West Germany, and it was especially attractive to expellees insofar as it did not rule out the possibility of the 'return of the *Heimat*'.[165] They equated Europe with a broader conception of the 'Christian West' or 'Occident' (*Abendland*), which was implicitly opposed to the East, the Soviet Union and communism, and to which expellees claimed their *Heimat* had belonged before the Soviets had taken over. Therefore, the notion of Europe constituted both a useful alternative to the trope of the nation and a way of framing the Cold War without forsaking their cause, namely the right to the homeland and to return to their home.[166] Yet Bukovinian Germans were not merely portrayed as Europeans, but as the 'first Europeans'. These were the terms in which the Raimund-Kaindl-Association defined its raison d'être. In the third issue of its publication, published in 1952 – actually the last for several decades – one could read that 'Bukovinians, regardless of their ethnicity should be considered the first pan-Europeans': 'our continent is Europe and Bukovina was a small Europe' and therefore 'in the narrow *Heimat*, Bukovina, the Europe problem had already been solved'.[167] The implication was that both Bukovina and Bukovinians could therefore serve as models in contemporary Europe.

Hans Prelitsch (using the alias Muil von Melag) had explored this idea in an article in *Buchenland* as early as August 1950. There, he explained that the 'borderland' Bukovina had constituted 'order in diversity' and that what had begun as a *German* system had developed into an *international* and therefore a *European* one; he concluded that Bukovina should not be understood in merely geographical terms, but as a system, 'Bukovinism' (*Bukowinismus*), a 'pan-European cultural form', that could be emulated.[168] Drawing on an older Austrian concept, he argued that this had produced a different kind of person, *homo bucoviniensis*, 'the Bukovinian' (*der Bukowiner*). Bukovina was therefore the source of not only a regional, but a supranational and supra-ethnic identity and a new kind of human, which he described as a synthesis of Greek, Roman, Christian, German, Slav and even socialist culture.[169] These ideas were published in different places and different variations.[170] In some instances, Prelitsch even drew parallels between this conception of Europe and his idea of 'the white race', which, for him, was made up of three groups: Romans, Germanics and Slavs.[171] In the Bukovinian Germans' newspaper, starting in the early 1950s, the concept of Bukovinian Europeanness (or sometimes 'Danubian' and sometimes even 'Austro-Hungarian' Europeanness) was discussed with a range of images and metaphors. In this connection, Bukovina was described as 'a model', 'a bridge', 'Europe's centre', 'a school for Europeans', 'a textbook example', 'the Switzerland of wider Europe [*Gesamteuropa*]' and 'a European cultural landscape'.[172] On one occasion, when Bukovina was described as a 'cultural oasis', mention was made of Karl Emil Franzos, who, as the author emphatically noted, was 'a Jew!'[173]

These ideas did not remain on an abstract, theoretical level. Bukovinian German leaders tried to have a real impact on politics. In a report written in June 1954, Rudolf Wagner, who by then was a member of the Bavarian Parliament for the expellee party known as the BHE, outlined the main objectives of the Landsmannschaft's 'homeland political work' (*heimatpolitische Arbeit*). For him, it had two pillars: first, reporting on the situation in the expellees' former homes (the 'old homelands'); and, second, maintaining links with different groups and institutions within West Germany. He argued for the need to 'play out homeland politics on the level of society' and believed that, in this respect, the Landsmannschaft could make up for the government's failings. He described this as a new *Ostpolitik* that would not, in his own words, 'go wrong' like that of the Third Reich because it would be inspired by the 'European idea' that had dominated in Bukovina and had even enabled Ukrainians and Romanians to get along with one another.[174] When lobbying the government for funds, Bukovinian leaders also often stressed their ongoing friendly relations with Romanian and Ukrainian immigrants in postwar Germany. In a letter from 3 August 1953, asking for the financing of a meeting, they emphasized:

> Keeping in mind the future reorganization of the south European space in the context of an integrated Europe, there has never been a better moment to deepen the commemoration of our homeland in close contact with those who share our fate [*Schicksalsgefährten*], the Romanian and Ukrainian émigrés.[175]

Of course, he did not mention that these relations were with select individuals and could be traced back to his work during the war.[176]

A handwritten text by Wagner filed among the Landsmannschaft's correspondence from 1954 gives a yet deeper insight into his understanding of the political role and stance of Bukovinian Germans and what he presented as their political credentials.[177] The text summed up the experiences of Bukovinians before and during the war, their ideological dispositions, and provided a history of the Landsmannschaft until that date. Wagner did not dwell on resettlement: 'A contractual agreement resulted in the Germans of Bukovina ending up in Germany during the war.' He refuted the fact that Bukovinian Germans had been collectively conscripted into the SS: 'The young men were recruited to all parts of the German army. Unilateral conscription, for instance to the SS, did not take place.' He also did not say much at all about the years spent in Poland. In contrast, he provided considerable detail about the 'inhumane expulsions', even telling the story of his own father. He then explained at some length how having experienced first-hand the meaning of 'Bolshevism', not a single Bukovinian German had been or was a communist.[178] Wagner believed that in view of their experiences, 'expellees had been given the task, on the way, to defeat Bolshevism in Western Europe from a social perspective'.[179] For him, 'Bolshevism' was Russian nationalism and expansionism, and he consistently opposed 'Bolshevism' and the idea of 'Europe'. The text mentioned 'Europe', 'united Europe' or 'the European idea' (*der europäische Gedanke*) repeatedly and underscored that beyond the integration of expellees, the Landsmannschaft aimed to help Ukrainians and Romanians, as well as other national groups in Europe, overcome their differences. Finally, Wagner emphasized the independence of the Bukovinian German Landsmannschaft as one without 'egoistic' ulterior motives insofar as its members made no claim to return.[180]

As this shows, the discourse on Europe was not only aligned with but also served West German Cold War anti-communism as it brought together, and at times conflated, the division of Europe and the loss of the Eastern territories. As Pertti Ahonen has argued, expellees technically transformed 'a territorial dispute into a worldview'.[181] By equating revisionism with anti-communism, revisionism came to stand for peace and European unity. This thinking also conveniently aligned with former Nazi anti-Bolshevism. Many older ideas were reused after they were 'cleansed' of their most blatant racial and antisemitic elements. Appeals to the *Volk* remained frequent.[182]

It was no coincidence that it was formerly German- or Austrian-dominated areas – Bukovina, the Danube region, the Austro-Hungarian Empire – that were put forward to help Germany and Germans imagine their role in the 'new Europe'. As one could read explicitly stated in an article published in *Buchenland* in April 1951, 'the European principle was the pan-German idea ... adapted to the times [*den Zeitverhältnissen angepasst*]'. What might previously have been framed in national terms – now discredited or at least viewed with suspicion – was moved to different levels: the village, the region, the federation, the continent, the civilization or even the *Heimat*.[183] These discursive strategies allowed for a reradicalization of rhetoric, at least in the expellee press, by the mid 1950s. References to the former ethnic diversity of Bukovina simply offered a convenient cover of impunity and dissimulation for this nationalist trend.

If these questions preoccupied the intellectual elite and the leadership of the Landsmannschaft, the majority of Bukovinian Germans were arguably less concerned with rehabilitating the German nation as a whole, let alone achieving a revision of European borders, than they were driven in their activities by nostalgia or, at most, a traditional form of ethnic and regional particularism. They expressed these aspirations through the reviving of clubs and societies such as student fraternities or the *Jahn* sports organization[184] and the publication of *Heimat* books and village chronicles.[185] As others have pointed out, though highly ethnocentric in their focus and outlook, these books were ethnonationalistic rather than 'National Socialist' in content.[186] In fact, they might even be seen as attempts to defend the value of specific experiences, which the Nazis had effectively underplayed by generically labelling particular groups of ethnic Germans as *Volksdeutsche* or *Umsiedler*. The roots of this discourse, then, should be sought in the interwar period when the German minorities in Eastern Europe and their distinct histories were 'discovered' in the first place.[187] Moreover, if these publications were veritable 'monuments' to the different village communities with maps, names of residents and lists of those who fell in the war, they also embodied the link between then and now. The title of the main German Bukovinian publication of this sort dating from 1956, *Bukowina: Heimat von gestern* (*Bukovina: Yesterday's Homeland*) is a case in point. Sections on the situation and activities of Bukovinian Germans in Germany in the present and pictures of their 'living memorials' in Darmstadt, Büsnau and other locations were included too.[188] West Germany had become a substitute image for the perfect *Heimat*. In effect, these books reflected the acceptance that their homeland had been lost and the celebration that it had moved with them.

The West German authorities did not regard such particularism as a problem, as the existence and official endorsement of homeland organizations shows. From the outset, public statements at the highest level indicated that ethnic Germans were not perceived simply as refugees, but also as 'bearers of culture' (*Kulturträger*) with a unique and valuable heritage. In a letter to the State Secretary in 1951, for instance, President Theodor Heuss wrote that 'the expellees do not only [arrive] as afflicted and needy people but … also as carriers of a piece of German intellectual history'.[189] In the 1950s, the history of German settlements in Eastern Europe was considered as an essential part of the history of the FRG.[190] In his speech in 1955 in front of an audience of southeastern Germans, including some Bukovinian Germans, the politician Franz Thedieck argued that:

> For sure, we all regret that Hitler misused ethnic Germans' principles for the purposes of his megalomaniac policies and, with this, the noble pursuit of many ideals – and – let's be frank – discredited many European-minded people. But whoever denounces the emergence and century-long existence of the German people in the Southeast as German expansionism stands in contradiction to historical facts and adopts an utterly mistaken approach to the study of Southeastern Europe.[191]

The history of Bukovinian Germans was not merely rehabilitated; Germans as a whole reclaimed it as their own. Although the aims of commemoration and integration could have been considered to be at odds with one another, the transposition of the old in the new and, last but not least, the political uses to which 'the old' could be put neutralized this contradiction. This is how, in combination with the wider narratives of return and suffering, the narrative of German difference in West Germany ultimately became not a source of segregation, but instead a source of belonging.

Conclusion

The immediate postwar decade was a very difficult period for Bukovinian Germans, as it was for many other displaced Germans and residents of Germany in general. However, it was also a period of establishment. With large numbers of people competing over scarce resources, the future was very uncertain and in the short term, there were many existential and material problems, ranging from basic subsistence needs to finding relatives, through to securing civil rights. In a context where everyone was left to fend for themselves, some Bukovinian Germans – mostly members of the former elite – got together, founded institutions and launched initiatives to satisfy and defend this group's needs, interests and perceived rights and entitlements. For this, they drew on their origins (with the notion of a return to the motherland) and their experience of migration as 'settlers' centuries earlier.

However, they also drew on their experiences of suffering, displacement and loss. In particular, by invoking their sense of victimhood as Germans, they appealed to the notion of common national fate. In the process, this group tried to become an actor on the political scene of the early FRG. The past was mobilized and reshaped to fit the present, and this soon became the primary purpose and task of the group's central representational organization, the Landsmannschaft and its leaders. By drawing on a concept of German culture as stable, reified and ethnic (if not racial), adopting a staunchly anti-communist and pro-European stance, they even tried to bear influence on early Cold War politics.

The first decade after the war was a decisive time during which Bukovinian Germans' official discursive and visual repertoire was first developed and the main agenda was set for the following decades. In some sense, Bukovinian Germans might even be said to have been invented in this period, the most significant achievement being to have been accepted collectively as German. In this sense, this example gives us insight into the so-called process of integration of refugees and expellees in postwar Germany in general, as the result of a careful balance of sameness and difference, a combination of Germanness and otherness. This is also why there was no perceived contradiction between the aims of integration and commemoration.[192] Despite the claims and evidence of their integration, refugees continued to be politically represented, socially supported and compensated for their losses. Protecting the heritage of expellees was also legally enshrined; cultural gatherings (*Heimattreffen*), museums (*Heimatstuben* and *Heimatmuseen*) and publications (*Heimatbriefe*) were (and continue to be) publicly funded. As Sabine Vosskamp has argued, the experience of expellees served as a foil for the new order.[193] At times, some have claimed that the 'social explosiveness' of the expellees had been 'defused by means of its integration into a folkloric subculture and the promise of the 'right to the *Heimat*'.[194] Yet, the folkloric content was by no means trivial or insignificant as it helped to reinforce the new state's ethnic and assimilationist ideology and therefore its legitimacy.

Notes

1. 'Das Buchenland, unsere alte Heimat', in *Festschrift zur Feier des 25-jährigen Bestehens der Heimstättensiedlung Darmstadt Süd 1932–1957* (Darmstadt: n.p., 1957), 44. These words were adapted from the presentation given by Emanuel Turczynski at the meeting of Bukovina Germans in Darmstadt in 1951. See E. Turczynski, 'Die wirtschaftliche und kulturelle Leistung des Buchenlanddeutschtums in der alten und neuen Heimat', *Raimund-Kaindl-Bund: Das Bundestreffen 1951: eine Bestandsaufnahme des Buchenlanddeutschtums* 2 (1951), 6.

2. On these different movements of population, see P. Ahonen, *People on the Move: Forced Population Movements in Europe in the Second World War and its Aftermath* (Oxford: Berg, 2008).
3. For instance, this was the case in the region of Hesse, to which Darmstadt belongs. See e.g. R. Messerschmidt, *Hessen und die Vertriebenen: Eine Bilanz 1945 bis zur Gegenwart* (Wiesbaden: Stiftung Vertriebene in Hessen, 2010).
4. On this, see A. Demshuk, 'Citizens in Name Only: The National Status of German Expellees, 1945–53', *Ethnopolitics* 5(4) (2006), 383–97.
5. R. Brubaker, 'Migrations of Ethnic Unmixing in the "New Europe"', *International Migration Review* 32(4) (1998), 1047–65, here 1053.
6. See e.g. R. Münz, 'Ethnic Germans in Central and Eastern Europe and Their Return to Germany', in R. Münz and R. Ohliger (eds), *Diasporas and Ethnic Migrants: Germany, Israel and Post-Soviet Successor States in Comparative Perspective* (London: Frank Cass, 2003), 261–71; see also M. Borutta and J. Jansen (eds), *Vertriebene and Pieds-Noirs in Postwar Germany and France* (Basingstoke: Palgrave Macmillan, 2016).
7. On the issue of integration, see S. Wolff and D. Rock (eds), *Coming Home to Germany? The Integration of Ethnic Germans from Central and Eastern Europe in the Federal Republic* (New York: Berghahn Books, 2002). For an analysis of the discourse on the expulsions, see R. Ohliger, 'Menschenrechtsverletzung oder Migration? Zum historischen Ort von Flucht und Vertreibung der Deutschen nach 1945', *Zeithistorische Forschungen/Studies in Contemporary History* 2(3) (2005), 429–38.
8. On this, see R.G. Moeller, *War Stories: The Search for a Usable Past in the Federal Republic of Germany* (Berkeley: University of California Press, 2001); P. Ahonen, 'On Forced Migrations: Transnational Realities and National Narratives in Post-1945 (West) Germany', *German History* 32(4) (2014), 599–614.
9. See e.g. P. Ahonen, *After the Expulsion: West Germany and Eastern Europe 1945–1990* (Oxford: Oxford University Press, 2003); A. Demshuk, *The Lost German East: Forced Migration and the Politics of Memory 1945–1970* (New York: Cambridge University Press, 2012); C. Lotz, *Die Deutung des Verlusts: erinnerungspolitische Kontroversen im geteilten Deutschland um Flucht, Vertreibung und die Ostgebiete: (1948–1972)* (Cologne: Böhlau, 2007).
10. While some Bukovinians also settled in Austria or the GDR, both of which accommodated them as citizens in their own ways, in those countries they had nowhere near the same public visibility or degree of recognition. Besides, political developments, including the generous compensation in West Germany and the residential deadline of December 1952 for applying, encouraged a number of those who had settled elsewhere to move to West Germany before that date. See I. Nargang, *Die Deutschen aus der Bukowina: Herkunft, Umsiedlung/Flucht, Neubeginn* (Vienna: Österreichische Landsmannschaft, 2013), 74–75. By 1964, only 5,339 Bukovina Germans were believed to be living in the GDR. See M. Hausleitner, *'Viel Mischmasch mitgenommen': Die Umsiedlungen aus der Bukowina 1940* (Berlin; Boston: Verlag Walter de Gruyter, 2018), 216.
11. Numbers from 'Deutsche aus der Bukowina', in D. Brandes, H. Sundhaussen and S. Troebst (eds), *Lexikon der Vertreibungen: Deportation, Zwangsaussiedlung und ethnische Säuberung im Europa des 20. Jahrhunderts* (Vienna: Böhlau, 2010), 137–38. For a more detailed account of the events of the end of the war, see Hausleitner, *'Viel Mischmasch mitgenommen'*, 202–16.
12. In the Landsmannschaft sources, this is usually depicted as forced migration back, but there is evidence that in some cases ethnic German refugees insisted on going back. See A. Bauernkämper, 'Assimilationspolitik und Integrationsdynamik: Vertriebene in der

sowjetischen Besatzungszone/DDR in vergleichender Perspektive', in M. Krauss (ed.), *Integrationen: Vertriebene in den deutschen Ländern nach 1945* (Göttingen: Vandenhoeck and Ruprecht, 2008), 22–47, here 26. This resulted in a rather paradoxical situation insofar as they were regarded as foreigners by the Romanian authorities, their properties were not returned, and some were even deported to Siberia for forced labour. Most of them then managed to obtain 'repatriation' back to Germany within a few years, but some remained in Romania for years or even decades. See O. Kotzian, *Die Umsiedler: die Deutschen aus West-Wolhynien, Galizien, der Bukowina, Bessarabien, der Dobrudscha und in der Karpatenukraine* (Munich: Langen Müller, 2005), 179. On this, see also Hausleitner, 'Viel Mischmasch mitgenommen', 204–5.

13. These synthesized remarks are based on a range of oral history interviews conducted by the author with Bukovinian Germans from 2012–16, as well as on a range of published and unpublished first-hand accounts. For a list of such resources, see http://bukowina.phil.uni-augsburg.de/wp-content/uploads/2018/05/Interview-Sammlung-Deutsche-und-Polen-aus-der-Bukowina.pdf (retrieved 20 September 2019).

14. This was the case for many of the inhabitants of the village of Alt-Fratautz, for example, who had been resettled as a group to Lorraine and settled in the Palatinate, from which they believed they had originated. As Mariana Hausleitner describes, Herbert Mayer played an instrumental role in this process. See Hausleitner, *'Viel Mischmasch mitgenommen',* 203.

15. Most notoriously, in 1951, 150 Bukovinian Germans left with the priest Kurt Bensch and founded a settlement in Venezuela. See 'Bericht aus Venezuela', *Buchenland*, July 1951. See also E. Massier, J. Talsky and B.C. Grigorowicz (eds), *Bukowina: Heimat von gestern*, (Karlsruhe: Arbeitskreis Bukowina Heimatbuch, 1956), 314–16.

16. Bundesarchiv Koblenz (hereinafter BArch-K), B 106 (Bundesministerium des Innern) /27364, fol. 329, 330: Information regarding the organization of the Homeland Society of German Resettlers from Bukovina (Landsmannschaft der deutschen Umsiedler aus der Bukowina), 1952–53.

17. E. Harvey, 'Management and Manipulation. Nazi Settlement Planners and Ethnic German Settlers in Occupied Poland' in C. Elkins and S. Pedersen (eds), *Settler Colonialism in the Twentieth Century: Projects, Practices, Legacies* (New York: Routledge, 2005), 95–112.

18. See B. Filaretow, *Kontinuität und Wandel: Zur Integration der Deutsch-Balten in die Gesellschaft der BRD* (Baden-Baden: Nomos Geschichte, 1990), especially 306–16.

19. BArch-K, B 122 (*Bundeskanzleramt*) /2090, seven-page historical overview of the experiences of Bessarabian Germans, no date. See also U. Schmidt, *Die Deutschen aus Bessarabien: Eine Minderheit aus Südosteuropa (1814 bis heute)* (Cologne: Böhlau, 2003), especially 278–310.

20. M. Weber, 'Hilfskomitees', in *Online-Lexikon zur Kultur und Geschichte der Deutschen im östlichen Europa*, 2015. Retrieved 20 September 2019 from ome-lexikon.uni-oldenburg.de/p32815.

21. H. Rudolph, *Evangelische Kirche und Vertriebene 1945 bis 1972* (Göttingen: Vandenhoeck and Ruprecht, 1985), 147.

22. M. Kopp-Müller, '50 Jahre Hilfskomitee für die evangelischen Deutschen aus der Bukowina', in *Wer sind die Buchenlanddeutschen?* (Augsburg: Landsmannschaft der Buchenlanddeutschen, 1996), 13–14, here 13.

23. Weber, 'Hilfskomitees'.

24. Wagner, who was born in Duliby in Galicia but grew up in Gura-Humorului (Gura Humora), had studied in both Cernăuți and Marburg/Lahn, where he obtained his

doctorate in 1938. He became a German citizen and joined the SS in early 1940, before helping with the resettlement operation later that year. During the war, Wagner had worked for the Wannsee-Institut in Berlin, which, in 1941, became part of the Reich Security Main Office. He also worked for the Security Police and the SD in Paris and Belgrade, before being sent as a soldier to the Eastern Front, where he was wounded in 1942. He became a member of the NSDAP in 1942 and, by January 1945, had achieved the rank of *Obersturmführer*. In his personnel file, a note from September 1944 described him as a promising member of the SD: 'Wagner's attitude towards National Socialism is clear and uncompromising.' Though he was released from British custody in 1946, another arrest warrant was issued in 1947 due to his presumed role in the National Socialist regime. This led him to step back from many responsibilities within the Bukovinian organizations and take a back seat within the homeland society in the following years too. He even went back to Romania for a few months in 1948 before returning to Germany as a refugee. Arrested near Munich in early 1949, he was first classified as belonging to group 1, 'heavily implicated in the National Socialist regime', but then managed to have the classification downgraded to group 4 ('fellow traveller') by appealing and arguing his case. That same year, he was recruited by the West German Secret Service (Bundesnachrichtendienst). On his wartime biography, see Bundesarchiv Berlin, SSO file Dr. Rudolf Wagner 18.7.1911: R9361-III/561822; and Hausleitner, *'Viel Mischmasch mitgenommen'*, 223–25. On his activities from 1945 to 1949, see Staatsarchiv München, Spk K 1893 (Rudolf Wagner, 18 July 1911). For more on his postwar career in the secret service, see S. Nowack, *Sicherheitsrisiko NS-Belastung: Personalüberprüfungen im Bundesnachrichtendienst den 1960er Jahren* (Berlin: C.H. Links, 2016), 262–67.
25. For more on these individuals and their backgounds, see Hausleitner, *'Viel Mischmasch mitgenommen'*, especially 216.
26. H.P. [Hans Prelitsch], 'Gründung der "Landsmannschaft der Umsiedler aus der Bukowina in Deutschland"', *Buchenland*, November 1949.
27. Prelitsch, 'Gründung der "Landsmannschaft"'. As later sources show, they mutually recommended each other and exculpated each other, by, for instance, insisting that recruitment to the SS among Bukovinian Germans had been the result of obligation and that no Bukovinian German had belonged to a National Socialist organization before 1940. Archive of the Bukovina-Institute in Augsburg (hereinafter BI), Allg. Korrespondenz Bundesverband, especially 1953.
28. This was dealt with on a case-by-case basis until the wholesale categorization of 'resettlers' (*Umsiedler*) as German citizens was decided upon in 1950.
29. Landesarchiv Baden-Württemberg, Abt. Hauptstaatsarchiv Stuttgart, J152 BXI 1948 Nr. 10: Charter (*Satzung*) of the Association of German Resettlers from Bessarabia and Dobrudja, 1948.
30. For more on the case of Darmstadt, see G. Fisher, '*Heimat* Heimstättensiedlung: Constructing Belonging in Postwar Germany', *German History* 35(4) (2017), 568–87.
31. Stadtarchiv Stuttgart, 20/1 6790-2: Siedlungsgenossenschaft Buchenländer, Stuttgart-Vaihingen-Büsnau. Geschäfts- und Prüfungsberichte, Jahresabschlüsse 1948–1964.
32. This account was published several times, including in Metzger's own autobiography: L. Metzger, *In guten und in schlechten Tagen: Berichte, Gedanken und Erkenntnisse aus der politischen Arbeit eines aktiven Christen und Sozialisten* (Darmstadt: Reba Verlag, 1980), 102–3. See also M. Horn and P. Rothermel, *Heimat in der Fremde: Dokumentation zur Geschichte der Vertriebenen in der Stadt Darmstadt und im Landkreis Darmstadt-Dieburg*

(Darmstadt: Reba-Verlag, 1993), 24; F. Czernawski, 'Die Bukowiner in Darmstadt', in *Wer sind die Buchenlanddeutschen?*, 10.
33. Metzger, *In guten und in schlechten Tagen*, 102.
34. Ibid.
35. A number of smaller Bukovinian settlements, especially in Bavaria, soon followed.
36. Quoted in S. Scribiac, 'Büsnau: Das Siedlungswerk der Buchenländer im Schwabenland', *Südostdeutsche Vierteljahresblätter* 10 (1961), 17–21, here 18.
37. Stadtarchiv Stuttgart, 17/1 2450: Speech by the Mayor (Arnulf Klett) at the ceremony of the Bukovina German Landsmannschaft in Büsnau, 21 October 1961.
38. See Metzger, *In guten und in schlechten Tagen*, 71. See also S. Kiraly, *Ludwig Metzger: Politiker aus christlicher Verantwortung* (Darmstadt: Historische Kommission für Hessen, 2004), 100–10.
39. Hess. StADA, H1 (Regierungspräsident Darmstadt), 1620: Letter from the Mayor (OB) Ludwig Metzger to State Commissioner for Refugee Matters at the Ministry of Work and Welfare, concerning the 'settlement of Bukovinian builders in Darmstadt' (*Ansiedlung von Buchenländer Bauhandwerkern in Darmstadt*), 18 September 1948. See also the Mayor of Darmstadt to the President of the Regional Government (Regierungspräsident) regarding the 'settlement of Bukovinian builders in Darmstadt' (*Ansiedlung von Buchenländer Bauhandwerker in Darmstadt*)', 6 July 1948 and 13 July 1948, and response from the President of the Regional Government to the Mayor of Darmstadt, 25 August 1948.
40. Stadtarchiv Stuttgart, 863/1, 112: Transcript of the letter from the SPD fraction to the regional authorities (*Bezirksamt*) in Stuttgart-Vaihingen, no date, but reporting on a visit from 19 March 1948. See also Extract from the protocol about the negotiation on 2 April 1948, with the regional committee (*Bezirksbeirat*), 6 pages; Extract from the transcript of the meeting of the regional committee on Friday 13 May 1949, §224 *Siedlung Büsnauer Hof*.
41. I. Connor, *Refugees and Expellees in Post-war Germany* (Manchester: Manchester University Press, 2007); A. Kossert, *Kalte Heimat: Die Geschichte der deutschen Vertriebenen nach 1945* (Munich: Siedler, 2008); R. Schulze with R. Rohde and R. Voß (eds), *Zwischen Heimat und Zuhause: Deutsche Flüchtlinge und Vertriebene in (West-) Deutschland 1945–2000* (Osnabrück: Secolo Verlag, 2001).
42. Interview by the author with inhabitants of the Heimstättensiedlung, Darmstadt, and with a long-time inhabitant of Büsnau, Mrs Deller, September 2012. See also oral history interview collection with Hungarian-German inhabitants of the Heimstättensiedlung: Stadtarchiv Darmstadt: Transcripts Krisztina Kaltenecker (1999).
43. Stadtarchiv Stuttgart, 863/1, 112: Extract from the protocol about the negotiation on 2 April 1948.
44. 'Trotz aller Hindernisse wird am Büsnauer Hof weitergebaut. Wie sich die Siedlungsgenossenschaft Buchanländer hilft – Auch der "kleine Mann" kann zu einer Wohnung kommen', *Filder-Zeitung*, 21 September 1949.
45. Stadtarchiv Stuttgart, 863/1, 109: 'Open council' (*Bürgerversammlung*) concerning the 'the problem of housing in the area of Vaihingen – Rohr', 22 September 1949.
46. In 1953, of the 385 members, 232 lived in apartments and 113 in houses built by the housing association. Stadtarchiv Stuttgart, 20/1 6790-2.
47. Stadtarchiv Stuttgart, N 6.7 (Büsnau (*Vaihingen*)), Letter from the municipal councillor Betzler to the Bukovinian Housing Association, 5 July 1954.
48. *Festschrift zur Feier des 25-jährigen Bestehens der Heimstättensiedlung Darmstadt Süd 1932–1957*.

49. Stadtarchiv Stuttgart 125/1 (*Hauptamt Straßenbenennungen*) 15 and 14. The naming of *Buchenländerstraße* and *Radautzerweg* in Büsnau took place in 1951. Suggestions for further names were made in 1953. See BI, Allg. Korrespondenz Bundesverband, 1953 (June–September), letter from Landsmannschaft der deutschen Umsiedler aus der Bukowina to regional branch of the Landsmannschaft in Baden-Württemberg regarding the naming of streets in Büsnau, 10 July 1953. See also 'Verständnis für die Situation der Vertriebenen: In Darmstadt sollen mehr Straßen nach Städten der verlorenen Ostgebiete benannt werden', *Darmstädter Tagesblatt*, 25 September 1956.
50. 'Siedlung Büsnau – lebendiges Denkmal: Zum Bundestreffen der Buchenland-Deutschen in Stuttgart-Vaihingen', *Stuttgarter Nachrichten*, 23 May 1953.
51. 'Ein Abend bei den Buchenländern: Ehrung für Dr. Klett und Baumeister Adolf Engster', *Stuttgarter Zeitung*, 23 October 1961.
52. SA.St. 863/1 (*Bezirksamt Vaihingen*), confidential report of a visit of Büsnauer Hof commissioned by the local authorities, 18 November 1949.
53. Scribiac, 'Büsnau', 19.
54. Ibid.
55. On this, see e.g. J. von Moltke, *No Place like Home: Locations of Heimat in German Cinema* (Berkeley: University of California Press, 2005).
56. See e.g. Stadtarchiv Stuttgart, 863/1, 112: Letter from the Vaihingen regional office of the city of Stuttgart to the cultural office of the city, 28 October 1950, concerning: 'The cultural support of our settlement in Büsnau' (*Kulturelle Betreuung unserer Siedlung in Büsnau*), celebrating the meeting of 'different branches' of the German people in Büsnau. See also 'Die Heimat ist edelstes Besitztum. Viel Anerkennung, Glück- und Segenswünsche für die Heimstättensiedlung', *Darmstädter Echo*, 3 June 1957, mentioning 'the real community of the people'. See also 'Die Entstehung eines neuen Volkes aus Heimatvertriebenen und Binnendeutschen', *Buchenland*, December 1950.
57. L. Metzger, 'Ansprachen der Behördenvertreter', in *Raimund-Kaindl-Bund: Das Bundestreffen 1951: eine Bestandsaufnahme des Buchenlanddeutschtums* 2 (1951), 20–21.
58. H.P. [Hans Prelitsch] 'Heinrich Kipper: zum 75 Geburtstag', *Buchenland*, December 1950, emphasis in original.
59. This happened in 1941, but the story was published later; see Hans Dressler, 'Im Banne der Heimat', *Buchenland*, November 1950.
60. See Arbeits- und Sozialminister NRW (ed.), *Das Auslandsdeutschtum in Osteuropa einst und jetzt* (Troisdorf: Wegweiserverlag, 1963), 82.
61. On such agreements in general, see A. Demshuk, 'Godfather Cities: West German *Patenschaften* and the Lost German East', *German History* 32(2) (2014), 224–55; see also M. Beer, 'Patenschaften', in S. Scholz, M. Röger and B. Niven (eds), *Die Erinnerung an Flucht und Vertreibung: Ein Handbuch der Medien und Praktiken* (Paderborn: Ferdinand Schöningh, 2015), 329–44.
62. M. Beer, 'Zur Entstehung und Beharrlichkeit von Geschichtsbildern. Die Patenschaft des Landes Band-Württemberg über die "Volksgruppe der Donauschwaben"', *Donauschwaben und andere. Tübinger Südosteuropaforschung* 61 (2015), 105–34.
63. T. Zahra, '"Prisoners of the Post-war": Expellees, Displaced Persons, and Jews in Austria after World War II', *Austrian History Yearbook* 41 (2010), 191–215.
64. Ibid. See also S. Schippmann, '"Höchst unerwünschte": The Fate of Ethnic German Expellees in Post-war Austria', *Sprawy Narodowosciowe* 41 (2012), 7–21; and D. Bacher and N. Perzi, 'Die Chance auf eine neue Heimat: Zwangsarbeiter, DPs und Vertriebene auf dem Gebiet der Republik Österreich 1944–1950', in B. Kuzmany and R. Garstenauer (eds), *Aufnahmeland Österreich: Über den Umgang mit Massenflucht*

seit dem 18. Jahrhundert (Vienna: Mandelbaum Verlag, 2017), 175–205, especially 189–96.
65. Brandenburgisches Landeshauptarchiv Potsdam, Rep 256 [Umsiedlerlager Küchensee], 166, Kulturelle und politische Betreuung der Umsiedler aufgeschlüsselt nach Transporten, January 1947–January 1949.
66. On ethnic German refugees in the GDR, see M. Schwartz, *Vertriebene und 'Umsiedlerpolitik' Integrationskonflikte in den deutschen Nachkriegs-Gesellschaften und die Assimilationsstrategien in der SBZ/DDR 1945–1961* (Munich: Oldenbourg, 2004); see also Bauernkämper, 'Assimilationspolitik und Integrationsdynamik', 22–47.
67. M. Schwartz, 'Vertriebene im doppelten Deutschland. Integrations- und Erinnerungspolitik in der DDR und in der Bundesrepublik', *Vierteljahrshefte für Zeitgeschichte* 56(1) (2008), 101–51, here 103.
68. See Ahonen, *People on the Move*, 147.
69. H. Prelitsch, 'Gründung der Landsmannschaft der Umsiedler aus der Bukowina in Deutschland', *Buchenland*, November 1950.
70. K. Bensch, 'Meine lieben Schwestern und Brüdern aus dem Buchenland!', *Buchenland*, November 1950.
71. E. Müller, 'Liebe Landsleute!', *Buchenland*, November 1950
72. See S. Scholz, '"Opferdunst vernebelt die Verhältnisse" – religiöse Motive in bundesdeutschen Gedenkorten der Flucht und Vertreibung', *Schweizerische Zeitschrift für Religions- und Kulturgeschichte* 102 (2008), 287–313. See also E. Fendl (ed.), *Zur Ästhetik des Verlusts: Bilder von Heimat, Flucht und Vertreibung* (Münster: Waxmann, 2010).
73. Prelitsch, 'Gründung der "Landsmannschaft"'.
74. Ibid.
75. Most recently, see I. Nachum and S. Schaefer, 'The Semantics of Political Integration: Public Debates about the Term 'Expellees' in Post-war Western Germany', *Contemporary European History* 27(1) (2018), 42–58.
76. See e.g. the following leading articles: The board of the Landsmannschaft, 'Die Heimatvertriebenen und die deutsche Frage von heute', *Buchenland*, March 1950; 'Sechs Punkte Program zur Vertriebenenfrage', *Buchenland*, April 1950; Dr Gerstenmayer (member of the Bundestag), 'Die deutschen Vertriebenen in der internationalen Politik', *Buchenland*, May–June 1950.
77. Gerstenmayer, 'Die deutschen Vertriebenen'.
78. See e.g. 'Lastenausgleich', *Buchenland*, April 1950; 'Gewährung von Aufbauhilfe', *Buchenland*, May–June 1950; 'Die Würfel sind noch nicht gefallen: Lastenausgleich wird noch beraten', *Buchenland*, November 1950; 'Neuer Weg zum Eigenheim: Finanzierungshilfe für den Wohnungsbau aus Mitteln der Soforthilfe', *Buchenland*, December 1950.
79. See e.g. W. Benz, *Die Vertreibung der Deutschen: Ursachen, Ereignisse, Folgen* (Frankfurt am Main: Fischer, 1985).
80. M. Stickler, *'Ostdeutsch heißt Gesamtdeutsch': Organisation, Selbstverständnis und heimatpolitische Zielsetzung der deutschen Vertriebenenverbände 1949–1972* (Düsseldorf: Droste, 2004), 359.
81. A. Schildt, 'Mending Fences: The Federal Republic of Germany and Eastern Europe', in E. Mühle (ed.), *Germany and the European East in the Twentieth Century* (Oxford: Berg, 2003), 153–80, here 159.
82. A. Demshuk, 'What was the "Right to the Heimat"? West German Expellees and the Many Meanings of "Heimkehr"', *Central European History* 45 (2012), 523–56, here 536.

83. Stickler, *'Ostdeutsch heißt Gesamtdeutsch'*, 281.
84. See C. Goschler, '"Versöhnung" und " Viktimisierung": Die Vertriebenen und der deutsche Opferdiskurs', *Zeitschrift für Geschichtswissenschaft* 53(10) (2005), 873–84.
85. See M.L. Hughes, *Shouldering the Burdens of Defeat: West Germany and the Reconstruction of Social Justice* (Chapel Hill: University of North Carolina Press, 1999), 99. See also M. Hughes, '"Through No Fault of Our Own": West Germans Remember Their War Losses', *German History* 18(2) (2000), 193–213.
86. BI, Allg. Korrespondenz Bundesverband, 1953: Letter to the the directorate of the Bukovina German Landsmannschaft (Buchenlanddeutschen-Landsmannschaft), 27 March 1953.
87. In Austria, a national Landsmannschaft was founded shortly after this in 1954, but it never was officially endorsed by the state as in West Germany. See P. Tiefenthaler (ed.), *Festschrift zum 20-jährigen Jubiläums-Bundestreffen Pfingsten 1969; Zwanzig Jahre Landsmannschaft der Buchenlanddeutschen e. V. 1949–1969* (Planegg near Munich: Landsmannschaft der Buchenlanddeutschen 1969), 53.
88. BI, Allg. Korrespondenz Bundesverband, 1953. 1953 is the first year for which there are files.
89. BI, Allg. Korrespondenz Bundesverband, 1953: Letter from K.K. to the Landsmannschaft, 11 March 1953.
90. Hughes, *Shouldering the Burdens of Defeat*, 99.
91. BI, Allg. Korrespondenz Bundesverband, 1954: Letter from F.F. to the Landsmannschaft of Bukovinians, 31 March 1954.
92. R.G. Moeller, 'Germans as Victims? Thoughts on a Post-Cold War History of World War II's Legacies', *History and Memory* 17(1–2) (2005), 147–94, here 151.
93. Bavaria 1,900; Southwest 340; Lower Saxony 680; Hesse 320; Rhineland Palatinate 220; North Rhine-Westphalia 65; Berlin 5; Schleswig Holstein 8; Hamburg 5; Bremen 8. For these numbers, see BArch-K, B 106/27364, fol. 300. For the refusals to help, see BI, Allg. Korrespondenz, Bundesverband, 1953, 1954: various documents.
94. BArch-K, B 106/27364, fol. 300.
95. Such bureaus were created for most areas of Central and Eastern Europe in which Germans had lived before the war – there were thirty-four in total. The first director of the Romanian branch, Peter Blaß, was a Bukovinian. See W. Spielhaupter, *51 Jahre Heimatauskunftstelle Rumänien: 1953–2004* (Munich: n.p., 2005).
96. Some of those deciding about compensation were even the same people who had been responsible for confiscating the goods of Poles and Jews and redistributed them to German 'resettlers' during the war. Many of the community leaders had experience in defending Bukovinian Germans' rights and Germanness in the face of the National Socialist authorities during the war. On this, see A. Strippel, 'Race, Regional Identity and *Volksgemeinschaft*: Naturalization of Ethnic German Resettlers in the Second World War by the Einwandererzentralstelle/Central Immigration Office of the SS', in C.W. Szejnmann and M. Umbach (eds), *Heimat, Region, and Empire Spatial Identities under National Socialism* (Basingstoke: Palgrave Macmillan, 2012), 185–98, here 193. M. Hausleitner has even shown that the requests of former Nazis were dealt with more generously and quicker; Hausleitner, 'Viel Mischmasch mitgenommen', 229–30.
97. Instituts für Volkskunde der Deutschen des östlichen Europa (formerly the Johannes Künzig Institut), Freiburg i. Br. (IVDE), *Tonarchiv* (hereinafter IVDE/TA). The collection comprises fourteen different interviews with Bukovinians – sometimes individual people and sometimes groups, couples or families. Due to the basic technology of the time, these have been cut into small audio sequences of up to ten minutes. On Künzig,

see W. Mezger, 'Dokumentation und Forschung unter den Rahmenbedingungen des 96 BVFG', in C. Schmitt (ed.), *Volkskundliche Großprojekte: Ihre Geschichte und Zukunft* (Münster: Waxmann, 2005), 85–98.
98. See W. Oberkrome, 'Regionalismus und historische "Volkstumforschung" 1890–1960', in M. Beer and G.Seewann (eds), *Südostforschung im Schatten des Dritten Reiches: Institutionen - Inhalte – Personen* (Munich: Oldenbourg, 2004), 39–48; E. Mühle, 'Der europäische Osten in der Wahrnehmung deutscher Historiker. Das Bei Hermann Aubin', in G. Thum (ed.), *Traumland Osten: Deutsche Bilder vom östlichen Europa im 20. Jahrhundert* (Göttingen: Vandenhoeck and Ruprecht, 2006), 110–37.
99. See e.g. IVDE/TA, 0175-1/007: Familie M. (Pleutersbach, 1953).
100. IVDE/TA, 0014-1/0001: Jakob M. (Peterstal, 1953).
101. IVDE/TA, 0007-1/0023: Jakob H. (Kaiserslautern, 1952).
102. IVDE/TA, 0007-1/0023: Jakob H.
103. IVDE/TA, 0014-1/0002: Jakob M.
104. IVDE/TA, 0007-1/0027: Johannes D. (Kaiserslautern, 1952).
105. IVDE/TA, 0014-1/0001: Jakob M.
106. IVDE/TA, 0172-2/0003: Christian A. and Jakob K. (Karlsruhe 1955).
107. IVDE/TA, 172-1/001: Jakob K. and Johann G. (Karlsruhe, Lager 1955).
108. IVDE/TA, 0160-1/0001: Anton S. and Karoline S. (Shapbach, 1955). The newspaper also often ran horror stories about the old homeland: see e.g. 'Nach der Umsiedlung', *Südostecho*, October 1952.
109. IVDE/TA, 0286-2/0004: Peter and Jakob E. (Darmstadt, 1958).
110. D.L. Bergen, 'The Volksdeutsche in Eastern Europe and the Collapse of the Nazi Empire', in A. Steinweis and D.E. Rogers (eds), *The Impact of Nazism: New Perspectives on the Third Reich and Its Legacy* (Lincoln, NE: University of Nebraska Press, 2003), 101–28, here 119.
111. This is corroborated by some of the letters sent to the Landsmannschaft that demonstrate that for many, the distinction between West German and National Socialist institutions, policies and terminology was not clear at all. BI, Allg. Korrespondenz Bundesverband, 1953–54: various documents.
112. BI, Allg. Korrespondenz Bundesverband, 1953: Letter from Schindelar to the directorate of the Landsmannschaft, 6 July 1953.
113. Ibid., Schindelar to the directorate of the Landsmannschaft, 6 July 1953.
114. G. Margalit, *Guilt, Suffering, and Memory: Germany Remembers its Dead of World War II* (Bloomington: Indiana University Press, 2010), 214.
115. BI, Allg. Korrespondenz Bundesverband, 1954: Letter from K. Dressler to the directorate of the Landsmannschaft, 11 March 1954.
116. BI, Allg. Korrespondenz Bundesverband, 1954: Letter from Konrad Gross to the directorate of the Landsmannschaft, 18 February 1954.
117. Konrad Gross to the directorate of the Landsmannschaft, 18 February 1954.
118. BI, Allg. Korrespondenz Bundesverband, 1954: Letter from Oskar Beck to the Landsmannschaft der Buchenlanddeutschen, 13 March 1954.
119. Beck to the Landsmannschaft der Buchenlanddeutschen, 13 March 1954.
120. Most of the members of the postwar Bukovina German elite were involved in the process, many as members of the 'Resettlement Commission'. On this, see R. Wagner, 'Die Umsiedlung der Deutschen aus der Bukowina', in F. Lang (ed.), *Buchenland: hundertfünfzig Jahre Deutschtum in der Bukowina* (Munich: Verlag des Südostdeutschen Kulturwerks, 1961), 509–26.
121. See R. Wagner, 'Probleme zur Umsiedlung der Deutschen aus der Bukowina', *Südost-Heimatblätter* 4 (1955), 168–74. As Hausleitner argues, Wagner controlled the narrative

regarding resettlement: Hausleitner, 'Viel Mischmasch mitgenommen', 237. Parts of this section have been published earlier in G. Fisher, 'Schweigen, Störung und Stimmigkeit: Erinnerungen an die Umsiedlung "Heim ins Reich" unter den Buchenlanddeutschen', in H.W. Retterath (ed.), *Germanisierung im besetzten Ostoberschlesien während des Zweiten Weltkriegs* (Münster: Waxmann, 2018), 273–304.
122. Wagner, 'Probleme zur Umsiedlung', 168–70.
123. Ibid., 169.
124. Ibid.
125. On this, see H.H. Hahn and E. Hahn, *Die Vertreibung im deutschen Erinnern: Legenden, Mythos, Geschichte* (Paderborn: Schöningh, 2010), especially 200–3.
126. Wagner, 'Probleme zur Umsiedlung', 172.
127. Ibid., 169.
128. See e.g. the propaganda books of the series *Volksdeutsche Heimkehr* (Berlin; Leipzig: Nibelungen-Verl., 1940–42), such as M. Schwarz, *Die Umsiedlung und die Sowjets: Erlebnisse einer deutschen Frau* (Berlin-Leipzig: Nibelungen Verlag, 1942).
129. This was not the discourse adopted by all 'resettler' groups. See e.g. Schmidt, *Die Deutschen aus Bessarabien*, 289.
130. On these circumstances, see BArch Berlin, R9361-III/561822.
131. See R. Wagner, 'Mein Lebenslauf', in R. Wagner, P. Tiefenthaler and A. Armbruster (eds), *Vom Moldauwappen zum Doppeladler: Ausgewählte Beiträge zur Geschichte der Bukowina* (Augsburg: Hoffmann-Verlag, 1991), 563–65. On this, see also M. Hausleitner, 'Die Geschichte der Bukowina in der ersten Hälfte des 20. Jahrhunderts aus der Sicht von Deutschen, Juden und Rumänen', *Die Bukowina: historische und ethnokulturelle Studien. Beiträge der IV. internationalen wissenschaftlichen Konferenz 'Kaindlische Lesungen'* (Chernivtsi: Selena Bukowina, 2007), 122–35, here 124–25; and Hausleitner, 'Viel Mischmasch mitgenommen', 226. He even concealed his past from the secret service that he worked for after the war; Nowack, *Sicherheitsrisiko NS-Belastung*, 263–65.
132. See Bundesministerium für Vertriebene, Flüchtlinge und Kriegsgeschädigte (ed.), *Dokumentation der Vertreibung der Deutschen aus Ost-Mitteleuropa*, 5 vols (Bonn: Bundesministerium für Vertriebene, Flüchtlinge und Kriegsgeschädigte, 1953–1962). For the volume on Romania, see Bundesministerium für Vertriebene, Flüchtlinge und Kriegsgeschädigte (ed.), *Das Schicksal der Deutschen in Rumänien*, vol. 4 (Bonn: Bundesministerium für Vertriebene, 1957). On the interview with Wagner, see Hausleitner, 'Viel Mischmasch mitgenommen', 97. On the Ost-Dokumentation project as a whole, see M. Beer, 'Im Spannungsfeld von Politik und Zeitgeschichte: Das Großforschungsprojekt "Dokumentation der Vertreibung der Deutschen aus Ost-Mitteleuropa"', *Vierteljahrshefte für Zeitgeschichte* 46(3) (1998), 345–89; see also Moeller, *War Stories*, 51–87. The last volume of the Ost-Dokumentation was never published and the debates among the editors reflect the growing concerns over its use as an *Entschuldigungszettel* ('apology note') for foreign policy purposes.
133. BArch-K, N 1188 (Schieder Nachlass) /3157: Schieder Report on the Ost-Dokumentation Rumänien.
134. Document no. 6: *Erlebnisbericht des S. K. aus Czernowitz (Cernăuți) in der Nord-Bukowina*. Original 26 February 1957: 'Die Auswirkungen der sowjetischen Besetzung in Czernowitz; die Abwicklung der Umsiedlungs-Aktion; Transport und Aufnahme der Umsiedler in deutschen Lagern', in Bundesministerium für Vertriebene, Flüchtlinge und Kriegsgeschädigte, *Das Schicksal der Deutschen in Rumänien*, 30–35.

135. Document no. 6: *Erlebnisbericht des S. K. aus Czernowitz*, 35.
136. Document no. 2: *Bericht des Dr. Rudolf Wagner aus Gurahumora (Gura Humorului, Județ Câmpulung (Kimpolung) in der Bukowina*. Original 29 January 1957: 'Die Umsiedlung der Volksdeutschen aus der Bukowina im Jahre 1940', in Bundesministerium für Vertriebene, Flüchtlinge und Kriegsgeschädigte (ed.), *Das Schicksal der Deutschen in Rumänien*, 13–17.
137. An example of this is the text by the then young history student, later well-known German historian of Eastern Europe, Hugo Weczerka, which he wrote with the assistance of key figures from the Landsmannschaft. H. Weczerka, 'Die Deutschen im Buchenland', in *Schriftenreihe der Göttinger Arbeitskreis* 51 (1955), 1–41. Hausleitner connects the dominance of the narrative to the control exerted by former National Socialists and members of the Landsmannschaft over the institutions and sources of funding for research on this topic: Hausleitner, *'Viel Mischmasch mitgenommen'*, 232.
138. BI, Allg. Korrespondenz Bundesverband, 1953: Letter from Armbrüster to Beck, 23 March 1953.
139. Stickler, *'Ostdeutsch heißt Gesamtdeutsch'*, 142.
140. See BI, Allg. Korrespondenz Bundesverband, 1953–54.
141. This was the case for Johann Christian Dressler, who published J.C. Dressler, *Chronik der bukowiner Landgemeinde Illischestie* (Freilassing: Pannonia-Verlag, 1960).
142. For instance, they all contributed pieces to Franz Lang's book *Buchenland* and were given prizes and funding from the Landsmannschaft for their work. There even was a youth branch, which tried to make links to the Deutsche Jugend des Ostens of which E. Turczynski and then E. Beck were the leaders; BI, Allg. Korrespondenz 1953–54, e.g. Letter from Beck to the *Landsmannschaft*, 28 May 1953. They all specialized in different periods: Weczerka on the early modern period, Turczynski on the Habsburg period, Rein on linguistics and Beck on economics.
143. This included plans for the establishment of a university for *Ostforschung* and cooperation with the Südostdeutsches Kulturwerk, which was founded by Fritz Valjavec and other related organizations and institutions. Wagner was also a member of the Rat der Südostdeutschen. On these activities, see M. Beer, 'Die deutsche Südosteuropa-Forschung zwischen Nationalsozialismus und Bundesrepublik: Kontinuität-Bruch-Neubeginn', *Südosteuropa Mitteilungen* 4 (2014), 28–45. See also Hausleitner, *'Viel Mischmasch mitgenommen'*, 233–37.
144. Its subtitle was *Zeitung der Deutschen aus Südosteuropa (Newspaper of the Germans from southeastern Europe)* and it included a section called *Buchenland*. It was renamed *Der Südostdeutsche* in May 1953. When the other groups left the alliance, the Bukovinians kept the name.
145. See https://www.gesetze-im-internet.de/bvfg/__96.html (retrieved 20 September 2019). See also H. Prelitsch, *10 Jahre Landsmannschaft der Buchenlanddeutschen 1949–1959: Gründung, Werdegang, Jubiläum* (Munich: Landsmannschaft der Buchenlanddeutschen, 1959), 24.
146. BI, Allg. Korrespondenz Bundesverband, 1953: Letter from E. Turczynski to the directorate of the Landsmannschaft der Umsiedler aus der Bukowina, 12 June 1953.
147. J. Luppes, 'The Commemorative Ceremonies of the Expellees: Tag der Heimat and Volkstrauertag', *German Politics and Society* 30(2) (2012), 1–20, here 3.
148. 'Raimund Friedrich Kaindl: der Karpatendeutsche', *Raimund-Kaindl-Bund* 1 (1950).
149. Ibid., 3.
150. Ibid.

151. *Raimund-Kaindl-Bund*: *Das Bundestreffen 1951: eine Bestandsaufnahme des Buchenlanddeutschtums* 2 (1951), 3.
152. F. Lang, 'Eröffnung', in *Raimund-Kaindl-Bund* 2, 4.
153. Ibid., emphasis in original.
154. See F. Lang, 'Sprache und Literatur der Deutschen in der Bukowina', *Südostdeutsche Heimatblätter* 4 (1955), 192–219, especially 208.
155. H. Prelitsch, 'Heiligtümer und ihre Abwandlungen', in *Raimund-Kaindl-Bund* 2, 11–19.
156. Ibid., 15–16.
157. Ibid., 16–17.
158. Ibid.
159. Ibid., 18, emphasis in original.
160. E. Turczynski, 'Die wirtschaftliche und kulturelle Leistung des Buchenlanddeutschtums in der alten und neuen Heimat', in *Raimund-Kaindl-Bund* 2, 5–6.
161. Ibid., 6. This speech provided the basis for the text quoted at the start.
162. Most famously K. Jaspers, *Die Schuldfrage* (Heidelberg: Schneider, 1946); R. Wagner, 'Das Jahr 1940: Ende und Anfang einer historischen Entwicklung des Buchenland-Deutschtums', in *Raimund-Kaindl-Bund* 2, 7–10.
163. Wagner, 'Das Jahr 1940', 9.
164. Ibid., 10.
165. S. Vosskamp, *Katholische Kirche und Vertriebene in Westdeutschland: Integration, Identität und ostpolitischer Diskurs 1945–1972* (Stuttgart: Kohlhammer, 2007), 224–28. On this, see also Hahn and Hahn, *Die Vertreibung im deutschen Erinnern*, 476–84.
166. Vosskamp, *Katholische Kirche und Vertriebene*, 228.
167. H. Prelitsch, 'Warum Raimund-Kaindl-Bund?', *Raimund-Kaindl-Bund* 3 (1952), 7.
168. Muil von Melag, 'Der Bukowiner', *Buchenland*, August 1950.
169. Ibid.
170. See e.g. Hans Prelitsch 'Homo Bucoviniensis', in Massier et al. (eds), *Bukowina: Heimat von gestern*, 333–37. This was a reprint of Hans Prelitsch, 'Der Bukowiner Mensch', *Brücke zum Westen* 4–5 (1954).
171. Prelitsch, 'Warum Raimund-Kaindl-Bund?', 7.
172. See 'Die Rückführung der Buchenlanddeutschen in ihre Urheimat – Das Modell Europas', *Buchenland*, October 1951; 'Das Buchenland als volks-u. sprachdeutsche Brücke Europas', *Buchenland*, November 1951; 'Europa aus der Mitte gesehen – Das Buchenland – ein gesamteuropäisches Beispiel', *Südostecho*, June 1953; 'Der Donauraum – eine Schule für Europäer', *Der Südostdeutsche*, issue 2, July 1953; 'Probefall Europa am Rande der Steppe: Bukowiner Geschichte als Schulfall für die heutigen Europa Pläne', *Der Südostdeutsche*, issue 1, March 1954; 'Das Buchenland – die Schweiz Gesamteuropas', *Der Südostdeutsche*, December 1955; 'Das Schicksal der europäischen Kulturlandschaft Bukowina', *Der Südostdeutsche*, January 1956.
173. 'Eine Kulturoase am Karpatenrand', *Der Südostdeutsche*, May 1953.
174. BI, Allg. Korrespondenz Bundesverband, 1954: untitled typed report, 26 June 1954.
175. BArch-K: B106/27364, fol. 324: Homeland Society of German Resettlers from Bukovina to the Ministry of Intra-German Relations regarding 'the funding of a cultural conference of the Landsmannschaft for the promotion of partnerships and cooperation with Romanian and Ukrainian émigrés from Bukovina', 3 August 1953.
176. Wagner's contacts were linked to the fact that had written his doctoral dissertation, submitted in Berlin in 1938, about the Ukrainians, 'Die ukrainisch-reformatorische

Bewegung in Ostgalizien', and from 1939, he was employed as an expert for Eastern Europe by institutions planning the war, including the Institut für Raumforschung. See Hausleitner, 'Die Geschichte der Bukowina', 124–25. In 1940, Wagner had also helped anti-Soviet Ukrainians and Romanians with sympathies for the Legion to leave Bukovina. On this, see Hausleitner, '*Viel Mischmasch mitgenommen*', 81–113.

177. BI, Allg. Korrespondenz Bundesverband, 1954: Undated handwritten 7-page text, probably written for some official purpose insofar as it also listed the names of further witnesses.
178. Ibid., 5.
179. Ibid., 4.
180. Ibid., 7.
181. Ahonen, *After the Expulsion*, 47.
182. These can be found in a wide range of sources in the 1950s, from the local archives in Stuttgart and Darmstadt to the publications of the Bukovinian German Landsmannschaft quoted throughout this chapter.
183. Cf. A. Confino, *The Nation as a Local Metaphor: Württemberg, Imperial Germany, and National Memory 1871–1918* (Chapel Hill: University of North Carolina Press, 1997); C. Applegate, *A Nation of Provincials: The German Idea of Heimat* (Berkeley: University of California Press, 1990).
184. Prelitsch, *10 Jahre Landsmannschaft der Buchenlanddeutschen*, 50.
185. See e.g. C. Armbrüster, *Deutsch-Satulmare: Geschichte eines buchenländischen Pfälzerdorfes* (Karlsruhe: n.p., 1962). The book *Bukowina: Heimat von gestern* ('Bukovina, Yesterday's Homeland') from 1956 specifically addressed 'common Bukovinians'. The preface stated it arose from 'the deeply felt necessity of a book about Bukovina, our unforgettable former Heimat, by men of the people for the people [*von Männern aus dem Volke für das Volk*]'; 'Vorwort', in *Bukowina: Heimat von gestern*, 6.
186. See e.g. J. Faehndrich, *Eine endliche Geschichte: Die Heimatbücher der deutschen Vertriebenen* (Cologne: Böhlau Verlag, 2011).
187. See Stickler, '*Ostdeutsch heißt Gesamtdeutsch*', 430. Others have noted the continuities; see P. Maeder, *Forging a New Heimat: Expellees in Post-war West Germany and Canada* (Göttingen: Vandenhoeck and Ruprecht Unipress, 2011).
188. Massier, *Bukowina: Heimat von gestern*, 299–316.
189. BArch-K, B 122/2091 (*Bundeskanzleramt, Landsmannschaften und Bund der Vertriebenen*), Letter from Theodor Heuss to the State Secretary von Bismark, 14 December 1951.
190. The subject *Ostkunde* ('East studies') was even taught in schools in the 1950s and 1960s. See B. Weichers, *Der deutsche Osten in der Schule: Institutionalisierung und Konzeption der Ostkunde in der Bundesrepublik in den 1950er und 1960er Jahren* (Frankfurt: Peter Lang, 2013).
191. Franz Thedieck quoted in R. Wagner (ed.), *Alma Mater Francisco Josephina: Die deutschsprachige Nationalitäten Universität in Czernowitz: Festschrift zum 100. Jahrestag ihrer Eröffnung 1875* (Munich: Menschendörfer, 1979), 358.
192. The best illustration of this is the fact that the Interior Ministry published in the early 1950s both the multivolume 'Documentation on the Expulsions' known as the Ost-Dokumentation, which denounced the crimes committed against Germans in their homelands, and a multivolume work on 'expellee integration', which celebrated the success of their new start. See Eugen Lemberg (ed.), *Die Vertriebenen in Westdeutschland* (Kiel: Ferdinand Hirt, 1959).
193. See Vosskamp, *Katholische Kirche*, 217.

194. The 1973 brochure from the Bundeszentrale für politische Bildung quoted in Christian Habbe, 'Der zweite lange Marsch', in S. Aust and R. Augstein (eds), *Die Flucht: Über die Vertreibung der Deutschen aus dem Osten* (Augsburg: Weltbild, 2013), 254.

Chapter 3

'A REMARKABLE BRANCH OF THE JEWISH PEOPLE'

Survivors from Bukovina between Romania and Israel after the Second World War

In 1952, a *shikun* (a block of apartments) for Bukovinian immigrants was founded in Rishon LeZion, a town eight kilometres south of Tel Aviv. On the day of the *shikun*'s inauguration ceremony, Mayer Ebner, a famous Zionist politician and intellectual, originally from Bukovina, delivered the opening speech. Though he referred to Israel as their ancestral homeland by mentioning the Exodus, he also spoke about their more recent history and described Bukovinians as a tribe: 'Bukovinians constitute a kind of tribal group' (*so bildet das Bukowinertum einen stammartigen Zusammenhang*). He explained that they felt connected by their losses, but also by their achievements: 'Our fate as Jews also includes our fate as Bukovinians, which we commemorate here with the founding of a settlement.'[1]

A representative from the Israeli Ministry of Interior then took over and continued along the same lines. He argued that Bukovinians, as 'new citizens', were 'a productive element that would increase the economic and intellectual strength of the Rishon area':

> In their homeland Bukovina, Jews were at the crossroads of different cultures, between East and West and had the opportunity to oversee the blending of the Jewries of different cultures and will contribute to such a 'fusion of the exiles' [*misug hagalujoth*] here as well.[2]

He then encouraged Bukovinians to do justice to their 'good name' as 'a remarkable branch of the Jewish people' in both their ancestral and new homeland. In recognition for this, the streets and squares were to be named after famous Bukovinians.[3] Even if the homeland Bukovina was their 'former home', the notion of 'Bukovinian' was now closely associated with their current lives and future in Israel.

Just a few years earlier, such a discourse and event would have been quite unthinkable. The immediate postwar period, following the 'liberation' by the Soviets, remained a period of considerable risk, insecurity and hardship for the majority of Bukovinian Jews. With Bukovina divided between Romania and the Soviet Union, the approximately 50,000 survivors from the region did not know where to go. While some managed to leave the area straight away, many men were drawn into the Red Army and most of the others were repatriated to Romania, where they lived as refugees. Although this country became a gateway for immigration to Palestine (so-called *Aliyah Bet*) after the Second World War, until the creation of the State of Israel in 1948, this remained both illegal and a quite uncertain choice.[4] Thereafter, the division of Europe and the communist government's ambivalent stance towards the Jews constituted a major hindrance to Jews leaving the country.[5] Furthermore, Zionism, the prevailing doctrine in the early State of Israel, posited not only the 'ingathering of exiles', namely unrestricted Jewish immigration, but also their 'fusion' as mentioned by the ministerial representative quoted above. This process was linked to the principle of 'absorption' – as social integration in Palestine and Israel was known – and the associated principle of the 'negation of the Diaspora'.[6] As Tom Segev has argued, Zionists envisioned a different society from that which had existed for Jews in exile.[7] New immigrants were supposed to shed their differences. As Dvora Hacohen has shown, 'it was also through immigration that the Zionists hoped to realize their dream of social reform … [*aliyah* –immigration to Palestine; also meaning 'to rise'] was both the goal and the means towards that goal'.[8] In other words, Zionism foresaw not only the dissolution of the Diaspora, but also of the cultures of exile its members brought with them.

Much of the scholarly literature has focused on denouncing this ideological stance and its inherent contradictions. Hacohen, for example, has emphasized the tension between the utopian principle of open doors and the application of a principle of selectivity in the treatment of new immigrants.[9] Indeed, as Segev has pointed out, those who came after the war from exile, with their alleged 'Diaspora mentality', were considered inferior and in need of re-education.[10] As Idith Zertal has argued:

> [T]he total rebellion against [the Diaspora] and all it represented, was a central, formative ethos of activist revolutionary Zionism. In fact, revolutionary Zionism negated not only the Diaspora's way of life; it intended to utterly

obliterate the Diasporic soul of the revolutionary Zionists themselves and along with it the past, the entire two thousand-year history of the Exile.[11]

The attitude towards Holocaust survivors, who were often sick and traumatized, was highly ambivalent. This realization has even led some historians to argue that Jewish authorities' promotion of Jewish emigration from Europe was self-serving and the attitude towards survivors patronizing.[12]

Yet, an increasing number of scholars have qualified these claims. For one thing, this situation needs to be viewed in light of the fact that emigration to Israel mostly resolved Europe's postwar Jewish refugee problem. Over half of all Holocaust survivors found a new home in Israel after the Second World War.[13] For another, as Hacohen has pointed out, the state was not patronizing from a position of strength, but rather out of a sense of moral obligation.[14] In her seminal work on the integration of Holocaust survivors in the early State of Israel, Hannah Yablonka has shown that while they were not offered much understanding or aid, the state did not actively discriminate against Holocaust survivors.[15] Unavoidably, therefore, there was a gap between the idealized image of Israel among refugees from Europe and the reality on the ground – they had to construct Israel as their home. But many of them did integrate and self-rehabilitate in the years following their arrival by drawing on a combination of old and new ideas and displaying, as Dina Porat and others have said, 'surprising energy'.[16] Porat has even described the rejection of the Diaspora as 'theoretical'.[17]

Most interestingly, perhaps, Hacohen has pointed to 'the influence of the immigrants' cultural background and their networks on the process of their absorption'.[18] She identifies a shift in attitude in the early 1950s as Israel developed into a diverse, immigrant society, something that reshaped both Israel and the Diaspora.[19] Moreover, as Liora Halperin has shown in her recent book on language use in pre-state and early-state Israel, there was an unavoidable gap between official rhetoric and lived practice. Halperin demonstrates how the issue of language was subject to a careful equilibrium whereby 'the embrace of the national did not seem inconsistent with a limited multilingual policy, one that tolerated or condoned language diversity in certain social spheres'.[20] This resonates with the case of Bukovinians, who continued to use German throughout the period of their establishment in Mandatory Palestine and later as well. As Yoav Gelber has argued, the contribution of Central European migrants was 'neither easily accepted nor taken for granted'.[21] And though he notes that they generally demonstrated astonishing 'self-reliance', he also admits that this was a highly diverse group.[22] This therefore raises the question, how did this ambivalence and this cultural negotiation play itself out in the case of Bukovinians?

This chapter explores the experiences of Jewish Bukovinians at the end and in the immediate aftermath of the Second World War, from their experiences in postwar Bukovina and Romania to their arrival in Mandatory Palestine and Israel. It describes the founding of a Bukovinian organization Chug Olej Bukovina (lit.: the Association of Immigrants from Bukovina) in Tel Aviv in 1944 and its development into the 'Organization of Immigrants from Bukovina' in Israel in the late 1950s. It discusses Jewish Bukovinians' specific experiences as 'repatriates' and 'refugees' in Romania and 'newcomers', 'immigrants' (*oleh, olim*), 'survivors' or part of *She'erit Hapletah* (the 'surviving remnant') in Palestine and Israel, but also their experiences as self-defined 'Bukovinians', and it looks at how these terms related to each other. This chapter places these experiences in the context of mass Jewish emigration from Romania after the Second World War and the so-called 'Great *Aliyah*', which saw some 200,000 immigrants arrive in Israel within the first year of statehood alone. It thus shows how Bukovinian Jews constructed a sense of belonging by negotiating between a Zionist stance and their past and present experiences, tracing the evolution of what it meant to be Bukovinian for Jews in the first decade after the end of the war.

'The Impossible Return': Bukovinian Jews in Romania after the Second World War

In late 1943, in an ironic turn of fate, the same Romanian regime that had deported over 100,000 Jews from Bukovina to Transnistria in 1941–42 decided to authorize the 'repatriation' of deportees.[23] With the military defeat of Axis-allied Romania, the wider 'liberation' of the area's camps and ghettos by the Soviets soon followed. Yet, the terms 'repatriation' and 'liberation' are somewhat misleading. While some 17,000 Jews had been able to survive in Cernăuți during the war and, according to Jean Ancel, 34,149 Jews from Bukovina were still alive in Transnistria as of 15 November 1943,[24] the rest of the population had perished due to cold, hunger, disease, exhaustion and summary executions. Nearly two-thirds of the 120,000-strong prewar community had been murdered during the war and the Holocaust. Moreover, many of those who survived were in a very challenging situation and, for them, the ordeal was not over. This was the start of what others have described as the 'violent' or 'brutal' peacetime that followed the end of the war.[25]

Indeed, for many survivors from Bukovina, the end of the war was a phase of continuing insecurity, risk and confusion.[26] The war did not end all at once: in 1944, the front was still moving across the region, bombings were taking place and the Soviets sought to recruit all young and able men and women into the Red Army or into doing hard labour. In addition, returning home was difficult, disheartening or even impossible. Years of malnourishment, maltreatment and illness had taken their toll. There were thousands of orphans and widows; many people were sick and disabled; almost all were destitute. Their property and goods had been either destroyed or taken and they were rarely restituted; some former neighbours displayed displeasure or even downright hostility at the Jews' return. The war and the Holocaust had completely destroyed and dismantled not only families but also entire communities and their structures. For many Bukovinian Jews, home was no longer home.

In many ways, this 'impossible return' of 'the living dead' to 'ghost towns' was similar to that of Jewish survivors elsewhere in Central and Eastern Europe.[27] Yet, there were particularities to the case of Bukovina too. First, this had to do with the character of the Holocaust in Romania: not only was the number of survivors higher, but as a group, they were also demographically more diverse than survivors from areas that had been occupied by the Germans; in particular, there were a higher number of children and elderly people. Second, the experiences of Jewish Bukovinians varied a great deal among each other, let alone compared to other Romanian Jews, who had been able to remain in the 'Old Kingdom'. There was little in common between the experiences of those – often the somewhat wealthier and better-connected people – who had survived in the city of Cernăuți, the young men who had been called up to forced labour and those deported to the devastated region of Transnistria, including almost all of the Jews from southern Bukovina. In Cernăuți, Jews had been able to work and, in some cases, even returned to their homes after the ghetto was dissolved in late 1941. Substantial differences also existed between different Transnistrian camps and ghettos. In Mogilev-Podolsk, for example, a semblance of normal life had been possible, while in the ghettos further east, such as Bershad, survival rates were very low. There too, wealth and connections had been instrumental to survival.[28] Accordingly, Bukovinians were in a highly variable situation as the war ended.

Furthermore, following liberation by the Soviets in 1944, the region was divided once again like it had been following the first Soviet invasion in 1940. The north became part of the Soviet Union and the south part of Romania. This made for a complicated situation, with the border cutting right through the middle of the historical region. The former capital, Austrian Czernowitz, Romanian Cernăuți and, by then, Soviet Chernovtsy, where many of the survivors were from and where many survivors who had been deported to Transnistria returned after the war, was in the north under direct Soviet rule. The south, with its sprinkling of small towns from which all Jews had been deported in 1941, remained Romanian; however, severed from its main economic and cultural centre, it seemed more peripheral than ever before, and many Bukovinian Jews did not know where they belonged.

According to many postwar accounts, in Soviet Chernovtsy after liberation in 1944, within the constraints of Sovietization, life and Jewish life in particular was returning to normal. Memoirs describe people reuniting with surviving members of their family and going back to school, university or work. Some even managed to recover their former homes. However, as Marianne Hirsch and Leo Spitzer have argued, 1944–45 can also be regarded as 'the bleakest of the "war" years in the city'.[29] It was a moment of realization and disappointment – the moment '*before* "After Auschwitz"' – 'when Jews all across Europe found they had nowhere to turn'.[30] Indeed, many Bukovinian Jews did not want to live in Romania, the country of their tormentors. However, having experienced Soviet rule once already in 1940–41, nor did they want to live in the Soviet Union. Among other things, they bitterly recalled the deportation of thousands Bukovinian Jews to Siberia in 1941, just before the Soviets withdrew from the area.[31] As a result, from 1944 to 1945, many Jews tried to cross the border into Romania illegally in the hope of moving on from there as soon as possible.

As it turned out, the Soviets did not want the region's Jews to stay anyway. According to Svetlana Frunchak, the Soviet authorities resented this population, who continued to speak German and who, in their eyes, had suspiciously managed to survive.[32] On 8 August 1945, a Soviet resolution allowed 'persons of Jewish nationality who are residents of northern Bukovina and were not Soviet citizens before 28 June 1940, according to documents presented by them' to leave for Romania.[33] This so-called 'transfer', which was rather a unilateral evacuation, took place in two phases in 1945–46.[34] An estimated 22,000 Jews left northern Bukovina for Romania during this short period, taking no more than what they could carry with them and forced to leave valuables behind.[35] Only a few thousand Bukovinian Jews are believed to have remained in the Soviet Union.[36] Within a year of the war's end, most Bukovinian Jews had, for better or for worse, 'returned' to Romania.

Displacement and homelessness thus caught up with both Bukovinian Jews who had been deported and those who had not. Most repatriates from northern Bukovina first sought refuge in small towns of southern Bukovina. However, the authorities there were rapidly overwhelmed by the situation and by the population numbers.[37] Many, therefore, travelled on further, mostly to the capital Bucharest and to other larger towns in Moldavia and Transylvania such as Iași or Cluj. In general, Romania experienced a veritable Jewish refugee crisis during this period. The number of Jews in Romania rose from 280,000 in 1944 to 428,000 in 1948; in Bucharest, the number of Jews more than doubled.[38] Many of them were so-called 'survivor-refugees'.[39] Some were Holocaust survivors from German concentration camps, originally from Transylvania, Poland and other countries, hoping to leave Europe via Romania. However, many were survivors from Bukovina and Bessarabia, who had survived Transnistria or been repatriated from northern Bukovina. Indeed, a large number of Bukovinians were considered stateless, having had their Romanian citizenship confiscated before the war and having lost their papers during the war. Up until 1947, the Romanian authorities automatically regarded northern Bukovinians as Soviet citizens and therefore foreign nationals, placing them at risk of further eviction and depriving them of civil rights.[40]

Among these people, severe economic hardship was widespread. Repatriates from Transnistria were in a very poor state. They were destitute, sick, homeless and socially isolated; they needed everything – food, medicine, clothing and housing.[41] The situation even attracted international attention. In November 1945, Kalman Stein of the Relief and Rehabilitation Department of the World Jewish Congress forwarded the translation of a Romanian article entitled 'An Impressive Appeal of the Transnistrians', which had appeared in the Romanian newspaper *Semnalul*, to the International Red Cross. The article read as follows:

> A large group of Jews, Romanian citizens, repatriated from the extermination camps of Transnistria, have been living, for a long time, a bitter life of privation and misery, in the capital as well as in some of the other cities of Romania … They have returned now to wander aimlessly, hungrily, without clothes or shoes, about the streets of the capital, or to nurse their weakened bodies in miserable shacks, while mourning their murdered parents and children, or to go around begging, begging for real help, which is constantly denied to them.[42]

Stein's accompanying letter explained that these were 'refugees' and 'victims of Nazi crimes' and asked what next steps were planned for the relief of Jews in Romania in general.[43] The reference to 'extermination camps' and 'Nazis' served to emphasize the seriousness of the situation, but the continued suffering of victims of wartime persecution in Romania was framed as a humanitarian emergency in its own right.

Some categories of people were particularly vulnerable. These included the elderly, orphans, single caregivers and the sick. Elias Hauster, for example, was a retired a civil servant who had been born in 1878 in Austrian Czernowitz and had survived the war in Cernăuți. Having been repatriated from northern Bukovina in 1946, he was living after the war as a refugee with his wife in the southern Bukovinian town Rădăuți. The letters he wrote between 1946 and 1949 to his son Julius, who was then living in Bucharest, capture the extent of his hardship. Elias Hauster and his wife were housed in a small, cold basement apartment and could not afford food or medicine.

When his pension was paid out after the war, it was one-fortieth of its previous value due to inflation, and the aid provided by the local Jewish community was insufficient to compensate for the difference. He repeatedly had to ask his son for money.[44] Another interesting case is that of the young Blanka Lebzelter, who was born around 1920 in a small Bukovinian town. She had survived deportation to Transnistria, but lost her elder brother, her father and her fiancé during the war. Though her mother had also survived, she had contracted tuberculosis in Transnistria and continued to suffer from the illness for the rest of her life. After the war, Blanka moved with her mother to the town of Constanța on the Black Sea and tried to make a new start. However, as her diaries reveal, taking care of her ailing mother alone, struggling to survive economically and plagued by gruesome memories, she felt incredibly depressed and isolated. She often wondered if it had been worth surviving the ordeal of deportation.[45]

Aid came mainly from fellow Jews, provided by relatives, friends, members of the Jewish community and Jewish international organizations such as the World Jewish Congress and the Joint Distribution Community (Joint). In Romania, the Joint funded initiatives at the local level across the country.[46] The Jewish community in Bucharest, for example, ran hostels, orphanages, hospitals and canteens financed by them. All around the country, Jewish communities mobilized to provide help to repatriated orphans from Transnistria in particular. Communities also prioritized the immigration of orphans and children to Palestine.[47] At this time, specialized relief organizations for 'Bukovinians' and so-called 'Transnistrians' or former deportees were founded.[48] These organizations solicited aid and sought to raise awareness of the situation beyond the Jewish circles.

In 1945, for example, Fabius Ornstein, the leader of the Association of Former Transnistrian Deportees, published a booklet entitled *The Suffering of Deportees in Transnistria: Think about Everything that Happened in Transnistria (1941–1944)*. It contained a detailed factual account of the persecution as well as expressive drawings and poems in Yiddish. In Romanian, Ornstein argued: 'The monstrous crime of Transnistria is equal in proportion to that experienced in Majdanek, Auschwitz or Lublin. It resulted in the death of around ninety per cent of those deported.'[49] He also explained that he had only depicted part of what had happened and he emphasized:

> I have not done this for those who survived this suffering, so that they relive it – by reading about it – at least in their imagination and in a considerably less powerful way. No! Bringing up this period of horror, with its chain of suffering and humiliation, which, to crown it, continues until now, is for each person with a conscience. We want to draw attention, public attention, to the fact that the liberation from the dark tyranny has not brought about a solution for

those who survived Transnistria and are former deportees and continue to be in a terrible material and moral situation to this day.⁵⁰

Although the reach of such a booklet was most probably limited, this publication testifies both to the fact that people would have known what Transnistria was and that it was still possible to discuss the matter for a short while in Romania after the war.⁵¹

Nevertheless, this source also captures the profound disappointment and dismay at the indifference to survivors' fate, as other documents do too. A report from a group of repatriates from the Soviet Union to the Romanian refugee committee of the World Jewish Congress in 1946, for instance, stated that the 40,000 Bukovinian and Bessarabian Jews, who had previously identified as Romanian and then been deported to Transnistria during the war, felt utterly let down by the regime. They had hoped that 'today's Romania, that condemns the regime of yesteryear, would understand its moral duty towards us … and would be aware of its obligation to repair the enormous material and moral wrongdoings committed by Antonescu's authorities against us'. Instead, however, they were now regarded as 'repatriates, namely foreigners and stateless people'.⁵² Similarly, both Elias Hauster and Blanka Lebzelter felt increasingly resentful towards and alienated from this regime that failed to address their problems. Elias constantly dreamed of a future for himself and his wife in Palestine and tried to convince his son to leave as well. He warned his son repeatedly about the risks the new regime appeared to present, drawing parallels to the recent past.⁵³ Similarly, in 1948, Blanka Lebzelter wrote to relatives in the United States to discuss emigration, but also considered Palestine and soon joined a Zionist organization, in which she became very active.⁵⁴ Many other Jewish survivors were considering their options at this time and an increasing number of people opted for emigration. Retrospective accounts often link the decision to a combination of factors, including ongoing economic difficulties, experiences of antisemitism and Romania's Soviet-inspired and increasingly undemocratic politics.

These statements and actions do not so much point to the effects of wartime Jewish suffering as to the passivity of the postwar Romanian government concerning Jewish hardship. To an extent, this was a consequence of the overall economic problems in the country after the Second World War, including uncontrolled inflation linked to the communization of the economy. Yet, antisemitism appears to have still been widespread in Romania in this period too. Ancel has argued that earlier antisemitic thinking was not challenged and that resentment towards the Jews even increased in Romania at this time, as people competed over scarce resources.⁵⁵ According to Hildrun Glass, the antisemitism of members of the historical parties is best recorded, but the communists were not immune to anti-Jewish prejudice either.⁵⁶ Indeed, in theory, the communists believed all citizens should be equal regardless of ethnicity. However, in practice, restitution of Jewish property, for example, was very limited. The authorities did not return what had been nationalized and were reluctant to dispossess ethnic Romanians. Moreover, 'egalitarian' policies were often duplicitous. Those affected by the war, for example, including Jewish deportees and forced labourers, were given priority access to education. Yet, one of the more or less implicit aims of this policy with respect to the Jews was 'restratification', a policy of re-education intended to alter the 'bourgeois' character of the existing Jewish social structure.[57] Finally, retribution for war crimes was completely inadequate. While trials against war criminals took place rapidly, they were instrumentalized for political purposes, and Jews were barely mentioned during them.[58] Denial and minimization of the crimes committed against Jews during the war also grew over time. Within a few years, the books recording the persecution of Romanian Jews during the war, such as the publications of Marius Mircu or Matatias Carp's *Black Book*, had disappeared from the shelves of bookshops and libraries. As Liviu Rotman has concluded: 'The Romanian majority viewed the rehabilitation of the Jewish minority as a gesture towards the Jews. It did not see restitution as the rectification of injustice and as such vital to the rehabilitation of Romanian society itself.' Therefore, as he concludes, , Jewish rehabilitation was 'only partial'.[59]

The result was a paradoxical situation. On the one hand, in a system aiming for conformity and assimilation, there was a negative attitude towards difference and religion. However, on the other hand, until 1947, Jewish organizations had considerable room for manoeuvre in terms of how they took care of the Jews. The creation, in June 1945, of an instrumental, state-controlled Jewish party, the Jewish Democratic Committee (CDE), embodies this paradox. Initially, it included left-wing Zionists and communists – basically atheists. But while some Jews climbed the echelons of the Communist Party – most notably Ana Pauker, the Foreign Minister of Romania from 1947 to 1952 – in general, their proportion in the ranks of the Communist Party has been overstated and only a small minority of Jewish Bukovinians identified with the new regime.[60] Communist Jews were a community within a community. As Ancel has argued, in Romania after the Second World War, not only did the Joint and the Zionist organizations it sponsored save the Jews from starvation and degeneration, but they were also 'the real authority' and reference point for Romanian Jews.[61] Ancel sees this as a 'mixed blessing', because while this helped members of the Jewish community survive, it also absolved the Romanian government of its responsibility towards them.[62] He even goes so far as to conclude that the authorities were nice to the Zionists in order to get rid of Jews, although they were fundamentally anti-Zionist.[63] Ultimately, while these organizations supported Jews, they also sought to prevent them from establishing themselves in Romania. In other words, Jewish self-sufficiency was essential, but it also encouraged Jews to identify as Jews rather than as Romanians.

In such a context, it is hardly surprising that Zionism and emigration were the most common responses among Romanian Jews in general and Bukovinian Jews in particular. Zionism had been quite strong in Romania before the war and its appeal only grew further during the war and in its immediate aftermath. After the war, a whole network of different local Zionist organizations developed throughout the country.[64] They offered not only aid but also Hebrew courses, Zionist education, cultural entertainment, summer camps for children and training camps (*Hachshara*) for young adults to prepare them for *aliyah*. They emphasized the Zionist message of redemption and the historical continuity of Jewish history. All of the Romanian Jewish newspapers apart from the organ of the party, *Unirea*, adopted a Zionist stance and presented the Holy Land as a paradise, especially for the young.[65] There, they would be able to make a new start and have a completely different life. The numbers speak for themselves. According to Ancel, there were 42,000 candidates for *aliyah* in March 1945, 105,000 a year later and, by July 1946, some 150,000 wanted to leave for Israel.[66] In view of the precarity of their situation, it is safe to assume that Bukovinian Jews were overrepresented among those who left or wanted to leave Romania in the immediate aftermath of the war.

Some scholars have viewed this trend as the consequence of the successful instrumentalization and exploitation of Jewish survivors on behalf of the Mossad and the Jewish government in Palestine, the Yishuv, who aimed to put pressure on the British in Palestine by recruiting fighters in Europe.[67] At the other end of the spectrum, Ancel, for example, argues that in the case of Romania, Jewish migration would have taken place even in the absence of the Zionist movement.[68] The motives of those who left most likely varied greatly. As Tom Segev has argued, these motives ranged from the belief in messianic redemption to the possibility to escape Stalinist Europe.[69] It is also probable, as Yehuda Bauer has argued, that given a choice, many survivors would probably not have gone to Israel. But as he goes on to explain about Displaced Persons (DPs) in general, their decision was not hard to understand: 'The murder of the European Jews seemed to vindicate the Zionist argument that there was no future for Jews in Europe' and 'America was closed'.[70]

What is certain is that the hardship and alienation many Jews experienced in Romania after the war reinforced ideological arguments and convictions. On 10 December 1947, for example, a group of Bukovinian Jews living in the town of Gheorgheni wrote to the Association of Support for Bukovinian Jews in Bucharest to inform them of their fate and situation. They were refugees 'without a possibility for earning money, without food, without clothes, without firewood, without windows, without furniture and without any trust in the future'. They explained to the addressees who were supposed to represent them that they were their 'only hope'. They wanted to leave with the next possible *aliyah*. As the letter continued: 'All our needs would be satisfied by life in our Holy Land ... we need to go to *Eretz*, and there we will be able to be humans once more. Here, we are only shadows.'[71] In this sense, Jewish emigration from Romania might be understood as preceded by what Rogers Brubaker has described as a process of, more or less, creative 'ethnic reidentification'.[72] Jews not only felt as though they did not belong in their homes any longer; they even believed they needed to leave their home to realize their true selves.

Of course, this did not happen overnight. As Pieter Lagrou has written about the homecoming of Jews to European societies in general, any return is a transition.[73] As Liviu Rotman has pointed out with respect to Romania in particular, 'unmasking the new regime was a lengthy process'.[74] This was all the more so because Romania had a large postwar Jewish population and many Jews had hope for a return to normality after the war. In the immediate aftermath of the war, for example, many Bukovinian Jews applied to join relatives elsewhere in Romania.[75] This suggests that, like Blanka Lebzelter, they were prepared to attempt a new start somewhere else. In many towns and cities, Jewish schools and institutions, such as ritual baths and Jewish theatres, reopened. Many, especially young adults, tried to rebuild their lives by going back to school, university or work. Some got married, had children and became more or less established and committed to the system. Even in retrospect, this 'life in transit' was not all bad. Pearl Fichman, for example, remembered her time in Bucharest after the war with considerable fondness, writing that it was 'a short but sweet interlude'.[76] For many people, it was a time of opportunity and rebuilding of the community. Marianne Hirsch remembers growing up in Bucharest after the war surrounded by a lively community of 'Czernowitz Jews', with whom her parents were friends.[77] At this time, a German-speaking and mostly Jewish literary scene developed there too, with a number of Bukovinian figures at its centre.[78]

In addition, from a logistical and pragmatic standpoint, there were major obstacles to leaving. In the first years after the war, ships were often overcrowded and in bad condition, and border crossings were dangerous and illegal. Besides, the future of Palestine was uncertain and the bureaucratic hurdles were significant. Indeed, Jewish emigration from Romania had its own conjuncture and is a topic in its own right.[79] Before May 1948, the British issued quotas on immigration to Palestine in line with the 1939 'White Paper'. For Romania, the number of permitted immigrants was set at 1,500. Certificates were therefore hard to obtain and as a result, many Jews tried to leave without. This, in turn, meant that ships with refugees from Romania were often turned away and the refugees detained in camps on Cyprus.[80] The 750 immigrants who were then allowed to leave Cyprus monthly were deducted from the total Romanian immigration quota. For many Jews, it soon became apparent that it was not worth leaving Romania. Many Bukovinian Jews also preferred other destinations, some insisting on remaining in Europe to keep their European heritage and traditions, others preferring North or South America. Here too, the only options were to wait for restrictions to be lifted and visas to be delivered or to leave anyway and risk illegality.

After 1948, the circumstances both of life in Romania and of immigration to Israel improved briefly, but the issue of emigration continued to divide families and cause considerable personal disruption. As Rotman has argued, '*aliyah* became an ongoing source of family crisis and community unrest'.[81] Here again, the example of Elias Hauster who favoured Palestine and his son who favoured South America is a case in point. Though Elias dreamt of Palestine, having already lost one son in the war, he did not want to be alone. The case of Blanka Lebzelter, whose unfulfilled aspiration to leave prevented her finding peace, is also intriguing. Later, she even asserted that the effort to leave prevented her from establishing herself in Romania – making friends, looking for a better job and even getting married.[82] In an ironic twist of fate, in 1950, her ailing mother obtained a visa for Israel, but Blanka did not.[83] Blanka was not able to leave Romania until 1961 and over the years, she came to regard her situation as a form of ongoing persecution. In another extreme case, Hedwig Brenner and her husband applied 130 times to leave Romania until the visa was eventually granted in 1982.[84] In general, applying for a visa was not an easy process. When, during an interview, leaving Romania was described as emigration, the interviewee retorted '"emigration" is a nice way to put it! We went through everything you could possibly go through'. The interviewee and her husband had spent four years in Bucharest and then had gone to Vienna before getting a ship to Haifa. When she arrived in Haifa, she was pregnant and she and her husband lived in a reception camp with hundreds of beds. Other Bukovinians had made similar journeys via Yugoslavia, Italy or even the Netherlands. The paths and experiences of immigration were highly diverse.

The postwar revival of Jewish life in Romania and in Bukovina especially, nevertheless coincided with its ultimate dissolution. An increasing number of Bukovinian Jews joined Zionist organizations in late 1946–47.[85] Many Jews left even before the creation of Israel in May 1948. In 1947, just before Romania itself shut its borders, there was a mass flight from Romania, known as the 'hunger flight', caused by the cold winter, drought, the shortage of food and the growing Sovietization of the economy and society.[86] Attendance of the Jewish kindergarten in Fălticeni, as small town south of Suceava, for the years between 1945 and 1948, for example, showed a steady decline: in October 1945, there were some fifty-five children registered and fifty attended; by April 1948, some forty-five were registered, but only sixteen attended.[87] As historians have shown, by 1948, the Jewish community in Romania had effectively been 'taken over' (*gleichgeschaltet*).[88] By 1949, in the context of an anti-Zionist campaign, Zionism was widely denounced as 'cosmopolitan', 'capitalist' and even 'fascist', and many Jews were arrested.[89] This only increased the desire to leave the country. A total of 50,000 Jews went to Israel from Romania in 1948 and, although in the following years the attitudes and policies towards the Jews, particularly regarding emigration, were contradictory and erratic, the Romanian government was not able to stop the haemorrhage. By 1956, there were fewer than 150,000 Jews still living in Romania and many of these wanted to go. In Romania just a few years after the Second World War, there was no more Bukovinian Jewish community to speak of.

Eretz Israel as 'Solution and Salvation': Bukovinians in Pre-State Israel

While some Bukovinian Jews attempted to return to their lives in Bukovina after the Second World War, others were convinced early on that there could be no future for the Jews in Europe. This was the case of Manfred Reifer, a historian and a lawyer by training, who had been a Jewish and Zionist politician in interwar Romania. Reifer had narrowly avoided deportation to Siberia at the hands of the Soviets in the summer of 1941 and had been among the Bukovinian Jews who had obtained a permit to remain in Romanian Cernăuți during the war. He then succeeded in escaping to Bucharest in 1943 and immediately set off on a risky journey through Bulgaria, Turkey and the Middle East. He arrived in British-ruled Mandatory Palestine in April 1944.[90]

As he later explained, when he arrived in Palestine, he had understood that his thirty-five years of engagement and work for the Jews 'in the Gola' (i.e. in the Diaspora) had come to an end.[91] But, in effect, this marked the beginning of a new task for him and for those he regarded as 'his people'. At the time, only a handful of Bukovinian Jews were living in Palestine and, with the war still raging, the future was very uncertain. Reifer thus made use of his journey via Istanbul and Ankara to speak with different people of influence – members of the Yishuv and other governments – about the situation of Romanian Jews and drew attention to their plight. He listed his priorities in the following order: the repatriation of the Jews from Transnistria, the freedom of movement of the Jews in Cernăuți, the facilitation of *aliyah* and the possibility of sending gift parcels to Romania.[92] Separately, he also lobbied for the repatriation of Bukovinian Jews who had been deported by the Soviets to Siberia in the summer of 1941.[93] Then, within a few months of his arrival in Palestine, he had written a two-hundred-page report in which he reiterated these demands and made the case again for the repatriation of Romanian Jews and the emigration of Bukovinian Jews in particular to Palestine. He sent a copy of this text to London.[94]

However, as Reifer soon realized, not only were there significant obstacles to leaving Romania and entering Mandatory Palestine, but further difficulties also awaited Bukovinian Jews once they reached the Holy Land. In the first place, these were logistical problems. Indeed, there was no real system of immigration in pre-state Israel. The constant flow of immigration placed considerable pressure on the area, which lacked the necessary infrastructure and had little in terms of administration. Upon arrival, newcomers known as *oleh* in the singular or *olim* in the plural (derived from the word *aliyah*) received aid in the form of temporary housing (in transit camps known as *ma'abarot*) and some financial support. But the former were extremely basic – mostly tents – and the latter largely insufficient and new migrants were encouraged to move out of the transit camps as soon as possible. Ideally, according to the Zionist logic at the time, they were to join collective agricultural settlements (*kibbutzim*).[95] But aside from the young, many did not want to, and suitable housing and employment outside these collectives were in particularly short supply.[96] Last but not least, after years of persecution, refugees were in a poor state and only some were able to adapt to the new circumstances, including a different climate, diet and language. These difficulties, it was feared, would encumber their 'absorption'.

The dilemma was also ideological. There was a gap between these newcomers and the existing population, which the authorities made little effort to bridge. As mentioned above, Zionism was conceived of as a victory over the Diaspora.[97] The Zionist doctrine was based on assimilationism and a belief in the rebirth of the Jewish spirit. Yet, this was at odds with the newcomers' diverse backgrounds and their need to work through their recent traumatic experiences. Already, the later phase of the fifth *aliyah* from 1929 to 1939, which had brought to Palestine diverse migrants with a range of different motives for immigrating, had confronted the Yishuv with an unprecedented challenge. Many, such as German-Jewish immigrants, had felt more like political refugees and forced emigrants than Zionist pioneers and clung to their cultural heritage. As Yonatan Shiloh-Dayan has even argued about a group of Central European German-speaking migrants from this period: 'They became displaced persons [in Palestine] in the sense that they neither belonged to their homelands nor to their new host society, whose language they did not master, whose national aspiration they negated and whose allegedly Eastern European politics they treated with disdain.'[98]

Similarly, many survivors of the Holocaust had only been drawn to Zionism because of the Holocaust, and the population of the Yishuv was wary of these 'post-catastrophe Zionists' who 'lacked a Zionist education, or were not even close to Zionism and were not organized within party or youth organization frameworks'.[99]

Overall, as Hannah Yablonka has argued, there was 'a general lack of faith in the human quality of Holocaust survivors'.[100] In the case of Bukovinians, their experiences in Romania during the war and immediately afterwards had taken their toll. Both retrospective accounts of life in pre-state and early-state Israel and contemporary documentation reveal that many were deeply shaken by what had happened to them, their families and their communities. In February 1948, a Bukovinian doctor, Dr Ungar, who was working in a DP camp in Munich, observed a number of Bukovinian Jews who had just arrived at the camp and commented that 'the persecutions that the Jews were subjected to and in particular the suffering in concentration camps have not remained without psychological consequences for the victims. Among some of them, a real sense of inferiority is notable'.[101] Such a disposition was also believed to pose a challenge to 'absorption'. New *olim* in Israel were expected to emulate the high self-esteem of the Sabra pioneers. They were supposed to shed their sense of victimhood for a narrative of resistance and heroism. As Zertal has argued in her book about the illegal immigration of Holocaust survivors to Mandatory Palestine, though the Mossad did everything in its power to bring as many survivors as possible over, it did not care about their stories of persecution. The victims, as she wrote, 'had to regard themselves as part of this collective on the collective's own terms, had to want to be a part of it in any way possible'.[102]

The discrepancy between the newcomers' experiences of displacement and victimhood, their desire to be rescued and the meaning attached to immigration by members of the Yishuv nurtured the initial prejudice and contempt of the population of the Yishuv towards Holocaust survivors mentioned earlier. Hacohen has described the state's attitude as utopian and condescending, and likened the alienation of veterans and newcomers to the development of an 'other' or 'second' Israel.[103] Zertal, for example, has described the arrival of the 'surviving remnant' in Palestine as a 'missed encounter'. According to her, the indigenous population 'turned away from the Diaspora' because it aroused 'anxiety' and 'fear', something akin to the Freudian idea of the 'uncanny' posing a threat to the Zionist subject.[104] To an extent, the case of Bukovinians illustrates this. In 1944, when Reifer arrived, a Bukovinian organization (Hitachdut Olej Bukowina) under the leadership of Markus Krämer already existed. It provided aid to Bukovinians in Palestine and sent parcels to Siberia. However, as of 1946, it only had 200 members because membership was restricted to 'veteran Zionists' or 'Zionist activists' – so-called *Vatikim* or *Askan* – who could demonstrate some twenty years of Zionist affiliation and their families.[105] The funding from the Committee of Zionist Veterans was based on this criterion and those who did not qualify could not join or receive assistance.

However, the case of Bukovinians also demonstrates the newcomers' degree of agency and the opportunities for self-rehabilitation. According to Reifer, all newcomers from Bukovina needed help, irrespective of their ideological orientation. The problems they faced included finding suitable employment, retraining and re-educating (especially in the Hebrew language) and searching for missing persons. He believed that 'the housing question' (*die Wohnungsfrage*), generally referred to as *shikun* (the term used to describe the four-storey buildings built at a low cost in this period) was the most pressing.[106] In a letter dating from September 1944 addressed to Chaim Weizmann, the President of the Jewish Agency based in London, Reifer attempted to convey the urgency of the situation. He outlined the fate of Bukovinian Jews who had survived years of persecution at the hands of the Nazis and the Soviets and who, as he claimed, had been faithful to Zionism throughout these critical times. He then described the issue of housing as 'the burning question'. He explained that Bukovinians had not expected to find 'palaces' in Palestine, but that the inaction of the Jewish Agency (Sochnut) and the passivity of the government of the Jews in Israel (Yishuv) were nevertheless appalling. He concluded by pointing out that the difficulty of the situation would ultimately hinder their 'absorption' (*Einordnung*, lit.: subsumption).[107] Implicit in this was the fact that dissatisfied people might even lose faith in the Zionist project.

The hopeless response Reifer received from Weizmann on 25 October 1944 strengthened his conviction concerning the necessity of self-administration and self-help.[108] He thus set out to solve the so-called '*olim* problem' in his own way by establishing his own organization. This initiative involved offering the newcomers financial and material assistance (housing and small loans) and advice, informing them about their rights and ensuring their representation, as well as helping them to find or keep in touch with each other. In effect, the aims of his efforts were similar to those of the existing Bukovinian organization, but insofar as political credentials were not a condition for membership, this new organization's reach was to be wider. Indeed, Reifer wanted to register and help *all* Bukovinians following their arrival in Palestine, irrespective of their past political affiliations. In late 1944, therefore, Reifer founded Chug Olej Bukovina (lit.: the Association of Immigrants from Bukovina). It was part of the Association of European Immigrants (Irgun Olej Merkas Europa) and was affiliated with the Organization of Romanian Jews (Hitachdut Olej Romania), but it had its own office in Tel Aviv. Reifer also decided to launch a monthly newsletter (*Informationsblatt*).[109] He gave responsibility for this to Elias Weinstein, the former editor of the major daily *Czernowitzer Morgenblatt*.[110] The first issue of this paper appeared on 13 December 1944, bearing the title *Chug Olej Bukowina* in large Hebrew letters above a small transcription of the name in the Latin alphabet.[111] A few months later, it was renamed 'The Migrant's Voice' (*Die Stimme des Oleh*) and eventually came to be known as simply *Die Stimme*.

This organization, like other, smaller ones created in those years, was not diasporic in the traditional sense. The message was incontestably Zionist. Reifer cast himself as a longstanding Zionist and presented Bukovinians as a group as such as well. As one could read in the first issue of the newsletter: 'The majority [of Bukovinians] are Zionists who have been leading activists in the Zionist movement of this land for decades and, in the last four years, constituted the illegal Zionist organization of Bukovina.'[112] As he later pointed out in an argument with the existing organization, they had been the ones who ran the Zionist organization in Bukovina under the 'Hitler and Antonescu regimes', participated in the saving of Jews from Poland and organized the rescue of Jews in Transnistria by their own means, without asking for any help. He stressed that: 'Many of our veterans went to prison and stood at the head of Zionist work in the most difficult hours in the history of the Jews in Romania.'[113] As scholars have remarked about DPs elsewhere, they may be 'post-catastrophe Zionists', but this made them 'Zionists in their very essence'.[114]

Reifer also tried to convince Bukovinian Jews who might have still had doubts that Zionism was the answer to their problems. In this first issue, he addressed readers with the words: 'You have lost everything for which you worked hard your entire life. Only in *Eretz Israel* can you be faithful to your ideal and remain unshakably true to Zion.' This was the case, even if, as he also conceded, 'the Yishuv and all the other Zionist administrations are not making it easy for you'.[115] At the same time, despite representing one specific group, the aims were believed to be consistent with those of the authorities who thought the 'ingathering of exiles' should bring about one ethnic, national community and the end of Jewish dispersion across the world. As Reifer explained, it was precisely *because* they were all fully aware of their national responsibility that this organization would take on the rescuing role that the Sochnuth was failing to fulfil. At first, this involved being critical of the current situation in Palestine and putting pressure on the authorities to recognize their plight, but ultimately, this would facilitate their integration:

> It must be said straight up that the union of the newly arrived *olim* from Bukovina, who have come in the past year, in an independent 'Chug' [Association, lit.: circle] is not a political alliance but has set itself its only goal, task and purpose the integration of these *olim*.[116]

The need for the organization, like the fact that most Bukovinians were, at this point, not fluent in Hebrew, would therefore only be temporary. The newsletter was to address Bukovinians across the world, but appear 'provisionally' (*vorläufig*) in the German language.[117] The first issues regularly displayed articles in Hebrew on the cover page.

The creation of an organization for Bukovinians separate from that of Romanian immigrants was primarily justified by the specific situation of Bukovinian Jews, both during the war and the Holocaust and after. These experiences were also regularly dealt with in the newsletter. In June 1946, for example, the headline article in *Die Stimme* written by Reifer was entitled: 'The History of Suffering of Bukovinian Jews: Deportation and Mass Murder. Words of Commemoration'. For one thing, this pointed to the fact that most Bukovinians were, at this point, still in Romania or in the Soviet Union in a particularly precarious situation, especially following the division of the region and the closing of the border between Romania and the Soviet Union. For another, this drew attention to the fact that Bukovinian Jews had their own particular stakes and position with respect to wider, international discussions concerning retribution, restitution and compensation (known as *Entschädigung, Schadensanspruch* or *Wiedergutmachung*) in relation to the crimes committed during the Second World War. Reifer aimed to draw attention to these distinct experiences because this explained why Bukovinian Jews needed rescuing and representing. Initially, the distinction of the group as 'Bukovinians' was not yet explicitly linked to the fact that they spoke German or to a particular prewar cultural identity, but rather to these immediate priorities.[118]

In effect, Reifer was not only concerned with the situation of Bukovinian Jews in Palestine but also with that of Bukovinian Jews abroad, who were still the majority. The first step in this direction was to draw attention to their situation. Thus, in practice, the newsletter not only dealt with the social issues faced by new immigrants such as housing or international developments relating to the Middle East and affecting Bukovinians in Palestine; it also reported extensively on Bukovinians elsewhere, primarily in their 'former home'. Regular sections included 'Bukovinians in Erez [*sic*]' or 'Remarks on the situation [in Palestine]', but also 'What one hears *from Czernowitz*', 'News from Bucharest' or 'The situation in Romania'. A whole page in Romanian, by Fred Șaraga, who had carried out relief work in Romania during the war and had many contacts among Jews from the 'Old Kingdom', gave a detailed update on the political and economic situation in Romania, including exchange rates and governmental decrees. Whatever news could be obtained concerning Bukovinian Jews deported to Siberia by the Soviets in 1941 was also published and assistance was organized. Contributions by Bukovinian Jews detained on Cyprus and Bukovinians who had managed to emigrate elsewhere – South America, Austria, Germany or the United Kingdom – also featured in the newsletter. Often, authors were introduced along with their former hometown – for example, so and so 'formerly Czernowitz' (*früher Czernowitz*). Obituaries and anniversary pieces discussed experiences during the war in detail as well as summarizing people's prewar achievements. In a sense, by both linking Bukovinian Jews wherever they were and the lives of Bukovinian Jews before and after the war, the newsletter created a sense of continuity despite widespread displacement and gave the impression that a cohesive Bukovinian-Jewish community continued to exist despite its members' dispersion across different countries and continents.

Palestine nevertheless unquestionably functioned as the new and real centre for the community. In the eyes of the Jewish Bukovinian leadership, Palestine was the present and the future. For Reifer, remaining in Europe was out of the question. For example, when he discussed the help obtained from select Romanians during the Holocaust, he underscored that this did not mean staying in Romania was an option.[119] News from the 'old homeland' published in *Die Stimme* always stressed the difficulty of the situation there. It is hardly a coincidence that the letters the editors received from Karl Horniker, who was living in Rădăuți – a town near the border, where many of the repatriates from northern Bukovina resided in dire conditions after the war – and which described how wretched the situation was there, were published in full. In October 1945, for example, Horniker explained that Bukovinian Jews' lives were now 'nothing more than memory' (*nur noch Erinnerung*). He suggested that the youth might still be able to make a new start in *Eretz Israel*, but for the elderly, 'the future lies in the past'.[120] In contrast, and despite Bukovinian Jews' political and social struggles, the news from Palestine published in *Die Stimme* mainly highlighted progress and achievements. This news stood for hope: new arrivals were celebrated; local adverts and notifications indicated Bukovinians were recovering a certain degree of normalcy – establishing themselves, opening businesses, reuniting with relatives. In October 1946, the first informal Bukovinian settlement in Palestine, built by the construction company Rassco, was inaugurated, and others soon followed. In the Bukovinian newsletter, as in other publications from this period, the real hardship experienced by many new migrants and the tensions with the Arab population were downplayed.[121] The contrast between the depictions of the desperate situation of Jewish Bukovinians in Romania and the new lives of Bukovinians in Israel therefore seemed all the more remarkable.

The editors of the newsletter not only closely watched and reported the situation in Romania but also took positions on what they should learn from it. According to them, both past experiences of persecution and the present situation proved that home was no longer home. In his text 'Exodus from

Czernowitz: The Final Act of a Tragedy', published as the Jews were evacuated from Soviet Chernovtsy, Weinstein, for instance, described the city not only as his hometown, but also as the town from which deportations to Transnistria had started and where Rabbi Jacob Mark, among others, had been brutally murdered. He added that in spite of this, he had nevertheless hoped, for a while, that he would see it again one day. However, he had now understood that this hope was in vain. Under the Soviets, not only had the Jews been driven out, but this town was now no longer even accessible; it had simply ceased to exist. On this basis, he concluded: 'History has proved to us and the proof is unquestionable, that there can only be one *Heimat* for us Jews and it is called Eretz Israel'.[122]

The deterioration of the social, economic and political situation in Romania throughout 1946–47 strengthened the conviction that the future of Bukovinian Jews could only be in Israel and the sense of urgency of the situation. As Reifer wrote in September 1946:

> The situation of the Jews in the European Diaspora [*golah*] has become untenable. Among the masses of those still alive in Eastern and Central Europe, the widespread belief is that Jews can only develop freely and develop as a people [*sich völkisch ausleben*] in Palestine and in the midst of a sovereign Jewish community. Hundreds of thousands of Jews are on the move; they, who made the biggest of sacrifices in this most frightening of wars, are still living in camps one and a half years after the armistice; they still have not found their path to the restoration of their being, because the world keeps its gates closed to Jewish emigration.[123]

One month later, in October 1946, Weinstein wrote:

> The situation of the 300,000 Romanian Jews remains critical whether they have citizenship or not. Antisemitism is a daily occurrence, and the experienced eye can see today already the signs that one unfortunate day will lead to terrible events. The big wide world that is not entirely free of guilt regarding Auschwitz, Majdanek and Transnistria must finally grant the Jewish people the right to their own soil and open the doors to its homeland. There is only one destination for Romanian Jews, in the same way as there is only one destination for Jews all over the world.[124]

As this shows, as time passed, an ever more complex combination of social, historical and ethnic arguments was drawn from and woven together in a compelling narrative of cause and effect to argue in favour of Jewish immigration to Palestine and eventually Jewish statehood. This reflected the wider growing recognition of the dramatic fate of the Jews both during and after the war in Europe. It cast a shadow on small achievements such as the wholesale granting of Romanian citizenship for Jews from northern Bukovina in 1947. For the Bukovinian leaders in Palestine, the situation of Bukovinian Jews in Europe exemplified a much broader set of problems: their hardship, homelessness and statelessness several years after the end of the war demonstrated acutely the need for a Jewish state in general.

This mixture of mystical arguments (the notion of national historical destiny) and immediate political concerns (the notion of humanitarian emergency) was characteristic of Jewish political discourse in this period. Historically, Zionism as a movement was ideologically diverse.[125] Now in practice, different factors like historical continuity, ethnic identity and messianic thinking came into play and reinforced each other to make arguments about power and interpret recent history and contemporary political developments in a single manner.[126] Particularly in the context of the War of Independence, Jewish national consciousness was strong and the growing self-confidence and hardening discourse among the leaders of the Bukovinian Jews was noticeable. As Weinstein wrote in 1945, according to him, the most destructive wars had revealed the 'Jewish spirit and Jewish will to live'.[127] From this perspective, sovereignty would not only mean rescue but would also bring about the regeneration of the Jewish people as a whole. Therefore, there was not just a political but also a spiritual dimension to what was happening. Similarly, over the course of 1947, Reifer discussed the creation of the Jewish state and established a line of historical continuity reaching back to Exodus and comparing the Holocaust to other episodes of persecution from which 'the Jewish people' – by implication identified as a coherent group – had recovered.[128] In ethnonational terms, this closed the circle. He even argued this marked the coming of the Messiah.[129]

Ethnonational thinking also shaped the interpretation of the current geopolitical situation, putting the Jews in Palestine in opposition to the British and to the Arabs. In an article about the end of British rule upon the Land of Israel and the War of Independence, Reifer argued that the loss of Jewish blood in this land would renew the indelible bond to the soil.[130] He spoke like this even though he was aware, in his own words, 'of the dangers of ethnic generalizations'. He concluded this same article with the comment: 'We as a people suffered a lot under the principle of generalization and must refrain from committing the same error in our approach to other peoples.'[131] The struggle was nevertheless depicted as a sacred fight for freedom and independence – literally 'their own piece of land' (*eigene Scholle*) – and as something that transcended the present situation by being both historically justified and a necessary task for the wellbeing of future generations.[132] Bukovinians did not merely need saving now; their fate was part of both an older and larger plan.

The extent to which readers were receptive to this narrative is difficult to gauge. What is certain is that for many Bukovinians, Israel increasingly appeared as the 'solution and salvation' (*Lösung und Erlösung*).¹³³ The combination of these two terms, one pragmatic and the other religious and spiritual, pointed to the fact that Israel not only offered Bukovinians a safe haven after persecution but also resolved the issue of belonging. Jews were portrayed as both a 'community of destiny' (*Schicksalsgemeinschaft*) and an 'ethnic community' (*Stammesgemeinschaft*), and both elements mattered and supported each other. This gave a sense of historical inevitability and self-evidence to the realization of the Zionist nationalist dream. As Reifer explained in the foreword to his biography of Mayer Ebner published in 1947, he was concerned to show that 'the return to Jewishness had preceded the return to the Jewish homeland'.¹³⁴ Yet, as the case of Bukovinians also shows and as Zeev Sternhell has argued, 'even if Israeli society was largely an ideological creation, one should not forget that it sprang up to an equal extent as a result of the upheavals that took place and are still taking place in Europe'.¹³⁵ This link was evident in the lead article of the Bukovinian newsletter published in May 1948, at the time of the Israeli Declaration of Independence. Entitled 'Jewish Statehood – Reality: From the Yellow Stain to Independence!', the article celebrated the development of Jews 'from a people to a state-people' (*von Volk zu Staatsvolk*) by emphasizing the unlikely transition, within four years, from wearing the yellow star to having national sovereignty.¹³⁶

The case of Jewish Bukovinians thus gives insight into the complicated relationship between notions of belonging and victimhood, displacement and self-realization among Jews after the Second World War. While it shows the range of ideological arguments deployed, it also demonstrates the centrality of the experience of suffering in justifying the Jewish 'return' to their ancestral home and Jewish statehood itself. As Idith Zertal has argued, the Holocaust was inseparable from Israeli politics of nationhood – the link between the murder of the European Jews and the Jewish state was indissoluble.¹³⁷ Zertal even connects victimhood and empowerment: 'An essential stage in the formation and shaping of a national community is its perception as a trauma-community, a "victim-community" and a creation of a pantheon to its dead martyrs, in whose images the nation's sons and daughters see the reflection of their ideal selves.'¹³⁸ This was also present in what Dina Porat has described as the 'mixed message' conveyed by the wording of the Israeli Declaration of Independence:

> The Holocaust ... in which millions of Jews in Europe were forced to slaughter again proved beyond doubt the compelling need to solve the problem of Jewish homelessness and dependence by the renewal of the Jewish state in the land of Israel, which would open wide the gates of the homeland to every Jew.¹³⁹

Statehood was understood as a means to overcome what had happened during the Holocaust, but simultaneously that experience was established as the key source of legitimation for the state's existence. Ultimately, Jewish statehood achieved two different things: it offered a solution to the problems of the Jews, but also substantiation for the argument that the Jews were a people. This was the basis for a series of creative reidentifications, including Romanians into Jews, Jews into Israelis and Israelis into survivors.

From 'a Jewry in Bukovina' to 'a Bukovinian Jewry' around the World

The Declaration of Independence in May 1948, including the declaration that 'the State of Israel shall be open to every Jew', opened the gates of emigration to Palestine. The 'Law of Return' officially granted every Jew in the world the right to settle in Israel, and the right to claim citizenship was voted for only two years later, in 1950.[140] However, it was between 1948 and 1951 that Israel experienced the peak of the mass emigration that has come to be known as 'the Great *Aliyah*'. Three-quarters of a million people are believed to have arrived within the first five years after the establishment of the state – 200,000 in the first year alone. At the time, this was a society at war, which was facing an economic crisis and had limited infrastructure. The gaps between predictions and reality were enormous, with the main problems being housing, employment and the health of the migrants. As Hacohen has argued, 'absorption was encumbered by the large percentage of elderly, sick and disabled persons requiring special attention manpower and budgets'.[141] And yet, although it presented the new state with a considerable challenge, David Ben-Gurion, the first Israeli Prime Minister, insisted on the principle of unrestricted immigration. Believing firmly in the principle of the fusion of exiles, he was fundamentally opposed to the introduction of limitations.[142]

Many of these newcomers came from the Middle East. But over 70% of the newcomers in the first two years were Holocaust survivors.[143] Among them were thousands of Jews from Romania and from Bukovina. This was a victory for Zionism and a victory for the leaders of Chug Olej Bukowina, who had fought for emigration. However, this did not mean that the Landsmannschaft, as the organization had come to be known among its members, had lost its purpose; if anything, these developments led it to specify its role further. First, the open borders policy was grounded in idealistic thinking rather than political realism. The state had not reckoned with such levels of immigration in practice and could only cope with difficulty. After 1948, the takeover of houses from which Arab families had been expelled or fled led to an improvement of the housing situation for Jews. However, amid mass emigration and while the war was still ongoing, resources were limited and new immigrants were increasingly forced to take care of themselves. The fact that a relatively high rate of newcomers subsequently left Israel again within the first few years demonstrated the need for structure of support.[144] The Landsmannschaft thus continued to provide vital social assistance.

Second, among the numerous different kinds of newcomers, from Europe and from Middle Eastern countries, there was a growing tendency among Bukovinians to emphasize their distinctive identity and their difference. This may be understood as going against the Zionist principles of fusion and ingathering, but, in general, the combination of statehood and mass emigration had led to a gradual shift within Israeli society and with respect to how absorption was understood. With the establishment of the state, not only did the degree of recognition for the newcomers' electoral potential grow, but, as Moshe Lissak notes, doubts also started to develop regarding the concept of the 'melting pot': 'there were calls to limit the involvement in the lives of the immigrants, to forgo shortcuts and to respect the principle of social and cultural pluralism, which in effect had already taken shape in *Yishuv* society'.[145] The cultural autonomy of immigrant groups was being recognized. As Lissak explains further on, in this period of mass immigration, social solidarity changed 'from the ideological solidarity of people who had chosen a certain direction as individuals, to familiar and ethnic solidarity of a very traditional and particularistic nature'.[146] Tellingly, this coincided with the official refounding of the Jewish Bukovinian homeland society in the early 1950s.[147]

Finally, the erratic character of Romanian emigration policy meant that new immigrants from Bukovina kept arriving in small numbers over the following years and decades – in greater numbers throughout the 1950s, but later too. In theory, therefore, there was an ongoing need for such an organization. The fact that in the late 1940s, the newsletter regularly featured articles defending the cause of the Landsmannschaften as a type of organization is indicative of the pressure it was under in this period. The sustaining of a Diasporic, let alone *German*, cultural identity in early-state Israel was undoubtedly controversial. But the continued existence of the organization also testifies to the conviction and perseverance with which the leaders pursued their agenda. As Weinstein explained in an article published in the summer of 1949, according to him, the tasks of the organization ranged from dealing with existential to psychological needs. He also pointed out that homeland societies fulfilled a critical bridging function among members of these communities inside and outside Israel, and there should be as many of them as there were lands of origin. He concluded that the organizations would be needed as long as a *gola*, namely a Jewish Diaspora, still existed.[148]

The formation and endurance of a self-conscious Bukovinian community also had to do with the demographic, social and cultural specificities of Bukovinian Jews both before the war and among those identifying as Bukovinian in Israel in this period in particular. Indeed, if one considers who participated in the activities of the Landsmannschaft, it becomes clear that the sense of community was not simply a matter of speaking German (rather than Romanian like many other Romanian Jews) or even of distinct experiences during the war in comparison to other Romanian Jews or even other survivors of the Holocaust. Jewish Bukovinians' sense of distinction was the result of different factors and what might be described as a matter of habitus in the sociological sense. It is worth noting that at the start, members of the older generation were overrepresented within the organization. The young were more likely to live in collective settlements, learn a trade or join the army, and adapt quicker to the new environment and circumstances. Besides, they were more likely to be willing to leave the past behind, as was expected of them. As others have noted, the system of Israeli integration worked better for some.[149] Indeed, older Bukovinians faced decisively different problems than members of the younger generation, which meant that they found particular solace in the existence of the organization.

The newsletter itself, for example, was run and written by Bukovinian Jews who had, for the most part, constituted the social and economic elite in their native region. Many of those who survived – for instance, in Cernăuți – had indeed belonged to the urban educated elite. This social component was evident in the themes they discussed in the newsletter. The care of the elderly, for example, was a major concern. In August 1949, an article entitled 'What Will Happen to the Parents?' ('Was geschieht mit den Eltern?') discussed the need for a home for the elderly.[150] Besides, since this was also the demographic most severely affected by unemployment, underemployment and 'downward social mobility' (*Deklassierung*) as a result of emigration, this topic was also often addressed. Weinstein, for instance, discussed this in the October/November 1948 issue in a headline article entitled 'Emigration and Absorption: The Problem of Uprooted Intellectuals'. He bemoaned that aside from doctors and engineers, whose diplomas were recognized, other academics were assigned jobs without any regard for their qualifications. He went on to outline several policy recommendations. This article, which was later republished in the national daily *Ha'aretz*, triggered a political response.[151] A few months later, in the April/May 1949 issue, Weinstein took up the issue once again. He argued that looking after such people was a social and national duty. He emphasized that many of them had been leading Zionists and that the generation of people who founded the Jewish state could not ignore their significance.[152]

The newsletter presented Bukovinians as a whole as both a homogeneous and a somewhat separate social group. They cast themselves as better immigrants – Zionists and more. Reifer had already argued along these lines in 1947 when he had addressed what he saw as the loss caused by the 'melting pot' in Palestine and argued in favour of 'individuality' and respecting the diverse backgrounds of the new immigrants.[153] However, at the time, this had been in relatively abstract terms. In the issue of *Die Stimme* from December/January 1949, the quality of Bukovinian immigrants as compared to others was explicitly posited:

> Bukovinians represent, in *Eretz Israel*, a group that is willing and able to work. If you have a look towards Jaffa-Ghibelia, you will see that they resent idleness. They turn to all sorts of professions and are concerned not to be a burden to anybody. If one were to make a selection among them, one would find much useful material that could contribute significantly to the building of the new state. One sees with satisfaction how they all hurry to their Hebrew classes after a day's work in order to catch up with what they missed. For many of them it is simply a matter of remembering the words and phrases that have disappeared from their memory over the years. The language is not foreign to them. This is the state of the new immigrant from Bukovina in Israel. He wants to forget what he suffered and lived through until yesterday, he wants to start a new and productive life. Giving him the opportunity to do this is in his and everybody's interest.[154]

Aside from the obvious generalization and exaggeration contained in this statement, it is interesting to note how elements from the 'two homelands' were integrated to present Bukovinians as better citizens, who were both the same and different. The past was a useful resource that enabled them to distinguish themselves as a group, but enabled them to have more control over their present situation too.

Yet, over time, Bukovinians also increasingly asserted themselves more specifically as a group of German-speaking Central European Jews. Already in 1947, when Reifer had published a German-language biography of Mayer Ebner, Bukovina's foremost interwar Jewish politician, he had described himself in the foreword as 'the translator of the feelings of Bukovinian Jews wherever they are' and had done so in German.[155] Further on, while Reifer had explained that Ebner had been deeply affected by the growing rift between Germans and Jews over the course of the nineteenth century and opposed assimilation and identification with Germanness, he also showed how instrumental German writers had been for Ebner's intellectual development.[156] By November 1949, the newsletter had changed quite significantly in this direction as well. The title was reversed, presenting the short German title *Die Stimme* (*The Voice*) in large letters above the smaller title in Hebrew. From then on, articles always appeared in German and no longer occasionally in Romanian or Hebrew. Besides, over time, an increasing number of articles dealt with memories of the region in a somewhat nostalgic tone. The authors reminisced about significant figures, features and events of the region's history. In December 1949, an article even described Czernowitz as 'The Austrian Jerusalem'.[157] During the course of the 1950s, articles included recollections of the activities of the Hasmonaea or the Maccabi sports associations in Bukovina and members even met again in Israel.[158] *Die Stimme* aimed to counteract what the authors called the sense of 'cultural impoverishment' experienced by many European immigrants in Israel.[159] For this, practices from the Diaspora were not only maintained, but were also revived and given a new incarnation and even a new meaning.

To an extent, the self-consciousness of this group as a group and its own definition – and demarcation – by means of language and culture was a historical legacy. Indeed, the texts contained in *Die Stimme* and the general degree of organization of Bukovinians reflected the tradition of social engagement, philanthropy and political participation of the Jews as an influential minority in Habsburg and Romanian Bukovina. The actual influence of Bukovinians on the politics of early-state Israel is difficult to evaluate. But reading the leading articles of *Die Stimme* shows how convinced Jewish Bukovinians were of both the value of their experiences and their ability to comment on or even shape Israel's future. In his biography of Mayer Ebner, Reifer summarized the politician's answer to the Arab-Israeli conflict as 'Austro-Hungarian dualism': 'This dualistic form would be beneficial to both sides. It would entail reciprocal respect and friendship. In this way, each could be the master in their own house.' Austria and Hungary, he emphasized, had never gone to war against one another.[160] Past experiences were not rejected, but, as in the case of this power-sharing situation, were revisited as solutions to contemporary problems. The opinion pieces written for a range of Israeli newspapers by Ebner himself offer further evidence for this. In them, Ebner tackled all of the 'big questions' that had preoccupied Jews and Zionists in Europe for decades – 'Who counts as a Jew', 'How religion and government should relate to each other' and 'What the place of the German language in Israel should be' – and applied them to the present. He drew comparisons to the Habsburgs and confidently spoke in the name of 'we Central Europeans' (*wir Mitteleuropäer*) as a distinct voice in Israeli society.[161]

The use of German and the Central European habitus may also be seen as an effort on behalf of Bukovinians to distinguish themselves from Yiddish-speaking, Middle Eastern or even Romanian-speaking Jews. This need for distinction was something they had brought with them from their homeland too. Marianne Hirsch and Leo Spitzer have pointed to the widespread mixture of arrogance and insecurity among Bukovinian Jews born out of the fear of being identified as 'semi-Asian'.[162] Such attitudes persisted after immigration to Israel, where differences between groups of Jews and migrants were significant and marked by prejudice.[163] One of my interviewees, born in 1937, described his father, who had been a successful businessman before the war, as someone who always tried to look his best, even after immigrating to Israel: 'in a suit, *perfekt, genau, wie man soll*' (perfect, exact, as one should be; in German in original). What he described was a stereotypical *Yekkes* – the name given to German Jews in Israel, presumably due to the characteristic European-style jackets they insisted on wearing despite the weather. According to him, his father had had a hard time in Israel, working in Tel Aviv harbour and being nicknamed *Yankele* by his colleagues. It had been a real demotion. Yet, he also emphasized on several occasions that his father's friends in Israel had all been 'from Bukovina and spoken German' and kept their distance from other *olim* – Yiddish-speakers and Romanian-speakers. Jokingly conveying his father's prejudices, he added that 'you know, those, they don't wash!' and mentioned how he had been prevented from playing with Yiddish-speaking children as a child in Cernăuți as well. According to him, his father's friends spoke all the time about Czernowitz. If the paper *Die Stimme* did not arrive on time, he would be sent to fetch it. As he concluded, 'my parents, they were part of a group. They were not in Israel; they were in Czernowitz, Austria. The food … my dad, until he died, did not know the difference between hummus and tahini'.

While this shows the gap between the generations, it also shows how practices and beliefs were transferred into the new state, sustained and, with this, transmitted to members of subsequent generations. This interviewee, for instance, explained that as a boy, he used to think: 'Oh no! Not Czernowitz again! I don't want to hear these stories! I have already heard these stories!' But it had nevertheless shaped him and, in the present, he spoke about 'Czernowitz' too and wished dearly that he could hear the stories again. As this also shows, even if the Landsmannschaft was not a fully representative group, it was nevertheless the public voice of Bukovinians, and by controlling the narrative about the past, the Landsmannschaft in Israel – just like the West German one – determined both *what* it meant to be Bukovinian in the present and ensured *that* it remained a relevant category of identification. In this connection, it is worth quoting the reader letter of Sabine Ruckenstein, a woman from Haifa, published in *Die Stimme* in February 1955. Having explained that she had arrived in Palestine eighteen years earlier, she then wrote:

> Your newspaper, Dr Weinstein, is like a balsam to all Bukovinians and it would be wonderful if it were to become a weekly, so that the old and the new *Heimat* merge into one and also so that the young can learn something about the Jewish traditions of their parents.

Such a statement points to the power of the reconstruction and re-enactment of Jewish Bukovina in Israel after the war.

Similarly, the writer Aharon Appelfeld, who survived the Holocaust in Bukovina in hiding as a child and came to Israel when he was just fourteen years old in 1946, said that after a few years in Israel, he 'gave up [his] ambition to become an Israeli writer' and accepted his position as an émigré writer, despite the fact that that he wrote in Hebrew.[164] He belonged to what he described as a club of Bukovinians and Galicians, and explained that he went there every evening and that it functioned as a surrogate home for orphans such as himself.[165] He even argued that: 'Sometimes it seems to me that all my writing derives not from my home and not from the war, but from the years of coffee and cigarettes at the club.'[166] In other words, this was what made him Bukovinian. The fact that many of the people I interviewed in Israel, even those born in the 1930s and some of their children, continued to speak German was further evidence of this transmission. A couple I interviewed in a care home in 2013 told me they always spoke German to their children in public, even in the 1950s when the opposition to this was significant and tangible. When I met them, not only did they speak German to me, but they were still greeting their fellow residents in this language too.

Acceptably framed, 'Bukovinian' thus remained or became a positive source of identification in Israel. This entailed paying more attention to the earlier past before the Holocaust and even before the interwar period, rather than the period of the war and the Holocaust. Indeed, over time, less and less concern was shown for Bukovinians' recent experiences of suffering. To an extent, victimhood was always central to the activities of the Landsmannschaft. There were regular ceremonies to commemorate the dead (*haskore*); the newsletter and later *Die Stimme* regularly referred to the victims (*Opfer*) with the words and expressions 'Transnistria victims', 'Nazi victims' (*Naziopfer*), 'casualties' (*Todesopfer*) and 'martyrs'. In the early years, the words 'Hitler', 'murder', 'concentration camps' and 'the extermination' (*die Vernichtung*) were also frequently employed. The issue of reparations – interchangeably described as *Wiedergutmachung* or *Entschädigung* – with reference to potential claims against both Germany and Romania was very present too.[167] The few new works regarding the Holocaust in Romania that appeared in those years, such as Arnold Daghani's diary or Matatias Carp's book, were also discussed briefly in *Die Stimme*.[168] However, it is also notable that these works were published abroad and hard to obtain in Israel and that the articles on this topic were short, somewhat hidden and generally quite rare. In general, over time, the discussion of Jewish suffering in *Die Stimme* became increasingly mechanical, ritualized and marginal. It was more about the duty of memory than it was about discovering new facts or even achieving recognition.

Upon arriving in Israel, both Reifer and the former leader of Suceava's Jewish community, Meier Teich, had written about their experiences during the Holocaust. According to an article in *Die Stimme* that mentioned Reifer's initial account of this period, the intention had been to provide the starting point for further research into what had happened in Romania during the war. Yet, while Reifer's text about persecution appeared in Hebrew, it was never published in the German original or translated into English as planned. Instead, in 1953, his autobiography *People and Ideas* (*Menschen und Ideen*), was published in German in Tel Aviv. While it covered his whole life in some detail, it only had a short chapter on the events of the war and the Holocaust.[169] It ended with a chapter entitled 'The Rebirth of the Nation' ('Die Auferstehung der Nation'), in which Reifer described the events of recent years and recounted the mass emigration of Bukovinian Jews from Romania to Israel in an emphatic and emotional tone. Reifer depicted the 'return' to Israel of Bukovinian Jews as the culmination of their history and the highpoint of the millennial history of his people. This put everything else, from the failed struggle for emancipation and acceptance to the recent suffering in Europe and the losses caused by the conflict with the Arabs or during the Israeli War of Independence, into perspective.

Nearly a decade after the war, the Holocaust in Romania, let alone the situation in Transnistria, were still not well known and not well understood in Israel. When the Yad Vashem historian Kurt Jakob Ball-Kaduri started trying to put together documentation on Transnistria in the early 1950s, he faced many difficulties.[170] Not only had the situation in Transnistria been extremely complex – with the conditions in different camps and ghettos varying a great deal – but the lack of secondary literature, the mix of languages required to study this topic, the challenge of finding sources and witnesses, and the tension among survivors regarding the conditions under which some had managed to survive while others had not, as well as the Cold War situation, all constituted major impediments to researching the subject. The case of Bukovinians highlights the well-known fact that although there was no real silence about the events we now think of as the Holocaust in postwar Israel, gaining a comprehensive and differentiated understanding of what had happened was very difficult. For one thing, the Zionist narrative, with its expectations of assimilation and narratives of bravery and heroism, silenced many survivors. For another, as others have argued, there was a tension between the aims of research and documentation, and those of commemoration.[171] As a result, although the Landsmannschaften should have been natural allies of official institutions and historians, they were considered to have a different approach and were barely used as a resource.[172] As Dina Porat, who analysed the issue of survivor guilt, explains:

> because they found the inner essence of the Holocaust events too intimate to share, the survivors viewed those Israelis who did take an interest and try to

understand as intruders. The survivors, tired of being different, needed time to heal and to forget.[173]

The handful of accounts on the Holocaust in Romania dating from this period held by the archive in Yad Vashem, the central Israeli institution for research on the Holocaust (remarkably called the Martyrdom and Heroism Remembrance Authority), testify to this. Not only are there just a few accounts, but they are eclectic and lack context.[174] Some interviewees mainly accounted for the history of their hometown before destruction rather than the events of persecution per se; others only listed the names of the dead as though to offer a substitute gravestone, but did not want to discuss in detail what had happened; others focused on a particular episode of rescue or even framed their remarks by saying it was 'not as bad as Poland', illustrating the fact that their experiences were, for a long time, 'in the shadow of Auschwitz'.[175] There was no equating of 'Bukovinian' with 'Holocaust survivor' or the development of a clear picture of a 'Bukovinian Holocaust experience'. Even in *Die Stimme*, Bukovinians' experiences during the war tended to be referred to in general and somewhat vague terms, with reference to notorious perpetrators and primarily to the dead and not the living. Over time, the discussion of Jewish suffering became increasingly rare, muted, symbolic and private. As among other communities of survivors, information about what people had gone through was shared with select individuals and restricted audiences.[176] An article in *Die Stimme* in December 1949 entitled 'No Atonement for Transnistria?' ('Keine Sühne für Transnistrien?') bemoaned not only the absence of compensation, but also the lack of knowledge in Israel about what had happened in Romania. Yet, this was not least the result of the fact that, once in Israel, Jewish Bukovinians ceased to be regarded or to think of themselves primarily as victims.[177]

Ultimately, experiences of violence and suffering were a contested way for Bukovinjan Jews to define themselves. This tension is perhaps best illustrated by the two-volume book *History of the Jews in Bukovina* (*Geschichte der Juden in der Bukowina*), edited by Hugo Gold and published in 1958 and 1962. This book belongs to the genre of *Yizkor* books, described by Annette Wieviorka and Itzhok Niborski as a crossover between the Jewish tradition of 'memory books' and the work of the Institute of Jewish research, YIVO.[178] Indeed, the first volume offers a detailed history of the Jews and Jewish life in the region up until the end of the First World War, and the second offers detailed accounts of experiences made in Bukovina during the interwar period and during the war. The second book, dedicated to those who had died in Siberia and during the Holocaust, thus lists what happened in nearly every small town and village. In a sense, therefore, it documents details and constitutes a kind of substitute monument to the deceased.[179] However, in this book, many sensitive issues were not tackled, and different political and religious trends were not given equal representation; some even suggested that the authors might have written it with an eye to the issue of reparations.[180] At the very least, this book served to inscribe the history of Bukovinian Jews in a decidedly Zionist tradition for the sake of the present and the future. If it was a 'monument of paper', it was at least as much a memorial to the living as one to the dead.[181]

In effect, the book served to show, in Weinstein's words, that Bukovinians had ceased to be 'a Jewry in Bukovina', but remained 'a Bukovinian Jewry'.[182] Despite the Zionist stance and Mayer Ebner's foreword, in light of the homogenizing and anti-Diaspora stance in Israel at this time, this should have been a controversial enterprise.[183] However, the editors had pre-empted some of these accusations. For example, they argued that 'absorption' actually made such a publication all the more essential:

> In a few years, the natural integration process may make the work of the Landsmannschaft look dispensable because the generations of those who have grown up in the country will surely struggle to show understanding for the problems of the emigrants from our home in the *galuth*. But it therefore seems all the more important to record in writing the memory of these problems, in order to ensure that a consciousness of historical continuity is maintained.[184]

This statement captured the growing self-confidence of Bukovinian Jews and a changing attitude towards the Diaspora in Israel in general.[185] However, it also draws attention the immigrants' own role in bringing about this transformation. And in this respect, Gold's book also contains the account of a telling episode. In 1961, David Ben-Gurion, the then Prime Minister of Israel, had invited the Jaffa Giwat-aliyah members of the Bukovinian Landsmannschaft, headed by Markus Geller, to an audience. They had been very honoured and accepted the invitation. Ben-Gurion had then asked them how long the services of the organization would still be required. Not knowing what he should say, Geller had answered 'for another five years' – 'the time for the Bukovinians who are still arriving in large numbers to be regarded as integrated [*als eingeordnet angesehen werden können*]'.[186] Ben-Gurion is then said to have stated that he was 'incredibly satisfied with the Bukovinian immigrants', that they were a 'wonderful element' and had 'secured a great place for themselves and occup[ied] leading positions in [the] country'. He concluded that 'they have the right to assert themselves'.[187] This corresponded to what many Bukovinians already believed and did, but it was an important official endorsement nonetheless: Ben-Gurion effectively condoned the identification of Bukovinians as Bukovinians.

Conclusion

The first decade after the end of the Second World War saw the end of the existence of a Bukovinian Jewish community in Bukovina. After the Second World War, Jews in the Soviet Union and Romania faced considerable difficulties. In this context, the Holy Land was construed as 'solution and salvation', both as a new and ancestral home. The experience of violence and persecution and the ongoing hardship after the war validated rather than challenged the significance of ethnic belonging, and as a result, the majority of Bukovinian Jews left the region. However, for many Bukovinian Jews, like Jews elsewhere, emigration was neither a self-evident decision, nor a straightforward process. After leaving Bukovina, Jewish Bukovinians often experienced years of insecurity, homelessness, instability and personal disruption. First, there was the challenge of emigration and then the challenge of immigration. The arrival in Palestine and integration in Israel was associated with distinct problems. The new state had to absorb hundreds of thousands of immigrants, and Bukovinians, with a strong sense of heritage and identity, did not become Israelis overnight. Many struggled to feel at home; a significant number later chose other destinations, revealing that emigration was not so much a choice in favour of Israel as a choice against their former home. Tellingly, Hugo Gold's seminal *History of the Jews in Bukovina*, published in 1958 and 1962, offered an impressive inventory of communities of 'Bukovinians abroad' ('Bukowiner im Ausland'), from Caracas to New York and London. However, it is worth noting that it did not include or mention Jews who had remained in Romania or the Soviet Ukraine. By the mid 1950s, not only had most Bukovinian Jews emigrated from Romania or the Soviet Union, but the identification as Bukovinian was also limited to what was identified as the 'free world'. This conveyed the fact that, in many Bukovinian Jews' view, it was no longer even possible to be Bukovinian in Bukovina.

However, what is perhaps more surprising is that Bukovina and 'Bukovinian' remained a source of identification at all after the territorial link was broken and many Jewish Bukovinians made *aliyah*. Looking at the development of the Landsmannschaft in Israel reveals how this identity remained relevant and even became a source of belonging and self-worth for Jews after the war and after their displacement. 'Bukovinian' was defined anew by drawing on a mixture of history and experience. On the one hand, their leadership emphasized the particular circumstances of Bukovinian Jews during and in the immediate aftermath of the war; on the other hand, they were inspired by the history of this group before the war, as a self-conscious and self-reliant Jewish group, and this history was both reinterpreted as a pre-history of Zionism and translated into something useful for the new Jewish state. In other words, the concept of Bukovinian was made compatible with Zionism, and past experiences and practices were used to identify as Israelis. The case of Bukovinians thus provides a unique view of Israeli society in this period. In particular, it gives insight into the degree of acceptability of Jewish difference and how such difference could be expressed and negotiated. There was neither a wholesale rejection of Europe nor a complete silence about the Holocaust. Yet, ultimately, both migrants and the society of the Yishuv agreed about the practical necessities needed to realize the messianic dream; while Bukovina could still be cherished, it was nevertheless regarded as irremediably lost. The case of Bukovinians thus highlights that this identification was not simply about memory and commemoration, but very much about drawing on the past for the sake of the present and the future. And, indeed, in this establishment period, the Landsmannschaft in its first decade set the tone and the discourse for Bukovinian Jews elsewhere and for the decades to come.

Notes

1. Ansprache von Mayer Ebner, 'Ein Shikun für Bukowiner Olim', *Die Stimme*, May 1952.
2. 'Ein Shikun für Bukowiner Olim', *Die Stimme*, May 1952.
3. Ibid.
4. This period is known as the Bricha. On this, see I. Zertal, *From Catastrophe to Power: Holocaust Survivors and the Emergence of Israel* (Berkeley: University of California Press, 1998). As others have argued, if anything, the Holocaust seemed to have made achievement of a Jewish state not more but rather less likely. See M. Brenner, *Israel: Traum und Wirklichkeit des jüdischen Staates: von Theodor Herzl bis heute* (Munich: Verlag C.H. Beck, 2016), 135.
5. On this, see L. Rotman, *History of the Jews in Romania*, vol. 5: *The Communist Era until 1965* (Tel Aviv: Tel Aviv University Press, 2004); R. Ioanid, *The Ransom of the Jews: The Story of the Extraordinary Secret Bargain between Romania and Israel* (Chicago: Ivan R. Dee, 2005).
6. I. Zertal, *Israel's Holocaust and the Politics of Nationhood* (Cambridge: Cambridge University Press, 2005), 140
7. T. Segev, *The Seventh Million: The Israelis and the Holocaust*, translated from Hebrew by H. Watzman (New York: Hill & Wang, 1994), 42.
8. D. Hacohen, *Immigrants in Turmoil: Mass Immigration to Israel and its Repercussions in the 1950s and after* (New York: Syracuse University Press, 2003), 1.
9. Ibid., 5.
10. Segev, *The Seventh Million*, 167–68.
11. See also Zertal, *From Catastrophe to Power*, 8.
12. See Zertal, *From Catastrophe to Power*; see also Z. Mankowitz, *Life between Memory and Hope: The Survivors of the Holocaust in Occupied Germany* (Cambridge: Cambridge University Press, 2002).

13. D. Ofer, 'Introduction', in D. Ofer, F.S. Ouzan and J. Tydor Baumel-Schwartz (eds), *Holocaust Survivors: Resettlement, Memories, Identities* (New York: Berghahn Books, 2012), 1–9, here 6.
14. Hacohen, *Immigrants in Turmoil*, 248.
15. See Hanna Yablonka, *Holocaust Survivors: Israel after the War* (New York: New York University Press, 1999).
16. D. Porat, 'The Role of European Jewry in the Plans of the Zionist Movement during World War II and in its Aftermath' in Y. Gutman and A. Saf (eds), *She'erit Hapletah 1944–1948: Rehabilitation and Political Struggle* (Jerusalem: Proceedings of the Sixth Yad Vashem International Historical Conference October 1985, 1990), 286–303, here 296. See also A. Patt, *Finding Home and Homeland: Jewish Youth and Homeland in the Aftermath of the Holocaust* (Detroit: Wayne State University Press, 2009).
17. Porat, 'The Role of European Jewry', 296.
18. Hacohen, *Immigrants in Turmoil*, 255.
19. Ibid., 263.
20. L. Halperin, *Babel in Zion: Jews, Nationalism and Language Diversity in Palestine, 1920–1948* (New Haven: Yale University Press, 2015), 227.
21. Y. Gelber, 'The Historical Role of the Central European Immigration to Israel', *Leo Baeck Institute Year Book* 38 (1993), 323–39, here 329.
22. Ibid., 337.
23. Parts of the following section have been published previously in G. Fisher, 'Between Liberation and Emigration: Jews from Bukovina in Romania after the Second World War', *Leo Baeck Institute Year Book* 62(1) (2017), 115–32.
24. J. Ancel, 'Statistik des Holocaust in Rumänien', *Halbjahresschrift für Südosteuropäische Geschichte, Literatur und Politik* 17(2) (2005), 29–44, here 44.
25. See M. Mazower, *Dark Continent: Europe's Twentieth Century* (New York: Random House, 1998), 410; and P. Gatrell et al., 'Violent Peacetime: Reconceptualising Displacement and Resettlement in the Soviet East-European Borderlands after the Second World War', in P. Gatrell and N. Baron (eds), *Warlands: Population Resettlement and State Reconstruction in the Soviet-East European Borderlands, 1945–50* (Basingstoke: Palgrave Macmillan, 2009), 255–68.
26. Both contemporary documentation and retrospective accounts of the end of the war testify to the significance and ambivalence of this moment in the life of many Jewish Bukovinians. The following remarks are based on a broad sample of postwar accounts of Bukovinian Jews from various sources, including the USC Visual History Archive, USHMM and my own interviews with Bukovinian Jews in Israel carried out between 2012 and 2016. For relevant interviews from the 'Visual History Archive' USC Shoah Foundation, see https://sfi.usc.edu/vha (retrieved 20 September 2019). Some published accounts are also a rich resource on this topic; see e.g. R. Glasberg-Gold, *Ruth's Journey: A Survivor's Memoir* (Gainesville: University Press of Florida, 1996); P. Fichman, *Before Memories Fade* (New York: Pearl Fichman, 2005).
27. See N. Aleksiun, 'Returning from the Land of the Dead: Jews in Eastern Galicia in the Immediate Aftermath of the Holocaust', *Kwartalnik Historii Żydów* 2 (2013), 257–71; A. Cichopek-Gajraj, *Beyond Violence: Jewish Survivors in Poland and Slovakia, 1944–1948* (Cambridge: Cambridge University Press, 2014).
28. For a synthesis of these events, see R. Ioanid, *The Holocaust in Romania: The Destruction of Jews and Gypsies under the Antonescu Regime, 1940–1944* (Chicago: Ivan R. Dee, 2000). See also M. Hausleitner, Brigitte Mihok and Juliane Wetzel (eds), *Rumänien und der Holocaust: zu den Massenverbrechen in Transnistrien 1941–1944* (Berlin: Metropol,

2001); W. Benz (ed.), *Holocaust an der Peripherie: Judenpolitik und Judenmord in Rumänien und Transnistrien 1940–1944* (Berlin: Metropol, 2009).
29. M. Hirsch and L. Spitzer, *Ghosts of Home: The Afterlife of Czernowitz in Jewish Memory* (Berkeley: University of California Press 2011), 238.
30. Hirsch and Spitzer, *Ghosts of Home*, 246.
31. Ibid., 232–58.
32. S. Frunchak, 'The Making of Soviet Chernivtsi: National Reunification, World War II and the Fate of Jewish Czernowitz in Postwar Ukraine' (D.Phil. thesis, University of Toronto, 2014), 352.
33. Quoted in Frunchak, 'The Making of Soviet Chernivtsi', 340.
34. On this, with documents, see M. Altshuler, 'The Soviet "Transfer" of Jews from Chernovtsy Province to Romania, 1945–1946', *Jews in Eastern Europe* 36 (1998), 54–75.
35. On this, see V. Altskan, 'The Closing Chapter: Northern Bukovinian Jews, 1944–1946', *Yad Vashem Studies* 43(1) (2015), 51–81.
36. Altshuler, 'The Soviet "Transfer"'; and Altskan, 'The Closing Chapter'.
37. See M. Olaru, 'Documente Rădăuțene IV', *Analele Bucovinei* 1 (2011), 279–303, here 301; see also N. Lazăr, 'Populația evreiasca din Rădăuți în timpul Holocaustului și imediat după', unpublished conference paper presented at the Conference of the Federation of Jewish Communities of Romania *Evreii din Rădăuți*, 25 July 2012.
38. H. Glass, *Minderheit zwischen zwei Diktaturen: zur Geschichte der Juden in Rumänien 1944–1949* (Munich: Oldenbourg, 2002), 71. Liviu Rotman estimates that by October 1945, there were some 41,000 Jewish refugees in Bucharest alone; Rotman, *History of the Jews in Romania*, 72.
39. Zertal, *From Catastrophe to Power*, 222.
40. This citizenship issue of northern Bukovinians was not resolved until the signing of the Paris Peace Treaties of 1947, following considerable lobbying on behalf of the Romanian Jewish community leadership and under international pressure. See J. Ancel, 'She'erit Hapletah in Romania during the Transition Period to a Communist Regime August 1944–December 1947', in Gutman and Saf (eds), *She'erit Hapletah 1944–1948*, 143–67, here 153. See also Arhivele Naționale Istorice Centrale, Bucharest (hereinafter ANIC), Fondul Comunități Evreiești din România, 1 (1946), 93: Letter from Wilhelm Filderman to the Romanian authorities dating from 19 March 1946.
41. See Archive of the Center for the Study of the History of Romanian Jews (hereinafter ACSIER), Fond VII Communism, 396; 193: Contemporary documentation concerning the Jewish community in Bucharest and around the country.
42. Central Zionist Archives (hereinafter CZA), C3\659: Translation into English of the article from 15 September 1945 for the International Red Cross in Washington DC.
43. Ibid., Letter from Kalman Stein to the International Red Cross, 9 November 1945.
44. These letters are available online: 'Briefe von Elias Hauster', http://radautz.blogspot.de (retrieved 20 September 2019). They have been transcribed by Elias's grandson, Edgar Hauster. The bulk of the correspondence was between Elias and his son Julius. They range from 26 April 1946, when Elias arrived in Rădăuți from Chernovtsy with his wife, to 10 April 1949, by which time he had joined Julius in Bucharest. Elias passed away in Bucharest a few months later.
45. 'Blanka Lebzelter Collection, 1942–1961', AR 25437, Leo Baeck Institute New York. On this, see J. Dawson, 'Finding Blanka: A Story of Sorrow and Strength in Post-war Romania', *Holocaust: Studii și Cercetări* 6(1) (2013), 87–99. These sources have been discussed in more detail in Fisher, 'Between Liberation and Emigration'.

46. On the activities of the Joint in Romania, see N. Lazăr and L. Benjamin (eds), *American Jewish Joint Distribution Committee în România: Documente* (Bucharest: Hasefer, 2017).
47. See e.g. Glasberg-Gold, *Ruth's Journey*.
48. There was a range of organizations, including, for example, the Association of Support for Jews of Bukovina (Asociația pentru sprijinirea Evreilor din Bucovina; ASEB) and the Association of Former Transnistrian Deportees (Asociața Foștilor Deportați în Transnistria).
49. F. Ornstein, *Suferințele Deportaților în Transnistria: Gândiți-vă la tot ce s-a petrecut în Transnistria (1941–1944)* (Bucharest: Editura Asociației, 1945), 69.
50. Ibid., 64–65.
51. Both of these claims are supported by further evidence: material at the National Archives in Suceava where frequent references to deportation to Transnistria can be found in administrative documents. See Serviciul Județean al Arhivelor Naționale Suceava (hereinafter SJAN-S), Fond 233, Inventar 103, 27 – (o)/1948; Fond 697, Inventar 452, 1/1945: Liceul evreiesc particular Suceava. Ruth Glasberg-Gold was encouraged by a teacher to write an account of her experiences in Transnistria in December 1944 (Yad Vashem Archives (YVA), O.33, 2339) and a shortened version was then published the Romanian daily newspaper *România Liberă*, 19 February 1945. See J. Alexandru et al. (eds), *Martiriul Evreilor din România: 1940–1944: Documente și Mărturii* (Bucharest: Editura Hasefer, 1991), 241–43. See also M. Mircu, *Progromul de la Iași* (Bucharest: Editura Glob, 1944); M. Mircu, *Pogromurile din Bucovina și Dorohoi* (Bucharest: Editura Glob, 1945); M. Mircu, *Pogromurile din Basarabia și Transnistria* (Bucharest: Editura Glob, 1947); M. Rudich, *La Brat cu Moartea: Vedenii din Transnistria* (Bucharest: Editura 'Hehaluț', 1945); M. Carp, *Cartea Neagră: Suferințele Evreilor din România, 1940–1944*, 3 vols (Bucharest: Editura Diogene, 1996 [first published 1945–1948]).
52. ACSIER, VII, 112: Memoriul adresat Comitetului de coordonare al asociațiilor de deportați, refugiati și repatriați [Congresul Mondial Evreiesc] de pe lung CME București, secție din România (no date; probably 1946).
53. See Fisher, 'Between Liberation and Emigration', 126.
54. See ibid., 128.
55. J. Ancel, '"The New Jewish Invasion": The Return of the Survivors from Transnistria', in D. Bankier (ed.), *The Jews are Coming Back: The Return of the Jews to Their Countries of Origin after WWII* (New York: Berghahn Books; Jerusalem: Yad Vashem, 2005), 231–56.
56. See Glass, *Minderheit*, 239.
57. ACSIER, VII 144, diverse documents. On restratification as a concept, see also Rotman, *History of the Jews in Romania*, 129.
58. Based on a survey of the articles published on the subject in *Scânteia*, the mouthpiece of the communist party, in 1944–45.
59. Rotman, *History of the Jews in Romania*, 62.
60. See Glass, *Minderheit*, 282–84.
61. Ancel, '*She'erit Hapletah*', 157.
62. Ibid.
63. Ibid., 166.
64. ACSIER, VII, diverse files.
65. This is based on a sampling of various postwar Jewish newspapers: *Curierul Israelit, Mântuirea, Neamul Evreesc, Renașterea* and *Viața Evreiască*.
66. Ancel, '*She'erit Hapletah*', 159
67. Zertal, *From Catastrophe to Power*.

68. Ancel, 'She'erit Hapletah', 161.
69. T. Segev, *1949: The First Israelis* (New York: Holt Paperbacks, 1998), 114.
70. Y. Bauer, 'The DP Legacy', in M.Z. Rosensaft (ed.), *Life Reborn: Jewish Displaced Persons, 1945–1951* (Washington DC: U.S. Holocaust Memorial Museum, 2001), 25–36, here 28.
71. ANIC, Fondul Comunității Evreiești din România, 1 (1946), 94: letter written by the local subsidiary of the ASEB to the Bucharest organization concerning a group of twenty-eight Bukovinians in the town of Gheorgheni, 10 December 1947.
72. R. Brubaker, 'Migrations of Ethnic Unmixing in the "New Europe"', *International Migration Review* 32(4) (Winter 1998), 1047–65, here 1053.
73. P. Lagrou, 'Return to a Vanished World: European Societies and the Remnants of Their Jewish Communities, 1945–1947', in Bankier, *The Jews are Coming Back*, 1–24, here 21.
74. Rotman, *History of the Jews in Romania*, 10.
75. ANIC, Fondul Comunități evreiești din România, 14 (1946): diverse documents.
76. Fichman, *Before Memories Fade*, 122.
77. Hirsch and Spitzer, *Ghosts of Home*, 255.
78. For more on this, see Chapter 5 below.
79. There is quite a lot of research on the issues, especially in Romania. For an overview of key issues, see Ioanid, *The Ransom of the Jews*; see also Radu Ioanid (ed.), *Securitatea și Vânzarea Evreilor: Istoria Acordurilor Secrete dintre România și Israel* (Bucharest: Editura Polirom, 2015).
80. Some 50,000 Jews were detained on Cyprus by the British. On this, see D. Ofer, 'Holocaust Survivors as Immigrants: The Case of Israel and the Cyprus Detainees', *Modern Judaism* 16(1) (1998), 1–23.
81. Rotman, *History of the Jews in Romania*, 89.
82. Fisher, 'Between Liberation and Emigration', 130.
83. Ibid.
84. C. Wollmann-Fiedler and H. Brenner, *'Czernowitz ist meine Heimat': Gespräche mit der Zeitzeugin Hedwig Brenner* (Brugg: Munda Verlag, 2009), 9.
85. For membership papers to various Zionist organizations, see e.g. ACSIER VII, 96, 464.
86. This included legal and illegal emigration. See Ancel, 'She'erit Hapletah', 160. See also R. Ioanid, 'Precisări preliminare', in Ioanid (ed.), *Securitatea și Vânzarea Evreilor*, 45.
87. SJAN-S: Fond 250, inventar 82: Grădinița Israelita de copii Fălticeni, 1945–48, 1/1945 Program de școală.
88. See Glass, *Minderheit*.
89. Ibid., 184. On the anti-Zionist campaign and the use of these terms, see ACSIER, VII 446, diverse documents. See also R. Vago, 'The Unexpected Cosmopolitans: Romania's Jewry Facing the Communist System', *European Review of History: Revue européenne d'histoire*, 17(3) (2010), 491–504.
90. This journey is depicted in M. Reifer, *Menschen und Ideen* (Tel Aviv: Edition Olympia, 1953), 238–61.
91. Ibid., 261.
92. Ibid., 260.
93. Ibid.
94. The text appeared in Hebrew with the title 'Journey to Death': M. Reifer, *Massa Hamaweth*, translated from German by J. Tulkes (Tel Aviv: Am Owed, 1945). The original German text, entitled 'The Tragedy of the Romanian Jewry', is as an unpublished manuscript: CZA: K13\47.

95. See Yablonka, *Holocaust Survivors*, 273.
96. Hacohen writes that: 'One-quarter of a million people – one-sixth of Israel's Jewish population – were still living in ma'abrot and immigrants camps in mid-1952'; Hacohen, *Immigrants in Turmoil*, 231.
97. Zertal, *Israel's Holocaust*, 40.
98. Yonatan Shiloh-Dayan, 'On the Point of Return', in B. Bannasch and M. Rupp (eds), *Rückkehrerzählungen: über die (Un-)Möglichkeit nach 1945 als Jude in Deutschland zu leben* (Göttingen: Vandenhoeck und Ruprecht Unipress, 2018), 35–56, here 37.
99. See Porat, 'The Role of European Jewry', 296.
100. Yablonka, *Holocaust Survivors*, 275.
101. 'Bukowiner in München', *Die Stimme*, February 1948.
102. Zertal, *From Catastrophe to Power*, 274.
103. Hacohen, *Immigrants in Turmoil*, 249, 244.
104. Zertal, *From Catastrophe to Power*, 10.
105. Many of these had been deported to Siberia by the Soviets in 1941. See CZA: S5\10882: Romania. Organization of Romanian Migrants, Bukovinian Migrants.
106. Reifer, *Menschen und Ideen*, 265.
107. Ibid., 302–3.
108. Ibid., 265, 305.
109. See ibid., 265.
110. Ibid., 265.
111. This changed in May 1946 when the inscription in Latin letters was placed above.
112. Die Leitung, 'Chug Olej Bukowina', *Chug Olej Bukowina*, December 1944.
113. CZA: S5\10882: Letter from 28 March 1946, Manfred Reifer to the Committee of Veteran Zionists.
114. See Porat, 'The Role of European Jewry', 296.
115. 'Chanuka 5705'; ibid.
116. Die Leitung, 'Chug Olej Bukowina', *Chug Olej Bukowina*, December 1944.
117. Ibid.
118. Interestingly, only in May 1946 did the journal's German-language title become larger than the Hebrew one.
119. 'Aus der Leidensgeschichte der Bukowiner Juden: Deportierung und Massenmord. Worte des Gedenkens', *Die Stimme*, June 1946.
120. 'Unser Leben ist nur noch Erinnerung … wie die transnistrischen Rückkehrer leben. Karl Horniker, Rădăuți', *Chug Olej Bukowina*, October 1945.
121. See Segev, *1949*.
122. 'Auszug aus Czernowitz: Schlussakt der Tragödie der Bukowina Juden', *Die Stimme*, May 1946, emphasis in original.
123. 'Gedanken zu Rosch Haschanah', *Die Stimme*, September 1946.
124. 'Gefährdete Staatsbürgerschaft', *Die Stimme*, October 1946.
125. M. Brenner, *Geschichte des Zionismus*, 4th edn (Munich: C. H. Beck, 2016).
126. On this, see Z. Sternhell, *The Founding Myths of Israel: Nationalism, Socialism and the Making of the Jewish State* (Princeton: Princeton University Press, 1998).
127. 'Czernowitz - Tel Aviv: Ein Jahr in Erez Israel', *Chug Olej Bukowina*, March 1945.
128. 'Untergang und Auferstehung des Judenstaates', *Die Stimme*, December 1947.
129. Ibid.
130. '30 Jahre britische Verwaltung in *Eretz Israel*', *Die Stimme*, March 1948.
131. Ibid.
132. 'Rückblick auf drei Jahrhunderte 1648–1948', *Die Stimme*, February 1948.

133. E. Weinstein, 'Rumänische Juden in Jaffa', *Die Stimme*, September 1948.
134. M. Reifer, *Dr. Mayer Ebner: Ein jüdisches Leben* (Tel Aviv: Edition Olympia, 1948), 46.
135. Sternhell, *The Founding Myths of Israel*, 12.
136. E. Weinstein, 'Judenstaat – Wirklichkeit: Vom gelben Fleck zur Unabhängigkeit!', *Die Stimme*, May 1948.
137. Zertal, *Israel's Holocaust*, 2.
138. Zertal, *Israel's Holocaust*.
139. Quoted in D. Porat, *Israeli Society, the Holocaust and its Survivors* (Portland: Vallentine Mitchell, 2008), 346.
140. Article 1 of the set of laws governing the State of Israel reads that 'every Jew has the right to return to his country as an *oleh*'. For these purposes, a Jew was defined as someone whose mother was Jewish. In 1970, the law was amended to include all of those who would have been persecuted under the Nuremberg Laws, namely people with at least one Jewish grandparent and non-Jewish spouses. On this, see D. Hacohen, 'The Law of Return as an Embodiment of the Link between Israel and the Jews of the Diaspora', *Journal of Israeli History* 19(1) (1998), 61–89.
141. Hacohen, *Immigrants in Turmoil*, 61.
142. See ibid., 246.
143. 'In 1948, 118,993 immigrants arrived in Israel. Of these, 102, 498 (86 percent) had survived the Holocaust: In 1949, 141,608 arrived, 95,165 of whom were Holocaust survivors, constituting 67 percent of that year's immigrants'; Yablonka, *Holocaust Survivors*, 9.
144. A total of 46.6% of those who left Israel had emigrated between 1948 and 1951, and some 15.4% were from Romania; ibid., 15
145. M. Lissak, 'The Demographic Revolution in Israel in the 1950s: The Absorption of the Great *Aliyah*', *Journal of Israeli History* 22(2) (2003), 1–31, here 13.
146. Ibid., 19.
147. H. Gold (ed.), *Geschichte der Juden in der Bukowina: ein Sammelwerk*, vol. 2 (Tel Aviv: Olamenu, 1962), 210. There were a number of local groups as well as splits among Bukovinians. According to *Die Stimme*, by 1948, there were at least three branches of the Bukovinian Landsmannschaft in Israel and there were repeated attempts to join them. See e.g. 'Bukowiner in Israel', *Die Stimme*, March–April 1951.
148. 'Parteien und Landsmannschaften: Ihr Beitrag zu Einwanderung und Einordnung', *Die Stimme*, June–July 1949.
149. See Yablonka, *Holocaust Survivors*, 258.
150. *Die Stimme*, August 1949.
151. *Die Stimme*, February–March 1949.
152. 'Noch einmal: die entwurzelten Intellektuellen', *Die Stimme*, April–May 1949.
153. 'Menschen an die man nicht vergessen soll', *Die Stimme*, June–July 1947.
154. 'Neue Olim aus der Bukowina', *Die Stimme*, December–January 1949.
155. Reifer, *Dr. Mayer Ebner*, 10.
156. Ibid., 18–19.
157. 'Czernowitz, das österreichische Jerusalem und Dr Benno Straucher', *Die Stimme*, December 1949.
158. 'Hasmonaea-Czernowitz in Tel-Aviv', *Die Stimme*, August 1949.
159. Yablonka, *Holocaust Survivors*, 27.
160. Reifer, *Dr. Mayer Ebner*, 225, 240.
161. CZA: S1\389.
162. See Hirsch and Spitzer, *Ghosts of Home*, 40.

163. See Hacohen, *Immigrants in Turmoil*.
164. See A. Appelfeld, *The Story of a Life: An Extraordinary Memoir of Survival*, translated from Hebrew by A. Halter (London: Penguin, 2004), 124.
165. Ibid., 184.
166. Ibid., 197.
167. See e.g. leading articles: 'Wo bleibt die Entschädigung? Ein Wort an den jüdischen Weltkongress', *Die Stimme*, September 1949; 'Entschädigung!', *Die Stimme*, January–February 1950.
168. On Daghani, see 'Tagebuch: Transnistrien', *Die Stimme*, January/February 1950; on Carp, see Mayer Ebner, 'Rumänische Schwarzbücher 1940–1944 von Matatias Carp', *Die Stimme*, April–May 1949.
169. Reifer did mention having written at more length about this in Hebrew elsewhere; Reifer, *Menschen und Ideen*, 238.
170. YVA: O.1 (Ball-Kaduri Collection), e.g. no. 218 Bemerkungen von Dr Ball-Kaduri zum Zeitzeugenbericht von Ernestine Rosengarten, 1–3; no. 190: Einige grundsätzliche Bemerkungen über die Lage der Dokumentation für Transnistrien im Zusammenhang mit einer kurzen Zeugenaussage von Isaak Panner über Transnistrien, 1–17.
171. As scholars have argued, after 1948, the Israeli state gave Holocaust research less importance due to other concerns. See B. Cohen, *Israeli Holocaust Research: Birth and Evolution* (Abingdon: Routledge, 2013), 9, 66.
172. Ibid., 146
173. Porat, *Israeli Society, the Holocaust and its Survivors*, 346.
174. The following remarks are based on a handful of accounts. See YVA: O.33, Testimonies, Diaries and Memoirs Collection on Romania, e.g. 890, 891, 893, 894, 896.
175. On the comparison with Auschwitz, see e.g. Glasberg-Gold, *Ruth's Journey*, loc. 4160.
176. As Pamela Ballinger has argued, people withdrew into survivor circles: P. Ballinger, 'Culture of Survivors: Post-Traumatic Stress Disorder and Traumatic Memory', *History and Memory* 10(1) (1998), 99–132, here 118.
177. *Die Stimme*, December 1949.
178. A. Wieviorka and I. Niborski, *Les Livres du Souvenir : Mémoriaux Juifs de Pologne* (Paris: Gallimard, 1983), 15.
179. Ibid., 47. See also Ballinger, 'Culture of Survivors', 114–15. Nicole Lapierre argues that Jews write books rather than build monuments; N. Lapierre, *Le Silence de la Mémoire: A la Recherche des Juifs de Plock* (Paris: Plon, 1989), 251.
180. On the book's critical reception, see the foreword to the second volume: H. Gold, 'Vorwort', in H. Gold (ed.), *Geschichte der Juden in der Bukowina*, vol. 2 (Tel Aviv: Olamenu, 1962). A harsh review bemoaning the disregard for Orthodox traditions appeared in the German-language newspaper for Nazi victims published in Tel Aviv, *Weg und Ziel*, in December 1958. For more on the issue of material compensation, see Chapter 4 below.
181. This is also the perspective adopted by those who see the books as 'an assertion of belief in the existence of community': J. Kugelmass and J. Boyarin (eds), *From a Ruined Garden: The Memorial Books of the Polish Jewry* (New York: Shocken Books, 1983), 18.
182. As Weinstein proclaimed in 1950: 'We have stopped being a Jewry in Bukovina, but we have remained a Bukovinian Jewry.' See 'Sie sind da!', *Die Stimme*, December 1950.
183. As Judith Baumel has argued, such regionalisms were dismissed as folklore; J. Tydor Baumel, 'In Everlasting Memory: Individual and Communal Holocaust Commemoration in Israel', in R. Wistrich and D. Ohana (eds), *The Shaping of Israeli Identity, Myth, Memory and Trauma* (London: Frank Cass, 1995), 149.

184. W. Kiesler, 'Hitachduth Olej Bukowina, Haifa', in H. Gold (ed.), *Geschichte der Juden in der Bukowina*, vol. 2 (Tel Aviv: Olamenu, 1962), 213.
185. See Porat, 'The Role of European Jewry', 297.
186. L. Teitler, 'Hitachduth Olej Bukowina, Jaffa – Giwat Alijah', in Gold (ed.), *Geschichte der Juden in der Bukowina*, vol. 2, 214.
187. Ibid., 124.

Part III
ENTANGLEMENTS

Chapter 4

'LOST HOME' AND 'AREA OF EXPULSION'

Compensating for Loss at the Height of the Cold War

In the mid 1960s, the Austrian, Bukovinian-German writer Georg Drozdowski wrote a letter to the Bukovinian Jewish writer Alfred Gong, who was by then living in New York. Drozdowski's attention had been drawn to Gong, whom he had never met, after reading two of his poems about Bukovina in an Austrian literary journal. Drozdowski began by praising the work of this colleague and stressed that they were also fellow countrymen – albeit adding as '*Bukowiner* (not "*Buchenländer*")', as Bukovinian 'ethnic Germans' like himself tended to describe themselves. Drozdowski then proceeded in suggesting changes to Gong's published poems on two counts. First, according to him, the region Gong had referred to in his poem *Bukowina* with the German neuter pronoun 'es' should instead, based on the character of its features, be given the feminine pronoun 'sie'. Second, Drozdowski took issue with the last verse of the poem *Topographie* and the claim that 'half of the Jews [of Bukovina had] kicked the bucket in Novosibirsk and the other half later in Antonescu's concentration camps'. Drozdowski acknowledged the millions of Jewish victims, emphasized his closeness to many Jews and even insisted he had no intention of offsetting Jewish against German victims as many tried to do. Nonetheless, he felt the need to point out that 'two halves constitute a whole' and thereby suggested that the claim in the last verse was overstated. As he explained, he himself had countless Jewish friends from the region. Evidently, therefore, many but not *all* of them had been murdered.[1]

Unfortunately, Gong's side of the correspondence has been lost. Yet Drozdowski's next letter suggests that Gong had answered and been open to discussion. And the fact that it ended with an invitation to Gong to visit Drozdowski in Austria, together with Gong's friend Paul Celan, shows that the tone remained cordial.[2] However, what we also know is that while Gong took on the first change, he rejected the second.[3] He and others had perhaps survived, but this was the exception, not the rule, as his own family's fate proved.

This exchange of letters, like the one quoted at the start of this book, constitutes quite a rare example of direct and personal interaction between a Bukovinian German and a Bukovinian Jew during the first decades of the Cold War. But like the one at the start, it captures critical aspects and problems of this relationship in general: the importance of the shared homeland, memories of the same time period and common acquaintances, but also the incommensurability of the experiences of Bukovinian Germans and Bukovinian Jews during the war and of the meaning being drawn from them. In this exchange, Drozdowski even hinted at this incommensurability by drawing attention to the difference between the inclusive concept of *Bukowiner* and the ethnoregional concept of *Buchenländer*. In short, this exchange points to a developing tension at the heart of what it meant to be Bukovinian – a tension caused by the uneasy combination of nostalgia and guilt and the contested meaning of Germanness.

This dilemma was not new. The issue of how to reconcile the violent past, the pain of displacement, complicity under the Nazis, feelings of nostalgia, and different types and conceptions of identity (national, regional, ethnic and cultural) was a problem Bukovinian communities and the societies they belonged to had faced since the end of the Second World War. Yet, as was described in the previous chapter, such debates had until then mostly been dealt with internally, within the communities and within their respective national arenas. However, as this example shows, as time passed, it became an increasingly public, entangled and international matter. Tellingly, for example, Drozdowski and Gong were awarded the same Austrian literary prize just one year apart in 1965 and 1966, respectively.[4]

The narratives, practices and activities of German and Jewish Bukovinians in the first half of the Cold War were typified by two simultaneous, contradictory trends along with a number of related problems. On the one hand, Bukovina came to be seen as a metaphorical space, invoked to refer to past places, individuals and events – a universe that no longer existed – a deterritorialized space.[5] In other words, Bukovina, as the lost *Heimat*, became an object of both a physical and 'temporal dislocation' – an object of nostalgia.[6] However, on the other hand, this period was characterized not only by attempts to idealize the past, but also attempts to achieve distance and closure, and by efforts to compensate for the past in a more practical sense, which necessitated reckoning with what had happened. In fact, the primary justification for the continued existence of the representative organizations of Bukovinians in Germany and Israel was the issue of financial indemnification. In both countries, these organizations represented the claimants and offered them guidance concerning West German legislation – both the Equalisation of Burdens Act (Lastenausgleichsgesetz (LAG)) and the law on reparations for the victims of National Socialism (Bundesentschädigungsgesetz (BEG)). For this purpose, Bukovina was even defined legally as an 'area of expulsion' (*Vertreibungsgebiet*). Compensation for the past was therefore both figurative and literal. On the one hand, it was a matter nostalgically remembering what had been lost to make up for the trauma of war and displacement, but, on the other hand, it was a matter of obtaining justice, recognition and reparations to make up for past damages and wrongs.

This situation resulted in a range of contradictions. First, there was a contradiction between positive nostalgic memories and memories of violence and suffering. This is the reason why Jewish nostalgia for Bukovina, in particular, is often described as 'ambivalent'.[7] Second, there was a contradiction between nostalgia and the imperative of taking responsibility for the past. Indeed, while nostalgia has been defined as 'history without guilt', a sentiment devoid of shame,[8] reparations required a significant revisiting of 'what had existed' and 'what had happened' and a confrontation with notions of collective responsibility. At the same time, the pervasive character in this period of the discussion of shame and guilt in West Germany often backfired and resulted in feelings of stigmatization and defensive attitudes, including denial and repression.[9] Finally, there was a contradiction between the visions and aims of Bukovinian Jews and Bukovinian Germans, despite both groups using the same language, German. Indeed, if these groups gave up on the pursuit of immediate and practical political aims, they did not abandon what some have called their 'ethnified collective memory' and 'culturalization of spatial features'.[10] Their memories of the lost homeland were therefore often very selective, if not exclusive or even incompatible, and so were the associated perceptions and definitions of the group to which they belonged and, with this, of Germanness in general.

This chapter explores the characteristics, overlaps and frictions resulting from different attempts to compensate for loss during the 1960s and 1970s. Indeed, as Norbert Frei has argued, the battles for belonging fought out in national arenas were followed by an international 'battle for memory'.[11] The case of Bukovinians illustrates this in a striking way. This was not only because both German and Jewish Bukovinians represented and engaged with the same space in the same language, but also because they dealt with many of the same issues, albeit from very different perspectives. The case of Bukovinians thereby reflects, on its scale, much broader debates and questions. Indeed, commemorating the past is never a neutral undertaking. But this dilemma was even more acute in West Germany and Israel in the late 1950s and early 1960s, where and when the recent past was intrinsic to the politics of identity and recognition as well as to the relationship between the two states – and, with this, to the relationship between West Germans and Israelis in general.[12] The discourse about Bukovina in the 1960s developed against the backdrop of a highly politicized climate of engagement with the recent past. This atmosphere was created and spurred on by repeated controversies relating to the war and the Holocaust and linked, among other things, to the advancing investigation of Nazi crimes, high-profile trials and scandals, and the ongoing discussion of the domestic and foreign policy issue of reparations. Ultimately, tracing how German and Jewish Bukovinians discussed, presented and conceived of Bukovina during the early Cold War thus not only gives a privileged insight into the German and Jewish identities and interactions in this period, but also helps explain how and why changes to this relationship occurred.

Idealized Visions of the 'Lost Home'

By the end of the 1950s, most Bukovinians had accepted that the 'old *Heimat*' was unquestionably lost. Both Germans and Jews who travelled back to the region argued that it had been transformed beyond recognition.[13] Those they knew who had remained behind were still pressing to leave; this confirmed that there was no future for Bukovinians in what was once Bukovina and reinforced their sense of belonging as Bukovinians in their new homelands. Isolated behind the Iron Curtain, the region was declared 'out of reach', 'vanished', 'sunken' (*untergegangen*) and irremediably lost.

In both cases, a new chapter of their history had begun. In August 1954, *Die Stimme*, the newspaper of the Organization of Immigrants from Bukovina published in Tel Aviv, headlined the issue with an article titled 'Ten Years' ('Zehn Jahre').[14] It recapitulated not just the history of Bukovinian Jews during the war, but also the process of immigration and the setting up of institutions in what was to become Israel. This date was not merely the anniversary of a tragedy; what they had done in those ten years was something they celebrated proudly. Similarly, in 1959, the Bukovinian German Landsmannschaft in West Germany published an anniversary booklet celebrating ten years of the organization's existence and outlining its various achievements.[15] It pointed to different activities, such as the cultural work, political agreements and settlement building; it even identified different phases within the Bukovinian Germans' postwar history.[16] This period itself was being historicized. The year 1940 might have been the end of one thing, but it was also the beginning of something else. The Second World War had not marked the end of Bukovinians' history in either West Germany or Israel.

Accepting that the *Heimat* was lost did not mean that it should be forgotten, and as the survival of these organizations and their activities proved, it certainly was not. This acceptance triggered a new wave of memorialization. Since, in both countries, 'integration' and commemoration were no longer regarded as incompatible, there was a notable drive in the second decade after the war to compensate publicly for loss. Not only did 'being integrated' not mean that one should forget what had preceded, but the transformation of the old *Heimat* also made the preservation of what it had once been even more essential and urgent. In turn, this also meant that these were memories that could be enjoyed. The foreword of the *Heimat* book of the village of Deutsch-Satulmare (Satu Mare near Suceava), for instance, read as follows: 'Deutsch-Satulmare is perhaps definitively lost as a *Heimat* for us, but this book should ensure that it lives on forever in our memory and in our hearts.'[17] Around this time, *Der Südostdeutsche*, the newspaper of Bukovinian Germans, also started displaying an increasing number of photographs of landscapes, cityscapes and buildings in Bukovina alongside its texts, providing its readers with visual elements to keep the region's past image alive. *Die Stimme*, in turn, published a growing number of articles about the prewar Jewish institutions and personalities. This type of material was what their readers wanted. In 1961, for example, a professor from Caracas wrote to the editors of *Die Stimme* to say:

> I am using this opportunity to tell you how grateful I am to *Die Stimme*, as so many other readers who come from our old *Heimat* must be as well. It connects us to our past and keeps alive in us the memory of ideals that we now experience for real. This is our great fortune. I read *Die Stimme* with particular pleasure and when the postman brings it, I put everything aside to be confronted for a while with people with whom I shared a piece of my life.[18]

With other newspapers dealing with the present, reporting on the past was *Die Stimme*'s and *Der Südostdeutsche*'s main remit and purpose.

To some extent, this nostalgia was contentious. Could Jews feel nostalgic for a place of suffering? Could the Germans feel nostalgic for a place they had willingly abandoned or, indeed, that they had contributed to destroying? Some authors addressed these problems directly. Hermann Sternberg, the author of the small book entitled *On the History of the Jews of Czernowitz*, described *Czernowitzers* as 'prisoners of their memories' because it was both 'only human' and 'unavoidable' to feel longing for one's youth: 'the connections may be severed for good but there is a deep melancholy that cannot be gotten rid of'.[19] However, Sternberg did not comment on the use of

German, which, as in many other Jewish Bukovinian publications, was a matter of course. As for the *Heimat* book regarding the town of Radautz (Rădăuți), entitled *Radautz: The Most German Town in Bukovina* (*Radautz: die deutscheste Stadt der Bukowina*) and published in 1966, the author's aim was 'to teach all *Radautzer* about the most important events from the life of their hometown and about the creation and constitution of political, cultural and economic institutions' and, in particular, 'to keep alive the memory of their dear old *Heimat*'.[20] For the author, the Germans had 'not forgotten their dear hometown of Radautz and still remembered it fondly'. But they had not forgotten what had led them to leave either: 'the lack of rights, persecution, demotion, contempt and abuse' they had endured after Bukovina became part of Romania.[21] In short, this was nostalgia without homesickness.

Accordingly, this new trend did not challenge the political status quo. The *Heimat* book about the village of Alt-Fratautz (Frătăuții Vechi) was described in its preface as a 'memorial book' (*Gedenkbuch*).[22] Its subtitle read 'about the development and the extinction of a German village community in Bukovina', clearly asserting that this history had ended. As Mordechai Rubinstein, the author of *The Jewish Vatican in Sadagora 1850–1950* – a title that incidentally exemplarily captures the exercise of reimagination – explained: 'The sole purpose of this book is just to temporarily amuse my friends from Bukovina – hand them over a mirror of their happily experienced youth – so that they can enjoy recalling stories and anecdotes about the place where they themselves and their forefathers played a role in good times and in bad.'[23] The dates in the title of his memory book made clear that life in Bukovina was well and truly over; the back cover even featured contact details of Bukovinian organizations in Tel Aviv and New York. Besides, Rubinstein, like Hugo Gold, the editor of the Bukovinian Jews' main memory book *History of the Jews in Bukovina*, dealt with this tension between the 'good' and the 'bad' memories by splitting the work into two volumes.[24] The separation made it possible to identify, isolate and celebrate positive legacies such as the student and sports organizations Hasmonaea, Hebronia and Maccabi, which were even later re-formed in Israel.[25]

In the case of *The Jewish Vatican*, the author's use of humour, irony and different genres created additional distance from the 'bad' experiences. The section on the war was entitled 'Expelled from Paradise' (*Vertrieben aus dem Paradies*), and this sarcastic tone was maintained throughout the text. One could, for instance, read: 'In the "Hitler-Stalin" war of the gods, many millions had to bleed to death – half a world collapsed into ruin – and humanity's most significant achievements were thrown to the dogs.'[26] As he explained:

> It hurts to have to leave the *Heimat* that one spent a whole life constructing. But such was the will of the godlike Stalin, who fears the sunlight of the free

world and hid behind an 'Iron Curtain'. Now we are free! He, however, is not because the murderous gang that are his friends is closer to him than he suspects.[27]

Rubinstein's way of addressing survivors' inner conflict between remembering and forgetting was also interesting. He set up a fictional dialogue between a 'Jored' (a migrant to Israel) and 'reason' (*die Vernunft*). The former would say 'I want to forget, I want to forget all the horror' and the latter would respond 'don't forget, don't forget who destroyed your happiness'.[28] However, in the end, this meant that experiences were discussed in rather general and abstract terms. The poems published in Rubinstein's work dealt with the question of Jewish suffering and mentioned the Nazis, the millions of victims and the persecution they experienced. Yet specifically *Bukovinian* Jewish experiences such as the deportations to Transnistria or persecution under the Antonescu regime, were not tackled.[29]

Discussing experiences of violence in more detail and, especially, attributing blame more precisely would have distorted the idealized memory of the lost home and detracted from Jewish Bukovinians' aim of lighthearted or at least positive reconstruction. It would have forced them to describe a more complex social reality. As others have noted, Jewish memory books aimed to create an ideal Jewish world in its totality.[30] In particular, the authors emphasized the usefulness of the Jews for the functioning of society. Although this was justified by the desire to re-create what had been destroyed, in the process the homeland became a place without Gentiles – a Zionist dream, a Jewish utopia, 'an island of Jewishness'.[31] As others have noted, these books created a Jewish geography.[32] In the case of Bukovinians, this was a Jewish-German geography. Hugo Gold's two-volume history of the Jews of Bukovina alongside his books on the Jews of Vienna and Bohemia are key examples of this phenomenon. The journal, *Zeitschrift für die Geschichte der Juden* (*Journal for the History of the Jews*), which he launched in 1964 and appeared in German in Tel Aviv until his death in 1974, is also a case in point. Despite its broad title, the journal focused almost exclusively on Jews in Germany and German-speaking Jews of the former Habsburg monarchy such as Bukovinian Jews. In effect, it brought together the history of German Jews and the history of German-speaking Jews from Central and Eastern Europe, tracing a direct line from the Jewish past in Europe to the present in Israel. Not only did it thereby create a 'German-Jewish' space that had never really existed, but it also removed and isolated the history of Jews from different areas from the history of the respective societies, in which they had lived in Central, Eastern and Southeastern Europe, as well as that of their brethren who spoke other languages (such as Romanian-speaking or Hungarian-speaking Jews).

For quite different reasons, a similar pattern emerged in the writings of some of the Germans from the region. This development had to do with the genre of *Heimat* books that not only contained memories and experiences, but primarily sought to reproduce a vision of the social space of the *Heimat*. As Jutta Faehndrich has shown, the story these books told often functioned as a founding myth for the groups of ethnic Germans, mostly members of village or local communities, and relied on an idealized, even canonized and often also highly ethnocentric, memory of their lost homes.³³ These depictions also entailed creating a new political geography – this time, one that was expressly German. For example, on the hand-drawn street and house map of the village of Alt-Fratautz, which was included in the sleeve of the village's *Heimat* book, the Romanian and Jewish neighbours were nameless.³⁴ Similarly, on the introductory page of his book *Student in Czernowitz*, Hans Prelitsch described the city as the 'Heidelberg of the East' and called on everyone to recall that the two world wars had put an end to German influence in the region.³⁵ The phenomenon of German presence was regarded as more significant than the homeland's multiethnic character or the lives and activities of the remaining 90% of the population. Diversity was a merely folkloric feature. In *Bukowina: Heimat von gestern*, for example, the first section was entitled 'Geography of Bukovina', the second 'The Germans in Bukovina' and the third 'German Achievements and Accomplishments'. Only in section four, 'Bukovina – a Multiethnic Land', on page 223, over halfway into the book, were members of other ethnicities mentioned at any length. As for the 'Prominent Bukovinians of our Time', they were almost all ethnic Germans.³⁶

Faehndrich also notes that it was typical for books belonging to the *Heimat* genre to avoid or elide contentious themes such as the war, interethnic relations, the Holocaust and even, in some cases, the postwar period.³⁷ Indeed, most Bukovinian-German authors steered clear of writing about difficult questions altogether, concentrating on the description of a timeless image of the *Heimat*. Franz Wiszniowski, for example, the author of the *Heimat* book about Radautz, did not tackle the fate of the Germans during the Second World War; he simply stated that the vast majority had been resettled and that, as of 1944, just 230 remained in the town.³⁸ As for the author of the *Heimat* book on Illischestie (Ilişeşti), Johann Christian Dressler, while he mentioned resettlement, he refused to take a position on its motives or consequences, arguing that:

> Whether resettlement was in the interest of the people or whether the only reason for what happened was cold political calculation will not be discussed here and should also not be asked of Germany [*sic*]. The whole resettlement operation, built on the premise of victory in a great war, is still far too shrouded that one could judge it clearly today.³⁹

Dressler nevertheless concluded that the resettlement had ultimately saved many lives: 'And this commits us to thankfulness towards Germany.'[40]

For others, writing about prewar Bukovina was even a means of rehabilitating the image of the Germans in general and in the face of ascriptions of guilt in particular. As Peter Blaß wrote, for example, in the preface to the village chronicle of Deutsch-Satulmare, echoing almost word for word the discourse of the Landsmannschaft: 'We Germans know too little about our past. Particularly in the current climate of haste and agitation, we should ask in contemplative silence about the direction of our people.' Specifically, he addressed 'the Germans from the Reich' (*Binnendeutsche*) who should know that 'in all of the southeastern states, the German settlers brought culture, carried progress, supported the state and, last but not least, were the main bearers of the burdens of the state'. He also stressed they had made great sacrifices in the war, 'even if this did not suffice to save the *Heimat*'.[41]

The foreword to the collection of essays about Bukovina *Buchenland: hundertfünfzig Jahre Deutschtum in der Bukowina*, written by the editor, the Bukovinian professor Franz Lang, even had a distinctly defensive tone. Lang first explained that the aim was to give insight into the history of Bukovinian Germans as a group while emphasizing their 'Germanness' and their 'tolerance', which had facilitated their smooth integration. He said he regretted that there had not been enough room in this volume to include contributions on 'other groups', which he named as Romanians and the Ukrainians. He then continued:

> If it was only a matter of welfare and comfort, we could easily draw a line under the past. The fact is that there is more to it than this: it is about the highest value of a people, about its responsible independence in freedom, and as our fate is inseparable from the fate of our people as a whole, we are not permitted and should not simply carry the memory of the loss of faraway Bukovina in our hearts, but soberly reflect on how it can counterbalance on the side of credits the large bill that the German people have been given to shoulder after 1945.[42]

He concluded that it would be nice to forget, but that this would not constitute a 'true peace'. He encouraged Bukovinians to make sure that their children developed love and gratefulness towards their ancestors and their people.[43] These statements amounted not only to a direct rejection of the so-called 'topos of collective guilt' but also to a direct attempt to counter it.[44] In general, such a publication focusing on Bukovinian Germans as a reified group reflected the perpetuation and endurance of old practices, ideas and beliefs about their identity and superiority, something also embodied by the refounding of Bukovinian branches of fraternities and student organizations such as Frankonia, Teutonia and Arminia zu Czernowitz in this period in Austria and West Germany.[45]

Idealization and the attendant gaps and silences were therefore features of both German and Jewish Bukovinian accounts in the second decade after the war. In both cases, discussions of victimhood, suffering and violence retreated into the background, if they appeared at all. Resettlement was narrated according to the Bukovinian German Landsmannschaft's leaders' sanitized version – it was 'ultimately for the best' – and detached from ideological tenets and the political context of its occurrence. The pictures of resettlement in Lang's book, for example, were carefully chosen to avoid featuring any swastikas or National Socialists in uniform.[46] The fact that hardly any books were published about Transnistria during the Cold War suggests that among Jews too, compensating for loss involved treating Bukovina as an object of idealization or only discussing the causes of its destruction indirectly.[47] Bukovinian Jews also had to face a lack of interest in and understanding of their unusual experiences on behalf of the wider public. The history of the publication and reception of Edgar Hilsenrath's autobiographical, documentary novel about Transnistria, *Night* (*Nacht*), is a case in point. The book, which he wrote in German while living and working in New York in the early 1950s, was not published until 1964, when Munich-based Kindler finally accepted it. Yet, most of the 1,000 copies printed were never distributed because the depiction of Jews was deemed too negative for a German-speaking audience. As a result, hardly any notice was taken of the novel until its translation into English and publication in this language in 1967 and its re-publication in the German original in 1978.[48]

In a sense, both groups were very protective of the image of the region. An interesting illustration of this is another literary phenomenon, namely the reception of the works of Gregor von Rezzori. Having been born in the region in 1914, Rezzori was himself a 'Bukovinian' and, as the son of a Christian member of the Habsburg administration, was widely considered to be of German descent.[49] His sarcastic writings about the region, starting with the *Tales of Maghrebinia* (*Maghrebinische Geschichten*), first published in German in 1953, provocatively and humorously parodied the genre of nationalist *Heimat* literature, and were by far the most popular representations of Bukovina available and circulating at this time in German-speaking Europe.[50] Initially, Bukovinian Jews in Israel ignored his work, but in West Germany, Bukovinian Germans could not be quite as dismissive of Rezzori's success. In 1955, Franz Lang published a review of Rezzori's 1954 novel *Oedipus at Stalingrad* (*Oedipus siegt bei Stalingrad*) in *Der Südostdeutsche*.[51] While Lang acknowledged the quality of Rezzori's writing, he vehemently denounced the content. He argued there was nothing Bukovinian about the hero, Traugott von Jassilkowski, aside from the name. He continued:

His meaningless and aimless way of being, his nihilistic view of life, if he has any, is a feature of big-city literature. The Bukovinian expellees who, despite all the strokes of fate, say yes to life and master it, are rightly entitled to reject this Traugott and his entire universe. Rezzori clearly did not write his novel for them. But how about next time he took Bukovina, his hometown Czernowitz and its inhabitants into account and in such a way that their fate and being should be fairly represented. They were not all 'Maghrebinians'![52]

With this last comment, Lang was referring to Rezzori's previous work in which Bukovina was described as *Maghrebinia* – a cheerful, chaotic and diverse area bearing a resemblance, as the name suggested, to the Orient. This depiction was at odds with the Europeanness that Bukovinian Germans claimed, and, as the review reveals, they felt personally attacked and insulted.

The release of Rezzori's next novel, *An Ermine in Czernopol* (*Ein Hermelin in Tschernopol*), heightened tensions further in 1958.[53] The nicknames 'Teskovina' and 'Czernopol' hardly concealed Rezzori's real focus. Yet, when it came to characters, he did not even bother to change the names. This book thus led Rezzori to be prosecuted and fined for libel in Austria by Ariadne Buchenthal, who believed he had besmirched her parents' reputation. However, by then, Rezzori had already made a name for himself on West German TV and had appeared on the cover of the major German weekly magazine *Der Spiegel*, with a ten-page feature inside.[54] This sudden popularity as well as the novel itself triggered a series of articles, comments and reviews in both *Der Südostdeutsche* and *Die Stimme* and beyond. Both papers reported on the trial.[55] They also published reviews and republished the corrective response of a Ukrainian Bukovinian living in Vienna, Wladimir Zalozieckyi, entitled 'What Czernopol Was [Really] Like', which had first appeared the Viennese daily *Die Presse*.[56] Bukovinian Germans accused Rezzori of 'throwing dirt', and Bukovinian Jews blamed him for 'blaspheming the world of yesterday'.[57] *Die Stimme*, in particular, published a series of outraged responses, including a review by the Bukovinian Austrian writer Georg Drozdowski, which bemoaned the book's success and posed the question: 'What can a country do against its defilement?'[58] Later, they also published the letters exchanged between Rezzori and Zalozieckyi, debating the relationship between historical accuracy and artistic licence.[59]

The most virulent and articulate response was a review in *Die Stimme* by Walter Kiesler from Haifa – a response that was met with widespread approval by readers.[60] Kiesler conceded that the book was 'humorous' and written with 'virtuosic style'. However, he also reminded Rezzori, whom he addressed directly, of his responsibility as the author of 'the only report of the memory of Bukovina in the free world': 'For the sake of historical truth', he wrote, 'the other Czernowitz also deserves mentioning', and this included 'the peaceful coexistence of the five nationalities, Romanians, Germans, Poles, Ruthenes and, *last but not least*, Jews, who contributed so much to the cultural and industrial flourishing of Bukovina and its capital'. Beyond this, Kiesler noted Rezzori's stereotypical depiction of Jews as comical traders and merchants. Yet, he was even more bewildered by Rezzori's depiction of his own group, the Germans, whom he had described as 'Germany's larva-like people' (*Larvenmenschen Deutschlands*). Kiesler had begun his review by mentioning Rezzori's own shady biography and credentials – in particular, that he had supposedly volunteered to the Wehrmacht in 1938, though he eventually remained a civilian in Berlin and thus, in the author's words, avoided a 'hero's death' (*Heldentod*). Thereby, Kiesler underscored the hypocrisy of Rezzori's uncompromising stance towards Bukovinian Germans in particular and Germans in general.[61] He concluded by saying that while Rezzori might be making money or making people laugh, he had not earned their 'respect' (*Achtung*).

Conflicting Visions of Bukovina

However, this short-lived congruence of opinions concerning Rezzori's work did not mean that Bukovinian Jews and Bukovinian Germans agreed with each other concerning what was lost or how to represent it. While in both cases the region was depicted as exceptional – 'an oasis of civilization' – for the Germans, it had been 'an island of Germanness', and for the Jews, it had been 'a Jewish Atlantis'. The main feature of the depictions of the region remained their exclusive nature. Both communities attempted to glorify the role of their own group and members, even problematically projecting backwards contemporary reified and hardened conceptions of ethnonational identity. As a result, they also had different spatial and historical reference points. As such, these were two radically opposed visions of what was there, who had lived there and what had happened. Indeed, invocations of the region mostly ignored the existence of 'ethnic others' – in particular, that of *other* German-speakers. Since this amounted to an inscription of culture on a particular space, Bukovina not only appeared as two very different places, but also corresponded to and underwrote two very different conceptions of Germanness.

Yet while Gold's, Rubinstein's and Sternberg's publications did not give any space to the region's 'ethnic others', they also did not claim to offer a comprehensive and exhaustive picture. By equating 'German' and 'Austrian', and therefore 'Bukovinian' and 'German', German narratives often took ethnocentrism to another level. Franz Lang's *Buchenland: One Hundred and Fifty Years of German Culture in Bukovina* with its sole focus on the German ethnic group, despite the title, is a prime example. In effect, 'German culture' (*Deutschtum*) had been equated with German ethnicity. However, Erich Beck's book of photographs, *Bukovina: Land between Orient and Occident*, which remained at the top of the list of books to purchase from the Bukovinian German Landsmannschaft for decades, constitutes another interesting case.[62] Beck, who was born in 1929 in Rădăuți, had studied business and economics in West Germany and lived, after the war, on the Bukovinian settlement of Büsnau near Stuttgart. He neither had much experience of the 'old home', nor was he a historian, so his book mainly relied on existing literature. Yet, it therefore provides a unique insight into what particular aspects of Bukovinian Germans' history were transmitted to subsequent generations and a wider audience. Indeed, this book demonstrates both the place of Bukovinian Germans' narratives in West Germany's highly politicized climate and landscape of memorialization and how, in turn, the politicization of 'the East' resulted in a small handful of people obtaining the monopoly and the prerogative over this history. In this sense, it sheds light on West German politics of memory and commemoration in the 1960s, offering a plastic illustration of issues of visibility, marginalization and interpretative authority other scholars have also noted.[63]

At nearly 200 pages, Beck's book was a modern and well-made 'coffee-table book' (*Bildband*), containing over 150 captioned black-and-white photographs, as well as a historical overview and description of the region and its people. Contrary to the *Heimat* books previously discussed, this publication was neither primarily about constructing a sense of belonging in West Germany, nor did it serve to record the history of Bukovinian Germans as a group in specific localities. Instead, it sought to provide a history of Bukovina on the ground since time immemorial and offer a comprehensive account including all its diverse peoples, landscapes and traditions. At the outset, Beck claimed that this book was not about the present, but was about the past: 'Bukovina is a land of the past.' Yet, as he went on to say, 'its present is composed of memories' and 'its future is the hope for the return of freedom'.[64] Its future was therefore a return to the past. This publication was not a history book in a conventional sense, but a book that collapsed the timeframe. It was a timeless, ahistorical vision the main aim of which was to bring to life an idealized, yet contemporarily relevant vision of an imagined past.

The influence of existing narratives, especially those promoted by Beck's elders within the Bukovinian-German homeland organization was tangible. Beck, for example, did not conceive of Bukovina or Austria-Hungary as a power-sharing political system, but in terms of an organic mixture of peoples (*Völker*).[65] At the same time, Bukovina was not only a land of 'encounters' (*Übergänge*) between Central and Eastern Europe but also a smaller yet 'true reflection' of the Habsburg monarchy; therefore, it might also be a model for Europe.⁶⁶ The region's diversity was openly discussed. In fact, 'The peaceful coexistence of randomly thrown together different ethnic groups' was described as the hallmark of Bukovina,⁶⁷ and the large portraits of members of different ethnicities throughout the book illustrated this impressively. However, this was a diversity of a specific kind. Both the text and the photographs exoticized the inhabitants and the region's 'ethnic others' in a somewhat primitive manner. The images captured individuals in traditional dress or performing traditional tasks: Romanian and Ukrainian peasants staking hay, Romanian and Ukrainian women washing clothes or painting Easter eggs, 'hardworking' German farmers and craftspeople, Jewish traders standing around at the marketplace and wandering Roma. Those pictured were not only supposed to be generic and stereotypical representations of their ethnicity, but also of their gender and socioeconomic group. Beck especially drew attention to the 'beauty of the women' and the region's 'numerous beggars'.⁶⁸

Even the featured 'Germans' were ostentatiously *Schwaben* (Swabians) and farmers, not city-dwellers, as the author himself or his family had been. There were no members of the middle or upper classes. In general, city inhabitants were not portrayed. Urban life was limited to the few shots of the cityscapes of Suczawa/Suceava and Czernowitz/Cernăuți, including the latter's most famous sites and landmarks such as the town hall, the market square, the university building (formerly the residence of the metropolitan bishop) and the 'German House' – the German (national) cultural centre located on the main pedestrian high street. However, these were captured from a distance and without any people. Mostly, Bukovina was depicted as a picturesque and bucolic rural landscape; the implication was that its diverse rural population was harnessed by a civilizing German culture embodied in a few rather grand but deserted urban centres.

In the opening section on the history of 'Czernowitz' since the Middle Ages, one could read that 'Czernowitz had always been a German city'.⁶⁹ Beck then explained that Germanization had occurred unwittingly, because Austria had never pushed for it and all groups were equal:

> The German language was employed by the members of the other nationalities by choice. This was because, on the one hand, they thereby could come closer to the achievements of the West and, on the other, because among the many everyday languages, German was the only and natural means of mutual understanding.⁷⁰

The policy of Romanization of the interwar period was omitted entirely:

> Nothing changed in the Romanian period ... In the years until the integration into the Ukrainian Soviet Republic, Czernowitz was a small Babylon, a

mixture between Orient and Occident ... a Black Forest village, a Podolian ghetto, a small suburb of Vienna, a piece of deepest Russia, a piece of the most modern America.⁷¹

As Beck meant to show, Bukovina was a 'land of contradictions'.⁷² However, the nostalgia was not for this, or even for the German presence, but for a premodern world characterized by a fantasy of benevolent German domination over these other peoples that spanned the period of Austrian rule both backwards and forwards.

Most notably, Bukovina was presented as an exclusively Christian region and Bukovinians as Christians. Not only was a cross prominently displayed on the book's front cover, but the main focus of attention was the German areas of settlement and the churches, as well as the famous Bukovinian painted Orthodox monasteries. Sadagora/Sadagura, in contrast, the major centre of Hasidic Judaism just outside Czernowitz/Cernăuți, did not feature at all. The only synagogue photographed was that of Rădăuți captured seemingly by accident in the background of the view of the town's market square.⁷³ Although the majority of the photographs presented rural, traditional, agricultural areas and small towns, there was not a single picture of a Jewish shtetl, let alone a Jewish cemetery.

The absence of Jews in this vision of Bukovina was made explicit in Beck's list of those who were regarded as 'Bukovinian' (*Bukowiner*) – a non-national ideal – from which the Jews were remarkably missing:

> Romanians, Ukrainians, Germans, Poles, Hutsuls and the smaller groups of Hungarians, Lipovans, Slovaks, Armenians and, *last not least* [in English in original], gypsies were each with all of their particularities and singularities a variation of the theme 'Bukovinian'. The harmony of these variations was the consciousness of the *Heimat* that was stronger than the national consciousness across generations and world wars.⁷⁴

Beck then explained that 'the fate of Bukovinians during the Second World War had been worse than that of other peoples'. To illustrate his point, he explained that: 'The Germans had been resettled to Germany as early as 1940 but had not been able to establish themselves until after 1945.'⁷⁵ Despite the definition of 'the Bukovinian' given above, this succession of points largely equated 'Bukovinian' with 'German'. Besides, given the assertion that the fate of Bukovinians had been 'worse than that of other peoples', the omission of Jews was all the more astonishing.

Jews were mentioned later on in the text. On page 96, one could read that Jews 'were the group that had taken the least to Bukovinian customs'.⁷⁶ The description of the Jews' characteristics that followed constituted a striking mixture of philosemitic and antisemitic stereotypes:

Afflicted by a certain aversion to hard physical work, they turned to professions that did not involve any physical exertion ... Their fathers taught them to do commerce in all of its variations. It is therefore no surprise that the Jew held a monopoly position in banking in Bukovina. The contribution of the Jews to the cultural life of the region was significant. Equipped with a distinctive ethnic consciousness, they created their own theatres, schools, hospitals and orphanages. The Jews of Bukovina now belong to the elite of the State of Israel.[77]

Aside from the latent racism underpinning the curious mishmash of ethnic characteristics listed here, this cursory outline of the Jews' history also gave absolutely no sense of their experiences, suffering and losses during the war and the Holocaust; on the contrary, it made it sound as though they had fared better than others. As such, not only did the combination of 'civilization', 'Christianity' and 'primitiveness' echoing authentic German understandings of the *Heimat* preclude including the Jews in the picture, but this statement also captures the extent of the author's lasting prejudice towards this group.

None of this was lost on the reviewer of the book in *Die Stimme*, Meier Teich, the former head of the Jewish community in the southern Bukovinian city of Suceava and editor of *Die Stimme* from 1965 until his death in 1975. As he explained, he had at first approached the book with 'great excitement' (*Herzensfreude*), but this had soon turned into 'sorrow and anxiety' (*Leid und Beklemmung*).[78] He noted all of the above text passages, saddened that this was, as the review of the title read, 'Bukovina's legacy from a German perspective'. For him, this kind of 'mastering of the past' (*Bewältigung der Vergangenheit*) was both 'immature' (*kindisch*) and 'unbelievable' (*unfassbar*). But most problematic in his view were the images used, which added insult to injury. He noted that there was only one labelled portrait of a Jew – that of a sad-looking bearded man wearing a black hat and carrying a wooden stick.[79] The caption on the previous page simply read 'Jew from Czernowitz'. Then, on page 38, Teich identified the remains of the synagogue burnt down by the Germans in 1941. The confusing caption below it suggested it had been destroyed in the First World War or perhaps under Soviet rule in 1940–41. On the next page, together with the caption 'Czernowitz on 16 August 1941',[80] there was both a picture of a destroyed building and the picture of a man sweeping the streets. In view of the date, Teich suspected that he too was probably a Jew, though this was not referred to in the caption. Yet, above all, this had led Teich to ask himself where Beck had found these photographs and who had taken them. The answer, according to him, was obvious: some at least had most probably been taken by German troops following the joint Romanian-German attack on the Soviet Union in the summer of 1941.[81]

Beck must have known where the images came from. Moreover, as of the early 1960s when the book was published, he can hardly have been unaware of the implications of using them. The first volume of his ambitious *Bibliography of Bukovina*, which appeared just a few years later and aimed to be comprehensive, included the occasional Bukovinian Jewish author.[82] Yet, he made neither any mention of the photographs' provenance, nor did he comment on their ideological content or try to make up for their biases in other ways. In fact, the text itself was often evocative of National Socialist literature. Aside from overlooking the contributions of Jews to the region's German culture, Beck backed up the claim of Bukovina's Western identity by mentioning that German soldiers who had been posted there during the Second World War had felt 'at home' in this 'unknown province' and that they described it to this day as one of the most interesting places in Europe.[83] He even justified his memorial undertaking primarily with reference to these same German soldiers of the Second World War, some of whom had fallen in the region: 'German people in a foreign soil – missing but not forgotten!'[84] The text ended with this emotional plea, reminiscent of an earlier discourse and period.

Unsurprisingly, the book was well received by members of the Bukovinian German Landsmannschaft. Bruno Skrehunetz-Hillebrand, the then editor of *Der Südostdeutsche*, who reviewed it, celebrated it as evidence that members of the younger generation were interested in the land of their ancestors, that 'small Europe could be a model for big Europe' and that Bukovina 'was truly unique!'. He explained that 'all issues have been dealt with concisely, but very accurately, enthrallingly, and handled clearly', going on to say:

> For older Bukovinians, seeing the many pictures will unavoidably elicit feelings of love and melancholy, as they document this beautiful and happy time powerfully . . . There are also two sad pictures from August 1941 after the liberation of the city from the Bolshevist rule of terror [*Schreckensherrschaft*]. They depict poorly dressed people [*sic*] and the ruins of houses [*sic*] on the *Ringplatz* [the main square] (on the corner of Temple Street).

Skrehunetz concluded his review by saying this book 'should not be missing in any household', an expression that remained the slogan in the adverts for the book in *Der Südostdeutsche* in the following years.[85] The book's positive reception among individual Bukovinians as well as in the wider West German media only served to reinforce this evaluation. A special feature on the book's reception even appeared in *Der Südostdeutsche* two years later.[86] No mention was made of Teich's review in *Die Stimme*.

Beck's book was unique insofar as there was no other such comprehensive and illustrated account of the region's history. However, its tone and orientation were typical of representations from this period with respect to how uncritically many expellees mourned their lost *Heimat*.⁸⁷ In particular, it reflected, as others have noted, the exoticism with which Jews were discussed in West German society up until the 1970s.⁸⁸ But it also showed the extent of the continuities in thinking after 1945 in some milieus, including the deflection of German responsibility and guilt and even hardly veiled antisemitism. It is worth noting that when, ten years later, the book was out of print and the idea of making a second edition was floated, Beck was against it, since in his view the text (though not the photographs) needed updating.⁸⁹ Until then, the majority of German publications grossly underplayed the role of Jewish inhabitants as part of the region's German character, let alone the gravity of their experiences during the war. And since no one except the members of this group dealt with this history in West Germany in this period, this version of the past was also largely unquestioned and unchallenged.

One of the ways in which this exclusive interpretation of the region's history was justified was by insisting that Jews should be regarded as a separate ethnic group. In the *Heimat* book on Radautz, a town where 30% of the population, namely the majority of the inhabitants, had been Jews, the author called them 'Israelites' to make sure they were identified as a distinct group.⁹⁰ Similarly, in *Bukovina: Yesterday's Home*, one could read that one should not mistakenly confuse the two groups as nineteenth-century Austrian historians had done.⁹¹ This stance also meant that the depictions of Jews' and Germans' activities and organizations were to be segregated too – something which sometimes proved difficult. In his short history of the press in Bukovina published in 1962, Vienna-based Bukovinian Erich Prokopowitsch warned the reader not to assume that all German-language newspapers in Bukovina were *German*, as many of them had been published by Jews. These, he explained, had been 'Zionist in their outlook' and, according to him, it was this 'Zionism' that had created a rift between Germans and Jews. This happened, he emphasized, before the creation of the Christian Social Party, while conceding that this party had contributed to deepening the differences.⁹²

Despite the famous diversity of the media landscape in Bukovina, Prokopowitsch's small book was largely an excuse to discuss the *Czernowitzer Deutsche Tagespost*, which had been the mouthpiece of the region's ethnic Germans. Prokopowitsch argued that it had been 'one of the most important German-language newspapers in Romania'⁹³ and had benefited from an ethnically diverse readership because it had always stood 'for rights of minorities'.⁹⁴ He used this opportunity to congratulate the two editors, Bruno Skrehunetz and Fritz Poppenberger, and to mention that the former was by then the editor in chief of the Austrian *Salzburger Nachrichten* (as well as the editor of *Der Südostdeutsche* after Prelitsch's death in 1967).⁹⁵ The fact that the *Czernowitzer Deutsche Tagespost* and its editors had supported the far right, spread ethnocentric and antisemitic ideas and ideals from the turn of the century onwards, and that the paper had been utterly Nazified from the onset of the so-called 'Movement of National Renewal' (*Erneuerungsbewegung*) in the mid 1930s, clearly eluded him.[96] This is all the more remarkable as Prokopowitsch, who had been an administrator at the University of Cernăuți, had himself, like Skrehunetz, been an especially active proponent of National Socialist ideas in Bukovina between 1934 and 1940.[97] As Mariana Hausleitner has argued, this ultimately also made him part of the network of people whose works received funding after the war.[98] Indeed, although he lived in Vienna, Prokopowitsch was friends and remained close to the West German Landsmannschaft's leaders.[99] This book was therefore very similar to many other of the Landsmannschaft's publications.

The vast majority of publications about Bukovina in Germany reflected not only the conservatism and *völkisch* worldview of the Landsmannschaft, but also often the unchallenged antisemitism of its elite and leadership. There had been no 'denazification' of the Bukovinian German Landsmannschaft, so there was neither any re-evaluation of the wartime actions and attitudes of the group as a whole, nor of those of particular individuals.[100] In the 1960s, these people continued to constitute the group's close-knit intellectual elite. It is hardly surprising, therefore, that the Landsmannschaft generally ignored the existence of Jewish authors from the region. Despite appearing in German and in Germany, the novels of the Jewish Bukovinians Siegmund Last and Jacob Klein-Haparash were not acknowledged by the Bukovinian German Landsmannschaft or in *Der Südostdeutsche*.[101] However, there is evidence that both Last, who lived in Vienna after the war, and Klein-Haparash, known as 'Kubi Klein', were known *Landsmänner* (fellow countrymen).[102] The success of Klein-Haparash's book, which was even translated into English in 1963, did not go completely unnoticed.[103] Yet the 'book catalogue' of the Landsmannschaft dating from 1963 only contained one Jewish author, the nineteenth-century Germanophile Karl Emil Franzos.[104] Paul Celan, who had received the Bremen Literature Prize in 1958 and the prestigious Büchner Prize in 1960, and was by far the most famous writer from the region – and even regarded as one of the most influential postwar German-language poets – was not listed there either.

The case of Celan is genuinely revealing. Bukovinian-German leaders were obviously aware of him and his success. In his response to a request for information from the Institute for Political Science of the Technical University of Rhineland-Westphalia in 1965, for a listing of prominent Bukovinians, Rudolf Wagner included him while specifying that he was 'a Jewish Bukovinian' 'without any links to the Landsmannschaft'.[105] But in a letter to the representative organization Bund der Vertriebenen (BdV) that same year, for example, the then managing director (*Bundesgeschäftsführer*) of the Landsmannschaft Otto Lachmund argued that their *Landsmann* Franz Lang 'would deserve, in their view, more attention' than Paul Celan did.[106] In Franz Lang's own contribution on the topics of language and literature in his book *Bukovina: One Hundred and Fifty Years of German Culture*, he mentioned Celan's 'hypermodern literature', but said that though Celan was born in 1920, he had 'soon turned away from Bukovina' (*schon früh der Bukowina entfremdet*).[107] Although Celan's poems were published in West German national newspapers and his obituary after his suicide in Paris in April 1970 was broadcast on German national television (ZDF), *Der Südostdeutsche* did not even refer to his passing.[108] A rare mention of Celan in a reader's letter in 1971 bemoaned the fact that the Transylvanian Saxon writer Dieter Schlesak had described Celan as the only famous writer from Bukovina. The author of the letter protested that there were significant others, such as Rezzori, who, in contrast, were 'ethnic Germans' (*Volksdeutsche*).[109] Unsurprisingly, none of Celan's texts were ever published in *Der Südostdeutsche*.

In fact, with the notable exceptions of the Jewish writer Rose Ausländer and German writer Georg Drozdowski, the German and Jewish Landsmannschaften only published texts by members of their own ethnic group.[110] This crossover in the case of Ausländer and Drozdowski was only possible because of the character of some of their writings and subjects – in Ausländer's case, her bucolic poems about the Bukovinian landscape and, in Drozdowski's case, his generic reflections on the pain of displacement and nostalgia for the Habsburg period – which happened to be suitable for both audiences. However, it is worth noting that only their texts on these topics were reproduced in the respective papers. The writings of German *Heimat* poets such as Heinrich Kipper, Johanna Brucker or Marianne Vincent, with their depiction of Bukovina as an idyllic German homeland, or those of the Jewish writers Immanuel Weissglas, Alfred Gong or Alfred Kittner, with their more direct engagement with the Holocaust, the Jewish experience or Bukovina as a place of suffering, in contrast, were never subject to such a crossover.[111]

The selection of poems published by *Die Stimme* and *Der Südostdeutsche* was symptomatic of their radically opposed approaches to the past and to politics. The two editors of *Der Südostdeutsche* in the 1960s, Hans Prelitsch and Bruno Skrehunetz (in addition to Wagner, who remained important behind the scenes and took on the role of editor of the paper in 1977), were members of the Landsmannschaft, with tainted pasts and unquestionable ongoing sympathies for National Socialist thought. They had close links to the Romanians and Ukrainians in exile in Germany, who were notoriously right wing. They also cooperated with Friedrich (also known as Fritz) Valjavec, a historian and founder of the Südosteuropa Gesellschaft in Munich in 1952 and the Südostdeutsche Historische Kommission in 1957, who, as a member of the SS and the *Einsatzgruppe D*, had participated in the murder of the Jews of Cernăuți in 1941.¹¹² Beyond this, regular headlines denounced not only the loss of the Eastern territories and the German 'capitulation',¹¹³ but also subverted the discourse on German guilt and shame by turning it against 'Germany's enemies': the Left, the Allies and the Jews. In *Der Südostdeutsche* in the 1960s, incidences of Holocaust minimalization, relativization and denial were frequent.¹¹⁴ Occasional mentions of the Jewish suffering by some of their members were even deleted from their contributions.¹¹⁵

In 1961, the Eichmann trial triggered a string of articles in *Der Südostdeutsche*, which called into question the evidence put forward at the trial, set out to challenge 'the myth of the recent past' and denied the existence of gas chambers.¹¹⁶ The contrast with the reaction to the trial among Bukovinian Jews could not have been greater. Since the mid 1950s, *Die Stimme* focused almost exclusively on the issue of retribution and reparations for Nazi crimes, from which Bukovinian Jews were long excluded. This quest for compensation and recognition of their suffering and, by the same token, for the recognition of German collective guilt was of extreme importance to them. The editors of *Die Stimme* followed the unfolding of the Eichmann trial and antisemitic reactions to it in Germany closely.¹¹⁷ The perspectives of German and Jewish Bukovinians were truly incompatible: Bukovinian Germans sought exculpation, and Bukovinian Jews sought an apology for what was ultimately the same crime. The election of Willy Brandt in 1969 further confirmed the opposite political positions adopted by the two newspapers and their editors. While *Die Stimme* celebrated Brandt's election as the symbol of a new Germany, the editors of *Der Südostdeutsche* saw in Brandt the face of what was known as 'renunciation' (*Verzicht*) – the abandonment of revisionism – and a national disgrace.

Such stances towards the past undoubtedly led some Bukovinian Germans to distance themselves from their representative organizations. As Pertti Ahonen has argued regarding West German expellee organizations in general, much of the elite came across to many West Germans and potential members as fanatics.¹¹⁸ In the 1960s, the term *Heimat*, associated with the expellee lobby in West Germany, started to acquire negative connotations. At this time, the Landsmannschaften in West Germany experienced significant losses, especially among members of the younger generations.¹¹⁹ In Israel too, if the Eichmann trial raised the status of witnesses, it also heightened many Israelis' wish to get on with their lives and leave the past behind them. The attitude towards the Diaspora, particularly its German-speaking incarnation, remained highly ambivalent.¹²⁰ But the marginalization of the topic of the former homes in both societies also meant that the communities and their active members maintained their monopoly over representations of the region and were hardly challenged. The few first-hand accounts of Bukovinians, which were not written by or for the purpose of the

Landsmannschaften, substantiate this claim and provide further evidence of the extent of these organizations' influence on the discourse of their members and beyond.[121] Indeed, these narratives highlight the existence of a significant gap, not only between the leaderships and constituencies of the two groups, but also between the perceptions and beliefs of German and Jewish Bukovinians who were not members of these organizations and perhaps even between many non-Jewish Germans and Jews in general. Contact or friendship between German and Jewish Bukovinians, as the exchange of letters between Drozdowski and Gong quoted at the start of this chapter suggests, were rare, emotionally charged and regarded as exceptional.[122]

The Framework of Material Compensation

Bukovinians' contrasting visions of Bukovina not only corresponded to different understandings of what Bukovina had been but also of community and belonging. With the issue of reparations, therefore, the consequences of this opposition became very real and tangible. Indeed, according to postwar West German legislation, both Bukovinian Germans and Bukovinian Jews were entitled to claim reparations for the damages they sustained during the war – as 'expellees' and as 'victims of the Nazis', respectively. As such, these were two separate procedures. But as scholars have argued, the issue of reparations encouraged contact between the societies of 'the perpetrators' and of 'the victims', not least because the former decided on the parameters of restitution.[123] Moreover, in both cases, the assessment of the losses depended not only on a specific interpretation of the circumstances under which they had suffered, but also on specific understandings of both the region's and the claimants' identity. In other words, indemnification relied on an understanding of 'what had existed', 'what had happened' and 'who was a German'. In this context, therefore, Bukovinian Germans' and Bukovinian Jews' differing conceptions of community became extremely important, and the issue even brought members of the two communities into direct contact and conflict.

If it had not been for the question of material compensation, the contrasting visions of Bukovinian Germans and Bukovinian Jews might not have been confronted directly in this period. Yet, while this was an area of confrontation, it also became a field of negotiation and helps explain how their positions could evolve. Indeed, the issue of compensation helped change come about insofar as it became a crucial arena of arbitration of the categories of belonging. In this sense, it was fundamental to recasting Bukovinian and broader German and Jewish identities after the Second World War: just like judicial procedures in postwar West Germany in general, it induced new knowledge and approaches to the recent past. Both the shortcomings of the reparations policy and the paradigm shift of the mid 1960s have been widely noted.[124] As Constantin Goschler has argued, whereas the 1950s and 1960s were characterized by an 'integrationist discourse' for the victims of the war and the Holocaust, the 1970s were marked by increasing differentiation among victims.[125] According to Jannis Panagiotidis, 1965 marked the beginning of a transformation period.[126] As he argues, from this perspective, 'the post-1965 development ... can be interpreted as a process of progressing entanglement within a common international context'.[127] This was also the year in which the FRG took up diplomatic relations with Israel. The case of Bukovinians substantiates these claims, giving further privileged insight into the nature of the debate and what heralded the change of political and cultural attitudes, as well as rare insight into the perspective of the victims.[128]

The efforts for compensation of Bukovinian Jews and Bukovinian Germans were the result of two different sets of legislation: the 1953 Equalisation of Burdens Act (Lastenausgleichsgesetz – LAG) for the 'war-damaged', including 'expellees' (*Vertriebene*), and the Federal Law on Restitution to the Victims of National Socialist Persecution (Bundesentschädigungsgesetz – BEG – more widely known as Wiedergutmachung) for the victims of National Socialist persecution, which followed three years later in 1956. While both sets of legislation in some sense reflected West Germany's adoption of the role of 'successor to the Nazi regime', the implications and rationale for the two laws could not have been more different. The first was related to the consequences of military defeat and a conception of 'Germans as victims'. The LAG claimants were encouraged to present the image of innocent and deserving victims, and therefore to produce exculpatory accounts and shirk responsibility for the past. This law was mainly perceived as a domestic matter and treated as a West German 'solidarity tax'.[129] The second, in contrast, was linked to a conception of 'Germans as perpetrators' and appealed to a German collective responsibility of a very different kind – namely, collective guilt for the past. In other words, the LAG and the BEG had conflicting aims: the first compensated 'Germans as victims', while the second compensated the 'victims of the Germans'.

Yet, this distinction between 'Germans as victims' and 'victims of the Germans' was not as easy to establish in practice as it was in theory. On the one hand, the fact that the legislation for each developed in response to the other demonstrates that the two kinds of victims were perceived to be in competition with one another. But, on the other hand, the wider postwar West German political culture with its 'politics of the past' (an awkward combination, as Norbert Frei has argued, of apology and amnesty),[130] the politics of identity and integration outlined in the previous chapters and the contrasting visions of the communities outlined above all contributed to blurring the distinction. As Goschler has argued, technically the rehabilitation of the victims and the punishment of the perpetrators should have gone together.¹³¹ But in the context of the 1950s, most Germans felt that the war of annihilation had been an injustice done unto the German people.¹³² Besides, if anything, many conceived of these reparations as a means of achieving distance from the past. In practice, there was a fundamental misunderstanding between the Germans who believed that the payments would reduce their share of guilt and the Jews who felt that the two should not be conflated.¹³³ Indeed, initially at least, reparations to the victims were seen 'less [as] a moral obligation than an onerous burden'.¹³⁴ Moreover, as the fact that they were exclusively for Jewish victims of the Nazis indicates, reparations were primarily construed as a foreign policy matter, essential to achieving the recovery of West Germany's international image.¹³⁵ In this sense, as others have argued, reparations can be said to have served less the rehabilitation of the victims than that of the perpetrators.¹³⁶

The complexity of making this distinction was also the result of the difficulty of turning a moral wrong into material compensation within a pragmatic political framework.¹³⁷ While there was obviously a gap between the framework of a past crime and the framework needed to deal with present claims, there was nevertheless a risk of applying the same principles that had led to the injustice in the first place in order to vindicate the wrongdoing.¹³⁸ To avoid this, an overlap between the different categories of victims was inadvertently embedded in the legislation – a conundrum later revealed in legal practice. Indeed, since both laws were conceived of as inner-German legislation, in both cases not only the experience but also the ethnic and territorial belonging of the claimants was taken into account (§141 of the BEG and §11 of the LAG).¹³⁹ In other words, a basic concept of the BEG (and obviously the LAG too) was that only 'Germans' should receive restitution.¹⁴⁰ This had two somewhat curious and unforeseen consequences. First, this meant that German-speaking victims were in a better position to claim reparations and that, as others have shown, victims claiming compensation were often required to demonstrate closeness to the culture of their tormentors.¹⁴¹ Second, since in both cases conceptions of victimhood and ethnicity played a role, there was significant terminological overlap (for instance, between 'expellee' (LAG) and 'expellee persecutee' (BEG)). There was therefore also potential for BEG claimants to feel that they were also entitled to claim via the LAG.

Indeed, although after the Second World War 'expellee' had rapidly become a synonym for 'ethnic German expelled from Eastern Europe', from a legal point of view, 'expulsion' and 'expellee' had relatively broad definitions.¹⁴² First came a territorial reference – namely, originating in 'areas of expulsion' (*Vertreibungsgebiete*). These included all areas that had belonged to the German Reich or the Austro-Hungarian monarchy as of January 1914 or later to Poland, Estonia, Latvia and Lithuania, and to the Soviet

Union, Czechoslovakia, Hungary, Romania, Bulgaria, Yugoslavia, Albania and China – that is, most communist states. Then, a number of points explained what *Vertreibung* (lit.: 'expulsion' or 'driving out') was supposed to mean. These conditions included the forced relocations approved at Potsdam, as well as 'resettlement' (*Umsiedlung*) beforehand. However, it also referred to 'flight' – a rather vague idea – reflecting a concern not to exclude individuals who had left Germany after the Nazis had come to power. The first point thus included those who had left after 30 January 1933 'as a result of political opposition to National Socialism or because they were subject to or threatened by National Socialist persecution on the grounds of race, faith or beliefs', and the victims of National Socialism were thereby included in the official definition of 'expellee'. This created what has been described as a 'legal fiction', opening the door to applications for compensation on behalf of so-called 'fictive expellees' who had in fact been victims of the Nazis.[143] Although being both a victim of Nazism and of the expulsions was quasi-impossible, the legislation made this legally feasible and hence created the categories of 'Jewish expellee' and 'Jewish ethnic German migrant' (*jüdische Aussiedler*).

In turn, the 'ethnocultural' dimension of the definition of 'expellee' was left open to interpretation. Created in the context of the need to integrate millions of ethnic Germans – many of whom had never been German citizens – into Germany after the war, it was intended as a synonym of the Nazi concept of *Volksdeutscher*. However, due to the concept's well-known 'overtones of blood and race', the definition of *Volkszugehörigkeit* used after the war and included in §116a of the Basic Law (Grundgesetz) did not make this as clear as this suggests.[144] Paragraph number 6 of the Federal Law on Expellees (Bundesvertriebnengesetz (BVFG)) explained: 'From a legal perspective, a German member of the people is someone who commits themselves [lit. "confesses" (*sich bekennen*)] to "German culture" [*Volkstum*] insofar as this commitment is confirmed by markers such as descent, language, education and culture.'[145] However, as it would not have been reasonable to require victims of the Nazis to display 'a commitment to German culture', the ethnocultural dimension had two permutations. While the LAG relied on the concept of *Volkszugehörigkeit* ('ethnic belonging', 'ethnic nationality' or literally 'membership to the people'),[146] the BEG relied on the slightly different notion of belonging to the *deutscher Sprach- und Kulturkreis* (German linguistic and cultural sphere; hereinafter DSK). The BEG stated that 'an explicit commitment to German culture is not a condition for belonging to the German linguistic and cultural sphere'. This condition was different from the LAG, which required 'the explicit commitment'. The distinction was therefore a matter of objective and subjective disposition or, in other words, a matter of active practice and performance of Germanness versus a passive claim to Germanness.

Of course, the fluidity of these terms was at odds with the rigidity with which the law was implemented in practice. This rigidity had several causes, and the case of Bukovina offers a unique illustration of the problems. The first was the reluctance and pusillanimity with which the question of reparations for the victims of National Socialism was approached in general.[147] Indeed, if these definitions were the basis on which millions of expellees, including Bukovinian Germans, almost immediately benefited from generous LAG compensation, they were used to reject outright the claims of thousands of 'non-German persecutees', including many Bukovinian Jews. The second, however, was the persistence of narrow and exclusive understandings of German culture and belonging. Since the existence of Bukovinian Germans as a group was acknowledged, there could be no doubt that Bukovina was indeed a *Vertreibungsgebiet*, an 'area of expulsion', but some other elements meant that Bukovinian Jews were considered 'doubtful cases' (*Zweifelsfälle*) and thus subject to deliberation. This included whether Bukovinian Jews had been 'expelled' from their homeland (or left voluntarily), whether West Germany could be held accountable for the persecution of Bukovinian Jews at all, since it had happened at the hands of the Romanians, and, last but not least, their Germanness – whether they belonged to the 'German linguistic and cultural sphere' (DSK) and later, for those who applied for compensation via the LAG, to the 'German people' (*deutsche Volkszugehörigkeit*).

Not only did compensation laws include a range of conditions, for example, concerning residency and deadlines, but they were also subject to different interpretations, which led to continuous additions and amendments. As Jannis Panagiotidis, for example, explains:

> In theory, being 'of the Mosaic faith' did not prejudice or preclude belonging to German culture [*Volkstum*]. Yet a 1958 commentary to the Federal Expellee Law added a restrictive condition: 'Those Jews cannot be considered German Volkszugehörige who belonged to a separate minority which existed alongside the German minority (like, for example, in Galicia and Romania).'[148]

The result was that although after 1962, Bukovinian Jews could claim compensation for imprisonment (*Freiheitsentzug*), they could still not claim for damage to their life, work and health like other Jewish victims, let alone for lost property and goods, something that was not covered by the BEG. Only in 1966, after a decade-long battle, was a wholesale territorial principle introduced by which Bukovina obtained the status of 'linguistic island' (*Sprachinsel*) for the purposes of the BEG, and applicants' requirement to prove their belonging to the DSK on a case-by-case basis lifted. Not until 1970 was the reference to belonging to the German *Volk* removed from conditions to qualify as an expellee for the purposes of the LAG.[149] As for the question of responsibility, only in 1965 (§43 of the 1965 BEG-Schlussgesetz (Final Act)) was the law amended to state that from the spring of 1941 onwards, racist measures in the states of Bulgaria, Romania and Hungary had been implemented under German influence (*Zeitpunkt für den Beginn der deutschen Veranlassung*).[150] Therefore, only from then on were Jews who had been subject to persecution in these countries after April 1941 theoretically entitled to make a claim to the German authorities and benefit from German reparations.

Contesting Germanness

In time, compensation claims thus became the object of vivid and ongoing contests. A triangular relationship developed between the Jewish claimants (backed by their lawyers and representatives of the community, and later the Claims Conference, the United Restitution Organization (URO) and staff of the Israeli Ministry of Finance), the West German compensation authorities and members of the informal 'Homeland Information Bureau for Romania' (Heimatauskunftstelle Rumänien; hereinafter HASt) – an advisory body composed of members of the Bukovinian German Landsmannschaft. Indeed, in 1953, when the HASt had been created, its purpose had been to check the authenticity and veracity of LAG applications with regard to the extent of material losses of individual ethnic German expellees living in West Germany. However, over the course of the late 1950s and 1960s, they were increasingly called upon to take a position on the background and credentials of people seeking to emigrate from Romania as 'ethnic Germans' (*Aussiedler*) and thereby making a claim to the status of 'expellee', as well as Jews claiming compensation as Germans or as expellees. Bukovinian Jews' battle for justice and compensation, which had been ongoing since the end of the Second World War, became, during the 1950s and 1960s, a dispute between Bukovinian Germans and Bukovinian Jews.

The HASt's members' main task was to issue advisory statements, based on whether they knew the applicant or not and their evaluation of the validity of the information provided, as to the latter's *Volkszugehörigkeit* ('ethnic belonging') and *Vertriebeneneigenschaft* ('expellee status'). However, for them, the situation was clear: Hitler had resettled the region's Germans in 1940 and, echoing the logic of the Nazis at the time, those who had not been resettled were therefore not German. Besides, an expellee was an ethnic German and an ethnic German was a Christian. Apart from in some very rare cases, they did not regard Bukovinian Jews as belonging to the same cultural realm, let alone as entitled to the status of 'expellee of the homeland'.[151] As they reiterated in the affidavits they wrote for the compensation authorities, 'the German group [in Bukovina] had nothing in common with the Jewish group, whether in the folkloric, cultural or political sense. Therefore, there were in Romania no German Jews but, rather, Jews residing in Romania'.[152] In essence, they equated Germanness with belonging to a reified and exclusive ethnic community reminiscent of the National Socialist 'people's community' (*Volksgemeinschaft*). Furthermore, despite the delivery of over fifty judgments regarding German participation in the persecution of the Jews of Romania and Bukovina in West Germany between 1954 and 1970,[153] they insisted that the Germans and Nazi Germany had no influence over the fate of these people insofar as Romania had been a sovereign state during the war with its own policy towards Jews.[154] There was therefore a fundamental discrepancy between the views of Bukovinian Jews who submitted the claims and those called on to evaluate their applications.

The reports exchanged between the then director of the HASt for Romania, the Transylvanian Saxon Erhard Plesch, and a lawyer employed by the Jewish Bukovinians, Dr I.D. Evian, in 1957 give insight into these split, respective perspectives on the issue of Jewish compensation.[155] The areas of disagreement concerned German responsibility in Bukovina (or rather the lack thereof), the character of Bukovinian Jews' displacement (whether it constituted expulsion) and finally the question of their Germanness.

Evian emphatically insisted on the necessity and righteousness of the recognition of Bukovinian Jews as expellees by emphasizing their Germanness, their suffering at the hands of both the Romanians *and* the Germans, and their unique contribution to the Germanness of the region as members of the urban and educated middle class. He even argued that their displacement was caused 'by the confiscation of the German-European cultural spirit and their determination to chase after it'.[156] Yet, Plesch countered every single one of these arguments in turn. He made the point that Romanian antisemitism had deep roots that bore no relation to Nazism. He also argued that the fact that Jews had been allowed to leave Romania for Israel after the war not only proved they had not been 'expelled', but also that they were not German, since ethnic Germans were not allowed to leave Romania in this period. His main argument concerned the fact that Jews had constituted a 'national minority' in their own right in Bukovina. According to him, despite their widespread proficiency in German as their 'language of everyday use' (*Umgangssprache*), their native language was the Yiddish 'jargon'.[157]

Finally, drawing on a mixture of philosemitic and antisemitic arguments, Plesch retorted that: 'The existence of a Jewish culture, a culture a few millennia older than the German one, which was consciously cultivated, both massively by those speaking jargon or by the smaller percentage of the German-speakers, is not mentioned. If it manifested itself religiously during the liberal Austrian period, the Jews became a nation around the turn of the century.'[158] From his perspective, therefore, only a tiny fraction of Bukovinian Jews could be considered German – namely, those who had converted, intermarried or were members of ethnic German institutions or German fraternities. He also argued that the town's 17,000 ethnic Germans had been the cornerstone of Czernowitz/Cernăuți's German character. On this basis, Plesch underscored his duty to take a position as representative of the expellee organizations and oppose the application of Bukovinian Jews as expellees both on the basis of the BEG and the LAG.[159]

This argumentation did not settle the dispute. Both sides proceeded in mobilizing further historical sources and arguments for their purposes and sending these to the compensation authorities as evidence. The Jews quoted the former German envoy in Cernăuți, the Consul General Fritz Schellhorn (a figure many Bukovinian Germans admired), who had argued in a report dating from 1937 that 'cultural life [in Cernăuți] was completely dominated by the Jews' and that the city 'would never have maintained the character of a German town without the Jews'.[160] The Germans, in turn, pointed to the census of 1930, when the vast majority of the Jews had declared that Yiddish was their mother tongue rather than German. However, Bukovinian Jews countered this with an appeal from the Zionist *Ostjüdische Zeitung* dating from 24 December 1930, calling on the Jews to declare Yiddish as their mother tongue for the sake of Jewish representation in the face of growing Romanization.[161] Besides, they drew attention to the census of 1910, when 70% of Jews had declared that their mother tongue was German and stressed that they had not had Yiddish schools and had rejected assimilation to Romania.[162]

Finally, Bukovinian Jews pointed out that their 'belonging to the German linguistic and cultural sphere' was not only something of the past. In 1962, some of the applicants' lawyers forwarded to Plesch an invitation in German to the Hebronia student organization summer party and emphasized that it was not taking place in Vienna in 1913 but in Tel Aviv in 1960.[163] In April 1965, members of the Landsmannschaft of Bukovinian Jews wrote a seven-page letter to the district representative in Cologne, in which they stated:

> Today we have a large Bukovinian Landsmannschaft in Israel and we have Bukovinian Landsmannschaften in New York, Montreal, in Sao Paulo, Buenos Aires and Santiago, in Sydney and Melbourne and many other parts of the world. Everywhere they have brought their German linguistic and cultural sphere with them. At the social events of all the Landsmannschaften, presentations and speeches are given in German, the protocols of the meetings of these organizations are carried out in German, and it is certainly not a superficial sign of our belonging if we point out that still today – a quarter of a century after 1940 – there is a central instrument of Bukovinian organizations that is published in German, the newspaper *Die Stimme*, which appears in Tel Aviv and cannot be unknown to you.[164]

They concluded that 'German language and culture had no role to play in the crimes of the Third Reich against our people'. Nonetheless, there could hardly be any better evidence of a genuine 'commitment to Germanness' than Jews who continued to use German despite and after what they had been through.¹⁶⁵

Eventually, the authorities decided to call upon the expertise of historians and a series of reports (*Gutachten*) were requested from the Institute for Contemporary History (Institut für Zeitgeschichte – IfZ) in Munich. The question of German responsibility for Bukovinian Jews' 'expulsion' was settled in 1958, at least for northern Bukovina. Nazi Germany was said to have exerted considerable influence on Romania, and the imposition of the yellow star was to be considered a '*Vertreibungsmaßnahme*' (a measure amounting to expulsion). Further, the report read that:

> It must, therefore, be said that the Third Reich bears a general co-responsibility for the Romanian policy towards Jews in the years 1940–44 because it was a stronger power [*überlegene Großmacht*] and did not limit itself to exploiting the political, military and economic potential of its subordinate allies but also *authoritatively* elevated the persecution and excision of the Jews into a central feature of the European new order and used it as a measure of Romanian loyalty and allegiance.¹⁶⁶

According to the historians, then, the German state shared the responsibility for the persecution of northern Bukovinian Jews.

A second report, dating from 1963 and written by the later Director of the IfZ, Martin Broszat, and entitled 'The National Cultural and National Political Character and Development of the Bukovinian Jewry before 1933', tackled the issue of the Germanness of Bukovinian Jews.¹⁶⁷ Broszat set out to establish whether the concept of *Volkszugehörigkeit* as defined in §6 of the BVFG could be applied to the German-speaking Jewry in Bukovina. In other words, he debated the existence of a separate Jewish national minority in Bukovina and the degree and prevalence of Jewish assimilation to German culture in the region. In this paper, he acknowledged the specific historical conditions under which the census of 1930 had taken place and recognized the historical contingency of the notions of *Volkstum* and *Kulturkreis*, as well as the arbitrariness of their definitions. However, he nevertheless adopted a very narrow stance. He argued that the DSK could only be applied to around 60% of Jewish Bukovinians. With this, he meant those of the older generation, born before 1910, who had been less exposed to Zionism and Bundism and had been educated in German. With regard to actual 'belonging to the German people' or German 'ethnic nationality' (*Volkszugehörigkeit*), he considered that only about 620 of those who had not declared Yiddish as their mother tongue in the census of 1930 – namely, around 5% of the Bukovinian Jewry – could be included in this category.

Therefore, Broszat's report did not resolve the issue either. For one thing, it was interpreted differently by the two sides: the HASt focused on the narrow definition of ethnic belonging and continued to underscore the validity of the census of 1930.[168] From their perspective, Broszat had endorsed their view, as he had stated that, any 'Jewish, German *Volkszugehörige*' would have been known to members of the German minority. The Jews, in turn, highlighted the fact that Broszat had ascribed the majority of the Jews of Bukovina to the DSK, refusing to acknowledge the difference between this and 'ethnic nationality'. But, in effect, Broszat's conclusions perpetuated the distinction between the conditions for the BEG and the conditions for the BVFG or the LAG, namely, that a passive 'belonging to the DSK' fell short of an active 'commitment to German culture'. Indeed, although Broszat spoke of a *Deutschtum jüdischer Provenienz* ('German people of Jewish extraction') in the region, he maintained the distinction between the 'claim to' and the 'practice of' Germanness.

This reasoning did not prevent 'doubtful cases' from multiplying and from the early to mid 1960s onwards, they grew exponentially. An ever-larger number of Bukovinian Jews started claiming compensation for their property and material losses (*Hausratsentschädigung*) that were not covered by the BEG in its version for 'foreign Jews', by claiming via the LAG as 'expellees' (*Vertriebene*) and therefore German *Volkszugehörige*. Since the forms were not even designed for their purposes, the result was often incongruous. Applicants were, for example, required to choose from three kinds of damage: 'East damage', 'war damage' or 'expulsion damage' (i.e. flight, eviction or resettlement), but not from 'National Socialist persecution' or 'deportation'. Everything in the form revolved around a non-Jewish, German experience of the war. Applicants were, for instance, asked to provide their address as of December 1944 or the date of their resettlement (*Zeitpunkt der Umsiedlung*). The implication was that the suffering had been at the hands of the Soviets in the midst of the Wehrmacht's retreat. Reflecting the confusion, one Jewish applicant wrote in his affidavit: 'My claim results from damage caused by National Socialist persecution …', before crossing out the word 'National' so that all that remained was 'Socialist persecution'.[169] In general, Jews' explanations concerning persecution – expropriation, ghettoization, deportation – often fitted awkwardly in the spaces available. Capturing understandable exasperation, one applicant completed the section introduced with the words 'The damage occurred through …' with the statement 'complete abandonment with deportation' (*durch im Stiche gelassen bei der Deportation*).[170] This practical hindrance only added to the absurd character of the entire procedure.

Enhancing the Kafkaesque character of the scenario was that stakeholders with antagonistic views and goals were involved in the process of deliberation. Until the introduction of the territorial principle, the applications of Bukovinian Jews were considered on an individual basis. It was up to the Israeli authorities (up until 1965, the Ministry of Finance) processing the claims to take a position as to applicants' 'expellee status' and cultural belonging. As José Brunner and Iris Nachum, who analysed these sources, argue, the Israelis assumed that anyone whose mother tongue was German belonged to the 'German cultural sphere'. A language test was therefore deemed sufficient. And since, from their perspective, an applicant could belong to several 'cultural spheres' at once, they approved and forwarded most of the applications.[171] But the final decision rested with regional West German authorities (the regional Ausgleichsamt or the Amt für Wiedergutmachung). Not only did the positions and decisions vary across regional offices, but they also tended to adopt a more exclusive and monolithic understanding of culture: 'the belonging to the German linguistic and cultural sphere prevented the connection to another people'.[172] As such, for these authorities, proficiency in German was not enough and belonging to another culture acted as a disqualification.

Another similar misunderstanding underlay Jewish applications to the LAG. If, from the perspective of German lawmakers, the distinction between belonging to the DSK and *Volkszugehörigkeit* was key to differentiating between claims via the BEG and the LAG, it was largely lost on Jewish applicants, as evidenced by the fact that some would write 'belonging to the German linguistic sphere' in response to *Volkszugehörigkeit* on the form.[173] Moreover, many supported their claim to the status of 'expellee', not with a number from a *Vertriebenenausweis* (expellee identification card) as expected, but with the file number of their previously successful claim for damage to their person filed under the BEG. They also justified their claim to 'ethnic nationality' in a similar way as they had previously justified their belonging to the DSK: speaking German at home, regularly reading in German or attending a German-language school. However, for the authorities, this was not sufficient: 'Ethnic nationality' required 'full assimilation' and 'speaking German' was regarded as 'neutral from an ethnic standpoint' (*volkstumsneutral*). Yet, the subjective and performative dimensions of *Volkszugehörigkeit* were difficult to establish for the authorities too. Witnesses were called upon, but the criteria they used varied significantly. In some cases, it was a matter of 'spending time in German company'; in others, of having 'shared with a third party the will to belong exclusively to the German people and be treated as a German';[174] in others still, it required 'marriage with a German' or 'study at a university in Germany, Austria or Prague'.[175] Ultimately, however, both the DSK and *Volkszugehörigkeit* relied on the same objective criteria: language, culture, sphere and belonging. The Israeli authorities thus continued, as with the DSK, to consider belonging to multiple ethnicities as possible. For this reason, the contentious cases accumulated, and the debates continued.

From the perspective of Bukovinian Germans – and not only them – Bukovinian Jews and others were knowingly committing fraud and distorting the past for this purpose. In 1969, following the publication of a positive review of Hugo Gold's book in the *Frankfurter Allgemeine Zeitung* (FAZ), none other than the man the Jews so eagerly quoted as a reference for their Germanness, the former German Consul General in Romania Fritz Schellhorn, publicly accused Bukovinian Jews of hypocrisy and opportunism for claiming to be Zionists and members of the German cultural sphere at the same time, and for trying to make Germany look responsible or complicit in their persecution for the sake of financial compensation.[176] Some Jews might indeed have put in false or exaggerated claims. Some, for instance, claimed to have belonged to the Jahn sports organization despite the fact that this was highly unlikely and could be confidently refuted by the Bukovinian Germans.[177] Some also tried to join the German Landsmannschaft for the sake of compensation.[178] But the framework of the law itself was confusing and flawed. In turn, the fact that members of the Bukovinian German Landsmannschaft lobbied for years for the rights of Bukovinian Germans who were Austrian citizens to claim compensation in West Germany via the LAG proves that their opposition to Jewish compensation had nothing to do with the financial burden this may have constituted.[179] The principled rejection of Jewish claims was primarily a rejection of responsibility for the war and the Jewish persecution.

Over time, a link was established between recognizing Jewish Germanness, taking responsibility for the past and accepting the verdict of collective guilt. This development came across in the speech given by Rudolf Wagner at the West German national meeting (*Bundestreffen*) of Bukovinian Germans in June 1969. Entitled 'Bukovina: Land of Encounter between Different Cultures and Religions', the speech mentioned Bukovina's Jews, though Wagner kept them until last because, as he explained, 'they were not Christians'. Wagner acknowledged the contribution of the Jews to the region's German culture, but he insisted, echoing Prokopowitsch's thesis, that they had distanced themselves with Zionism. In this sense, 'the National Socialist excesses in Germany in the Romanian period had only caused an acceleration [of the process of separation] but not the fact in itself'. The fact that this 'acceleration' had not constituted a mere cultural gap or distance, but culminated in genocide was conveniently elided, if nevertheless implicit. Indeed, to illustrate his point, Wagner added that the death of the singer Josef Schmidt (a famous Jewish opera singer from Bukovina who died in a refugee camp in Switzerland in 1942) was 'deplorable', but 'it [could] not be put on Bukovinian Germans' tab'. Viewed in such a narrow way, responsibility could indeed be evaded. He concluded: 'The German-Jewish symbiosis became history because it already no longer existed in that location.'[180] While this was all but a concession, it reflected both how the process of reparation and reckoning was understood, and the growing sense of self-consciousness and need for justification among many non-Jewish West Germans.

For Bukovinian Jews, the process of demanding compensation was transformative too. The length and character of the procedure was a source of outrage, disappointment and dismay. Some believed that Germany was hoping for a so-called biological solution to the problem, as people often died before their claims were settled. As some scholars have argued, this whole process may also have been a source of retraumatization.[181] The case of Bukovinians certainly resonates with Ralph Giordano's concept of 'second guilt' and Regula Ludi's argument that the errors of compensation had, if inadvertently, magnified the wrongs.[182] To many Bukovinian Jews, the process was at the very least humiliating and, later, many said they had never submitted claims for this very reason. As Meier Teich stated in his 1961 book on compensation, in which he pleaded for a revision of the Luxemburg Agreement, 'we stand as beggars at the door of the Germans'.[183] Similarly, in a memorandum sent to the Office of the Chancellery in the 1960s, Elias Weinstein, at the time the head of the Association of Jewish Immigrants from Bukovina in Israel, argued that 'there is no legal, moral or financial reason to treat us differently to any of the other persecuted groups. On the contrary: the collective judgement presents an unfathomable wrong'.[184] These feelings repeatedly found expression in *Die Stimme*, which was dominated by this topic throughout the 1960s. Experts attempted to make sense of the regulations, defined and redefined 'expellee', 'expulsion', 'DSK' and '*Volkstum*', and the conditions for making claims for the benefit of their readers. In the 1960s, a group of Jews from Eastern Europe even founded their own Landsmannschaft in West Germany in order to defend their rights.[185]

The process of compensation left an imprint in other ways too. In 1970, the author of a long cover article in *Die Stimme* entitled 'Life without a Homeland' ('Leben ohne Heimat') contested the use of the word 'immigrant' to describe the situation of Jews in Israel, since this suggested that their displacement had been voluntary and they were merely trying their luck elsewhere. On the contrary, they argued, they had been forced to leave and had been technically 'refugees' (*Flüchtlinge*) and 'expellees' (*Vertriebene*) even before they were expelled (*vor der Vertreibung*).[186] Not only was this quite different from the Zionist narrative of Israel as a land of immigrants and settlers, but it also showed how they adopted and appropriated West German terminology to rethink their situation. Moreover, with the centrality of the question of identity, the irony was, of course, that decades of protest had indeed reinforced Bukovinian Jews' 'commitment' to their Germanness. In effect, Bukovinian Jews came to think of themselves with ever more conviction as standing for the German humanist tradition versus the *völkisch* mentality associated with the figure of *Turnvater Jahn* and their opponents in the process. It strengthened their sense of distinction from Bukovinian Germans or other ethnic German migrants from Eastern Europe with their flawed German language skills.[187] As an article in *Die Stimme* in 1963 stated:

> Who went to the German theatre? The Germans from Rosch [a village outside of Czernowitz] – or the Jews of Czernowitz? To whom did the Romanian government forbid the use of German? … No serious German scholar or cultural expert would contest the belonging of even the less educated Bukovinian Jews to the German intellectual world. The whole truth must for once be told: with the exception of a ridiculous minority of Germans from the West who were 'sent' to Bukovina, the majority of the Germans in the province at best belonged to the linguistic sphere and, even then, not all of them, while the majority of the Jews belonged to the German linguistic *and* cultural sphere.[188]

The author then went on to quote Goethe, Hölderlin, Schoppenhauer and even Nietzsche, and to mention Buber, Rosenzweig and Einstein. In the 1960s, 1970s and 1980s, West Germany featured ever more prominently in *Die Stimme*. On some level, this was a watchful eye, but on another, it reflected an interest in 'the right kind of German', a search for a cultural home and a welcoming of West Germany's democratic development.

Starting in the 1960s, an increasing number of Bukovinian Jews emigrating from Romania also chose West Germany over Israel. While this certainly had to do with the Six-Day War, it also reflected a growing faith in Germany's democracy and the lessening taboo about Jewish immigration to this country.[189] This migration was made possible by the recognition of Jews as *Aussiedler* (ethnic German migrants), which derived from their classification as *Vertriebene* and *Volkszugehörige*, and therefore their recognition as part of the German people, governed by the same rules as compensation. In turn, these developments and their tangible consequences also forced non-Jewish Germans to reconsider their own 'identity politics'. As other historians have argued, German–Jewish–Israeli relations were a decade-long 'learning process' in which the issue of reparations was central.[190] It was only a matter of time before 'being the right kind of German' also meant defending the cause of Jewish claimants in Germany too. Therefore, with a substantial delay, change did occur. The guidelines the compensation authorities received in March 1980 stated that Judaism was a marker of faith rather than nationality, that Zionism should not be a criterion of exclusion and that one should be careful not to apply the 'National Socialist definition of culture and belonging in contemporary Germany'.[191] The same document also reminded the administration that the HASt merely had an advisory role and that a non-Christian name, immigration to Israel or non-participation in Hitler's 1940 resettlement did not constitute sufficient grounds to disqualify a claimant.

This clarification is indicative of both the recognition of the impossibility of defining Germanness in any definitive manner and of the growing sense of unease among Germans surrounding the use of an exclusive concept of Germanness for the implementation of compensation or immigration policies. Enacting such change was not easy. Indeed, as Günther Hockerts has argued:

> The legal figure of the 'damaged national' was judicially fuzzy and is historically questionable, because a particular cause of persecution, 'nationality', could hardly be separated from the racist or political context of the National Socialist regime of occupation in Eastern Europe.[192]

Yet, if the terms of the debate could not be altered, their use and interpretation, at least, could. By the mid 1980s, the absurdities of the compensation process were being publicly discussed.[193] In 1988, an article on the case of a Jewish *Aussiedler* in a major West German paper was not only remarkably empathetic, but also took the use of the notion of 'Jewish ethnic German' for granted.[194] In the same year, the Berlin Regional Authorities appealed to a professor of law from Darmstadt to advise on the case of a Romanian Jew asking to be recognized as an *Aussiedler* and hence a *Vertriebener*. As the professor put it in the conclusion to his advisory report, in the strict legal sense, being a German from Romania required sharing the typical fate of an ethnic German. Yet, he challenged the authorities, as he put it, 'in the interest of German culture and the German cultural nation' to tolerate this interpretation and to put it into practice.[195] This statement reflected the extent of the shift not so much in the law itself, but in the modalities and context of its enforcement.

Conclusion

During the Cold War, Bukovina became the object of both heightened idealization and increasingly virulent contestation. The self-understandings of Bukovinian Jews and Bukovinian Germans – as Jews, Germans and Bukovinians – derived from their attempts to construct belonging in their respective new homelands in the first decade after the war and resulted in highly ethnicized and exclusive visions of the region's past. Human losses featured ever less prominently in these accounts, and the focus was increasingly on the Habsburg and interwar periods, which they had in common. However, perceptions of what was lost, in either case, were very different.

For the Germans, it was a German-dominated Europe and national pride. For the Jews, in contrast, the loss was that of towns bustling with Jewish life, German-Jewish Central European culture and a Europe in which Jews had a place and a home. Not only were these different visions, but explaining how such 'losses' had occurred – and certainly compensating for them – made the acknowledgement of the other perspective virtually impossible. As Anthony Kauders has argued, while most Germans accepted criminal and individual guilt, they did not accept moral guilt.[196] And yet this dimension – the endurance of antisemitism in West German society at large – was precisely what Bukovinian Jews expected Germans in general and Bukovinian Germans in particular to acknowledge and 'make good'.

For a time, radically different visions of the region and the past coexisted with only sporadic interaction between the two groups. Yet, the antagonism was soon revealed and concretized within the framework of policies of material indemnification for the losses, damages and persecution incurred and experienced during the war. This process opposed representatives of Bukovinian Jews and Bukovinian Germans directly. In the beginning, West German legal practice reflected the narrow conceptions of Germanness and responsibility propagated by Bukovinian Germans after the Second World War. In particular, it equated German culture with German ethnicity. In turn, policies shaped mentalities by officially condoning a reading of history that was apologetic and discriminatory. Challenges to this attitude were linked to generational changes and were slow in coming. But the process of deliberation surrounding this issue also induced change and was transformative for all of those involved. If the Landsmannschaften became increasingly isolated and associated with their own interest groups, this episode nevertheless clarified their purpose and orientation. The focus of the Landsmannschaft in Israel became the defence of German-Jewishness in an ever more self-assured Israel. In turn, the radicalism of the rhetoric of the German Bukovinian Landsmannschaft decreased over time as the mood among the West German public grew increasingly self-conscious and contrite. Ultimately, both organizations moved away from politics and turned to culture.

Notes

1. Letter from Georg Drozdowski to Alfred Gong, 20 June 1964. The letter has been published in full in N. Shchyhlevska, *Verschränkungen: Leben und Werk von Autoren aus der Bukowina anhand von Briefen und Nachlässe* (Aachen: Rimbaud Verlag, 2011), 52–55.
2. Letter from Georg Drozdowski to Alfred Gong, 1 August 1964, published in Shchyhlevska. *Verschränkungen*, 56–58.

3. Shchyhlevska, *Verschränkungen*, 60, 64.
4. This was the Theodor-Körner-Preis; see ibid., 50.
5. This resonates with Andrew Demshuk's concept of 'Heimat of memory' as well as Florence Heymann's notion of Bukovina and Czernowitz as vanished, nonplaces for the Jews after the war. See A. Demshuk, *The Lost German East Forced Migration and the Politics of Memory, 1945–1970* (New York: Cambridge University Press, 2014); and F. Heymann, *Le Crépuscule des Lieux: Identités Juives de Czernowitz* (Paris: Stock, 2003).
6. E. Keightley and M. Pickering, *The Mnemonic Imagination: Remembering as Creative Practice* (Basingstoke: Palgrave Macmillan, 2012), 113.
7. See M. Meng, *Shattered Spaces: Encountering Jewish Ruins in Postwar Germany and Poland* (Cambridge, MA: Harvard University Press, 2011), 221; M. Hirsch and L. Spitzer, '"We Would Not Have Come without You": Generations of Nostalgia', in K. Hodgkin and S. Radstone (eds), *Contested Pasts: The Politics of Memory* (London: Routledge, 2014), 79–96, here 82.
8. See M. Kammen quoted in S. Boym, *The Future of Nostalgia* (New York: Basic Books, 2001), xiv. See also F. Davis, *Yearning for Yesterday: A Sociology of Nostalgia* (New York: Free Press, 1979).
9. See 'Kollektivschuldthese', in T. Fischer and M.N. Lorenz (eds), *Lexikon der 'Vergangenheitsbewältigung' in Deutschland: Debatten- und Diskursgeschichte des Nationalsozialismus nach 1945* (Bielefeld: Transcript, 2015), 45–49. Most famously, the social psychologists Alexander and Margarete Mitscherlich spoke of Germans' 'inability to mourn': A. Mitscherlich and M. Mitscherlich, *Die Unfähigkeit zu trauern* (Munich: Piper, 1968). This is a contested thesis, but Aleida Assmann, for example, has argued that the period 1945–57 was characterized by 'communicative silencing' and a rejection of memory. See A. Assmann and U. Frevert, *Geschichtsvergessenheit Geschichtsversessenheit: Vom Umgang mit deutschen Vergangenheiten nach 1945* (Stuttgart: Deutsche Verlags-Anstalt), especially 143–44.
10. H. Süssner, 'Still Yearning for the Lost *Heimat*? Ethnic German Expellees and the Politics of Belonging', *German Politics and Society* 22(2) (2004), 1–26, here 7, 8.
11. N. Frei, *Adenauer's Germany and the Nazi Past: The Politics of Amnesty and Integration*, translated from German by J. Gold (New York: Columbia University Press, 2002), 311.
12. On this, see I. Zertal, *Israel's Holocaust and the Politics of Nationhood* (Cambridge: Cambridge University Press, 2011). See also Frei, *Adenauer's Germany*; and Frank Stern, who also argues that German–Jewish relations were a foreign policy factor: F. Stern, *The Whitewashing of the Yellow Badge: Antisemitism and Philosemitism in Postwar Germany* (Oxford: Pergamon Press, 1992), 334. On the relationship with each other, see D. Diner, *Rituelle Distanz: Israels deutsche Frage* (Munich: Deutsche Verlags-Anstalt, 2015); and J. Hestermann, *Inszenierte Versöhnung: Reisediplomatie und die deutsch-israelischen Beziehungen von 1957 bis 1984* (Frankfurt: Campus Verlag, 2016). Diplomatic relations between West Germany and Israel were officially established in 1965.
13. See e.g. 'Die alte Heimat: eine wahre Hölle – Reisende berichten über das Leben im heutigen volksdemokratischen Rumänien', in *Der Südostdeutsche*, August 1956, or the summary of a talk entitled 'Czernowitz heute', *Bukowina Bulletin* 4 (New York: Bucovinaer Cultural Society, March 1968); for the GDR, see A. Haupt, *Meine Reise in die alte Heimat: Erinnerungen* (Eichwalde: Raku Verlag, 2007). This resonates with the findings of Demshuk, *The Lost German East*, who develops the concept of 'the *Heimat* transformed'.
14. 'Zehn Jahre', *Die Stimme*, August 1954.

15. H. Prelitsch (ed.), *10 Jahre Landsmannschaft der Buchenlanddeutschen 1949–1959: Gründung, Werdegang und Jubiläum* (Munich: Landsmannschaft der Buchenlanddeutschen, 1959).
16. Rudolf Wagner described 'the pre-*Landsmannschaft* period' (*die vorlandsmannschaftliche Zeit*) as 'the hardest period in the life of German resettlers from Bukovina' since 1945; R. Wagner, 'Die vorlandsmannschaftliche Zeit', in Prelitsch, *10 Jahre Landsmannschaft*, 7–9.
17. P. Blaß, 'Vorwort', in C. Armbrüster, *Deutsch-Satulmare: Geschichte eines buchenländischen Pfälzerdorfes* (Karlsruhe: n.p., 1962).
18. 'Unsere Leser schreiben', *Die Stimme*, September–October 1961.
19. H. Sternberg, *Zur Geschichte der Juden in Czernowitz* (Tel Aviv: Olamenu, 1962).
20. F. Wiszbiowski, 'Foreword', in F. Wiszbiowski, *Radautz: die deutscheste Stadt des Buchenlandes* (Waiblingen: F. Wiszbiowski, 1966).
21. Wiszbiowski, *Radautz*, 306.
22. E. Massier (ed.), *Fratautz und die Fratautzer: Vom Werden und Vergehen einer deutschen Dorfgemeinschaft in der Bukowina* (Pleutersbach: n.p., 1957).
23. M. Rubinstein (Ben Saar), *Der jüdische Vatikan in Sadagora 1850–1950*, vol. 1: *Werdegang und Glanzzeit 1850–1914. Historische Notizen, Humoresken und Lieder* (Tel Aviv: Verlag Olamenu, 1955); vol. 2: *Auf den Trümmern des Vatikans 1914–1950: Invasionskalender, Humoresken, Lieder* (Tel Aviv: Verlag Olamenu, 1958), here vol. 1, 3.
24. The first volume dealt with the period 1850–1914 and the second volume with 1914–50. In Gold's case, the cutting date was 1939. See H. Gold (ed.), *Geschichte der Juden in der Bukowina: ein Sammelwerk*, 2 vols (Tel Aviv: Olamenu, 1958; 1962).
25. See e.g. 'Festkommers der "Hebroniah": Aus Anlass des 120. Semesters seit Gründung der Verbindung', *Die Stimme*, January 1961.
26. Rubinstein, *Vatikan*, vol. 2, 78.
27. Ibid., 79.
28. 'Nicht Vergessen!', in ibid., 90–91.
29. See, for instance, M. Rubinstein, 'Infiltrantenmörde und das Welt-Gewissen', in ibid., 88; Emma Ausländer, 'Der gelbe Stern', in ibid., 93.
30. See A. Wieviorka and I. Niborski, *Les Livres du Souvenir : Mémoriaux Juifs de Pologne* (Paris: Gallimard/Julliard, 1983), 171.
31. Dan Miron, quoted in ibid., 140.
32. Wieviorka and Niborski, *Les Livres du Souvenir*, 55.
33. See J. Faehndrich, *Eine endliche Geschichte: Die Heimatbücher der deutschen Vertriebenen* (Cologne: Böhlau Verlag, 2011), 40.
34. Ibid., 228.
35. H. Prelitsch, *Student in Czernowitz: Die Korporationen an der Czernowitzer Universität* (Munich: Landsmannschaft der Buchenlanddeutschen, 1961).
36. E. Massier, J. Talsky and B.C. Grigorowicz (eds), *Bukowina: Heimat von gestern* (Karlsruhe: Arbeitskreis Bukowina Heimatbuch, 1956), 316.
37. Ibid., 15.
38. Wiszbiowski, *Radautz*, 306.
39. J.C. Dressler, *Illischestie: Chronik der Bukowiner Landgemeinde* (Freilassing: Pannonia-Verlag, 1960), 553.
40. Dressler, *Illischestie*, 553.
41. Blaß, 'Vorwort'.
42. F. Lang, 'Vorwort', in F. Lang (ed.), *Buchenland: hundertfünfzig Jahre Deutschtum in der Bukowina* Lang (Munich: Verlag des Südostdeutschen Kulturwerks, 1961), 2.

43. Ibid., 2.
44. Assmann and Frevert, *Geschichtsvergessenheit Geschichtsversessenheit*, 140. Interestingly, this quote was used in the adverts for the book too. See e.g. *Der Südostdeutsche*, issue 2, October 1961.
45. On this, see H. Prelitsch, 'Student in Czernowitz. Die Korporationen an der Czernowitzer Universität', in Lang, *Buchenland*, 357–80.
46. Lang, *Buchenland*, 45–47, 512–13.
47. One of the few exceptions is J. Fisher, *Transnistria: The Forgotten Cemetery* (South Brunswick, NJ: T. Yosseloff, 1969). However, it is worth noting that this small book was published in the United States, in English, with a small print run.
48. On this, see Archiv der Akademie der Künste, Vorlass Edgar Hilsenrath, 790. See also 'Grauen im Ghetto', *Der Spiegel* no. 36, 1978.
49. Rezzori prided himself on being of mixed descent and was allegedly stateless for many years after the war. On this, see C. Spinei, *Über die Zentralität des Peripheren: Auf den Spuren von Gregor von Rezzori* (Berlin: Frank und Timme, 2011), especially 25–28.
50. An English translation appeared in 1962: G. von Rezzori, *Tales of Maghrebinia*, translated from German by C. Hutter (San Diego: Harcourt, Brace & World, 1962). It was reviewed in a major German daily: 'Ein Maghrebinier', *Die Zeit*, 16 April 1953. On the parodying, see A. Corbea-Hoişie, 'Gedächtnisort Maghrebinien: Eine Lesehypothese', in M. Csáki and P. Stachel (eds), *Die Verortung von Gedächtnis* (Vienna: Passagen Verlag, 2001), 151–62.
51. G. von Rezzori, *Oedipus siegt bei Stalingrad: Ein Kolportageroman* (Hamburg: Rowohlt, 1954). This book was also reviewed in *Die Zeit*: 'Oedipus siegt bei Stalingrad: Gregor von Rezzoris "Kolportageroman"', *Die Zeit*, 2 December 1954.
52. *Der Südostdeutsche*, issue 1, June 1955, also published in: F. Lang, 'Sprache und Literatur der Deutschen in der Bukowina', *Südostdeutsche Heimatblätter* 4 (1955), 192–219, here 217–18.
53. G. von Rezzori, *Ein Hermelin in Tschernopol: Ein maghrebinischer Roman* (Hamburg: Rowohlt, 1958).
54. 'Der Idiotenführer', *Der Spiegel* no. 1, 1959.
55. "Maghrebinien' und die Justiz', *Der Südostdeutsche*, issue 1, March 1959; 'Ist Tschernopol identisch mit Czernowitz?', *Die Stimme*, April 1959.
56. W. Zalozieckyi, 'So war Tschernopol', *Die Stimme*, June 1959 and *Der Südostdeutsche*, issue 2, August 1959.
57. *Der Südostdeutsche*, issue 1, March 1959; L. v. Semaka, 'Schmähen wir nicht die Welt von gestern!', *Die Stimme*, September 1959.
58. See *Die Stimme*, August 1959 and the review by Drozdowski, *Die Stimme*, October 1959.
59. 'Der "väterliche Freund": zwischen Gregor von Rezzori und Dr Wladimir Zalozieckyi', *Die Stimme*, August 1959.
60. W. Kiesler, 'Was erzählt Rezzori über Tschernopol?', *Die Stimme*, March 1959.
61. Rezzori was indeed famous for having once declared on West German TV that 'whatever you try to do with the German youth, its conscience remains to be found in mass graves' and thus led the show host to cut the programme short. 'Der Idiotenführer', *Der Spiegel* no. 1 (1959).
62. E. Beck, *Bukowina: Land zwischen Orient und Okzident* (Freilassing: Pannonia-Verlag, 1963).
63. See e.g. M. Hausleitner, *'Viel Mischmasch mitgenommen': Die Umsiedlungen aus der Bukowina 1940* (Berlin; Boston: Verlag Walter de Gruyter, 2018), especially 203–45.

64. Beck, *Bukowina*, 5.
65. Ibid., 16.
66. Ibid.
67. Ibid., 5.
68. Ibid., 30.
69. Ibid., 20.
70. Ibid., 22.
71. Ibid. Although it is not acknowledged as such, this is largely a quote from Karl Emil Franzos.
72. Ibid., 16.
73. Ibid., 47.
74. Ibid., 84.
75. Ibid., 98.
76. Ibid., 96.
77. Ibid., 96, 98.
78. 'Die Bukowina als historisches Vermächtnis – in deutscher Sicht', *Die Stimme*, July 1965.
79. Beck, *Bukowina*, 93
80. Ibid., 39.
81. While this may certainly be true, some of the photographs appear to have been taken by Willy Pragher, a photographer who travelled a great deal in Romania before, during and after the war. His photographs are held in the archives in Freiburg: https://www2.landesarchiv-bw.de/ofs21/olf/einfueh.php?bestand=20677#_1 (retrieved 20 September 2019).
82. E. Beck, *Bibliographie zur Landeskunde der Bukowina* (Munich: Verlag des Südostdeutschen Kulturwerkes, 1966). Turczynski later described it as 'multiculturalism in practice'. See 'Vorwort', in E. Beck (ed.), *Bibliographie zur Kultur und Landeskunde 1976–1990* (Wiesbaden: Harrassowitz, 1999–2003). The first volume in particular referenced very few works by Bukovinian Jews. It was nevertheless quite positively reviewed in *Die Stimme*. See 'Zur Landeskunde der Bukowina', *Die Stimme*, May 1967.
83. Beck, *Bukowina*, 18.
84. Ibid., 190.
85. See e.g. *Der Südostdeutsche*, issue 2, May 1963.
86. 'Die Presse urteilt über den Bildband "Bukowina"', *Der Südostdeutsche*, issue 2, November 1965; Reader Letter, *Der Südostdeutsche*, issue 2, March 1968.
87. On this, see P. Ahonen, 'The Impact of Distorted Memory: Historical Narratives and Expellee Integration in West Germany, 1945–1970', in R. Ohliger, K. Schönwälder and T. Triadafilopoulos (eds), *European Encounters: Migrants, Migration and European Societies since 1945* (London: Ashgate, 2003), 236–54.
88. Y.M. Bodemann, 'The Uncanny Clatter: The Holocaust in Germany before its Mass Commemoration', in D. Michman (ed.), *Remembering the Holocaust in Germany 1945–2000: German Strategies and Jewish Responses* (New York: Lang, 2002), 43–54, here 47.
89. Archiv des Bukowina-Instituts, Augsburg (hereinafter BI), Allg. Korrespondenz Bundesverband, 1975: Letter from Erich Beck to the *Landsmannschaft der Buchenlanddeutschen*, 28 June 1975.
90. Wiszbiowski, *Radautz*, 134.
91. Massier et al., *Bukowina: Heimat von gestern*, 249.
92. E. Prokopowitsch, *Die Entwicklung des Pressewesens in der Bukowina* (Vienna: n.p., 1962), 28.

93. Ibid., 40.
94. Ibid.
95. Ibid., 40–41.
96. On Poppenberger in relation to National Socialism, see *Der Tag* no. 819, 25 December 1934. Retrieved 20 September 2019 from http://dertag.forenworld.com/viewtopic.php?f=40&t=282. Poppenberger became the chief editor of the *Frankenpost*. On Skrehunetz, see M. Hausleitner, 'Die Geschichte der Bukowina in der ersten Hälfte des 20. Jahrhunderts aus der Sicht von Deutschen, Juden und Rumänen', in *Die Bukowina: historische und ethnokulturelle Studien* [Beiträge der IV. internationalen wissenschaftlichen Konferenz 'Kaindlische Lesungen'] (Chernivtsi: Selena Bukowina, 2007), 122–35, here 123.
97. See Hausleitner, '*Viel Mischmasch mitgenommen*', 56–57, 238.
98. This was a group around Fritz Valjavec; ibid., 238
99. BI, Allg. Korrespondenz Bundesverband, 1964: Letter from Rudolf Wagner to Erich Prokopowitsch, 29 May 1964. Prokopowitsch had contributed four articles to Franz Lang's *Buchenland* and was named as one of the people who worked on it (*Mitarbeiter*). See Lang, *Buchenland*, 527. He also published a book: E. Prokopowitsch, *Das Ende der österreichischen Herrschaft in der Bukowina* (Munich: Oldenbourg, 1959).
100. In the biographies of important figures, the years 1938–45 were simply omitted or evasively summarized. This was, for example, the case for biographies of Rudolf Wagner. See the contributions to the book published for his eightieth birthday: R. Wagner, A. Armbruster and P. Tiefenthaler (eds), *Vom Moldauwappen zum Doppeladler: Ausgewählte Beiträge zur Geschichte der Bukowina. Festgabe zu seinem 80. Geburtstag* (Munich: Hofmann Verlag, 1991). See also his obituary: 'Das Leben seiner Gemeinschaft prägend mitgestaltet – Nachruf', *Kaindl-Archiv* 53/54 (2003). His membership to the SS only became public knowledge in 2006 when journalists obtained his personal file from the German National Archives. On this, see H.M. Kloth and K. Wiegrefe, 'Unbequeme Wahrheiten', *Der Spiegel* no. 33, 2006, 46–48. See also Hausleitner, '*Viel Mischmasch mitgenommen*', 226.
101. S. Last, *Die Letzten Juden* (Rothenburg ob der Tauber: J.P. Peter, 1960); J. Klein-Haparash, *... der vor dem Löwen flieht* (Stuttgart: Deutscher Bücherbund, 1961). Perhaps less surprisingly, Leo Katz's 1944 novel *Totenjäger*, a Socialist antifascist account published in Mexico in 1944, was not acknowledged either. Republished as L. Katz, *Totenjäger* (Aachen: Rimbaud Verlag, 2005).
102. Last was occasionally mentioned in *Der Südostdeutsche* (see, for instance, issue 2, January 197 and issue 2, August 1971). A text by him was published in R. Wagner (ed.), *Alma Mater Francisco Josephina: Die deutschsprachige Nationalitäten-Universität in Czernowitz. Festschrift zum 100. Jahrestag ihrer Eröffnung 1875* (Munich: Verlag Hans Menschendörfer, 1979), 352–54. A long obituary of Klein-Haparash was published in *Der Südostdeutsche* in March 1971, and the editor, Bruno Skrehunetz, mentioned that he knew him from school.
103. Klein-Haparash was mentioned in a list of books about Bukovina in *Der Südostdeutsche*, issue 1, September 1965. Klein-Haparash's book was reviewed in *Der Spiegel* no. 40, September 27, 1961 and appeared in English (and French) in 1963: *He Who Flees the Lion*, translated from German by C. Winston and R. Winston (New York: Atheneum, 1963).
104. BI, Bibliothek des Bukowina-Instituts Augsburg: 'Bücherkatalog (der Landsmannschaft)', 1963. Another notable entry in the list was an account of 'resettlement' dating from 1942 and introduced by an SS general. Interestingly, the date of

publication did not feature in the list. See W. Lorenz, *Der Zug der Volksdeutschen aus Bessarabien und dem Nord-Buchenland* (Berlin: Volk und Reich Verlag, 1942).
105. BI, Allg. Korrespondenz Bundesverband 1965–66: Letter from Rudolf Wagner, Landsmannschaft der Buchenlanddeutschen to the Institut für politische Wissenschaft der Rheinisch-Westfälischen Technischen Hochschule, 27 October 1965.
106. BI, Allg. Korrespondenz Bundesverband, 1965: Letter from Otto Lachmund to C.J.N., 9 June 1965.
107. F. Lang, 'Sprache und Literatur der Deutschen in der Bukowina', in Lang, *Buchenland*, 428.
108. See 'Entwurf einer Landschaft', *Die Zeit* no. 5, 30 January 1958; *Der Spiegel*, issue 20, 11 May 1970.
109. *Der Südostdeutsche*, issue 2, March 1971.
110. See e.g. the publication of Drozdowski's letters: 'Georg Drozdowski antwortet', *Die Stimme*, July 1959.
111. Drozdowski was aware of the exceptional circumstance of him publishing in both papers. As he wrote in his second letter to Alfred Gong on 1 August 1964, they constituted 'two completely opposed papers': See Shchyhlevska, *Verschränkungen*, 57.
112. On Valjavec's network and links to Bukovinians, see Hausleitner, 'Viel Mischmasch mitgenommen', 236. On Valjavec's role in Cernăuţi in 1941, see A. Angrick, 'Power Games: The German Nationality Policy (*Volkstumspolitik*) in Czernowitz before and during the Barbarossa Campaign', *Dapim: Studies on the Holocaust* 24(1) (2010), 89–135, here 113–16. Valjavec's death in 1960 was mentioned in P. Tiefenthaler (ed.), *Festschrift zum 20-jährigen Jubiläums-Bundestreffen Pfingsten 1969; Zwanzig Jahre Landsmannschaft der Buchenlanddeutschen e. V. 1949–1969* (Planegg: Landsmannschaft der Buchenlanddeutschen 1969), 25. See also 'Prof. Dr Fritz Valajvec zum Gedenken', *Der Südostdeutsche*, issue 1, November 1961.
113. On 'capitulation', see: 'Sechzehn lange Jahre: der schicksalschwerste Tag in der Geschichte der Deutschen', *Der Südostdeutsche*, issue 1, May 1961.
114. See e.g. 'Der verhängnisvolle Mythos – 'jüngste Vergangenheit' in anderen Dimensionen – Opfer des Hasses: Deutsche und Juden!', *Der Südostdeutsche*, issue 2, April 1961.
115. BI, Allg. Korrespondenz, 1965: Bericht von Anton Scribiac über den Besuch von Schellhorn in Büsnau, 2 September 1964.
116. 'Fragmente als Beweise der Dokumentation', *Der Südostdeutsche*, issue 1, April 1961; 'Augenzeugebericht über Massenvergasungen', 'Vergangenheitsbewältiger zwingen Naturgesetze', *Der Südostdeutsche*, issue 1, May 1961.
117. See e.g. E. Horowitz, 'Was sagen Sie?...', *Die Stimme*, January 1961; 'Prozess Eichmann – seine geschichtlich Bedeutung', *Die Stimme*, April 1961.
118. Ahonen, 'The Impact of Distorted Memory', 250.
119. It is estimated that only 10% of expellees were members of expellee organizations by 1955. See M. Stickler, *'Ostdeutsch heißt Gesamtdeutsch': Organisation, Selbstverständnis und heimatpolitische Zielsetzungen der deutschen Vertriebenenverbände 1949–1972* (Düsseldorf: Droste, 2004), 122.
120. See A. Wieviorka, *The Era of the Witness*, translated from French by J. Stark (Ithaca: Cornell University Press, 2006); see also T. Segev, *The Seventh Million: The Israelis and the Holocaust*, translated from Hebrew by H. Watzman (New York: Hill & Wang, 1994).
121. This is based on the evaluation of various accounts including the four submissions by Bukovinians to the 'Ältere Menschen schreiben Geschichte' competition and launched in 1976 inviting people born before 1920 to write about their experiences. Most

submissions date from 1977. Hauptstaatsarchiv Stuttgart, J175, 1518; 817; 1310; 1630, as well as testimonies from Yad Vashem Archives, O3 (Yad Vashem Collection of Testimonies; hereinafter YVA), 1732, 3562, 1130.
122. See e.g. the publication of the article signed 'from a grateful Bukovinian German' (*von einem dankbaren Bukowiner Deutschen*), 'Die Juden der Bukowina – Geniewinkel der Donau-Monarchie', *Die Stimme*, October/November 1963.
123. C. Goschler, *Schuld und Schulden: Die Politik der Wiedergutmachung für NS-Verfolgte seit 1945* (Göttingen: Wallstein, 2005), 8.
124. See C. Pross, *Paying for the Past: The Struggle over Reparations for Victims of Nazi Terror*, translated from German by B. Cooper (Baltimore: Johns Hopkins University Press, 1998); Goschler, *Schuld und Schulden*; R. Ludi, *Reparations for Nazi Victims in Post-war Europe* (Cambridge: Cambridge University Press, 2012), 114–15.
125. C. Goschler, '"Versöhnung" und "Viktimisierung": Die Vertriebenen und der deutsche Opferdiskurs', *Zeitschrift für Geschichtswissenschaft* 53(10) (2005), 873–84, here 878.
126. J. Panagiotidis, 'Laws of Return? Co-ethnic Immigration to West Germany and Israel (1948–1992)' (D.Phil. thesis, European University Institute, 2012), 16.
127. Ibid., 18.
128. On the difficulty in gaining access to the perspective of the victims, see Ludi, *Reparations*, 128.
129. The compensation for the war-damaged was subject to widespread approval. See M. Hughes, *Shouldering the Burdens of Defeat: West Germany and the Reconstruction of Social Justice* (Chapel Hill: University of North Carolina Press, 1999).
130. See Frei, *Adenauer's Germany*.
131. Goschler, *Schuld und Schulden*, 7.
132. M. Hughes, '"Through No Fault of Our Own": West Germans Remember Their War Losses', *German History* 18(2) (2000), 193–213, here 194.
133. Goschler, *Schuld und Schulden*, 215.
134. Ludi, *Reparations*, 94.
135. Frei, *Adenauer's Germany*, 28.
136. See Stern, *Whitewashing*, 265–384, especially 349.
137. Goschler, *Schuld und Schulden*, 8.
138. See E. Barkan, *The Guilt of Nations: Restitution and Negotiating Historical Injustices* (New York: Norton, 2000).
139. See I. Nachum, 'Reconstructing Life after the Holocaust: The Lastenausgleichsgesetz and the Jewish Struggle for Compensation', *Leo Baeck Institute Year Book* 58 (2013), 53–67.
140. Pross, *Paying for the Past*, 67.
141. See H.G. Hockerts, 'Wiedergutmachung in Deutschland: Eine historische Bilanz 1945–2000', *Vierteljahrshefte für Zeitgeschichte* 49(2) (2001), 167–214; J. Brunner and I. Nachum, '"Vor dem Gesetz steht ein Türhüter": Wie und warum israelische Antragsteller ihre Zugehörigkeit zum deutschen Sprach- und Kulturkreis beweisen mussten', in N. Frei, J. Brunner and C. Goschler (eds), *Die Praxis der Wiedergutmachung: Geschichte, Erfahrung und Wirkung in Deutschland und Israel* (Göttingen: Wallstein, 2009), 423–24.
142. See §11 of the LAG and §2 of the BVFG.
143. Brunner and Nachum, '"Vor dem Gesetz steht ein Türhüter"', 391–92.
144. This was in fact a merely amended version of the one used by the Nazis. The reference to 'blood and race' had been replaced with the more neutral word *Abstammung* ('background' or 'origin') and the sentence indicating that Jews could never be

Volkszugehörige had simply been removed. See Nachum, 'Reconstructing Life after the Holocaust', 56. On the concept of *Volksdeutsche*, see D.L. Bergen, 'The Nazi Concept of "Volksdeutsche" and the Exacerbation of Anti-Semitism in Eastern Europe, 1939–45', *Journal of Contemporary History* 29(4) (1994), 569–82.
145. §6(1) of the BVFG.
146. Brubaker uses 'ethnic nationality': see R. Brubaker, 'Migrations of Ethnic Unmixing in the "New Europe"', *International Migration Review* 32(4) (1998), 1047–65. Emphasizing the literal meaning, Ruth Mandel speaks of 'people belongingness' that should not be 'glossed as ethnicity': R. Mandel, *Cosmopolitan Anxieties: Turkish Challenges to Citizenship and Belonging in Germany* (Durham, NC: Duke University Press, 2008), 207. Nachum argues that it can hardly be translated; Nachum, 'Reconstructing Life after the Holocaust', 55.
147. See Pross, *Paying for the Past*; Hockerts, 'Wiedergutmachung'. Ludi also notes the obsession with 'compensation fraud' (*Wiedergutmachungsbetrug*); Ludi, *Reparations*, 109.
148. Panagiotidis, 'Laws of Return?', 170.
149. Brunner and Nachum, 'Vor dem Gesetz', 412.
150. On this issue see D. Siemens, 'Juristische Zeitgeschichte *avant la lettre*. Die Frankfurter Dissertation von Max Münz zur 'Verantwortlichkeit für die Judenverfolgungen im Ausland' (1958)', *Zeithistorische Forschungen/Studies in Contemporary History* 15(1) (2018), 184–92.
151. In some very rare cases, they approved the applications of Jews. See e.g. BI, Allg. Korrespondenz Bundesverband, 1964: Statement by Otto Lachmund (Ay.P 1501 – 9/64), 29 September 1964.
152. See e.g. BI, Allg. Korrespondenz Bundesverband, 1965–66: Otto Lachmund to the regional branch of the Landsmannschaft der Buchenlanddeutschen RHL/Pfalz regarding the establishing of the ethnic nationality of L.K. (*Feststellung der Volkszugehörigkeit des L.K.*), 10 September 1965.
153. H. Weber, *Die Bukowina im zweiten Weltkrieg: völkerrechtliche Aspekte der Lage der Bukowina im Spannungsfeld zwischen Rumänien, der Sowjetunion und Deutschland* (Hamburg: Metzner, 1972).
154. See e.g. BI, Allg. Korrespondenz Bundesverband, 1964: Otto Lachmund to the Compensation Office of the region of Rheinland/Pf. Regarding the compensation of J.W. (A. Z.: W-1473-5/64), no date, May 1964.
155. These reports were sent to the compensation authorities and are archived here. Bundesarchiv Lastenausgleichsarchiv (hereinafter BArch-LAA), ZLA7/03 – 1234 (*Extra-Dokumentation Rumänien, Jüdische Volkszugehörigkeit*). Plesch headed the HASt from 1957 to 1975. He was preceded by a Bukovinian, Peter Blaß (1953–57) and was replaced by Dr Franz Noll (1976–79), Fritz Krauss (1980–2000) and Wilhelm Spielhaupter (2001–4). It was then dissolved. See W. Spielhaupter, *51 Jahre Heimatauskunftstelle Rumänien: 1953–2004* (Munich: n.p., 2005) (Bibliothek des Bundesarchivs in Bayreuth).
156. BArch-LAA, ZLA7/03 – 1234: Letter and Memorandum from Dr I.D. Evian regarding the expellee status of persecutees from Bukovina (*Vertriebenen-Anerkennung Verfolgter aus der Bukowina*) to the regional office for compensation in Mainz, 11 July 1957.
157. BArch-LAA, ZLA7/03 – 1234: Report from Erhard Plesch regarding information about former relations in Bukovina to the regional Compensation Office in Mainz, 29 November 1957, and report to the regional government office for compensation in Neustadt an der Weinstraße regarding the reparations to the victims of National Socialism (*Bundesentschädigungsgesetz* (BEG)), 12 December 1957.

158. BArch-LAA, ZLA7/03 – 1234: Plesch report from 12 December 1957, 5; given in similar terms in the report from 29 November 1957, 5.
159. BArch-LAA, ZLA7/03 – 1234: Plesch report from 12 December 1957, 8–9 and report from 29 November 1957, 9.
160. BArch-LAA, ZLA 7/03 – 1234. This was also quoted in the memorandum addressed to the German Chancellery by the Landsmannschaft of Bukovinian Jews in 1963: BArch-K, B136/3310 (*Wiedergutmachung Bundesklanzeramt*), 9. Schellhorn was sometimes a guest at the events and meetings of Bukovinian Germans and in 1963 – for example, *Der Südostdeutsche* celebrated his seventy-fifth birthday with a large feature: *Der Südostdeutsche*, issue 2, December 1963.
161. Appeal published in the *Ostjüdische Zeitung* (Czernowitz), 24 December 1930.
162. See e.g. BArch-LAA, ZLA7/03 – 1234: Letter from the Landsmannschaft of Bukovinian Jews in Israel (Dr M. Weinberger and Dr J. Mann) to the regional government president (*Regierungspräsident*) in Cologne, 28 April 1965.
163. BArch-LAA, ZLA 7/03 – 1234: Letter from Dr Rossmeissl and K. Weidmann to Plesch, 17 December 1962.
164. BArch-LAA, ZLA7/03 – 1234: Letter from the Landsmannschaft of Bukovinian Jews in Israel (Dr M. Weinberger and Dr J. Mann) to the regional government president (Regierungspräsident) in Cologne, 28 April 1965.
165. BArch-LAA, ZLA7/03 – 1234: Letter from the Landsmannschaft of Bukovinian Jews, 28 April 1965.
166. BArch-LAA, ZLA7/03 – 1234: Report of the Institute for Contemporary History, 1958, 177, emphasis in original.
167. BArch-LAA, ZLA7/03 – 1234: Report by Martin Broszat for the regional court in Cologne, October 1963; later published with slight amendments as an article: M. Broszat, 'Von der Kulturnation zur Volksgruppe: die nationale Stellung der Juden in der Bukowina im 19. und 20. Jahrhundert', *Historische Zeitschrift* 200(3) (1965), 572–605.
168. BArch-LAA, ZLA7/03 – 1232: Letter from Plesch (*Heimatauskunftstelle*) to the President of the Compensation Office Bad Homburg and State Ministry for Work and Social Affairs, Compensation Office Munich, 23 September 1969.
169. BArch-LAA, ZLA1/2200286000: A. L. (born 1886 in Czernowitz) – living in Israel (Ramat Gan); demand received 10 April 1962; rejected 1969.
170. BArch-LAA, ZLA 1/ 2212946000: J. B. (born 1887 in Radautz) – application from 1962 by his daughter in Haifa (born 1908).
171. Brunner and Nachum, 'Vor dem Gesetz', 406.
172. Ibid., 411.
173. BArch-LAA, ZLA1/ 2212946000: J. B. (born 1887 in Radautz), claim made by daughter living in Haifa; application sent 1962.
174. BArch-LAA, ZLA1/2200286000.
175. BArch-LAA, ZLA1/ 2219716 K.K. (born 1871 in Radautz), claim made by daughter living in Holon Israel; application sent 4 October 1962.
176. Dr F.G. Schellhorn, 'Die Juden der Bukowina', *Frankfurter Allgemeine Zeitung* no. 114, 19 May 1969, a response to the book review by Salcia Landmann: S. Landmann, 'Juden der Bukowina: Eine geschichtliche Dokumentation', *Frankfurter Allgemeine Zeitung* no. 71, 25 March 1969. Two outraged responses to Schellhorn soon followed: Dr A. Schwarz, 'Ziemlich saures Leben', *Frankfurter Allgemeine Zeitung* no. 120, 27 May 1969. Dr J. Pfeiffer, 'Die deutsche Kulturzugehörigkeit der Bukowiner Juden', *Frankfurter Allgemeine Zeitung* no. 152, 5 July 1969. However, in his final response, Schellhorn defended his position: Dr F.G. Schellhorn, 'Jiddisch war die

Umgangsssprache', *Frankfurter Allgemeine Zeitung* no. 182, 9 August 1969. Schellhorn also published an article on this topic in *Der Südostdeutsche*: 'Rumänien und die Leiden der Bukowiner Juden', *Der Südostdeutsche*, issue 2, July 1969.
177. BI, Allg. Korrespondenz Bundesverband, 1973: Letter from Otto Lachmund to the reporter of chamber no. VI of the administrative court of the free city of Bremen (*Berichterstatter der VI Kammer des Verwaltungsgerichts der Freien Hansestadt Bremen*) regarding membership to the 'Jahn' Sports Organization in Czernowitz/Bukovina, 4 May 1973.
178. BI, Allg. Korrespondenz Bundesverband, 1966: Letter from the North Rhine–Westphalia regional branch of the Landsmannschaft of Bukovinian Germans to the national office of the Landsmannschaft of Bukovinian Germans regarding the membership in the Landsmannschaft of ethnic German migrants (*Spätaussiedler*) from Romania, 5 October 1966.
179. See e.g. 'Sind Vertriebene in Österreich Parias?', *Der Südostdeutsche*, issue 2, June 1961.
180. 'Bundestreffen: Der Festvortrag des Bundessprechers Dr Rudolf Wagner', *Der Südostdeutsche*, issue 1, June 1969.
181. See C. Pross, *Wiedergutmachung: Der Kleinkrieg gegen die Opfer* (Frankfurt am Main: Athenäum, 1988), 240.
182. Ludi, *Reparations*, 193.
183. M. Teich, *Für eine Revision der Luxembourger Verträge und der Wiedergutmachungs-Gesetze* (Tel Aviv: Selbstverlag, 1961).
184. BArch-K, B136/3310.
185. On this, see J. Panagiotidis, '"The Oberkreisdirektor Decides Who is a German": Jewish Immigration, German Bureaucracy, and the Negotiation of National Belongings, 1953–1990', *Geschichte und Gesellschaft* 38(3) (2012), 503–33, here 514–17.
186. 'Leben ohne Heimat', *Die Stimme*, November 1970.
187. M. Teich, 'Die Vertriebeneneigenschaft im Sinne der 11. DV zum Lastenausgleichsgesetz', *Die Stimme*, December 1970.
188. 'Die Zugehörigkeit der Juden aus der Bukowina zum deutschen Sprach- und Kulturkreis', *Die Stimme*, July–August 1963, emphasis in original.
189. On this trend, see also J. Panagiotidis, 'A Policy for the Future: German-Jewish Remigrants, Their Children, and the Politics of Israeli Nation-Building', *Leo Baeck Institute Year Book* 60 (2015), 191–206.
190. M. Brenner and N. Frei, 'Zweiter Teil: 1950–1967 Konsolidierung', in M. Brenner (ed.), *Geschichte der Juden in Deutschland von 1945 bis zur Gegenwart: Politik, Kultur und Gesellschaft* (Munich: C.H. Beck, 2012), 242.
191. BArch-LAA, ZLA 7/03, 1233: Guidelines for the implementation of §6 BVFG (*Richtlinien zur Anwendung des §6 des Bundesvertriebenengesetzes (BVFG)*), 27 March 1980.
192. Hockerts, 'Wiedergutmachung in Deutschland', 190–91.
193. See D. von Westernhagen, 'Wiedergutgemacht', *Die Zeit* no. 41, 5 October 1984.
194. See C. Wessel-Hanssen, 'Um frei zu leben unter Deutschen: Wie ein jüdischer Aussiedler an einem bundesdeutschen Sachbearbeiter verzweifelte', *Die Zeit* no. 43, 21 October 1988.
195. BArch-LAA, ZLA7/03, 1234: Letter from Dr Axel Azzola to the Regional Office for Central Social Affairs regarding the issuing of an expellee identification card of category A (*Vertriebenenausweises 'A'*), 15 August 1988.
196. A. Kauders, *Unmögliche Heimat: Eine deutsch-jüdische Geschichte der Bundesrepublik* (Munich: Deutsche Verlags-Anstalt, 2007), 16.

Chapter 5

'SUNKEN CULTURAL LANDSCAPE'

Reimagining Bukovina through the Lens of Literature

In May 1989, at the fortieth anniversary meeting of Bukovinian Germans, which took place in the Bavarian town of Augsburg, Professor Johannes Hampel, who had just become the chairman of the newly founded Bukovina-Institute in Augsburg, gave a speech entitled 'The Contribution of Bukovina to European Culture'. He started by mentioning that when the current Israeli ambassador in Bonn, Benjamin Navon, had been asked recently on German television why he spoke such good German, he had answered self-evidently: 'German is my mother tongue. I was born in Czernowitz.' Hampel used this anecdote to describe the unique character of Bukovina and, in particular, its exceptional ethnic and religious diversity. He mentioned the people's incredible 'industriousness' (*Gewerbefleiß*) and 'tolerance', the particularity of the Bukovinian compromise of 1909–10 and the university, where 'non-German sons of Bukovina' could benefit from 'the universal reach of German education'. Finally, he spoke about the literature of Bukovina, about which he said: 'even if one only considers what was written in German, it can be described as outstanding compared to other regions, with the exception, perhaps, of Vienna and Prague'. He then said a few words about Karl Emil Franzos, Raimund Friedrich Kaindl and Gregor von Rezzori and listed many other writers, including Paul Celan and Rose Ausländer. As he explained, it would be the Bukovina-Institute's task to popularize 'this exceptional diversity – this kaleidoscope of European culture'.[1]

The discourse on Bukovinian tolerance and multiculturality was not new as such. As others have noted, the Bukovinian-German historian Emanuel Turczynski was a prominent and persistent proponent of this narrative.[2] In their own ways, Hans Prelitsch and Erich Beck had also celebrated the region's ethnic diversity, as discussed in previous chapters. But until then, all three of them had discussed this in an abstract manner and without referring explicitly to the case of acculturated Jews. In so doing, they had often implied that the Austrian rulers and, by implication, the region's Christian German-speakers should take the credit for the region's exceptional German culture and harmonious atmosphere. With this in mind, Hampel's speech was quite different. Echoing a contemporary trend, he foregrounded the broader reach of German culture and the role of German-speaking Jews in particular. His words stood for the shift from the focus on Bukovinian Germans as the 'bearers of culture' (*Kulturträger*) in a lost *Heimat*, to Bukovina as a lost German-language 'cultural landscape' (*Kulturlandschaft*) in Eastern Europe.[3]

This shift reflected a new way of thinking about the space of Bukovina and its people in West Germany specifically and in the German-speaking space overall. Indeed, throughout the 1970s and 1980s, the notion of 'sunken cultural landscape' (*versunkene Kulturlandschaft*) came to replace that of 'lost *Heimat*' as the dominant metaphor used to talk about the region, a development that reflected a widening of the understanding of German culture and belonging. In general, the German notion of 'cultural landscape' points to the transformation of an area's natural features as a result of human activity and draws attention to both the landscape and agriculture, architecture and what one generally thinks of as heritage sites. Therefore, it is often used to refer to 'the existence of cultural institutions in a given space and the associated cultural life of this area'.[4] As others have noted, when used to describe areas of former German presence in Central and Eastern Europe, it often serves to emphasize a form of German influence on the area that was not primarily political, national or ethnic.[5] This might certainly be applied to the case of Bukovina, where German high culture and literature, both in the interwar period and after the Second World War, were primarily a feature of the Austrian legacy and predominantly carried by Jews. Thus, not only did the advent of the more comprehensive concept of 'sunken cultural landscape' mark the recognition of the significance of Habsburg rule for the German character of the region, but it also brought with it closer attention for the activities of German-speaking Jews and thereby also challenged existing exclusive conceptions of the *Heimat* as Christian.

In itself, the conception of Bukovina as a landscape was older. It had its origins in the works and self-perception of Bukovinian Jewish intellectuals, who sought to describe their relationship to their homeland and to German culture in a cultural rather than a national or political sense in the interwar period. The revival of this idea was therefore closely linked to the discovery and rediscovery, as the Cold War advanced, of German-speaking Jewish writers from the region. Indeed, despite the fact that Bukovinian Germans had their own literary figures, it was German-speaking Jewish poets such as Paul Celan and Rose Ausländer who contributed most to putting Bukovina back onto the map of Europe during the latter half of the Cold War, as they themselves became icons for the region as a whole. By 1989, for many people, Bukovina had become a synonym for German-speaking and mostly *Jewish* German-speaking culture and literature. This process, in turn, had some unintended and unforeseen consequences: as these writers' nostalgic and poetic visions of the region gained ground, the narratives of victimhood of Bukovinians as 'Germans' and as 'Jews' increasingly moved into the background, hence attenuating the strong distinction between Bukovinian Germans and Bukovinian Jews as separate communities of experience. Indeed, thinking of the region as a sunken cultural landscape led to the idea that what was lost in the Second World War was not so much a German or a Jewish *Heimat*, but rather the site of an exceptional German-Jewish symbiosis in a wider and now lost multicultural Central European world.

This reframing of Bukovina thus gives us insight into the development of different and more diverse interactions between Jews and non-Jews during the Cold War – in particular (but not only) in West Germany. Indeed, the popularization of the conception of Bukovina as a cultural landscape was closely bound up with the dynamics of engagement with the recent past, a process often described in German using the notoriously problematic expression 'coming to terms with the past' (*Vergangenheitsbewältigung*).[6] In this period, an interest in Jews and Jewish history developed among some members of the younger generation of West Germans and Austrians especially. This interest was part of their attempts to make sense of what had happened during the war and the Holocaust, and what their parents especially had done and experienced. Others have noted the distinctly philosemitic mood in West Germany among members of this age group – especially a section of the 1968 generation.[7] However, the case of Bukovina shows that this was a more international and transnational trend, involving people with Jewish heritage around the world as well as other Europeans. This thus also raises questions about the role of traditional stakeholders of Bukovinian identity in West Germany and Israel and their reactions to cultural change. As Anthony Kauders has shown for the case of West Germany, the rapprochement between German Jews and the non-Jewish German public was a two-way process, and Jews themselves were instrumental for this shift.[8] Did a similar process occur among German-speaking Jews in Israel and Bukovinian Jews elsewhere? What was the role of German-speaking writers who sought to publish their work and then became spokespersons for the larger group? How did this relate to the wider geopolitics of the Cold War and the tendency in this period, noted by others, to invent and imagine rather than understand the pre-World War past and the communist present?[9]

This chapter explores how Bukovina was reimagined and reinvented in the 1970s and 1980s, during the second half of the Cold War. It first focuses on Jewish writers and intellectuals from the region for whom, as their activities, personal statements and creative endeavours show, Bukovina remained an important point of reference after the war and the Holocaust. By outlining the main characteristics of their work, its reception and their relationships among each other, this chapter shows how this smaller, more informal, more diverse but also more international group of 'Bukovinians' than that making up the Landsmannschaften, came to the fore during the second half of the Cold War and, in turn, exerted significant influence on the wider image of Bukovina and even on the discourse of organized Bukovinians. Indeed, it is mostly thanks to them that Bukovina, by 1989, had come to be conceived of as a 'literary landscape', a 'sunken cultural landscape' and the site of an exceptional 'German-Jewish symbiosis'. However, as will be shown, this conception of Bukovina was also very much a product of Europe's division. Indeed, while it is impossible to understand why and how Bukovina was perceived during the Cold War without making sense of its writers and their impact, it is also the circumstances of the Cold War that made such a literary phenomenon possible – or at least seem so special.

Bukovina as a Literary Landscape

The conception of Bukovina as a distinct landscape, both physical and cultural, pre-dated the First World War.[10] However, this idea and expression acquired particular significance in the interwar period as a response to Romanization. Indeed, the notion of cultural landscape constituted a way of referring to surviving elements of the Austrian legacy – the use of the German language, the diverse culture and vibrant public life – that continued to distinguish the region even after the fall of the Habsburg Empire. The expression resonated with a handful of emancipated, liberal and educated Jews from the region in particular.

This was, for instance, the case for the German-speaking Jewish translator, writer and journalist Alfred Margul-Sperber, who was born in 1898 in the small north Bukovinian town of Storozynetz.[11] Having left Bukovina for Paris after the First World War and spending the early 1920s in New York, Margul-Sperber returned to Bukovina in 1924 and tried to establish himself as a key figure in the region's German-speaking cultural life. In the early 1930s, he worked as a journalist for the major daily newspaper, the *Czernowitzer Morgenblatt* (1927–33), and even founded his own short-lived weekly *Bukowinaer Provinzbote* in 1931.[12] In 1934, he was forced to take an administrative job in his hometown of Burdujeni, a suburb of Suceava. But he continued to correspond with writers, editors and intellectuals around the world and to promote local German-speaking writers, including Rose Ausländer (born 1901), Moses Rosenkranz (born 1904), David Goldberg (born 1904) and Alfred Kittner (born 1906), 'Alfred II', who became Margul-Sperber's closest associate.

Still writing in German, these writers embodied the ongoing and anachronistic attachment to the region's Austrian past and culture after the region had become part of Romania. For Margul-Sperber, what united them was not only the inspiration gained from a special relationship to a physical space, as a concept of 'regional literature' would do too, but also their isolation and their nostalgic orientation, embodied by their use of German. In other words, the Bukovinian literary figures he represented were shaped by their island-like, peripheral situation and the unlikely – if not resistant – character of their mode of identification as German-speaking Jewish writers. Not only were they far away from German culture's national core, surrounded by an array of different languages and influences, but this centre was not perceived as theirs, even before the rise of nationalism and antisemitism in Germany widened the gap further. *Their* centre, Vienna, the capital of the empire, was no more. At the same time, they stood apart from popular intellectual trends and political movements among the region's Jews such as Bundism, communism, Zionism and the use of Yiddish, all of which were gaining ground among some Jewish intellectuals in interwar Bukovina.[13] Therefore, as self-conscious but self-confident Bukovinian Jewish German-speaking poets, they were going against the tide.[14] From Margul-Sperber's perspective, this had tremendous creative potential, but he was under no illusions. Already at the time, he described this literature as the 'invisible choir' and as something ephemeral and 'doomed'.[15] When, in the late 1920s, together with Kittner, he started working on an anthology of German-language Bukovina poetry, his intention was to give the writers visibility, but also to record the last moments of this exceptional literary phenomenon.

Margul-Sperber's conception of a German literary landscape in Bukovina was therefore distinct from notions of a timeless, enduring and ahistorical *Heimat*. In fact, it might be understood as developed in response to such a notion and in response to a National Socialist concept of German culture. In 1931, in an essay entitled 'German Letter from Bukovina', he outlined his thoughts on the subject. He referred to figures such as Ernst Rudolf Neubauer, who founded *Bukowina*, the first German newspaper in Bukovina in the second half of the nineteenth century, the historian Raimund Friedrich

Kaindl and the 'Swabian poet' (*Schwabendichter*) Heinrich Kipper. He also wrote about the emergence of a 'marriage of convenience' between the region's Germans and Jews, which had, until then in his view, halted the spread of *völkisch* ideas. But according to him, since 1918, it was the Jews who had been the 'guardians of "Austrian" tradition' in the region.[16] As he wrote in one of the later draft introductions to his anthology in 1936, 'Bukovina was a distant eastern landscape, which was shaped by Jews in the German language'.[17] This was how he justified his exclusive focus on writers living in Bukovina and inclusion of only Jewish ones.[18] But this choice might also have reflected or been a reaction to the spirit of the times. In 1936, the Transylvanian Saxon Heinrich Zillich, editor of the journal *Klingsor*, wrote to Margul-Sperber that he would no longer publish texts by Jewish authors.[19] And while in 1932, the ethnic German Bukovinians Franz Lang and Alfred Klug had published texts by both ethnic Germans and German-speaking Jews, Alfred Klug's *Bukowiner Deutsches Dichterbuch* published in 1939 had notoriously only included 'Aryan' authors.[20] This ultimately also helps to explain why Margul-Sperber was unable to find a publisher for his anthology.

The Second World War appeared to have given this German literary landscape its final blow. While Margul-Sperber had described it as merely 'hidden' or 'invisible', it came to be known as 'forgotten', 'vanished' and 'immersed' or 'sunken' (*versunken*). It was Paul Celan and Rose Ausländer in particular who popularized these expressions and this vision of the region. Celan's conflicted relationship to the region of his birth has been widely noted and discussed.[21] By referring to Bukovina as a 'utopia', a 'landscape' and a region 'where people and books lived', Celan idealized his native region.[22] However, he also drew on the notion of its disappearance and 'sunkenness'. Celan described himself as 'background-less' (*herkunftslos*)[23] and the region of his birth as 'unknown', 'having fallen prey to history-less-ness' (*der Geschichtslosigkeit anheimgefallen*).[24] He labelled his disillusioned condition in the postwar world as '*post-kakanisch*', namely the aftermath of something that, in itself, was never real.[25] Similarly, Ausländer's poems often celebrated the beauty of Bukovina's countryside and the uniqueness of the region's cultural life and features. Her answer to the question of why she wrote was: 'Maybe because I was born in Czernowitz, because the world came to me in Czernowitz. This exceptional landscape. The exceptional people [*Jene besondere Landschaft. Die besonderen Menschen*]'.[26] But in her piece 'Memories of a Town' ('Erinnerungen an eine Stadt'), published in 1977, while she celebrated her hometown Czernowitz/Cernăuți up to 1944 as a place of German high-culture, she concluded with the words: 'A sunken town. A sunken world.'[27]

The notion of sunkenness captured the brutal and irrevocable character of a disappearance, something that underpinned discussions of the 'lost homeland' among Jewish intellectuals in general. Yet, while the 'sunken cultural landscape' pointed to a unique kind of loss, it also suggested a special kind of longing. It not only captured the place's significance, but also heightened the significance given to a place, which was not lost merely for a time but lost for good – not merely absent but extinguished. The belief in its exceptional character not only had implications, as we shall see, for the later reception of the works of these authors, but also, before that, for the surviving members, who nostalgically attempted to keep something of this spirit alive in their private relationships and writings.[28] Indeed, although the Bukovinian literary landscape, as Margul-Sperber had defined it, did not survive the destruction and dispersion caused by the Second World War, many of its surviving members maintained a connection to each other despite their displacement. Private correspondence reveals that friendships were rekindled, sustained and even newly developed with Bukovinians across the world after 1945 based on their shared background.[29] This was not only reflected in the large number of letters written, the intellectual exchange and the communities of Bukovinians that formed informally, but also in the poets' official dedication of poems to each other into the 1970s and 1980s, not to mention the controversies surrounding cross-references and even plagiarism in their writing.[30] As George Guțu has argued, central to this connection was the 'human dimension'.[31] The common roots and the shared breeding ground for their thoughts, which the idea of landscape embodied, was as important as the shared experience of displacement and exile, which the notion of Bukovina's sunkenness captured.

Bukovinian writers' postwar network relied on a mixture of longstanding relationships and newer ones. Margul-Sperber and Ausländer, for example, had met in 1921 when they both lived in New York City.[32] Celan and Ausländer, in contrast, only met at the end of the war, in 1944, and Ausländer and Alfred Gong, born Alfred Liquornik, only got to know each other much later when they both were living in the United States in the 1950s.[33] Margul-Sperber, who had survived the war in Bucharest and was able to pursue a relatively successful career as a journalist and a translator in Romania after the war, remained the central figure. In the immediate aftermath of the war, his apartment in Bucharest famously became a meeting point for displaced Bukovinians before they moved to Israel or to the West. In general, according to the Celan expert and literary scholar Andrei Corbea-Hoişie, not only could all political and intellectual tendencies that had existed in prewar Bukovina be found in Bucharest after the end of the Second World War, but for a time, the whole 'German-speaking cultural scene of Czernowitz' was reconstituted there too.[34] Celan, for example, spent almost three years in Bucharest between 1945 and 1947 before moving to Vienna and later Paris, as did Gong, who lived in Bucharest before moving to Vienna and later to the United States.[35] Moses Rosenkranz was there too before being arrested in 1947 on the streets of Bucharest and sent to a Gulag in the Soviet Union for ten years. Immanuel Weissglas went to Bucharest after the war as well and remained there until he died in 1979, and Kittner stayed until 1980, when he left for West Germany. Rose Ausländer spent a short time there in 1946 before making her way to New York once again. Before she left, Margul-Sperber organized a reading of her collection of poems *The Rainbow* (*Der Regenbogen*), which he had helped her publish in 1939. Attendees included Celan, Kittner and Edith Silbermann, another Bukovinian Jewish intellectual, as well as a range of Romanian literary critics.[36]

This group wrote to each other, met, promoted each other, helped each other, reviewed each other's work and shared publishers. Margul-Sperber came to be known as 'the father', 'the advocate' and 'the promoter' of 'Bukovinian literature' (*Bukowina Dichtung*, lit.: literature from Bukovina).[37] As he himself declared in a letter to a publisher in Austria in 1947: 'You will soon realize with dismay that there is such a thing as a Bukovinian poetry school of which, whether I like it or not and for better or for worse, I am the Opitz [a reference to the founder of the Silesian poetry school Martin Opitz].'[38] As others have noted, this group could hardly be described as a 'school' because its supposed members were so different.[39] But Margul-Sperber's wide-ranging correspondence nevertheless testifies to both his deep understanding of poetry and his dedication to the cause of Bukovinian literature both before the war and after.[40] Having not been able to publish it before the war, Margul-Sperber continued to work on the anthology of Bukovinian Jewish poetry afterwards. After his death in 1967, his close friend Alfred Kittner took over from him, pursuing Margul-Sperber's extensive correspondence and even acquiring the title of 'trustee' (*Sachverwalter*) of Bukovinian literature.[41] Kittner died in 1991 before completing the project of the anthology, but in 2009, some seventy years after Margul-Sperber and Kittner had started working on it, the anthology *Die Buche* was published based on their extensive notes and letters.

Not only did members of this group continue to write, but many of them were even more productive after the war than before. Indeed, one of the notable characteristics of Bukovinian literature is not only its *post facto* notoriety but also its delayed flourishing. The Bukovinian literary landscape was not simply something of the past. And, insofar as it was constituted by its re-enactment in a very different present, it became the source of something rather new. With Margul-Sperber and Kittner in Romania, Bukovinian literature came to be seen after the Second World War as embedded in the broader context of the so-called 'fifth German' – namely Romanian-German – literature. Margul-Sperber corresponded with an international network of linguists and German-language scholars on both sides of the Iron Curtain.[42] But the closest of these new relations were with Transylvanian Saxon and Banat Swabian writers and intellectuals, who belonged to the 400,000-strong ethnic German minority in postwar Romania. The Transylvanian Saxon writer Hans Bergel and the journalist Elisabeth Axmann both fondly remembered Margul-Sperber from their time in Bucharest.[43] He was very close to the intellectual Oscar Walter Cisek and the Transylvanian Saxon pastor and writer Erwin Wittstock. The wider circle around Margul-Sperber and Kittner included many others, such as Oskar Walter Pastior, Dieter Schlesak and even Andreas Birkner, a Transylvanian Saxon writer who had volunteered for the Waffen-SS.[44] As Paul Schuster, the former editor of the Romanian German-language literary magazine *Neue Literatur* commented in 1987: 'He, the Jew, was the mentor ... of all of the newcomers from Transylvania and the Banat, who were trying themselves out in German – a kindergarten teacher in the bleakest of times.'[45]

This openness had both to do with Margul-Sperber's friendly persona and the fact that the original circle around him was merely a loose association based primarily on a shared language.[46] As Corbea-Hoişie puts it, he was guided by a German humanistic cultural ideal.[47] The 'literary landscape' that Margul-Sperber and Kittner had in mind after the Second World War was not defined in ethnic terms; they placed emphasis on the use of German. Indeed, although the majority of the members were Jewish, the Jewish experience and the recent past only played a minor role. In part, this was due to political circumstances. In communist Romania, where Margul-Sperber and Kittner were active, the dominant attitude towards the Holocaust was characterized by relativization, silence and even denial.[48] As public figures, Margul-Sperber and Kittner were committed to toeing the party line. Margul-Sperber, in particular, was careful to avoid anything resembling 'ethnic particularism' (*Volkstümlichkeit*).[49] While Kittner, for instance, published a Holocaust memoir 1956, in his lifetime, Margul-Sperber did not publish his poems dealing with the war and Jewish persecution and did not discuss openly the members of his family and friends who perished during the war.[50]

Margul-Sperber's political stance has been subject to debate and it certainly influenced his reception in the West.[51] However, whether and how it may have informed the direction of his work is harder to determine. As Peter Motzan writes, 'Sperber did not reject the categorical call of the new regime of the People's Democracy'.[52] He wrote leading articles for the Romanian-German state newspaper *Neuer Weg*, worked for the state publisher Kunst und Literatur and became an editor for the official German literary magazine *Neue Literatur*. But the benefits, of course, were mutual: the state, which was short of German-speakers 'untainted by fascism' to satisfy the cultural needs of its relatively large German-speaking population, thereby had the support of a prominent German-speaking intellectual. In turn, Margul-Sperber as a writer was thereby able to publish and continue his work in a context with limited opportunities.[53] It is also worth noting that what we now think of as the Holocaust did not necessarily dominate the work of the writers in the 'democratic West' either. Paul Celan himself, despite being known first and foremost for his rendering of Jewish suffering and German guilt with his poem 'Todesfuge' ('Death Fugue'), famously resented speaking directly about his experiences.[54] It is telling in itself that this poem was associated with the German death camps and Auschwitz rather than the landmarks and features of the Holocaust in Romania, his own experience of forced labour or his parents' experience of deportation to Transnistria. While Celan's commitment to realism and the importance of his own experiences for his writing are unquestionable, he gave them an abstract form and expression.[55]

A similar tension was present in Ausländer's work in which the Holocaust also only featured indirectly. Both her oeuvre and personal statements reflect an ambivalent combination of nostalgia and bitterness towards the past that resulted in silence about its most painful episodes. In a private letter to Itzik Manger in 1947, Ausländer had answered the question about what had happened to her in their 'beloved' country by saying '[it] would be possible only in the form of a book, which I am not prepared to write quite yet'.[56] But that book was never written. In the decade-long correspondence between her and Kittner, the topic of suffering and persecution was hardly ever broached. There is no doubt that some of her work deals with the Holocaust. When she sent some unpublished 'collected poems' to Kittner in the summer of 1976, he commented that with the biographical epilogue she had 'created a monument to [their] unforgettable, poor, murdered and forever lost homeland', and for this Kittner thanked her 'in the name of the dead and the few living brothers and sisters'.[57] But this remained a sensitive topic. When she found out that Kittner had forwarded some of these unpublished 'ghetto poems' to a third party in June 1977, she was very upset. Her current plans, she explained, were for those to remain part of her 'estate' (*Nachlass*).[58] Not everything was meant to be 'unforgotten' publicly or while she was still alive.

Kittner's role with respect to the past and Holocaust memory was ambivalent too. He was one of the first to write about his experiences. His poems written in Transnistria appeared as early as 1944 in Soviet publications as well as in early issues of *Die Stimme*.[59] It was also Kittner who, in 1975, decided to publish Margul-Sperber's poem entitled 'On the Name of a Death Camp' ('Auf den Namen eines Vernichtungslagers') seven years after his death, which mentioned the uncanny resemblance between the names 'Buchenland' and 'Buchenwald'. In the epilogue to the collection, Kittner commented on the fact that though Margul-Sperber had described Bukovina as the site of peaceful interethnic relations, 'forty years later, hundreds of Jewish citizens, among them the parents-in-law and a sister-in-law of the poet himself, had been the victims of bloody carnage'.[60] The fact that Jewish suffering was one of the driving forces behind Kittner's preoccupation with Bukovina and its literature was made even more explicit in a private letter to Ausländer in 1976, in which he wrote about this same epilogue to Margul-Sperber's posthumously published poetry:

> I tried to give the reader a first fleeting insight into a poetic landscape that stayed hidden as a result of unfortunate historical circumstances and that consumed itself with painful inbreeding until the murderous heels of Hitler and Stalin sent some behind barbed wire and to their deaths, and the others into the somewhat liberating 'abroad', so that, in the first instance, their talents could develop. But that it was already too late, that the wounds would not heal, was demonstrated with dreadful clarity by Paul [Celan]'s fate. And wasn't Sperber's own ending also a form of – *spiritual* – suicide?? Posterity will acknowledge this, if there is still poetry then, something about which I have my doubts.[61]

For him, the landscape and its destruction were inextricably linked, and the lives of those associated with it needed to be viewed in light of this connection.

Yet if Kittner's endeavours did succeed in bringing the region's poets and their work into the open, they did not, in the short term, help shed light on their fate in the Holocaust or on the depths of the internal crisis many of them experienced and to which he referred in his letter to Ausländer quoted above. Kittner himself did not like to speak about his experiences during the war.[62] Besides, he was opposed to what he described as 'another form of ghettoization' of the Jews by separating their works from those of 'other Germans'.[63] Contrary to Margul-Sperber before the war, his efforts to put together an anthology of Bukovinian literature did not focus on the work of Jews alone.[64] He set apart the *völkisch* poets, whom he named as Heinrich Kipper, Alfred Klug and Franz Lang, but his list of German-language writers from Bukovina, for instance, included the Austrian Bukovinian-German poet and writer Georg Drozdowski, whom he described as sharing the 'exile situation' and belonging to the same 'community of fate'.[65] As Kittner explained in his memoirs, he saw himself not only as a Jew and a Holocaust survivor, but also as the defender of a better kind of Germanness: 'I have always had a comprehensive view of Germanness, even during the Third Reich. Bukovinian intellectuals always kept in spiritual contact with the positive section of the German people.'[66] This was also the reason why he felt close to a number of Romanian German writers and poets of the younger generation: not only did they share the experience of communism – oppression by the Romanian regime and cultural isolation – but he also considered that they 'had to bear the same burden' (*die gleiche Last zu tragen hatten*), consisting in a form uprootedness predicated on a radical break with the past, namely their Nazi fathers.[67]

In 1971, for example, Kittner put together a selection of Bukovinian poetry that was published in two consecutive issues of the Romanian

German-language magazine *Neue Literatur*, published in Bucharest with the title 'Echoing Choir of Voices: Poems from Bukovina' ('Verhallter Stimmen Chor: Gedichte aus der Bukowina'). In his introduction, Kittner explained that the death of the poet Celan had led to an increase in interest in Celan's work and life, and therefore also in the 'spiritual landscape' from which he came. According to Kittner, other famous writers from this area included Gregor von Rezzori or Jacob Klein-Haparash. But he now wanted to introduce the poets of this 'terra incognita' who had been 'forgotten' or who 'never achieved the fame they deserved' by publishing samples of their work. This wider group of authors were therefore described as 'a selection of highly talented, including significant poets, all of whom originate from the Bukovinian landscape and whose path to a wider reception was closed by adverse life circumstances or the untimely moment of their emergence'.[68] Kittner had only chosen poems from after the First World War, as he believed it was important that the authors had shared the experience of modernity, but he had published both Jewish and non-Jewish Bukovinians, and though thirty-two were Jews and only four were non-Jews, he did not emphasize the Jewish character of this 'landscape'.

It took time for these activities to receive attention abroad. But a decade later, in 1981, the year in which Kittner himself immigrated to West Germany as an ethnic German migrant (*Aussiedler*), Bukovina was described as a 'lyrical landscape' (*lyrische Landschaft*), this time in a West German journal.[69] In the 1980s, a growing number of articles appeared in major German-language media outlets such as *Die Zeit*, the *Frankfurter Allgemeine Zeitung* (*FAZ*) or the *Neue Zürcher Zeitung* (*NZZ*) about Bukovinian writers living in Germany such as Moses Rosenkranz or Rose Ausländer, who had also been the recipient of many literary prizes since the 1970s.[70] This became the primary context for the discussion of the region of Bukovina, and the writers became icons for their communities and for the region as a whole. As an article about Romania's Jewish communities published in the *NZZ* in 1982, for instance, read: 'The fact that Paul Celan, the great German poet, was born [in Czernowitz] says more about the significance of the Jewish community of Czernowitz than any numbers can.'[71] This was considered a self-explanatory statement. Yet, a further historical contextualization or explanation would have shown that when Celan was born in 1920, Czernowitz was already Cernăuți, German was very much a feature of the Jewish bourgeoisie, Bukovinian Jews' situation was already very precarious and Celan's survival was the exception rather than the rule. Overall, this would have painted quite a different picture.

By the late 1980s, different aspects of the Bukovinian 'literary landscape' and the 'literary metropolis' (*literarische Weltstadt*)[72] Czernowitz were the subject of academic theses, articles, conferences and books. Bukovina itself gradually came to be identified not as the homeland of a group of writers, but as the literary landscape that had produced them. This amalgamation had some curious consequences. On the one hand, the popularization of Bukovina's literature – the 'late discovery of a literary landscape' (*Spätentdeckung einer Literaturlandschaft*),[73] as Kittner put it – coincided with and even contributed to a wider resurgence of a general interest in Jewish history and heritage and Eastern Europe in West Germany and Austria in this period in general.[74] However, on the other hand, the growing attention over the course of the Cold War paid to these mostly Jewish German-speaking Bukovinian writers both individually and as group focused not on their experiences as Jews, but rather on their position as representatives of an exceptional and sunken German literary and intellectual phenomenon originating from a strange and unknown location in Eastern Europe. With their nostalgic and poetic images, these authors drew attention to the region's history but also reduced it to their memories, namely to select experiences and their artistic expression. Hence the promotion and eventually the prominence, of these mostly Jewish German-speaking writers reified the image of the region in a new way. In particular, the discovery of the region through a superficial reading of their works and biographies disseminated the oversimplified image of the region in the interwar period as a 'German-language island' (*deutsche Sprachinsel*) and a site of an exceptional German-Jewish symbiosis.

In general, throughout the 1970s and 1980s, the idea came to prevail that what had been remarkable about the region was less the nature of the people – Germans or Jews as 'bearers of culture' (*Kulturträger*), as the Landsmannschaften claimed – than the extent of cultural and artistic production coming out of the region in general. As the most prolific, but also because they were the best established in the West, Celan and Ausländer were by far the most prominent figures.[75] But those interested in these two writers would often discover other German-speaking authors or figures from the region through them.[76] The list of Bukovinians therefore varied and grew accordingly to include other contemporary Jewish writers such as Alfred Gong, Immanuel Weissglas and Itzig Manger, or much older ones such as Karl Emil Franzos.[77] Famous people in other professions or members of other ethnicities such as Mihai Eminescu, Georg Drozdowski and Gregor von Rezzori, and scientists and artists such as the biochemist Erwin Chargaff or the illustrator Ed Arno, both living in New York, widened the scope of the group.[78] These Bukovinians were therefore not so much taken to be spokespeople for the experiences of Jews, Germans or others (through deportation, resettlement and displacement), but collectively as emblems of the region's exceptional cultural life. In turn, Bukovina acquired the features associated with these people – multiculturality, cosmopolitanism and sophistication – despite the fact that these tended to be features of their postwar lives outside Bukovina rather than of the experiences they made when they still lived in the region.[79]

The 'Cultural Turn' of the Landsmannschaften in the 1970s

The World Organization of Bukovina Jews

The rising prominence of Bukovinian writers and the focus on literature and culture was mostly independent of the activities of the Bukovinian representative organizations, the Landsmannschaften. But insofar as it influenced members of the broader societies in which they operated, it affected them significantly as well. In the autumn of 1969, for example, a few months before he committed suicide, Celan visited Israel for the first and only time. The Israeli public and Israeli scholars had warmly welcomed him. The October 1969 issue of *Die Stimme* not only displayed a poem by Klara Blum, a poet born in Czernowitz who later lived in China, on its cover, but also included an article by the editors welcoming Celan to Israel and emphasizing how much they valued his work.[80] In the November issue, Israel Chalfen, a medical doctor by training but someone who had known Celan personally before the war, attended Celan's Jerusalem reading and reported on it for *Die Stimme* in a very positive manner.[81] Less than a year later, on 20 April 1970, Celan was found dead in the Seine in Paris. In the June issue of *Die Stimme*, Meier Teich published a lengthy and emotional obituary.[82] In July, the editors mentioned the fact they had received many comments and letters from members of the community and readers. They published two of them, including one by the Bukovinian writer and sculptor Manfred Winkler (born 1922).[83] The anniversary of Celan's death was mentioned and commemorated in *Die Stimme* at regular intervals thereafter.[84]

In 1979, Israel Chalfen published the first biography of Celan. Not only did he write this book in German, but he also presented the region as 'Celan's old *Heimat*', 'an unknown landscape' and the site of German-Jewish (in his words, Jewish-German) symbiosis: 'This is the way the life of people and books in this landscape ended after it had been a home to the Jewish-German symbiosis for one and a half centuries.'[85] It was also following Celan's visit that Manfred Winkler, who had emigrated from Romania to Israel in 1959, started translating Celan into Hebrew. This marked the beginning of Winkler's personal rediscovery and reconnection with his European heritage. As he explained in a letter to his German editor in 1978, his life consisted of two distinct phases: He described himself as 'a Hebrew poet', but, in what he called his 'European past', he said he had been a 'German poet in Romania'. And as he explained, 'sometimes I am a slave to my old sins' – namely writing in German.[86] Winkler's endorsement of his 'European past' was incremental. It began with the translations and attending weekly meetings to discuss Celan's work in the 1980s, and then culminated in his membership in the Jerusalem-based group of German-speaking poets and writers, Lyriskreis, and eventually his cooperation with West German institutions.[87] In the 1990s, he even rekindled his friendship with the Transylvanian Saxon writer Hans Bergel, whom he had met thanks to Margul-Sperber in Bucharest in the 1950s.[88]

In many ways, Winkler's path was characteristic of a wider trend among Bukovinian and German-speaking Jews in Israel. In 1975, Meir Marcell Faerber, who was originally from Moravia, established an 'Association of German-Language Writers in Israel' (Verband deutschsprachige Schriftsteller in Israel). They published two anthologies in 1979 and 1989, respectively.[89] The organization had thirty-nine members, and nine of them, including its last chairperson and later editor of *Die Stimme*, Josef N. Rudel, were from Bukovina.[90] The rationale given for the association was to counteract the isolation of German writers in Israel. As Faerber explained in the foreword to the first anthology:

> Among the majority of the population and especially among those organized in national circles in the country's cultural establishment, the German language was for a long time out of favour as the language of Hitler and his National Socialist following. The Hebrew writers' association, which brings together all of the country's literary writers, refused to take in colleagues writing in foreign languages, even though, in the end, the German language is not only that of the Nazis, but also the language of their first victims.[91]

They insisted they were Zionists and did not feel like migrants in Israel, but they nevertheless could not express everything they wanted in Hebrew, and they defended their right to use their native language: 'Even after the unprecedented atrocities we have seen in the past, Jews testify to their attachment to their mother tongue, with which they grew up, and express their free, disinterested humanistic spirit in awareness of their mediating role between their native land and their national homeland.'[92] The activities of Israeli German-speakers were unavoidably short-lived and impact of their efforts are difficult to measure.[93] But their aims were unquestionably broad and ambitious. As one could read in the anthology's afterword, this was about the need to acknowledge the importance of a 'European tradition' in the country: the recognition of the century-long contribution of the Jews in Europe was to be matched by an acknowledgement of the European dimensions of contemporary Israel.[94]

In this period, the self-perception and self-confidence of these German-speaking members of the Diaspora was growing together with their sense of entitlement to making a claim to their heritage and legacy. This approach was part of a wider process, a gradual shift in the approach not just to the German-speaking Diaspora in Israel, but to the Diaspora in Israel generally and to Holocaust survivors in particular. This reached its height in the 1990s with the development of post-Zionism, but, as Dina Porat has argued, in the 1970s and 1980s Israeli society's attitude towards this section of its population was already changing 'from contempt and criticism to empathy and identification'.[95] In 1973, a Center for Research on Romanian Jewry opened in Israel.[96] That same year, the Landsmannschaft of Bukovinian Jews was refounded as the World Organisation of Bucovinian [sic] Jews. It described itself in English as a 'Fund for social assistance and eternization of Bucowinian [sic] Jewry'. Indeed, over time, the organization increasingly adopted the form of a philanthropic body, offering social aid, bursaries and loans for those in need, and running a home for the elderly.[97] In its international appeal for supporters, published in German in 1973, it explained its purpose as providing aid to destitute and deserving Jewish Bukovinians, including new migrants and students, as well as organizing meetings and commemorative events. At this point, the creation of a cultural centre (Kulturzentrums [sic] (Heychal-Bukowina)) and an academic publication, a 'History of the Bukovinian Jewry' ('Geschichte des Bukowiner Judentums'), were being planned too.[98] The year 1973 was also that of the first 'Bukovinian world meeting' (Welttreffen der Bukowiner), which, although it took place in Israel, brought together Bukovinians from all over the world.

The organization's new name and the use of a mixture of German and English reflected the recognition that despite being based in Israel, the Landsmannschaft of Bukovinian Jews represented a global community. As an article published in *Die Stimme* in 1984 explained, a third of its readers lived abroad and one of its aims was to connect Israelis and Jews in the Diaspora.[99] Both the obituaries and articles published in *Die Stimme* in the 1970s and 1980s, as well as their authors, reflected this state of affairs. The author of a regular tribune entitled 'Streaks of Light and Streaks of Shade' (Streiflichter und Streifschatten), Lior Kunstadt, lived in New York, and other contributors were living in South America, Paris, Vienna and Düsseldorf. In 1975, the editors of *Die Stimme* introduced two new sections: 'The Man of the Month' and 'From the Diaspora' – a section that became longer over time and featured news from Germany and Austria in particular. In 1981, a Bukovinian meeting even took place in Düsseldorf.[100] Although the paper offered readers an Israeli perspective on Middle Eastern and international politics, as well as briefly commented on Israeli domestic politics, its main focus was German-language Jewish culture, history, literature, art, philosophy and religion, relating more or less closely to Bukovina. Political and cultural events in the West Germany and Austria dealing with the history and situation of the Jews were therefore unavoidably central. Often, the editors even reprinted or commented on articles from the German or Austrian press. In effect, the focus was less on the events of the Holocaust itself than on memory politics, and the editors dealt less with Romania and the Soviet Union, which were out of reach, than with Germany and Austria, which were responsive and accessible.[101] The fact that from the 1980s onwards, a group of Romanian and Bukovinian Jews travelled annually together from Israel to southern Germany for a holiday is further evidence of West Germany's centrality to Bukovinian-Jewish identity.[102]

What *Die Stimme* effectively offered during this period was a platform for the discussion of German-Jewishness in Israel and beyond after the Holocaust. Today, therefore, it offers an insight into the character and perception of German-Jewish, Austrian-Jewish and Gentile-Jewish interactions and relations during the Cold War. As then-editor Meier Teich had explained in an article from March 1970, they believed in a 'spiritual symbiosis' (*geistige Symbiose*) between Germans and Jews whereby the Jewish influence on Germans had been more significant than the other way around.[103] With the main social problems (even the issue of reparations) largely solved, the representatives of Bukovinian Jews' main agenda was to protect this legacy. They therefore often wrote about Bukovinian writers and the reception of their work. Insofar as the focus was on Jewish figures, Jewish Bukovinians necessarily noticed – and welcomed – the fact that these writers and artists – and Bukovina in general – were becoming so popular in the FRG. An article that appeared in *Die Stimme* in 1981 reported on the speech given by Ilse Rosenberg-Dubenski, a Jewish Bukovinian who was living in Düsseldorf. She had noted that: 'Recently there has been a development, a trend that seems to be leading towards the discovery or re-discovery of our Bukovina, our – once – Czernowitz.' She explained that she had one specific example in mind (the recent discussion of Erwin Chargaff's book in the German media), but that this was just one of many. In particular, she had noted the description of Bukovina as a 'genius-province' with an 'overflow of talent'. This expression, '*Geniegegend mit Talentschwemme*', was chosen as the title of the article.[104] In a way, therefore, Jewish Bukovinians embraced and contributed to the vision of Bukovina as a cultural oasis dominated by German-speaking Jews and thereby also to the illusion of a German-Jewish symbiosis in Bukovina before the Second World War.

The Homeland Society of Bukovinian Germans

If the notion of *Kulturlandschaft* did not replace the conception of the region as an ethnically German *Heimat,* it did come to challenge or at least influence representations of the Bukovinian-German *Heimat* – Bukovina. Significantly, the title of Erich Beck's bibliographies changed from *Bibliographie zur Landeskunde* (*Bibliography of Regional Studies*) in 1966 to *Bibliographie zur* Kultur *und Landeskunde* (*Bibliography of* Culture *and Regional Studies*) in 1985 (emphasis added).[105] In this period, the Bukovinian German Landsmannschaft started emphasizing aspects of Bukovinian-German 'high culture'. In 1975, Rudolf Wagner published a volume to celebrate the centenary anniversary of the university in Czernowitz, which coincided with the 200th anniversary of the region's acquisition by Austria. A booklet entitled *German* Cultural *Life* in Bukovina (emphasis added), with explorations of the parliamentary and school systems in the region and an illustrated book on the city of Czernowitz followed in 1981.[106]

While still often overstating ethnic Germans' contribution to the region's culture and stressing the Austrian 'civilizing mission' and German character of the area, these forays into the history of the region focused more than previous works had on the objective conditions of life in Bukovina, such as Habsburg rule, and less on the subjective character of the organic combination of peoples forming the *homo bucoviniensis*. At this time, the German Bukovinian Landsmannschaft also promoted and funded the publication of collections of *Heimat* poetry and even *Heimat* novels such as Johanna Brucker's Bukovinian trilogy.[107] The twentieth-anniversary booklet of the Landsmannschaft published in 1969, for example, ended with an extract from one of Drozdowski's short stories.[108] While here too, the cultural turn reflected a subsiding of social problems and practical concerns, it also constituted an attempt to compete with the multiplication of Jewish Bukovinian poets and the depictions of the region as a Jewish literary landscape by promoting those they saw as their own literary figures.

Another notable development was Irma Bornemann and Erich Beck's initiative, in 1972, to resurrect the Raimund-Kaindl-Association (Raimund-Kaindl-Bund), which had lain dormant since the mid 1950s. In 1974, it was relaunched as the 'Raimund-Friedrich-Kaindl-Society' (Raimund-Friedrich-Kaindl Gesellschaft) under the presidency of Herbert Mayer, a professor of physics and rector of the Technical University of Clausthal-Zellerfeld near Göttingen.[109] The Society's charter explained that it was 'a society for specialists and researchers' the aim of which was to 'organize scientific meetings, publications and research work'. As in the 1950s, the main output was to be an annual publication, which they called *Kaindl-Archiv*.[110] Officially, the Association's aim was 'the protection of knowledge of the relationships that led to a peaceful neighbourhood and coexistence among groups of different ethnicity and religion in East Central Europe, especially in the Carpathian and Danube regions'.[111] However, in practice, it was an outlet for Bukovinian-German intellectuals such as Mayer, Emanuel Turczynski (by then a professor of history in Bochum), Kurt Rein (a professor of linguistics in Munich) and others, who wrote most of the texts and who all took on official responsibilities. Bukovinian Germans were the focus of most of the contributions: these discussed the work of the Landsmannschaft and ethnic German literature from the region, called for genealogical research among Bukovinian Germans, and celebrated the achievements of historical Bukovinian-German personalities such as Kaindl and Heinrich Kipper, but also contemporaries such as Mayer himself (who aside from being a physicist had been a hobby genealogist since the interwar period) and the hobby historian Erich Prokopowitsch (who died in 1982). In turn, references to or discussions of the more recent past were rare.

This movement towards intellectualization and institutionalization was symptomatic of a wider trend in the area of 'East German cultural work' (*Ostdeutsche Kulturarbeit*) in this period in the FRG. 'The House of the German East' (*Das Haus des deutschen Ostens*) in Munich, for example, opened in 1970, as did several other similar institutions elsewhere in Germany.[112] In this period, Bukovinian Germans discussed creating a 'national archive' in Büsnau, on the largest settlement of Bukovinian Germans in West Germany or even in the Austrian town of Linz, in the Arminia fraternity house.[113] In 1972, following a long period of fundraising, a home for the elderly, the Buchenlandheim, with an imposing meeting hall, opened on Darmstadt's Bukovinian settlement in the Heimstättensiedlung. This trend was linked to changes to the work, purpose and real and putative constituency of the Landsmannschaft as an organization and reflected the desire to leave a legacy. Indeed, the 1970s was a paradoxical decade for such institutions. On the one hand, this was a period of stagnation. Members and the leadership had grown older and the organization was suffering, by their own admission, of fatigue.[114] They now had less money and fewer members. In 1969, the Landsmannschaft of Bukovinian Germans estimated that only around 1% of those they identified as Bukovinian Germans, namely resettlers and their descendants, were members.[115] In effect, little had changed since the immediate postwar period. In the 1960s, the activities, the narratives and many of their reference books remained the same as in the 1950s.[116]

By this time, everything was well rehearsed: the meetings were organized according to a tried and tested method, the networks and hierarchies were in place and their literary canon – Kaindl, Kipper, Drozdowski and a handful of others – was established.[117] But this also meant that there was absolutely no change to what was valued and no evolution to cater to a new generation and a changing sociopolitical environment. A sample of applications for the allocation of the 'badge of honour' (*Ehrennadel*), the Landsmannschaft's highest reward, submitted by the branch of the Landsmannschaft in Bavaria to the Landsmannschaft's national office in 1974 show that what mattered most was both what one had done for the community since the war, but also and especially having been active in 'German ethnic organizations' (*völkische Vereine*) before the war, having been 'a champion of German culture' (*ein Verfechter des Deutschtums*) or having 'publicly demonstrated a German mind and honesty' in the old homeland.[118] These wordings were remarkably reminiscent of the Nazi period and quite probably alienated many members of the younger generation and others as well. When, in 1978, a Bukovinian Jew tried to become a member, his application was rejected on the basis that 'according to its charter, [the] *Landsmannschaft* is *only* responsible for ethnic German resettlers from Bukovina' and people who had 'demonstrated their commitment to Germanness or been active in German organizations already back in Bukovina'.[119] It is worth noting here the use of the word 'resettler', pointing not only to Germanness but also to a specific experience.

Yet, on the other hand and in other respects, this was a period of subtle change. In 1967, when Wagner sent his report to the expellee umbrella organization, the Bund der Vertriebenen (BdV), he included a statement that reflected his sense of a changing public discourse, referring to Bukovinian Germans' good relations to all other 'Bukovinians', including Jews.[120] In general, the Bukovinian-German leadership recognized that the new political climate under the new Chancellor Willy Brandt, and the 'new Eastern policy' (*neue Ostpolitik*) in particular, rendered their political claims – especially their assertion of solidarity with other 'expellees' (*Vertriebene*) who wished to return to their homelands by sustaining the 'right to the homeland' – redundant and counterproductive.[121] From then on, their political lobbying, as reflected in *Der Südostdeutsche*, remained limited to helping Austrian Bukovinians obtain compensation (this was achieved in 1970), denouncing the treatment of ethnic German minorities in the Eastern Bloc and, in general, commenting on Cold War politics (especially GDR–FRG relations). While still staunchly anti-communist, they abandoned their revisionist stance and focused on the present, giving priority to information that would be useful to those, ever more numerous, visiting the 'old *Heimat*' in the context of what has come to be known as 'homesickness tourism'.[122] In so doing, they implicitly accepted the status quo, as did their constituents.

In this period, the Landsmannschaft and its leadership also took stock of the growing interest in Bukovina from beyond its ranks and its gradual loss of the monopoly over the history of the region, not the least due to the emergence of travel opportunities to Romania for Westerners in general, not just Bukovinian Germans. The publication of an article in the *NZZ* in 1974 entitled 'Artistic Journey to Bukovina' highlighting Bukovina's painted monasteries and Romania's Black Sea resorts, rather than the region's Austrian legacy and German culture, resulted in Rudolf Wagner writing in protest to the newspaper about all that was missing from the article.[123] The correspondence of the Landsmannschaft's national office reveals that a growing number of different people – researchers, travellers and descendants of Bukovinian Germans – were showing interest in the history of the region and asking for information and assistance.[124] Some were even publishing their own studies and books.[125] The Landsmannschaft's 'help' was limited to recommending in-house publications. Nevertheless, this forced them to reassert, and to an extent reconsider, their stance as well as address new themes in their speeches and texts.[126] The books *Bukowina: Landschaften – Bauten – Denkmäler* (*Bukovina: Landscapes, Buildings and Memorials*), published in 1986 and presenting many images of the area, *Czernowitz: eine Stadt im Wandel der Zeit* (*Czernowitz: A City through Time*), about the role of Germans in the city's development in 1988 and, last but not least, *Mit Fluchtgepäck die Heimat verlassen…* (*Leaving the Heimat with Flight Luggage…*), published to coincide with the fiftieth anniversary of resettlement in 1990, can be seen as responses to publications by others and the growing interest in the history of Czernowitz and the more recent past.[127]

Demographic changes were inevitably under way within the organization too. An increasing number of women were becoming active and vital in a structure, which, until then, had been largely dominated by men.[128] The thirtieth-anniversary brochure celebrated the work of many women.[129] In general, a new generation, which had somewhat different views and opinions, was coming to the fore. A small incident that took place in 1975 can serve to illustrate this point. The issue put a young regional cultural representative, Bogdan Fedorowytsch, in opposition with members of the Landsmannschaft's 'old guard', most notably Emanuel Turczynski. The problems started when Fedorowytsch had enquired why Romanian and Hungarian songs had been removed from the programme of one of the Landsmannschaft's meetings. At the next meeting, he had been reprimanded and reminded they should play only 'German songs'. Turczynski had emphasized that 'foreign music such as the Romanian Hora [the famous Romanian folkdance]' should not be included. He had then added that Fedorowytsch was in any case too young to stand up to him.[130] The problem escalated further when, following two speeches, one by Franz Specht on 'Bukovina as a model for a united Europe' and another by Turczynski himself on interethnic relations in nineteenth-century Bukovina, Fedorowytsch had dared say he did not agree with them. Again, however, Turczynski cut him off rudely.[131] The leadership supported the latter.[132]

In the ensuing discussion of the altercation with other leading members, Fedorowytsch explained that he could not understand the stance adopted on either issue and even linked them. As he pointed out in a letter to the directorate of the Landsmannschaft, many Bukovinian Germans had grown up in southern Bukovina, and Romanian culture had had a strong influence on them. He also mentioned the many 'mixed marriages'. According to him, introducing 'one or two songs from other groups' should not be seen as 'a betrayal of the fatherland', but as an expression of 'nobleness of heart' (*Herzensbildung*). He then accused the Landsmannschaft's leaders of hypocrisy. As he wrote, 'despite spending the last twenty-five years celebrating good neighbourly and human links and relations in multiethnic Bukovina and its great culture, some today clearly do not want to know anything about [these matters]. Why then do we speak of Bukovina as a prototype for a "miniature Europe"? This is how new tensions arise'.[133] The Landsmannschaft's position on the issue did not change, but Fedorowytsch did not budge either. When Irma Bornemann, who was responsible for cultural affairs on the national level, attempted to calm the situation by writing in a similarly idealized manner about Bukovina, Fedorowytsch answered with obvious annoyance: 'Oh, – this democracy, tolerance, respect, cooperation, equality that we are constantly prescribing to others – these wonderful things we falsely take credit for!'[134] From his perspective, a lack of democracy was precisely the problem, since the desires of the majority of the people were not being taken into consideration.

This incident is revealing on several levels. First, the escalation captures the resistance to dissidence and change among the leadership and members of the older generation. Second, it gives insight into the fact that by this point, such internal disputes and the organization of social events were the Landsmannschaft's central preoccupations and purpose. Finally, it shows that however resistant the 'old guard' was, change was unavoidable. In 1980, for example, the membership application of a Jew from Rădăuți was accepted. Admittedly, he had put together a persuasive file. Like many other Jewish Bukovinians, he had first moved to Israel and only later, in 1967, moved to West Germany, where he settled in Düsseldorf. In his cover letter, he avowed that he 'belonged to the Mosaic faith' and therefore 'did not know if it would be possible [to become a member]!' But he also included a whole range of additional documents. Aside from the friendly cover letter, he had copied proof of a donation of 300 Deutschmarks towards the construction of the Bukovinian old people's home, the Buchenlandheim, in Darmstadt in 1964, when he was still living in Israel, as well as a postcard also dating from 1964, from a Bukovinian-German friend from Rădăuți who had sought out other 'Radautzer' living in Israel. He explained he had remained 'in constant contact' with ethnic German friends from Rădăuți and included original pictures of postwar meetings with them to prove so.[135] This strategy appears to have been successful and led to his admission. Later correspondence reveals that members of the Landsmannschaft asked him to promote their book on Czernowitz among Israeli Bukovinians.[136]

The German-Jewish Symbiosis and Its Limits

The concept of an exclusive 'lost home' was therefore slowly being substituted by the notion of lost culture in a 'sunken (multi)cultural landscape' among Bukovinian Germans too. The memoir of Georg Drozdowski, the Bukovinian-German writer living in Austrian Carinthia, entitled *Back Then in Czernowitz and around* (*Damals in Czernowitz und rundum*), which appeared in 1984 on his eighty-fifth birthday, epitomizes this shift – even if it also reflects the fact that, as an Austrian, he was writing in a somewhat different context and subject to a different set of influences.[137] Drozdowski's focus was not the lost *Heimat* Bukovina; instead, it was the lost world of 'old Austria' of which Bukovina was believed to be a unique example. He said he wrote to discuss the harmonious coexistence of 'six different nationalities', and his use of the words 'past' (*vergangen*) and 'lost' (*untergegangen*) to describe Bukovina and the sense of loss were more reminiscent of how people spoke about the Habsburgs than about the *Heimat*.[138] He portrayed himself not as a Bukovinian, but as an 'old Austrian' (*Altösterreicher*) and concentrated not on the countryside, but on the region's urban character, ahistorically referring to the town as Czernowitz (not Cernăuți), the inhabitants, himself included, as *Czernowitzer*, their manners as *Czernowitzismen* and their language as *Czernowitzerisch*.[139] He even described *Czernowitzer* as 'a people' (*ein Volk*) and illustrated this with anecdotes of his encounters, many years after the war with Bukovinian Jews in Israel, who, as he emphasized, were *Czernowitzer* too and 'fellow countrymen' (*Landsleute*) to whom he felt especially close.[140]

Drozdowski's memoir, written explicitly 'to protect against the process of forgetting' (*vor dem Vergessenwerden zu bewahren*), mainly emphasized positive aspects of the past and what was now lost. As a result, he did not explain in detail or show any detailed interest in *how* this loss had occurred, let alone the fate of the region after it was 'swallowed' by 'the communist east'.[141] Yet, while Drozdowski's account was deeply nostalgic and romanticized and the text was loaded with ethnic stereotypes, it was not ethnocentric in the way in which earlier Bukovinian-German publications had been. A multicultural concept of 'Austrian' was distinguished from a monolithic kind of Germanness. In fact, it was the transition from Austrian to German that was said to have been the source of loss: 'The propaganda that seemed to proclaim the strength of everything German, slowly eclipsed what was Austrian … One thing was certain: politics had removed from the people what had remained in them from old Austria.'[142] This was a rather vague and rather abstract interpretation. Yet such an approach produced an unprecedented consensus amongst German and Jewish Bukovinians: nearly the entire novel was printed in consecutive issues of *Die Stimme* and it was welcomed by the

Bukovinian Germans too as the work of one of their own.[143] The first edition of the book was out of print within a year.

This consensual vision of a lost world attracted attention beyond the narrow remit of native Bukovinians. The notion of testimonies to a vanished world was a source of fascination. This interest was widespread among intellectuals of the so-called 1968 generation in the German-speaking space – Austria and Switzerland as well as West Germany – especially. As Aleida Assmann has argued, their political activism was gradually channelled into a new vision of the past.[144] With this came the development of a new perspective on Eastern Europe that was distinct from that of expellees, who, until then, had largely controlled the narrative. A typical and, as Anna de Berg has suggested, pioneering account in this respect is Martin Pollack's 1984 *To Galicia* (*Nach Galizien*).[145] In this book, Pollack, an Austrian journalist born in 1944 who had studied Slavic languages and history, drew on a range of authors from the region to take the reader on a literary journey through both space and time. His focus was on the period before the Second World War and all of the writers he drew on and wrote about, including Heinrich Kipper, Alfred Margul-Sperber, Manès Sperber and, in particular, Karl Emil Franzos, were no longer alive. He did not discuss Ausländer and Celan, and only mentioned Margul-Sperber's postwar activities briefly.[146] In the foreword, Pollack explained that the multiethnic world he described 'had disappeared' and 'was lost and could not be brought back' (*eine unwiederbringlich verlorene Welt*).[147] He pointed out that although it might be possible to book a trip to the region, what one would see there had little to do with what he wanted to describe.[148] Pollack himself suggested that he had not needed to travel to the region to write his account.

The reason Pollack gave for this approach was that his characters were real, but the places, as he saw it, were fictional. He pointed to this fact in his book's subtitle: *Of Hasidim, Hutsuls, Poles and Ruthenians: An Imaginary Journey through the Lost World of East Galicia and Bukovina* (*Von Chassiden, Huzulen, Polen und Ruthenen: Eine imaginäre Reise durch die verschwundene Welt Ostgaliziens und der Bukowina*). This situation was the consequence of the annihilation of many of these places and their inhabitants during the war and the Holocaust. However, he not only described the 'murdered shtetl [*Städtel*]',[149] but also the German villages revolving around 'work, the church and the inn' and their 'hardworking, prosaic and pious' inhabitants.[150] The Austrian connection was implicitly, yet continuously present too, if only in his choice of mostly German-speaking writers. Even if he was less naïve about the character of interethnic relations, Pollack, like Drozdowski, made only fleeting allusions to the source of the destruction. He mentioned the Gestapo and the Nazis each only once.[151] As de Berg has noted, Pollack conceived of the book as 'a literary epitaph', a 'reconstruction of the past' of the people who had lived there.¹⁵² His intention was to re-create the Central European world as a whole and in all of its diversity. He therefore gave priority to the everyday lives of Germans and Jews – to those who had made up the German cultural landscape he discussed and who were conspicuously no longer present – and wrote about them together.

In its first use by Ausländer, 'sunkenness' had a dramatic connotation and was linked to the irremediable loss and dislocation caused by the Holocaust. However, now mobilized to discuss a less precisely defined lost world or cultural landscape hidden behind the Iron Curtain, it effectively brought Germans and Jews together in the region at the end of the Cold War. There is perhaps no better illustration of this than Peter Stenberg's study *Journey to Oblivion: The End of the East European Yiddish and German Worlds in the Mirror of Literature*, which was published in 1991, but written and researched in the late 1980s.¹⁵³ Stenberg, a North American scholar, set out to look at the disappearance of the German and Yiddish languages in the region, together with the people who spoke them. He saw the two languages as linked not only by their Germanic roots, but also by their tragic fate.¹⁵⁴ For him, Czernowitz and Bukovina, with its large number of both German and Jewish writers, epitomized the scenario.¹⁵⁵ The scattering of Germans and Jews and the quasi-simultaneous disappearance of their languages from the region legitimized considering them together. He even argued that the Galician writer Manès Sperber's statement regarding the proximity of the memory of the lost shtetl could just as well have been made by some of the region's Germans.¹⁵⁶ The images he included at the start of his book were not only of Jews, who had been deported, but also expelled Germans during and immediately after the Second World War. Among them was also an image of a Romanian-German village in Banat. The picture dated from 1982, but the caption read that Germans had since deserted the village because of the Romanian Revolution of 1989. Although Stenberg emphasized the devastation of the Holocaust, the 'sunkenness' was understood as the result of the devastation of both communism and Nazism; the 'oblivion' was twofold as well: it was of both Germans and Jews.

This conflation had a range of different and loosely related yet mutually reinforcing causes. First, it captured the growing interest in Jewish history and the experiences of German and German-speaking Jews especially, together with their de-exoticization in West Germany and Europe more broadly.¹⁵⁷ Second, it reflected and coincided with a growing interest in the history of Eastern Europe and the Holocaust in this period.¹⁵⁸ Third, it captured West Germans' growing efforts to deal with and address the past, including the issue of the relationship between Nazism and communism, which would culminate in the famous 'historians' controversy' (*Historikerstreit*).¹⁵⁹ Finally, concerning the specific case of Bukovina, the phenomenon of ethnic migration from Romania to West Germany – its effects and perception in West German society – also played a role. From the late 1970s onwards, around 10,000 Germans left Romania every year, including some ethnic Germans and even some 'Jewish' ethnic Germans from Bukovina, such as Alfred Kittner. In the following years, a number of these individuals became active in West German academia and public life, drawing attention to their experiences and to the phenomenon of the 'fifth German literature' and, with this, to Bukovinian literature too.[160] Moreover, over time, emigration from Romania increasingly came to be framed as a de-ethnicized matter of human rights.[161] The attention attracted to the gradual destruction of the German minority's culture and institutions drew attention to the Ceaușescu regime's policies towards ethnic minorities in general and contributed to further connecting the experiences of Germans and Jews from the region.

However, as these diverse issues also show, this was also a moment of transition that revealed how polarized German society had become with respect to the recent past. A conflict that arose between the leadership of the Bukovinian German Landsmannschaft and the editor of a publication of the West German 'national expellee association' (the BdV) in 1984 can serve to illustrate this point. The issue concerned the inclusion of texts by Alfred Margul-Sperber under the heading 'Bukovina' in the BdV's *East German Reader* (*Ostdeutsches Lesebuch*). When she found out, Irma Bornemann, the cultural attaché of the Bukovinian German Landsmannschaft, contacted the editor to share with him both her surprise at not having been consulted about it and the Landsmannschaft's strong disapproval of the choice of Margul-Sperber on several counts. First of all, according to her, 'the fact that [Margul-Sperber] was born in Bukovina and lived there for a while [*sic*] without anyone even taking notice' (*von der Umwelt unbeachtet*) did not justify 'considering him as an example of German literature from Bukovina'. Instead, she suggested that they consider Heinrich Kipper, Georg Drozdowski or Marianne Vincent and even pointed them towards Alfred Klug's 1939 *Bukowiner Deutsches Dichterbuch*, which she argued offered 'a mirror image of poetry from the period'. Second, however, she also underscored Margul-Sperber's closeness to the communist regime, which had 'awarded him prizes' and 'granted him privileges'. In her view, therefore, choosing Margul-Sperber constituted a provocation towards Bukovinian Germans, but also Transylvanian Saxons, who had suffered under the postwar regime in Romania.[162]

A lively exchange ensued. In his response to Bornemann, the editor explained he understood her annoyance, but had also heard strong support for including Margul-Sperber from none other than a Transylvanian Saxon and the editor-in-chief of the Transylvanian Saxon newspaper, *Siebenbürgische Zeitung*, Hans Bergel, who assured him that Margul-Sperber had not been a communist. Besides, as he explained, the publication was not supposed to be a collection of 'expellee literature', but of German-language literature from abroad. Therefore, he was not prepared to remove Margul-Sperber based on ethnicity. He even added: 'Jew here, Jew there, our language is our common house and home, and therefore culture and not race or religion. This is, in fact, quite secondary when it comes to assessing the quality of literature.'[163] Finally, while apologising for his strong words, he stressed his responsibility to be true to his beliefs as an editor. Thereupon, Bornemann had a long phone conversation with Bergel and wrote a lengthy response. She maintained that, in her view, as someone who was openly Jewish (something that Bergel had confirmed) and who had been endorsed by the communists, Margul-Sperber could not represent 'German Bukovina', no matter how well he wrote. For Bornemann, he could be, at best, included among the German-speakers from Bucharest. As she explained, he may have written in German, but, in Bukovina, so had everyone else (Romanians, Ukrainians, Poles and Jews). She then addressed the fact that the editor had seemed to suggest her position was racist and she answered: 'maybe (hopefully) I misunderstood. The coexistence with so many other peoples in Bukovina, including Jews, was characterized by tolerance and reciprocal respect for all activities, including literature'. While the debate appears to have ended there, a few days later, Rudolf Wagner, having looked into the issue, had written Bornemann a supportive letter. He too disapproved of the choice of Margul-Sperber and would have favoured Karl Emil Franzos, who was Jewish but, as Wagner pointed out, 'had had a German mother'.[164]

This debate captured a fundamental difference not only of opinion but also of the premise – a different understanding of what German meant and what Germanness stood for. From Bornemann's perspective, drawing such a strict distinction between Germans and Jews, let alone between German and communist, was not wrong and not even contentious.[165] Yet, as Dan Diner has argued, in this period a shift was taking place that made the admission of guilt a matter of ethnos rather than politics – a process that would only become fully realized after Germany's reunification.[166] Indeed, by the early 1980s, the Holocaust was gradually replacing 'the expulsions' in West German popular opinion and public life as 'the crime of the century' and the ultimate moral benchmark.[167] At the very least, one had to commemorate *all* of the victims of the war.[168] Therefore, what this incident reveals is that German society at this time was changing. In a sense, a large section of the general public had turned against traditional expellee organizations and their discourse, though these might not yet have noticed or taken stock. This situation was therefore symptomatic of the challenge posed to the position of expellees in West Germany in this period in general and the ambivalence of their situation: although they were still vocal and had an established position, their views looked increasingly radical and outdated, and they were increasingly powerless and marginalized.[169] The BdV's *Lesebuch* appeared with Margul-Sperber's writings.[170] The following year, the members of the Landsmannschaft were appalled by the publication of *Niederungen*, a collection of short stories by the Romanian-German writer Herta Müller, which were critical of the *Heimat*, but this book was a success and made her famous in Germany and beyond.[171] In 1986, the 'House of the German East' in Munich hosted a talk on Celan by his childhood friend, fellow Czernowitzer and, herself a 'Jewish *Aussiedler*' (Jewish ethnic German migrant) from Düsseldorf, Edith Silbermann.[172] The Landsmannschaft was swimming against the current.

Ultimately, however, these same developments offered the Bukovinian German Landsmannschaft unprecedented visibility as well as a chance to reframe the group's identity and purpose and even a chance for the organization to reinvent itself. In general, the renewed interest in the history of the Second World War in the 1980s in the FRG brought new attention to the fate of expellees in West Germany.[173] In addition, Bukovinian Germans were able to capitalize on the phenomenon of ethnic German migration from Romania. In general, in the second half of the Cold War, the importance of the small Landsmannschaften of Romanian Germans, Banat Swabians and Transylvanian Saxons, of which many potential members were still living abroad and who were candidates for ethnic migration, grew in contrast to that of the other larger groups of 'expellees' such as Silesians, Sudeten Germans or East Prussians, whose main concern was still 'the expulsions' and territories long lost to Poland, Czechoslovakia and the Soviet Union. Since the late 1970s, the situation of the estimated 2,000–3,000 ethnic Germans in the 'old *Heimat*' Bukovina and their emigration or potential emigration as 'late ethnic German migrants' (*Spätaussiedler*) had become a fundamental justification for the ongoing financing of the activities of the Bukovinian Landsmannschaft in Bonn.[174] The history of resettled Bukovinian Germans was even reinterpreted in light of the new circumstances of the late Cold War and this phenomenon of 'ethnic remigration'. In a 1987 issue of *Kaindl-Archiv*, one could read that, had Bukovinian Germans not been resettled, they would have been forced to join the ranks of the current *Spätaussiedler*.[175] Not only did this reinforce and sustain the interpretation of resettlement as 'ultimately for the best', but it also underscored the contemporary political significance of this group and its experiences.

At this time, the Bukovinian German elite also started exploiting a discourse on the contemporary cultural and political relevance of Bukovinian Germans' experiences, based not only on the narrative of their cultural contribution, but also on Bukovina's history tolerance and peaceful coexistence with members of other ethnicities including Jews. This narrative of harmony was the main argument for the creation of a Bukovinian 'Research Centre'

(Forschungsstelle), which later became the Bukovina-Institute in Augsburg in the late 1980s. In 1985, at the annual meeting of Bukovinian Germans, Georg Simnacher, the President of Swabia's regional government, had spoken of the need to revive the thirty-year-old 'godparenthood' (*Patenschaft*) agreement between the district and the group of Bukovinian Germans, which dated from 1955.[176] Soon afterwards, together with Ortfried Kotzian, a young academic at the University of Augsburg, concrete steps were taken towards creating an interdisciplinary documentation and research centre for Bukovinian Germans.[177] In practice, this had to do with securing the legacy of the ageing Bukovinian German Landsmannschaft and finding a sustainable solution for the preservation of this group's heritage after members of the generation who could remember prewar Bukovina would have disappeared.[178] But the narrative the initiators offered was about European identity, peace and reconciliation and the contemporary relevance of Bukovina as historical multicultural idyll. According to them, before the Germans had left, Bukovina had been a 'bridge to Europe' and, as Hampel said in the quote at the start of this chapter, their model for the institute was to be the University of Czernowitz – 'the easternmost German university' – which had contributed to 'peace and reconciliation among the peoples of the southeast'.[179] Furthermore, as far as possible, parallels were drawn to the present. As Kotzian argued: 'Some of the problems in Austrian Bukovina are reminiscent of the problems we have today [in West Germany] with our guest workers. And other elements are simple political provisions that seem essential to living together reasonably in a future Europe.'[180] Drawing on the language of development aid and humanitarianism, he even highlighted the similarities between the Austrians' 'civilizing mission' in the past and West Germany's role in the divided Europe of the 1980s.[181]

At this time, Bukovinian Germans also briefly achieved the inclusion of their own writers and commentators in Bukovina's 'literary landscape'. Key evidence for this was the conference organized by Anton Schwob in Graz in October 1987, with the title 'Sunken Poetry from Bukovina'.[182] For a start, the peculiarity of this event is captured by the organizers' unusual use of the expression 'Bukovina-German poetry' (*Bukowinadeutsche Dichtung*) to describe German-language Bukovinian literature as a whole. Yet another remarkable feature is that the conference brought together experts working on the region's literature from across Europe and the world, including both Bukovinian Jews, such as Amy Colin and Edith Silbermann, and members of the Landsmannschaft of Bukovinian Germans, such as Paula Tiefenthaler and Kurt Rein, who incidentally and somewhat incongruously used his paper to argue that 'Bukovina literature' had not survived the Second World War.[183] The conference also included a discussion of the work of the *Volk* poet Kipper.[184] Even if the organizers mentioned his receptiveness to the 'brown

Zeitgeist' and the contribution about him emphasized his outspoken endorsement of National Socialism, in itself, as later commentators noted, the evaluation of survivors works by the same criteria as the work of non-survivors, not to mention their potential persecutors, was rather awkward.[185] Indeed, while Kittner had distinguished between the Transylvanian Saxons and Banat Swabians of the new generation and the earlier *Blubodichter* ('blood and soil poets'),[186] here, this distinction appeared to have been blurred. In effect, the concept of Bukovina as a literary or cultural landscape was being used to recreate the region's multicultural character, and a German-Jewish symbiosis in particular, *a posteriori*.

In itself, the consideration of German-speaking Bukovinian writers without differentiating among them based on the specific conditions of production of their respective works was problematic. Yet their retrospective uniting based on an alleged shared background was perhaps even more so. Indeed, this showed that the phenomenon of German-language Bukovinian literature itself had been misunderstood. As Corbea-Hoişie argued just a few years later:

> After 1918, when Bukovina became a Romanian province, it is possible to assert without further ado the existence of two Bukovinian cultures (or rather literatures) in the German language: on the one hand, a rural-provincial culture, with a similar profile to the culture of the Transylvanian Saxons and the Banat Swabians and increasingly legitimized by an ethnic [*völkisch*] and racist ideology imported from the Reich; and, on the other hand, a bourgeois urban and cosmopolitan culture, which was open to experimentation and engagement, and of which the efforts were in line with the new aesthetic sensibility of the modernism prevalent in German and European literature.[187]

Similarly, Valentina Glajar, in her work, distinguishes between different types of Germanness in Bukovina – Habsburg Austrians, Bukovina Swabians and German-speaking Jews – and their respective legacies and literatures. As she argues: 'Bukovina provides fascinating and challenging notions of "Germanness". Unlike the German-Romanians and Sudeten Germans who claim German ethnic and cultural heritage and who represent the emblematic Volksdeutschen, Germans in Bukovina belong to different German-speaking minorities, and not all can claim German ethnicity: they include former Habsburg Austrians, Bukovina Swabians, and German-speaking Jews.'[188] Glajar's choice of Gregor von Rezzori's autobiographical novel *Snows of Yesteryear* (*Blumen im Schnee*), published in 1989, to discuss the case of Bukovina in her book is no coincidence.[189] As she points out, he is one of the few Bukovinian writers whose work engages with the existence and coexistence of these different types of Germanness critically.

Conflating the three obfuscated not only the differences between them but also the remarkable fact of the survival of Jewish German-speaking

Bukovinians after 1918 and after 1945 especially. In other words, commentators took these writers' continued use of German despite the Holocaust for granted. Yet, for many of the Jewish members of this cultural landscape, their work was not so much influenced by the sheer peripherality or liminality of their belonging to a 'linguistic island', let alone their experience of ostracization in the interwar period, but also by a much more complex and contentious estrangement within their own culture and language after 1945. Herein resided the tension, as Celan put it, of language defining their home, yet their language being simultaneously their native language and the murderers' one.[190] This state concerned both those who wrote in German and settled in West Germany and those who did not. While Celan chose to live in France and declared that language was the one thing he had not lost, he was nevertheless most famous in West Germany and particularly paranoid about what he regarded as neo-Nazi tendencies in this country.[191] Similarly, failing to make a breakthrough, Alfred Gong in New York in the late 1960s tried to come back to Europe.[192] These writers were cosmopolitans not by choice, but by force. As Leo Sonntag put it when he was interviewed in 1979, 'the Jews were not the makers of exile but its victims. They did not become heroes voluntarily – it happened as they fled'.[193] Even what has been described as the 'incredible flourishing'[194] of German Jewish poetry in Cernăuți in the two decades before the Second World War can be seen as the result of Jews' 'displacement without moving' or, as Kittner put it, their unique position as 'emigrants in their native home' (*Emigranten auf angestammten Boden*).[195]

This inner conflict was no weaker among Jewish writers from Bukovina who used German and settled in West Germany. Ausländer always presented her choice of Düsseldorf as her last home as a coincidence;[196] Edgar Hilsenrath depicted his immigration from the United States to West Germany in 1974 as a fraught and reluctant decision. In an article published in 1980, he explained that his *Heimat* was Bukovina and that today 'I live somewhere. I don't want to live where I don't feel well such as America. I can't live in Israel because of the language. I don't want to move again. So Germany remains at least my linguistic homeland'.[197] Even Kittner, who moved to West Germany in 1980, explained in his memoir how easy it had been for him, as someone who was born in Vienna, to be considered 'a member of the German cultural circle' and an 'ethnic German migrant' (*Aussiedler*), but he was apparently never happy there.[198] Rosenkranz, who had also come to West Germany as an *Aussiedler*, gave the most banal but perhaps also the most appropriate explanation of the tension experienced by German-speaking Jewish writers in Germany after the war. In an autobiographical note dating from 1984, he wrote: 'I have been living in West Germany since the 2 August 1961. "This is how I came to be among the Germans" and I cannot leave. Among them, I have been able to remember and write down many of my lost poems.'[199]

As Anthony Kauders has argued, coming to Germany was not a given, but was something Jews had to justify repeatedly.[200] For many, it was not a gift, but a burden. Yet, the many other Jewish Bukovinian writers, such as Aharon Appelfeld, Norman Manea and Dan Pagis, who had chosen not to write in German and live elsewhere, were only rarely or sporadically included in the list of Bukovinian writers during the Cold War. They did not suit the image of the sunken and unequivocally *German* cultural landscape of 'Bukovina'. Making geography and language determining factors not only created the German-Jewish symbiosis retrospectively but also imposed a false sense of homogeneity and harmony. The idealization of the Habsburg period and the recollection of 'what was then' were deemed uncontentious and consensual. As a result, as the literary critic Winfried Menninghaus later noted, Bukovina, despite slowly making it back onto the map of Europe by the end of the Cold War, was for a long time not on the map of the Holocaust.[201] On the contrary, as the scholar Martin Hainz has argued, for 'the Germans', Bukovina provided a form of 'incongruent compensation' insofar as it seemed to prove that Germans and Jews had been able to get along at least *somewhere* in Europe.[202] The conception of the region as a sunken cultural landscape thus not only perpetuated assumptions of German cultural superiority by leaving older ethnocultural hierarchies unchallenged, but even had an exculpatory dimension.

Of course, this view of Bukovina was based on a selective and superficial reading of the region's past and poets and their politics. Yet, only after 1989 would the irony that, in Bukovina, as Amy Colin commented, 'not the Nazi poets but the persecuted Jewish writers were the custodians of German culture' be granted due attention.[203] As Herta Müller, for example, wrote in an article published in *Die Zeit* in 1996, the classification of Celan as 'Romanian-German' filled her with unease. She wrote that her own Banat Swabian background meant that she felt close to him, yet she could not help but see her connection as twofold: on the one hand, her country (Romania) and the shared Habsburg heritage (not least the common language, German), but on the other hand, her belonging to the Banat German minority that had supported Hitler. The second dimension of her connection prevented her from feeling unspoilt admiration, let alone unhindered identification:

> I always need both lenses to read the great poetry of a destroyed existence … My father was one of the many Transylvanian Saxons and Banat Germans in the country who, if they had been ordered to, would have sent the Bukovinian Jews to their death. They were fortunate not to receive this order. But it was only the luck of some of their children, because their fathers did not think about it. My father spent Sundays drunk, bowling with army comrades, playing cards and celebrating weddings and parish fairs. They sang the song,

'Where did they end up?' and with *them*, they meant their fallen fellow SS. Where Celan's parents had remained was not a question they ever asked.[204]

Conclusion

Writers and intellectuals, both with their work and its reception, had a significant impact on the image of Bukovina during the Cold War. The personal networks that survived the war, in particular among Bukovinian writers, challenged predominantly ethnic understandings of identity, the strict means of representation and the self-censored modes of commemoration of the past within the traditional Bukovinian representative organizations, the Landsmannschaften. The use of artistic devices, but also the sheer fact that their work gave them a public voice, meant that the influence of this group went far beyond that of the representative organizations and their constituencies. During the Cold War, Bukovina came to be primarily perceived as a 'literary' or 'cultural landscape', and this perception revolved around the use of German rather than a specifically or ethnically German or Jewish experience in the war. It therefore enabled German and Jewish Bukovinians to find some common ground. In a sense, nostalgia had produced a kind of German-Jewish symbiosis retrospectively. Yet, ultimately, the politicization of these issues prevented the experiences – let alone the suffering – of Bukovinians from being realistically evaluated and acknowledged. In other words, Bukovinians largely compensated for loss during the latter stages of the Cold War by ignoring its causes and consequences. Indeed, before 1989–90, the short-lived attempt to summon a consensual Bukovinian multicultural idyll, fitting with the period's politics of appeasement and glossing over decades of enduring antisemitism in West Germany, precluded the admission and engagement with the fact that Jews and Germans from Bukovina belonged to two different communities of experience and were treated very differently both during and after the war.

In the process, the fact that for the Germans, Bukovina remained merely a site of longing and, for Jews, a site of both longing and suffering – a *locus terribilis* – was conveniently overlooked.[205] As Marianne Hirsch has argued, there is a fundamental difference between 'the violent destruction of the Jewish communities and Jewish cultures of Eastern, Central, and Western Europe …[and] the displacements other Europeans had to suffer because of the two wars, painful though they must have been for many'.[206] In the midst of an undifferentiated discourse on the region's 'sunkenness', this difference was blurred and therefore, the Cold War was the breeding ground for new permutations of the 'Bukovina myth'. Bukovina, like Celan, was invoked in contradictory ways. John Felstiner, the author of Celan's first

English-language biography, showed that Celan became a 'contested commodity' in this period.[207] Romanians claimed him in terms of influence (he had, after all, changed his name from the German-sounding 'Antschel' to the Romanian sounding anagram 'Celan'), Germans because of his language, the French because of his choice of Paris as an adoptive home and Israel because of his Jewish roots.[208] He ironically described himself as coming from 'Czernowitz near Sadagora' (*Czernowitz bei Sadagora*), emphasizing the importance of the Hasidic small town a few kilometres outside of his large cosmopolitan hometown for the person he had become.[209] But it is worth noting that in this period, no one regarded him primarily as a Holocaust survivor or as a victim. Similarly, Bukovina was regarded as intriguing but not distressing, sunken but not destroyed. During the Cold War, the region was not forgotten, but the kind of 'remembering' that took place produced an impression of oblivion.

Notes

1. Archiv des Bukowina-Instituts, Augsburg (hereinafter BI), Allg. Korrespondenz, Bezirk Schwaben und Bukowina-Institut: Transcription of the speech in *Bukowina Press: ein Pressedienst der Arbeitsstelle zur Erforschung von Geschichte und Kultur der Bukowina*, 10 May 1989.
2. See S. Frunchak, 'Studying the Land, Contesting the Land: A Select Historiographic Guide to Modern Bukovina', *Carl Beck Papers in Russian and East European Studies* 2108(1) (2011), 31.
3. See e.g. A. Corbea-Hoişie and M. Astner (eds), *Kulturlandschaft Bukowina: Studien zur deutschsprachigen Literatur des Buchenlandes nach 1918* (Iaşi: Ed. Univ. Alexandru Ioan Cuza, 1990).
4. L. Gailing and M. Leibenath, 'Von der Schwierigkeit, "Landschaft" oder "Kulturlandschaft" allgemeingültig zu definieren', *Raumforschung und Raumordnung* 70(2) (2012), 95–106, here 102.
5. See K. Scharr, *'Die Landschaft Bukowina': das Werden einer Region an der Peripherie 1774–1918* (Cologne: Böhlau, 2010), 25. See also T. Weger, 'Cultural Landscapes – ein kulturwissenschaftliches Konzept', in A. Demshuk and T. Weger (eds), *Cultural Landscapes: Translatlantische Perspektiven auf Wirkungen und Auswirkungen deutscher Kultur und Geschichte im östlichen Europa* (Munich: De Gruyter Oldenbourg, 2015), 17–28, especially 26.
6. This term is sometimes translated as 'mastering the past'. On this, see C. Maier, *The Unmasterable Past: History, Holocaust, and German National Identity* (Cambridge, MA: Harvard University Press, 1988).
7. For an overview of these trends, see C. Goschler and A. Kauders, 'Dritter Teil: 1968–1989 Positionierungen', in M. Brenner (ed.), *Geschichte der Juden in Deutschland von 1945 bis zur Gegenwart: Politik, Kultur und Gesellschaft* (Munich: C.H. Beck, 2012), 295–375. On philosemitism, see also F. Stern, *The Whitewashing of the Yellow Badge: Antisemitism and Philosemitism in Postwar Germany* (Oxford: Pergamon Press, 1992).

8. See A. Kauders, 'West German Jewry: Guilt, Power and Pluralism', *Quest. Issues in Contemporary History. Journal of Fondazione CDEC* 1 (2010), 17–33, here 29. As Kauders explains elsewhere, in the 1970s, there was an emotional shift in the Jewish relationship to space and to Germanness; as he put it, by the end of the 1970s, 'on a symbolic level at least, prominent Jews [in West Germany] had gained a sense of place'. A. Kauders, 'The Emotional Geography of a Lost Space', in F. Eigler and J. Kugele (eds), *Heimat: At the Intersection of Memory and Space* (Berlin: De Gruyter Oldenbourg, 2012), 193–207, here 206.
9. On this, the most stimulating account remains: K. Schlögel, *Die Mitte liegt ostwärts: Die Deutschen, der verlorene Osten und Mitteleuropa* (Berlin: Siedler, 1986).
10. Habsburg scholars such as Raimund Friedrich Kaindl did a great deal for the conception of Bukovina as a self-contained and separate landscape. See also e.g. the travel guide to the region from 1907, reprinted in 2001: H. Mittelmann, *Illustrierter Führer durch die Bukowina*, edited by H. Kusdat (1907–8; reprint: Vienna: Mandelbaum Verlag, 2001).
11. He added Margul to his name after the Second World War and is known both as 'Sperber' and 'Margul-Sperber'.
12. See P. Motzan, 'Alfred Margul-Sperber (1898–1967), eine Portraitskizze', in A. Corbea-Hoişie, G. Guţu and M. Hainz (eds), *Stundenwechsel: Neue Perspektiven zu Alfred Margul-Sperber, Rose Ausländer, Paul Celan, Immanuel Weissglas* (Konstanz: Hartung-Gorre, 2002), 10–42.
13. See G. Guţu and P. Motzan, 'Nachwort', in A. Margul-Sperber (ed.), *Die Buche: Eine Anthologie deutschsprachiger Judendichtung aus der Bukowina* (Aachen: Rimbaud Verlag, 2009), 425–69, here 428.
14. He promoted them in Germany, Austria and Switzerland, but also among Romanian-Germans. However, his success was limited. Many of their works were self-published in Cernăuţi: Guţu and Motzan, 'Nachwort', 433.
15. A. Margul-Sperber, 'Der Unsichtbare Chor: Entwurf eines Grundrisses des deutschen Schrifttums in der Bukowina', in *Czernowitzer Morgenblatt*, 25 July 1928 quoted in Guţu and Motzan, 'Nachwort', 434. See also A. Margul-Sperber, 'Jüdische Dichtung in der Bukowina', original from 1936, reprinted in Margul-Sperber, *Die Buche*, 358–61, in which Margul-Sperber speaks of this literature's 'fourfold tragedy' (*vierfache Tragik*).
16. National Museum of Romanian Literature (Muzeul Naţional al Literaturii Române, Bucharest), Nachlass Alfred Margul-Sperber (hereinafter MLR, NS), 25000/51: *Deutscher Brief aus der Bukowina*, 5; republished in *Die Buche*, 351–57.
17. Margul-Sperber, 'Jüdische Dichtung in der Bukowina'.
18. Guţu and Motzan, 'Nachwort', 433.
19. G. Guţu, 'Im Trubel der Geschichte – Heinrich Zillichs Briefe an Alfred Margul-Sperber', in A. Schwob (ed.), *Die deutsche Literaturgeschichte Ostmittel- und Südosteuropas von der Mitte des 19. Jahrhunderts bis heute* (Munich: Verl. Südostdt. Kulturwerk, 1992), 206–15, here 214.
20. A. Klug, *Bukowiner Deutsches Dichterbuch* (Stuttgart: E. Wahl, Stuttgarter Volksdeutsche Bücherei, 1939).
21. See, for instance, P. Motzan and S. Sienerth (eds), *Wahrnehmung der deutsch(sprachig)en Literatur aus Ostmittel- und Südosteuropa – ein Paradigmenwechsel? Neue Lesearten und Fallbeispiele* (Munich: IKGS Verlag, 2009); most recently, see A. Corbea-Hoişie, *Paul Celans 'unbequemes Zuhause': Sein erstes Jahrzehnt in Paris* (Aachen: Rimbaud Verlag, 2017).

22. The expression is from the speech delivered upon his receipt of the Georg-Büchner Prize in Bremen in 1960. See P. Celan, *Der Meridian: Endfassung, Entwürfe, Materialen*, edited by B. Böschenstein and H. Schmull (Frankfurt am Main: Suhrkamp, 1999).
23. MLR, NS, 25002/19: Letter from Celan to Margul-Sperber, 8 February 1962.
24. P. Celan, 'Ansprache anlässlich der Entgegennahme des Literaturpreises der Freien Hansestadt Bremen (1958)', in *Gesammelte Werke in fünf Bänden*, vol. 3 (Frankfurt am Main: Suhrkamp, 1992), 185.
25. MLR, NS, 25002/24: Letter from Celan to Margul-Sperber, 7 December 1966.
26. Quoted in C. Helfrich, *'Es ist ein Aschensommer in der Welt': Rose Ausländer: Biographie* (Weinheim: Beltz, Quadriga, 1995), 32.
27. Originally published in R. Ausländer, *Gesammelte Gedichte* (n.p., 1977); quoted in R. Ausländer, 'Erinnerungen an eine Stadt', in H. Braun (ed.), *Rose Ausländer: Materialen zu Leben und Werk* (Frankfurt am Main: Fischer, 1991), 10.
28. See, for instance, the speech by Moses Rosenkranz about Margul-Sperber from 1946 quoted in G. Guțu, 'Nachwort von George Guțu', in M. Rosenkranz, *Briefe an Alfred Margul-Sperber 1930–1963*, edited by G. Guțu (Aachen: Rimbaud Verlag, 2015), 171–91, here 178.
29. Aside from the correspondences of Rose Ausländer, Alfred Margul-Sperber and others, informal groups of Bukovinians and, including, in some cases, Romanian Jews formed in Bucharest around Margul-Sperber, in New York City around Alfred Gong, in Paris around Celan and Leo Sonntag (e.g. the Romanian Jews Isac Chiva and Serge Moscovici and Jacques Schärf) and in Israel around Manfred Reifer and Elias Weinstein. On Bucharest, see P. Solomon, *Paul Celan: The Romanian Dimension*, translated from Romanian by E. Tegla (Syracuse, NY: Syracuse University Press, 2019); on Paris, see Corbea-Hoișie, *Paul Celans 'unbequemes Zuhause'*; on New York, see *Bukowina Bulletin: ein Nachrichtenblatt der Bucovinaer Cultural Society, inc. New York*, of which the first issue appeared in April 1967; on Israel, see *Die Stimme: Mitteilungsblatt für die Bukowiner*.
30. Two of Ausländer's poems published in 1985 were dedicated to Celan; in 1979, Drozdowski dedicated a poem to Immanuel Weissglas and three of Kittner's poems were dedicated to Drozdowski, Ausländer and Weissglas. See G. Guțu, 'Nachwort von George Guțu', in Rosenkranz, *Briefe an Alfred Margul-Sperber*, 179. On the accusations of plagiarism, see G. Guțu, 'Drinking the Milky Blackness, Romanian Journal of Artistic Creativity', *Romanian Journal of Artistic Creativity* 1 (2013), 138–48.
31. See G. Guțu, 'Dialogizität als Identitätsfindung deutschsprachiger Dichter in der Bukowina', in E. Dácz (ed.), *Räumliche Semantisierungen: Raumkonstruktionen in den deutschsprachigen Literaturen aus Zentral- und Südosteuropa im 20.-21. Jahrhundert* (Regensburg: Verlag Friedrich Pustet, 2018), 211–30.
32. N. Shchyhlevska, *Verschränkungen: Leben und Werk von Autoren aus der Bukowina anhand von Briefen und Nachlässe* (Aachen: Rimbaud Verlag, 2011), 11.
33. Shchyhlevska, *Verschränkungen*, 23.
34. A. Corbea-Hoișie, 'Bukarest als intellektuelle Hauptstadt der deutschsprachigen Bukowina: 1945–1947', unpublished conference paper presented at the conference *Bukovina and Bukovinians after the Second World War: (Re)shaping and (Re)thinking a Region after Genocide and 'Ethnic Unmixing'*, University of Augsburg, 14–15 September 2016.
35. Solomon, *Paul Celan*, 17–43.
36. Shchyhlevska, *Verschränkungen*, 19.
37. Motzan, 'Margul-Sperber', 35.

38. Quoted in ibid.
39. H. Stănescu, 'Der Dichter des "Nobiskruges", Immanuel Weissglas', *German Life and Letters* 39(1) (1985), 46–64.
40. Shchyhlevska, *Verschränkungen*, 13.
41. T. Buck, 'Nachwort', in A. Kittner and E. Silbermann (eds), *Erinnerungen 1906–1991* (Aachen: Rimbaud Verlag, 1996), 126.
42. Over the course of the 1950s, Margul-Sperber corresponded about his work with writers, publishers and institutions in Austria, West Germany but also the GDR and the Soviet Union. See e.g. MLR, NS, 25002/1118; 25002/626; 25002/1110/2; 25002/1096/1.
43. See E. Axmann, *Wege, Städte: Erinnerungen* (Aachen: Rimbaud Verlag, 2005); see also E. Axmann, *Die Kunststrickerin: Erinnerungssplitter* (Aachen: Rimbaud Verlag, 2010); H. Bergel, 'Erinnerungen an Alfred Margul-Sperber', in D. Goltschnigg, A. Schwob and G. Fuchs (eds), *Die Bukowina: Studien zu einer versunkenen Literaturlandschaft* (Tübingen: Francke Verlag, 1990), 187–98, especially 188.
44. Bergel, 'Erinnerungen', 191.
45. G. Guțu and P. Motzan, 'Editorischer Bericht', in Margul-Sperber, *Die Buche*, 21–43, here 21–22.
46. A. Kittner, 'Epilog', in A. Margul-Sperber, *Geheimnis und Verzicht: Das lyrische Werk in Auswahl* (Bucharest: Kriterion, 1975), 608. He was known, due to his height and kindness, as 'the friendly giant' (*der gütige Riese*). The expression comes from one of Rosenkranz's poems in which he called him 'Margul, der gute Riese': Guțu and Motzan, 'Editorischer Bericht', 21.
47. Corbea-Hoișie, 'Bukarest als intellektuelle Hauptstadt'.
48. P. Weber, 'Regime Changes, Public Memory and the Pursuit of Justice: The Case of German-Speaking Jews in Bukovina, 1920–1960' (D.Phil. thesis, University of Sussex, 2005), especially 160–63.
49. Motzan, 'Alfred Margul-Sperber', 37.
50. A. Kittner, *Hungermarsch und Stacheldraht: Verse von Trotz und Zuversicht* (Bucharest: ESPLA, 1956). See also O.W. Cisek, 'Gedichte von Trotz und Zuversicht', *Neuer Weg*, 8 March 1957.
51. On the reception of Margul-Sperber in West Germany, see P. Motzan, 'Der Lyriker Alfred Margul-Sperber: Ein Forschungsbericht. Nebst einer kurzen Nachrede', in Schwob, *Die deutsche Literaturgeschichte Ostmittel- und Südosteuropas*, 119–36, here 124–25. He notes that the first article published on Margul-Sperber in the FRG was his obituary and that he was more famous in the GDR. See also 'Das Lebenswerk eines Bukowiner jüdisch-deutschen Dichters', *Die Stimme*, February 1975.
52. Motzan, 'Margul-Sperber', 37.
53. Ibid., 35.
54. See A. Corbea-Hoișie, 'Die biographische Wende in der Celan-Forschung', in Corbea-Hoișie, Guțu and Hainz, *Stundenwechsel*, 143–164, here 144.
55. Corbea-Hoișie, *Paul Celans 'unbequemes Zuhause'*.
56. Heinrich-Heine-Institut, Rheinisches Literaturarchiv, Nachlass Rose Ausländer (hereinafter HHI, NRA): Letter from Ausländer to Itzik Manger, 4 February 1947.
57. HHI, NRA: Letter Kittner to Ausländer, 12 August 1976.
58. HHI, NRA: Letter from Ausländer to Kittner, 3 June 1977.
59. See e.g. *Die Stimme*, November 1946 and February 1948; see also Shchyhlevska, *Verschränkungen*, 73.
60. Kittner, 'Epilog', 592.

61. HHI, NRA: Letter from Kittner to Ausländer, 15 March 1976, emphasis in original.
62. At one of their meetings, Kittner told Guțu: 'The essence of my experiences is captured in my poems.' Quoted in G. Guțu, 'Nachwort', in Alfred Kittner, *Briefe/4: Briefe an Alfred Margul-Sperber 1932–1966* (Aachen: Rimbaud Verlag, 2015), 73.
63. See D. Goltschnigg, A. Schwob and G. Fuchs, 'Vorwort', in *Die Bukowina*, 9–13, here 12.
64. This was published posthumously: A. Colin and A. Kittner (eds), *Versunkene Dichtung der Bukowina* (Munich: W. Fink, 1994). Originally, it supposed to be entitled *An Anthology of Romanian German Poetry* (*Befassung mit der Anthologie rumäniendeutsche Lyrik*); see Shchyhlevska, *Verschränkungen*, 79.
65. Colin and Kittner, *Versunkene Dichtung*, 417–18.
66. Kittner and Silbermann, *Erinnerungen*, 115.
67. Ibid., 112–13.
68. See e.g. 'Gedichte aus der Bukowina: verhallter Stimmen Chor', *Neue Literatur* 11 (1971), 36–58 and *Neue Literatur* 12 (1971), 44–56, quoted in G. Guțu, 'Nachwort von George Guțu', in Rosenkranz, *Briefe an Alfred Margul-Sperber*, 174.
69. B. Kolf, 'Eine Gegend, in der Menschen und Bücher lebten: Die Bukowina als lyrische Landschaft', *Akzente* 4 (1982), 336–83.
70. R. Hoghe, 'Vergessen, wie macht man das? Begegnungen in einem jüdischen Altersheim', *Die Zeit* no. 12, 16 March 1979; R. Hoghe, 'Schreiben gegen Sterben', *Die Zeit* no. 27, 27 June 1980; G. Lindemann, 'Verse aus der Galgenzeit', *Die Zeit* no. 43, 17 October 1980; R. Hoghe, 'Sie hält fest an ihren Träumen. Jüdisches Altenheim, 4. Stock, Zimmer 419: Ein Besuch bei der Dichterin Rose Ausländer', *Die Zeit* no. 41, 7 October 1983; W. Hink, 'Genug Herz verschleudert: Gedichte aus Rose Ausländers letzten Lebensjahren', *Frankfurter Allgemeine Zeitung*, 22 October 1988. For the range of publications on Rosenkranz, see M. Rosenkranz, *Briefe an Kaspar Niklaus Wildberger, 1978–1933* (Aachen: Rimbaud Verlag, 2016).
71. 'Rumäniens Juden und ihr Verhältnis zum Staat', *Neue Zürcher Zeitung* no. 187, 15–16 August 1982.
72. K. Rein, 'Politische und kulturgeschichtliche Grundlagen der "deutschsprachigen Literatur der Bukowina"', in Schwob, Goltschnigg and Fuchs, *Die Bukowina*, 27–48, here 27.
73. See Kittner, 'Epilog'.
74. See M. Meng, *Shattered Spaces: Encountering Jewish Ruins in Postwar Germany and Poland* (Cambridge, MA: Harvard University Press, 2011), 5.
75. Celan wrote 800 poems between 1938 and 1970. See J. Felstiner, *Paul Celan: Poet, Survivor, Jew* (New Haven: Yale University Press, 1995), xvi. In the 1970s, several people, including George Guțu, wrote doctoral dissertations about Celan's work: Guțu graduated in 1977 in Leipzig. Klaus Voswinckel wrote a thesis on Celan in Munich: K. Voswinckel, *Paul Celan: Verweigerte Poetisierung der Welt: Versuch einer Deutung* (Heidelberg: Lothar Stiehm Verlag, 1974). Felstiner also says he discovered Celan around this time, in 1977.
76. Voswinckel discovered Leo Sonntag and Kaspar Niklaus Wildberger became interested in Rosenkranz after working on Celan; see Rosenkranz, *Briefe an Kaspar Niklaus Wildberger*; and also J. Stenzel, *Leo Sonntag: Ein jüdisches Emigrantenschicksal* (Essen: Verl. Die Blaue Eule, 1994).
77. K.E. Franzos and J. Strelka, *Erzählungen aus Galizien und der Bukowina* (Berlin: Nicolai, 1988).

78. See e.g. 'Leo Sonntag in Paris: Ein Portrait von Ulrike Voswinckel', *Bayerischer Rundfunk*, 13 March 1980.
79. On this, see also M. Hainz, 'Czernowitz/Bukowina als europäische Lektion', *Kakanien Revisited*, 17 August 2005. Retrieved 23 September 2019 from http://www.kakanien.ac.at/beitr/fallstudie/MHainz1.pdf.
80. 'Paul Celan zum Gruss!', *Die Stimme*, October 1969.
81. I. Chalfen, 'Paul Celan in Jerusalem', *Die Stimme*, November 1969.
82. M. Teich, '1920–1970: Paul Celan hat uns verlassen', *Die Stimme*, June 1970.
83. D. Müller-Altneu, 'Unser Paul' and Manfred Winkler, 'Epilog auf Paul Celan', *Die Stimme*, June 1970.
84. See e.g. I. Chalfen, 'Paul Celans Tod: "Ein Meister aus Deutschland"?', *Die Stimme*, April 1972; I. Chalfen, 'Paul Celan: Sieben Jahre Später', *Die Stimme*, August 1977.
85. I. Chalfen, *Paul Celan: Eine Biographie seiner Jugend* (Frankfurt am Main: Insel-Verl., 1979), 24.
86. IKGS, Vorlass Winkler (hereinafter IKGS, VW): Letter from Winkler to Mrs S., Deutsche Verlags-Anstalt, 10 March 1978.
87. On the *Lyriskreis*, see D. Wahl (ed.), *Lyris: deutschsprachige Dichterinnen und Dichter in Israel* (Frankfurt am Main: Beerenverlag, 2004); *Der Klang der Worte: Deutsche Sprache in Jerusalem*, directed by Gerhard Schick, DVD, Goethe Institut, 2008. On Winkler's cooperation with West Germany, see IKGS, VW, various documents.
88. For the original collection of letters, see IKGS, VW. A selection has been published in M. Winkler, H. Bergel and R. Windish-Middendorf, *'Wir setzen das Gespräch fort…': Briefwechsel eines Juden aus der Bukowina mit einem Deutschen von Siebenbürgen* (Berlin: Frank und Timme, 2012).
89. M.M. Faerber (ed.), *Stimmen aus Israel: Eine Anthologie deutschsprachiger Literatur in Israel* (Gerlingen bei Stuttgart: Bleicher, 1979); and M.M. Faerber (ed.), *Auf dem Weg: eine Anthologie deutschsprachiger Literatur in Israel* (Gerlingen bei Stuttgart: Bleicher, 1989). In 1983, another German-language anthology was published in Israel: A. Schwarz-Gardos (ed.), *Heimat ist anderswo: Deutsche Schriftsteller in Israel; Erzählungen und Gedichte* (Freiburg im Breisgau: Herder, 1983).
90. Rudel, who had left Romania in 1972, was also editor in chief of *Die Stimme* in the 1990s. The Verband was disbanded in 2005. For general information about the Association, see Verband deutschsprachige Schriftsteller in Israel (ed.), *Nicht das letzte Wort: Eine Dokumentation: 30 Jahre – 1975 bis 2005* (Berlin: Boesche, 2005).
91. Faerber, 'Vorwort', in *Stimmen aus Israel*, 9.
92. Ibid., 10.
93. A. Kilcher and E. Edelmann-Ohler, *Deutsche Sprachkultur in Palästina/Israel: Geschichte und Bibliographie* (Berlin: De Gruyter, 2017), 60–63.
94. W.P. Heyd, 'Nachwort', in *Stimmen aus Israel*, 250.
95. D. Porat, *Israeli Society, the Holocaust and its Survivors* (London: Vallentine Mitchell, 2008), 388–403, here 389.
96. Retrieved 23 September 2019 from http://www.jewishhistory.huji.ac.il/Centers/center_for_research_on_romanian_.htm.
97. See 'Aus der Tätigkeit des Weltverbandes der Juden aus der Bukowina', *Die Stimme*, May 1981.
98. Bundesarchiv Lastenausgleichsarchiv, ZLA7/03 – 1234 (*Extra-Dokumentation Rumänien, Jüdische Volkszugehörigkeit*), Bucovinian international appeal for supporters.
99. '40 Jahre Stimme', *Die Stimme*, December 1984.
100. On this, see *Die Stimme*, March 1981

101. In the 1980s, some articles appeared on people's trips to the region, but these were not depicted as easy experiences. See e.g. R. Beckermann, 'Vier Tage im jetzigen Czernowitz', *Die Stimme*, May–August 1986. Beckermann, whose father was from Bukovina, later made a film based on her 'search for the *Heimat*' and on her trip. See *Die papierene Brücke*, directed by R. Beckermann, DVD (Austria: R. Beckermann, 1987). On this, see also R. Beckermann, 'Erdbeeren in Czernowitz', in R. Beckermann and C. Ransmayr (eds), *Im blinden Winkel: Nachrichten aus Mitteleuropa* (Vienna: Brandstätter: 1985), 79–100.
102. Jakob Weiner (former Vice-President of the World Organization of Bukovina Jews), interview by the author, Tel Aviv, Israel, June 2013.
103. M. Teich, 'Von Buczacz nach Jerusalem', *Die Stimme*, March 1970.
104. I. Rosenberg-Dubenski, 'Geniegegend mit Talentschwemme', *Die Stimme*, April 1981.
105. E. Beck (ed.), *Bibliographie zur Landeskunde: Literatur bis zum Jahre 1965* (Munich: Veröffentlichungen des Südostdeutschen Kulturwerkes, 1966); E. Beck (ed.), *Bibliographie zur Kultur und Landeskunde: Literatur aus den Jahren 1965–1975* (Dortmund: Forschungsstelle Ostmitteleuropa, 1985).
106. See R. Wagner (ed.), *Alma Mater Francisco Josephina: Die deutschsprachige Nationalitäten-Universität in Czernowitz. Festschrift zum 100. Jahrestag ihrer Eröffnung 1875* (Munich: Verlag Hans Menschendörfer, 1979); R. Wagner, *Deutsches Kulturleben in der Bukowina* (Vienna: Schutzverein Österr. Landsmannschaft, 1981); R. Wagner, *Der Parlamentarismus und nationale Ausgleich in der ehemals österreichischen Bukowina* (Munich: Verlag 'Der Südostdeutsche', 1984); R. Wagner, *Das multinationale österreichische Schulwesen in der Bukowina* (Munich: 'Der Südostdeutsche', 1985–86). A chapter in *Deutsches Kulturleben* entitled 'Deutschsprachiges Schrifttum nichtdeutscher Autoren – Übersetzungen' briefly mentioned the region's Jewish writers; see 35–36.
107. J. Brucker, *Und immer wieder Hoffnung: Buchenlandtrilogie* (Munich: Landsmannschaft der Buchenlanddeutschen, 1984).
108. P. Tiefenthaler (ed.), *Festschrift zum 20-jährigen Jubiläums-Bundestreffen Pfingsten 1969: Zwanzig Jahre Landsmannschaft der Buchenlanddeutschen e. V. 1949 – 1969* (Planegg: Landsmannschaft der Buchenlanddeutschen, 1969).
109. On Herbert Mayer and his prewar work in particular, see M. Hausleitner, *'Viel Mischmasch mitgenommen': Die Umsiedlungen aus der Bukowina 1940* (Berlin; Boston: Verlag Walter de Gruyter, 2018), 222–23.
110. An issue appeared every year from 1978 apart from in 1980, 1981 and 1983.
111. BI, Bundesverband der Bukowiner Landsmannschaft. Landesverband Bayern, Nr. 7 (1972–74), Charter (*Satzung*) of the Raimund-Kaindl-Gesellschaft e. V. (no date).
112. Das Haus der Heimat in Stuttgart opened in 1976 and the Institut für Donauschwäbischen Geschichte und Kultur in Tübingen in 1979.
113. BI, Allg. Korrespondenz Bundesverband, 1975: Letter from E.B. to the national archive of Bukovina Germans (Bundesarchiv der Landsmannschaft der Buchenlanddeutschen e. V.), 20 September 1976; on the Arminia House, see BI, Allg. Korrespondenz Bundesverband, 1977–79: Letter from the Akademische Burschenschaft Arminia-Czernowitz zu Linz to the Landsmannschaft der Buchenlanddeutschen, 16 February 1978.
114. BI, Allg. Korrespondenz Bundesverband, 1977–79: Letter from Erich Beck to Max Zelgin, 12 April 1978.
115. BI, Allg. Korrespondenz Bundesverband, 1969: Letter from Otto Lachmund to the Regional Leader in Hesse, 18 June 1969.
116. Bücherkatalog. Landsmannschaft der Buchenlanddeutschen, Stand April 1966 (Library of the Bukovina-Institute).

117. BI, Allg. Korrespondenz Bundesverband, 1977–79: Letter from Bornemann to the Federal Ministry of Interior concerning cultural work (*kulturelle Breitenarbeit*), 14 September 1978.
118. BI, Bundesverband der Bukowiner Landsmannschaft. Landesverband Bayern, Nr. 7: various applications from October and November 1974.
119. BI, Allg. Korrespondenz Bundesverband, 1977–79: Letter from the Landsmannschaft directorate [signed Zelgin and Dombrowski] to Mr G., 31 August 1978, emphasis in original.
120. BI, Allg. Korrespondenz Bundesverband, 1967 (2), Rudolf Wagner, 'heimatpolitische Thesen', 3 May 1967.
121. BI, Bundesverband der Bukowiner Landsmannschaft. Landesverband Bayern, Nr. 7: Protocol of the meeting with the national organization (*Hauptverband Sitzung*) in Munich, 7 November 1970: 'Beim gegenwärtigen Stand der Ostpolitik müßte [Wagner] aber heimatpolitisch eine Drehung von 180 Grad vornehmen, um bei den Behörden in Bonn genehm zu sein.'
122. On so-called 'homesickness tourism' and the notion of acceptance, see A. Demshuk, *The Lost German East: Forced Migration and the Politics of Memory 1945–1970* (New York: Cambridge University Press, 2012). See also E. Fendl, 'Reisen in die verlorene Vergangenheit - Überlegungen zum "Heimwehtourismus"', *Jahrbuch für deutsche und osteuropäische Volkskunde* 41 (1998), 85–100.
123. 'Kunstreise in die Bukowina: Die Moldauklöster im Norden Rumäniens', *NZZ* no. 102, 1 March 1974. For Wagner's response, see Reader Letter signed 'R. W': 'Kunstreise in die Bukowina', *NZZ* no. 113, 8 March 1974.
124. A 'Bukovina Society of the Americas' was even created in 1988: http://bukovina society.org/about-us/bsa-file_history_the-bukowina-society (retrieved 23 September 2019).
125. See e.g. M. Bendas-Ast, *Die Bukowina heute* (n.p., 1981). While it presented a very similar discourse, its format with large contemporary pictures and little text was very different and it was not supported by the Landsmannschaft. See also BI, Allg. Korrespondenz Bundesverband, 1980–81: Letter from D.J. to Landsmannschaft der Buchenlanddeutschen asking for accounts of resettlement, 31 May 1981.
126. Speech by Norbert Gaschler about resettlement in 1981 published as: Norbert Gaschler, 'Die Umsiedlung der Buchenlanddeutschen im Spätherbst 1940 und ihre Folgen für die Katholiken und ihre Priester aus Bessarabien, der Bukowina und der Dobrudscha' (in two parts), *Analele Bucovinei* XVII(1) (2010), 301–42 and XVII(2) (2010), 427–36.
127. I. Bornemann (ed.), *Bukowina: Landschaften – Bauten – Denkmäler* (Munich: Landsmannschaft der Buchenlanddeutschen, 1986); I. Bornemann, P. Tiefenthaler and R. Wagner (eds), *Czernowitz: Eine Stadt im Wandel der Zeit: mit Berücksichtigung ihres deutschen kulturellen Lebens* (Munich: Bertsch, 1988); I. Bornemann, (ed.), *Mit Fluchtgepäck die Heimat verlassen … 50 Jahre seit der Umsiedlung der Buchenlanddeutschen* (Augsburg: Verlag 'Der Südostdeutsche', 1990).
128. By the early 1970s, Ottilie Blass was the women's representative (Bundesfrauenreferentin); Elfriede Reif was the leader in Swabia; Irma Bornemann was press attaché for Baden-Württemberg and later became the federal cultural attaché (Bundeskulturreferentin). Later still, Paula Tiefenthaler became the federal representative.
129. P. Tiefenthaler (ed.), *Festschrift zum 30-jährigen Jubiläums-Bundestreffen Pfingsten 1979: Dreißig Jahre Landsmannschaft der Buchenlanddeutschen e. V. 1949–1979* (Planegg: Landsmannschaft der Buchenlanddt, 1979), 29–30.

130. BI, Allg. Korrespondenz Bundesverband, 1975: Letter from Fedorowytsch to the directorate of the Landsmannschaft, no subject matter, no day, July 1976 (no day), summarizing the circumstances for members of the Landsmannschaft.
131. BI, Allg. Korrespondenz Bundesverband, 1975: Letter from Fedorowytsch, July 1976.
132. See BI, Allg. Korrespondenz Bundesverband, 1975: Letter from Max Zelgin to Bogdan Fedorowytsch, 31 May 1976.
133. BI, Allg. Korrespondenz Bundesverband, 1975: Letter from Fedorowytsch to Zelgin, no subject matter, 20 May 1976.
134. BI, Allg. Korrespondenz Bundesverband, 1975: Letter from Fedorowytsch to Bornemann, no subject matter, 30 July 1976.
135. BI, Allg. Korrespondenz Bundesverband, 1980: Letter from K.R. to the Landsmannschaft der Buchenlanddeutschen (Christian Armbrüster), 10 December 1979 and accompanying documents.
136. BI, Allg. Korrespondenz Bundesverband, 1986: Letter from K.R. to Landsmannschaft der Buchenlanddeutschen (Paula Tiefenthaler), 9 September 1986.
137. G. Drozdowski, *Damals in Czernowitz und rundum: Erinnerungen eines Altösterreichers* (Carinthia: Verlag der kleinen Zeitung, 1984).
138. It is, for instance, reminiscent of S. Zweig's *Die Welt von gestern* (*The World of Yesterday*). Drozdowski, *Damals in Czernowitz*, 11.
139. Drozdowski, *Damals in Czernowitz*, 16, 132, 149.
140. Ibid., 18–19.
141. He wrote: 'The name of the region today doesn't interest me. The Communist East which has swallowed it can call it what it likes'; ibid., 12. The interwar period was hardly discussed, and resettlement and the deportations to Transnistria were only mentioned in passing. References to the Nazis or German nationalism were, for instance, made with distancing irony and characterized by the use of passive forms, reported speech and separations from the main body of the text by a section (the epilogue) or brackets. See ibid., 26, 57, 112, 198.
142. Ibid., 198.
143. A positive review appeared in *Die Stimme*, October 1984. Excerpts were published in *Die Stimme* from March to September 1985: 'Die Stadt am Pruth', March 1985; 'Vor und hinter den Kulissen', April 1985; 'Vivat Academia!' July/August 1985; 'Von Armen und Schnorren', September 1985. A brief but very positive review, together with a letter from Rudolf Wagner to the author and Drozdowski's response, appeared in *Der Südostdeutsche*, June 1984.
144. A. Assmann, '1968 in Germany: A Generation with Two Phases and Faces', *Eurozine*, 22 June 2018. Retrieved 23 September 2019 from https://www.eurozine.com/1968-germany-generation-two-phases-faces.
145. M. Pollack, *Nach Galizien: Von Chassiden, Huzulen, Polen und Ruthenen: Eine imaginäre Reise durch die verschwundene Welt Ostgaliziens und der Bukowina* (Vienna: C. Brandstätter, 1984).
146. Ibid., 151.
147. Ibid., 7–8.
148. Ibid., 7.
149. The expression is borrowed from Manès Sperber, who described himself as 'the only survivor of the murdered Städtel'. Ibid., 117.
150. Ibid., 72.
151. Ibid., 48, 80.

152. A. de Berg, 'Nach Galizien': Entwicklung der Reiseliteratur am Beispiel der deutschsprachigen Reiseberichte vom 18. bis zum 21. Jahrhundert (Frankfurt am Main: Peter Lang, 2010), 105.
153. P. Stenberg, *Journey to Oblivion: The End of the East European Yiddish and German Worlds in the Mirror of Literature* (Toronto: University of Toronto Press, 1991), 3.
154. Ibid., 8, 46.
155. Ibid., 42–43.
156. Ibid., 173.
157. On this, see e.g. Goschler and Kauders, 'Dritter Teil: 1968–1989 Positionierungen'.
158. This famously culminated in the broadcasting of the *Holocaust* miniseries in West Germany in 1979. For a recent and broad overview of the dynamics of historical memory in West Germany, including this period, see J. Olick, *The Sins of the Fathers: Germany, Memory, Method* (Chicago: The University of Chicago Press, 2016). See also M. Fulbrook, *German National Identity after the Holocaust* (Cambridge: Polity Press, 1999).
159. See A. Hillgruber, *Zweierlei Untergang: Die Zerschlagung des Deutschen Reiches und das Ende des europäischen Judentums* (Berlin: Siedler, 1986); and the debate surrounding this: Maier, *The Unmasterable Past*.
160. In German-speaking circles in Banat in the 1970s, for example, readings of Celan's and Ausländer's poems had been popular; HHI, NRA: Letter from Kittner to Ausländer, 25 November 1975. On activities relating to literature, see e.g. 'Aus Paul Celans poetischer Provinz. Zwei Abende mit dem Bukarester Dichter Alfred Kittner', *Rein-Neckar-Zeitung*, 4 March 1981. The work and employees of the Südostdeutsches Kulturwerk, now the Institut für deutsche Kultur und Geschichte Südosteuropas (IKGS), of which many employees were ethnic Germans from Romania, is also a case in point. This institution published M. Rosenkranz, *Im Untergang: ein Jahrhundertbuch* (Munich: Südostdeutsches Kulturwerk, 1986). On this, see J. A. Stupp, 'Die 'Südostdeutschen Vierteljahresblätter' als Publikationsmedium für Literatur', in Schwob, *Die deutsche Literaturgeschichte Ostmittel- und Südosteuropas*, 58–63.
161. See e.g. R. Michaelis, 'Angekommen wie nicht da', *Die Zeit* no. 13, 20 March 1987; Dieter Schlesak, 'Ceaușescus Dorfzerstörung bedeutet das Ende der Jahrhunderte alten Tradition', *Die Zeit* no. 31, 29 July 1988 Dieter Schlesak, 'Unser Erbe, das Nichts: Die gestundete Zeit der Rumäniendeutschen und ihrer Literatur', *Die Zeit* no. 42, 14 October 1988.
162. BI, Allg. Korrespondenz Bundesverband, 1984: Letter from Irma Bornemann to E.E. Keil Kulturstiftung der deutschen Vertriebenen, no subject, 17 July 1984.
163. BI, Allg. Korrespondenz Bundesverband, 1984: Letter from Keil to Bornemann, 6 August 1984.
164. BI, Allg. Korrespondenz Bundesverband, 1984: Letter from Rudolf Wagner to Bornemann, 18 August 1984.
165. As others have noted, the pressure of political conformity among ethnic Germans, which included the perceived incompatibility between 'being German' and 'being communist', was very strong. On this, see J. Koranyi, 'Between East and West: Romanian German Identities since 1945' (D.Phil. thesis, University of Exeter, 2008).
166. D. Diner, *Beyond the Conceivable: Studies on Germany, Nazism, and the Holocaust* (Berkeley: University of California Press, 2000), 223.
167. M. Röger, *Flucht, Vertreibung und Umsiedlung: Mediale Erinnerungen und Debatten in Deutschland und Polen seit 1989* (Marburg: Verlag Herder Institut, 2011), 43–45, here

44. See also C. Goschler, '"Versöhnung" und "Viktimisierung": Die Vertriebenen und der deutsche Opferdiskurs', *Zeitschrift für Geschichtswissenschaft* 53(10) (2005), 873–84.
168. Röger, *Flucht, Vertreibung und Umsiedlung*, 47.
169. Most studies of expellees and their organizations end in the early 1970s, as this is regarded as a turning point. See e.g. P. Ahonen, *After the Expulsion: West Germany and Eastern Europe 1945–1990* (Oxford: Oxford University Press, 2003); Demshuk, *Lost German East*; C. Lotz, *Die Deutung des Verlusts: erinnerungspolitische Kontroversen im geteilten Deutschland um Flucht, Vertreibung und die Ostgebiete: (1948–1972)* (Cologne: Böhlau, 2007).
170. E.E. Keil, *Ostdeutsches Lesebuch: Vier Jahrhunderte deutscher Dichtung vom Baltikum bis zum Banat/2: Deutsche Dichtung der Jahrhundertmitte vom Baltikum bis zum Banat* (Bonn: Kulturstiftung d. Dt. Vertriebenen, 1984).
171. BI, Allg. Korrespondenz Bundesverband 1985: a photocopy of the text was archived with many sections of the text disapprovingly underlined and commented. It is worth noting that it was not well received among Banat Germans either.
172. BI, Allg. Korrespondenz Bundesverband 1985–89: Invitation to 'Paul Celan: ein Dichter aus dem Buchenland', 29 October 1986, Haus des deutschen Ostens.
173. A documentary on the topic of 'flight and expulsion' was broadcast on German television in 1981. It can be seen as a response to the 1979 *Holocaust* miniseries. On this, see M. Broszat, *Nach Hitler: Der schwierige Umgang mit unserer Geschichte* (Munich: Deutscher Taschenbuch Verlag, 1988), 185–88. At this time, the so-called 'Documentation of the Expulsions' was also republished: Bundesministerium für Vertriebene, Flüchtlinge und Kriegsgeschädigte, *Dokumentation der Vertreibung der Deutschen aus Ost-Mitteleuropa*, 5 vols (Munich: Deutscher Taschenbuch Verlag, 1984).
174. 'Die Sozialarbeit der Landsmannschaft hat sich schwerpunktmäßig auf die Betreuungs- und Eingliederungshilfe von Spätaussiedlern verlagert', in Tiefenthaler, *Festschrift zum 30-jährigen Jubiläums-Bundestreffen*, 19
175. J. Leugner, '40 Jahre seit der Umsiedlung aus dem Buchenland (Bukowina)', *Kaindl-Archiv* 6 (1987), 5–14, here 14.
176. O. Kotzian, 'Als vor 25 Jahren das Bukowina-Institut gegründet wurde…', *Der Südostdeutsche*, November/December 2013.
177. Kotzian himself was not a Bukovinian German; he was born in Germany in 1946. However, his parents came from the Sudeten region and he completed his thesis on the topic of German schools in Romanian Transylvania. He therefore identified with the subject and had close contact with the Homeland Society of Bukovina Germans, which supported him.
178. BI, Bukowina Institut, Registratur, Allg. Korrespondenz, no. 2 (1985–89): Draft of the protocol of the meeting of the working group for the creation of a collection of Bukovinian artefacts (*Entwurf von dem Protokoll der Besprechung der Arbeitsgruppe für den Aufbau einer Sammlung buchenländischen Kulturgutes*) in Augsburg, 6 November 1985, 5 pages.
179. BI, Allg. Korrespondenz Bundesverband, 1987: Letter from Kotzian to Simnacher's regarding his speech on 8 June 1987, 25 May 1987.
180. BI, Allg. Korrespondenz Bundesverband, 1987: 'Swabia and Bukovina': copy of Georg Simnacher's speech at the meeting of Bukovina Germans in Augsburg on 8 June 1987.
181. On this, see J. Hampel and O. Kotzian (eds), *Spurensuche in die Zukunft: Europas verges- sene Region Bukowina* (Augsburg: Bukowina-Institut, 1991); J. Hampel and O. Kotzian (eds), *Das Bukowina-Institut in Augsburg*, 2nd edn (Augsburg: Bukowina-Institut e. V.,

1994 [1990]). See also G. Fisher, 'Looking Forwards through the Past: Bukovina's "Return to Europe after 1989–1991', *East European Politics and Societies* 33(1) (2019), 196–217.
182. See the conference proceedings published as Schwob, Goltschnigg and Fuchs, *Die Bukowina: Studien zu einer versunkenen Literaturlandschaft*.
183. Colin, a descendant of Bukovinian Jews and an American literary scholar, did much to shed light on Bukovinian literature as 'Shoah literature'. See A. Colin, *Paul Celan: Holograms of Darkness* (Bloomington: Indiana University Press, 1991). Edith Silbermann was a childhood friend of Celan; Rein, 'Politische und kulturgeschichtliche Grundlagen'.
184. D. Kessler, '"Der ganzen Welt zum Vorbild": die Schriften Heinrich Kippers (1875–1959)', in Goltschnigg, Schwob and Fuchs, *Die Bukowina*, 89–100.
185. See the review of the conference proceedings by P. Demetz, 'Czernowitz, Paris, New York. Von der Schwierigkeit Literatur aus der Bukowina zu beurteilen', *Frankfurter Allgemeine Zeitung*, 12 July 1991, 32.
186. Kittner and Silbermann, *Erinnerungen*, 113.
187. Corbea-Hoișie, *Kulturlandschaft Bukowina*, 14–15.
188. V. Glajar, *The German Legacy in East Central Europe as Recorded in Recent German Language Literature* (Rochester, NY: Camden House, 2004), 15.
189. See G. von Rezzori, *Blumen im Schnee: Portraitstudien zu einer Biographie, die ich nie schreiben werde* (Munich: Bertelsmann, 1989); G. von Rezzori, *The Snows of Yesteryear: Portraits for an Autobiography*, translated by H.F. Broch de Rothermann (London: Penguin, 2010 [1989]). On this, see also G. von Rezzori, *Memoiren eines Antisemiten: Roman* (Munich: Steinhausen, 1979), which, it is worth noting, was published in English, as *Memoirs of an Anti-Semite*, nearly twenty years earlier, in 1961.
190. See Celan's concepts of '*Heimat* as a language', the 'loss of language' and the notions of '*Mutter-* and *Mördersprache*'. On this, see M. Braun, 'Paul Celan und die "Fremde der Heimat": Zum 90. Geburtstag und 40. Todestag des Dichters', *Die Politische Meinung: Zeitschrift für Politik, Gesellschaft, Religion und Kultur* 492 (2010), 70–75.
191. See the exchange of letters between Celan and his wife Gisèle Lestrange and son Eric Celan: P. Celan, *Correspondance: 1951–1970: Avec un Choix de Lettres de Paul à son Fils Eric* (Paris: Seuil, 2001). See also Solomon, *Paul Celan*, 123–48.
192. Shchyhlevska, *Verschränkungen*, 47.
193. L. Sonntag, 'Erinnerungen eines exilierten Juden. Leo Sonntag erzählt aus seinem Leben', in Stenzel, *Leo Sonntag*, 54.
194. See Corbea-Hoișie, 'Bukarest als intellektuelle Hauptstadt'.
195. Kittner and Silbermann, *Erinnerungen*, 112.
196. Helmut Braun explains that she even avoided Germany on her first trip back to Europe after the war in 1957. She went to Germany in 1965 after experiencing anti-semitism in Vienna and having returned to using German in her writing. In 1984, she received the Order of Merit of the FRG from the German President. H. Braun, '"Es bleibt noch viel zu sagen" – Zur Biographie von Rose Ausländer', in Braun, *Rose Ausländer*, 25–33.
197. Interview with E. Hilsenrath, *Kölner Stadt-Anzeiger*, 19–20 January 1980.
198. See A. Kittner, W. Kirsten and R. Kiefer, *Briefe/3: Briefe an Wulf Kirsten: Ausgewählte Briefe* (Aachen: Rimbaud Verlag, 2010).
199. IKGS, Nachlass Moses Rosenkranz: Autobiographical Note, 10 November 1984. This sentence echoes the famous phrase often used by ethnic Germans claiming they wished 'to live as Germans among Germans'.

200. Kauders, 'The Emotional Geography', 195.
201. W. Menninghaus, '"Czernowitz/Bukowina" als Topos deutsch-jüdischer Geschichte und Literatur', *Merkur* 53(3–4) (1999), 345–57.
202. M. Hainz, 'Nostallergie: Die Czernowitzer Inkongruenzkompensationskompetenz', *CAS Working Paper* 1 (2009), 1–23.
203. Colin, 'Introduction', in Colin and Kittner, *Versunkene Dichtung der Bukowina*, 16. See also E. Wichner and H. Wiesner (eds), *In der Sprache der Mörder. Ausstellungsbuch: eine Literatur aus Czernowitz, Bukowina* (Berlin: Literaturhaus, 1993).
204. H. Müller, 'Zungenspäße und Büßerschnee: wie Helmut Böttiger mich durch "Orte Paul Celans" führte', *Die Zeit* no. 50, 6 December 1996.
205. Shchyhlevska, *Verschränkungen*, 62.
206. M. Hirsch, *Family Frames: Photography, Narrative and Postmemory* (Cambridge, MA: Harvard University Press, 2012), 242.
207. Felstiner, *Paul Celan*, xvii.
208. The critic Heinz Stănescu, for instance, argued that it was impossible to understand Celan without taking into account Romanian influences. See e.g. Stănescu, 'Der Dichter des "Nobiskruges"'.
209. See P. Celan, *Die Gedichte: Kommentierte Gesamtausgabe* (Frankfurt am Main: Suhrkamp, 2005), 135.

Conclusion

By the time I began to seek out, meet and interview self-identifying German 'resettlers' and Jewish survivors from Bukovina from 2012 to 2016, the narratives they shared with me were quite different from those presented in the preceding chapters. The 'story of nationalities', as I came to think of it, with all of its inherent problems and politics (were there four, five, six or twelve different groups living together in Bukovina and Czernowitz?) was a great favourite of the German Bukovinians I spoke to and whose accounts I read. Often, it had since turned into or become conflated with a 'story of changing regimes and sovereignties': 'my parents were born in Austria-Hungary, I myself in Romania, then the Russians came in, then the Nazis, and now I am German and my hometown is in Ukraine'.[1] Bukovina was not the lost *Heimat* or a multicultural idyll, but rather a chessboard of history, and Bukovinian Germans had been just some of the unfortunate pawns.

The case of Jewish Bukovinians was even more remarkable. As the titles of several Bukovinian Jews' autobiographical accounts suggest, with their multiple experiences of displacement and persecution, their life stories were believed to be paradigmatic twentieth-century destinies.[2] In the meantime, these stories and their multilingual authors had become the object of a great deal of interest and fascination in the German-speaking space especially, but beyond as well. Their experiences of suffering and survival were considered exceptional, unbelievable, and most definitely worth hearing and recounting.[3] For many, Bukovinian Jews' experiences were regarded as emblematic of the region's history and even Europe's history as a whole; they had come to be perceived as the only 'real' Bukovinians and the only true 'Middle Europeans'.[4]

These versions of the past and the new questions they raised about identity and history were symptomatic of the post-Cold War period. The experiences of Jewish Bukovinians especially, but those of Bukovinians in general – including the region's contemporary inhabitants living among the physical traces of the past – resonated with perceptions of the postmodern condition: belonging everywhere and nowhere, being uniquely vulnerable in the face of political forces and events that could not be controlled, and feeling fundamentally alienated by the pace of historical change. The Bukovinian writer Gregor von Rezzori, who famously remained stateless for years after the war, claiming he was unable to identify with any single state or nation, even came up with the composite word *Epochenverschlepper* (lit. 'the one who drags epochs along behind him') to describe the unusual position of people like him in the world. He thereby sought to capture the anachronistic feeling of embodying 'yesterday's reality when it [had] become unreal'.[5] It is worth noting that the word, coined decades earlier, gained popularity only after 1989–91.[6]

In general, after 1989–91, with the collapse of communism and other global trends, Bukovina was first denounced as forgotten, then proclaimed as a place to be rediscovered, and finally creatively reinvented as the ultimate European and multicultural space.[7] This phenomenon of reinvention cast a shadow over the four preceding decades of activities, identifications and 'memory work' relating to Bukovina in West Germany and Israel in particular. By the turn of the twenty-first century, the meaning derived from the experiences of Bukovinian Germans and Bukovinian Jews was very different from what it had been fifty years before. It reflected completely new assumptions about the world – a new set of politics of belonging – whereby being a hybrid and an *Epochenverschlepper* was a source of interest and not opprobrium, of self-worth and not disgrace. Driving this trend and the associated new types of communities of identification was what others have described as a kind of 'redemptive cosmopolitanism'[8] – a discourse on race, ethnicity, national identity and history with completely new parameters and taboos.

Yet, this resurgence of interest along these lines after the end of the Cold War did not come out of nowhere. It was both very much a result of and a response to what had happened before. Indeed, this version of the past was only fascinating because it highlighted what had been previously silenced. Besides, it was only possible and valorizing because Bukovinians were by then so firmly established in their postwar national homelands, where their belonging was beyond question. In effect, this rediscovery was a symptom of the fact that, over the course of the postwar period, perceptions of what was 'normal' had changed so dramatically that a past of more fluid identifications and encounters was barely recognizable. The post-1989 Bukovina phenomenon, in this sense, was the outcome of the questioning and rethinking of the postwar order, but thereby also revealed how accepted and normalized this postwar order had become.

Therefore, tracing Bukovina as well as the activities of self-identifying Bukovinians during the alleged 'blind spot' of the Cold War has shed new light on a number of issues, including the reasons for the region's perceived oblivion, its alleged 'return' and the background of some of the key actors of its post-Cold War resurgence. However, this undertaking has also revealed that the history of Bukovinians away from their homeland after the war was not so much a story of displacement as one of successful emplacement. Indeed, Bukovina can serve as a prism through which to view a wider set of postwar relationships. These include relations between ethnic German refugees, locals and the West German state after the Second World War; Romanian society and Holocaust survivors in the immediate aftermath of the war; the Yishuv and new immigrants in Palestine and later Israel; West Germans, Austrians and Israelis; and all of these groups and the states of Eastern Europe behind the Iron Curtain. Moreover, this period had its own chronology, conjunctures and dynamics. Looking at Bukovina and Bukovinians in the decades following the Second World War thus tells us about societies in the aftermath of war and the legacies of mass violence, displacement and genocide, but also about experiences of migration and social integration, about ideals of community and justice, and about changing conceptions of culture, morality and history. In practice, it tells us about how Bukovinians and the wider societies in which they lived dealt with the residues of the ethnicized and ethnicizing violence of the Second World War and the Holocaust. But beyond this, it tells us about the modes, agents, causes and rhythms of social, political and cultural change in the postwar period, and therefore the much broader mechanics of meaning-making processes.

* * *

While the First World War transformed the map of Europe by redrawing borders, the Second World War and its immediate aftermath appeared to have ensured that peoples and borders coincided by moving peoples themselves across political boundaries. The effect this had on the lives of individuals and the fate of communities was all the more significant. The Bukovinians at the centre of this study – Bukovinian Jews and Bukovinian Germans – who were involved in and affected by the violence unleashed during the war, albeit in very different ways, were acutely marked by a sense of 'before' and 'after' the Second World War. Notwithstanding the huge differences between the circumstances of their 'displacement', in both cases, these events transformed any previously held idea of what was 'normal' or where they belonged. As the often-used and charged metaphor 'after Auschwitz' suggests, people not only lost their homes and loved ones, but their convictions and self-understanding changed as well. In other words, the war and the Holocaust radically altered the stories individuals and communities told and lived by; even the meaning of the categories people used to describe themselves did not remain the same.

The meaning of (Bukovinian) German or (Bukovinian) Jew was not identical before and after the Second World War and the Holocaust. These notions were reshaped by both these groups' respective experiences of wartime displacement and/or persecution and the need to start life anew – the need to rebuild societies and communities. These consequent and related communities of identification were then constantly rethought as the circumstances changed around them, and individuals and groups continued to work through their experiences by different means and in both separate and intertwined ways. This reciprocity and negotiation between Bukovinians' experiences and the broader circumstances – the infusing of their past with meaning for the sake of the present – has been the focus of this book, and insofar as this is about Bukovinians' postwar lives, beliefs and practices, it is not reducible to memory alone. Bukovinians made sense of their experiences by situating themselves with respect to different postwar options for identification and, in the process, contributed to what these modes of identification meant in different contexts. They were political actors on the scene of the Cold War, and their politics were primarily not politics of memory but politics of belonging.

In the first decade after the war, Germans and Jews from Bukovina focused on overcoming their hardship and experiences of uprooting. Many achieved this by emphasizing their belonging in new national homelands, what would become West Germany and Israel, and settling there within a few years of the end of the war. From a practical standpoint, for many Bukovinians, this was a difficult period, which required moving across international borders, finding new homes and starting over in a context of considerable personal disruption, economic shortage and political uncertainty. Yet, the conception of West Germany and Israel as not merely new states but also ancestral homelands to which Bukovinian Germans and Bukovinian Jews were merely returning after centuries and generations eased the process considerably. Moreover, in both cases, the rapid obtaining of political rights and representation alleviated the difficulties they faced as refugees and as immigrants. In both settings, Bukovinians founded representative organizations, the Landsmannschaften, to defend their rights and benefits as Germans and as Jews, and later as West German and Israeli citizens with specific experiences and attributes. Their origins and experiences in their native homeland of Bukovina thus continued to play an important role, and they even rewrote their history to suit the present. Not all Bukovinians joined the organizations, not all official readings of the past were necessarily subject to consensus, and discrimination undoubtedly did occur. Nevertheless, there was no fundamental question as to these groups' and individuals' belonging as Bukovinians, as Germans and as Jews in their putative national homes, as demonstrated by the fact that there was no perceived contradiction between the commemoration of their 'old homeland' and integration in a new one.

Looking at these organizations, their discourse and their leaders in this early period not only shows how a specific group of ethnic German expellees in West Germany and a specific group of European immigrants in Israel negotiated their belonging. It also provides privileged insights into the larger projects of state- and nation-building in postwar West Germany and Israel, and the social, political, cultural and symbolic spaces created in the process. Indeed, although the narratives of Bukovinians undoubtedly only had a limited influence on their respective wider societies, they were nonetheless symptomatic of contemporary politics of history, memory, identity and belonging in West Germany and Israel. Looking at these two groups in their respective national contexts also reveals a series of intriguing contradictions and ambivalences. In both instances, interwar particularist politics and wartime experiences inspired narratives about the past – especially narratives of suffering – and ethnic conceptions of identity remained the cornerstones in conceiving of new modes of identification, inclusion and participation. In both cases, social integration was achieved based on mixtures of similarity and distinction, tradition and novelty, victimhood and pride. In West Germany, while the protection of the heritage of ethnic Germans from Central and Eastern Europe was enshrined in law, their workforce and flexibility were put to the service of the country's reconstruction and a rapidly modernizing economy created new sources of identification and loyalty. In early-state Israel, the toleration of the use of German in private among many Bukovinians went hand in hand with the promotion of identification with the Zionist ideal, sidelining experiences of suffering, and harnessing and reinterpreting Jewish experiences in prewar Bukovina as a prehistory of the Jewish state.

Therefore, while they obtained representation, the activities of Bukovinians in the aftermath of the Second World War were nevertheless highly constrained by the new political circumstances and characterized by a constant game of give and take. In both locations, 'Bukovinian' remained a salient category of identification by being conferred a specific, narrow and ethnonational meaning. Within ten years of the end of the war, 'Bukovinian German' and 'Bukovinian Jew' had become equated with two distinct communities of experience from the war – 'resettlers' and survivors. Yet these also functioned as synonyms for 'good German citizen' and 'good Jewish Israeli', respectively, hence conflating separate – ethnic, historical and political – dimensions of identity and reinforcing the belief in the importance of the overlap and compatibility of these elements in society more generally.

By the early 1960s, with the region seemingly in irreversible isolation behind the Iron Curtain, the organized communities largely held a monopoly over representations of Bukovina in West Germany and Israel. Their publications, newsletters and *Heimat* and memory books depicted Bukovina as the exclusive space of their respective community. The early postwar politics of integration in West Germany and Israel thus resulted in the development and coexistence of parallel, conflicting – and at times downright incompatible – visions and representations of Bukovina and its past.

The Germans represented the region as 'an island of Germanness', a German-dominated idyllic *Heimat* in an ahistorical prewar past, where they were the sole representatives of Germanness. The Jews, in turn, depicted 'a Jewish Atlantis', focusing on Jewish institutions, communities and figures from the late Habsburg and interwar periods and their eventual destruction during the Holocaust, making a near-complete abstraction of the surrounding Gentile populations. The idiosyncrasies, contradictions and lacunae of these representations were not completely ignored or entirely unchallenged. Occasional and often indirect interactions resulted from German and Jewish Bukovinians' common use of the German language and their associated, overlapping claims to have been the sole representatives of the region's 'German' culture. Ultimately, they also shared an interest in nostalgically protecting the region's and their own communities' images and reputations. However, exchanges nevertheless remained rare, private and emotionally charged, shaped by geopolitics, different political outlooks and pre-existing prejudices and inhibitions. For a long time, Bukovinian Germans and Bukovinian Jews, like most non-Jewish Germans and Israelis in general, barely had any contact with one another. The conception of Bukovinian Germans and Bukovinian Jews as two different wartime communities of experience prevented the perception of any shared ground for identification among many members of these two groups. This situation and Bukovinians' parochial approaches also meant that there was limited interest in the region on behalf of people who were not from there.

However, in time, a conflict did arise between some of the representatives of Bukovinian Germans in West Germany and Bukovinian Jews in Israel, which resulted in more direct interaction and brought this situation to a head. The antagonism concerned the issue of West German reparations for Bukovinian Jews' material losses and suffering in the war. This debate, which continued over several decades, exposed not only opposing understandings of historical responsibility, guilt and justice – as well as variance in West German and Israeli legal, political and bureaucratic practices – but also fundamentally different conceptions of community, ethnicity and Germanness.

This issue thus highlighted concretely the significance of German and Jewish Bukovinians' diverging postwar politics of identity, history, memory and belonging. Yet, looking at the dynamics of this opposition also suggests that such debates and a range of concurrent developments heralded a slow shift among large sections of West German society – and, eventually, West German bureaucracy too – especially with regard to the perception of what had happened during the war and who the real victims had been. Not until the 1980s did many West Germans take responsibility for the Holocaust or at least embrace distancing themselves from National Socialist ideas part of their self- and collective identity and a matter of principle. However, the effects of generational change had started to make themselves felt in the 1960s already. Over time, the rejection of Jewish Bukovinian claims for West German compensation or citizenship based on ethnicity appeared increasingly questionable or even unacceptable. This trend also coincided with the marginalization of more conservative actors in public discourse, such as leaders of expellee organizations. Compensation for the past thus unfolded on several levels, and indemnification was one of several decisive developments.

Applying for reparations was transformative for Jewish Bukovinians too, insofar as they were required to demonstrate their closeness to German culture as well as detail their individual experiences of suffering and foreground their collective identity as victims. This procedure did not entail an immediate or particularly thorough confrontation with what had happened during the war. Nonetheless, Jewish Bukovinians' fight for recognition and indemnification not only reflected a shift in West German and Israeli popular historical consciousness, but also captured the kind of transnational development that contributed to altering views of the recent past during the Cold War. With this, it reflected the recasting of not just what it meant to be Bukovinian, but also what it meant to be German, Jewish and Israeli in general by the end of the Cold War.

By the 1970s, it was the realm of arts and culture and the phenomenon of 'Bukovinian literature' in particular – literary figures from the region and their reception – that had become the most significant arena of a renegotiation, re-evaluation, reimagination and reinvention of what Bukovina had been and what it meant to be 'German', 'Jewish' and 'Bukovinian' in West Germany and Israel. Indeed, over the course of the second half of the Cold War, the growing popularity of a handful of mostly Jewish German-speaking writers from the region transformed the image of Bukovina from that of the lost or destroyed *Heimat* of German and Jewish Bukovinians to that of an exceptional – though now sunken – German cultural and literary landscape. With this, the region also came to be perceived as the site of a unique German-Jewish symbiosis.

Its most prominent figures were Paul Celan and Rose Ausländer, who referred to their lost homeland of Bukovina publicly and rose to fame during the Cold War as two of the most important contemporary German-language poets. However, the conception of Bukovina as a cultural landscape and Bukovinian literature as an exceptional cultural phenomenon was linked to the activities and promotion of a larger and more international group of German-speaking writers, artists, intellectuals and their readers in West Germany, Austria and elsewhere. This trend, for instance, owed much to the efforts of Alfred Margul-Sperber and Alfred Kittner, two Bukovinian writers themselves, who had remained in Romania and continued to promote German literature from Bukovina after the Second World War. Their conception of Germanness, German culture and hence Bukovinian culture was inspired and shaped by their experiences in the interwar and wartime periods, their minority status in Romania before and after the war, and their situation behind the Iron Curtain in a divided Europe. Though they had suffered during the war and the Holocaust, they emphasized cultural and humanistic, rather than ethnic or national, elements of identification and did not make the experience of suffering, persecution and violence central to their work.

In the absence of any historical research and due to the difficulties of access to the region, these writers soon became the voices and even icons of the region's culture and history. Indeed, their success coincided with a growing interest in West Germany, Austria and Israel in German-Jewish history and Eastern Europe in general. The reimagining of Bukovina in the 1970s and 1980s thus both reflected and contributed to the widening conceptions of community and Germanness, and a new approach to the past in Israel and Europe as a whole. Initially, this trend constituted a challenge to the traditional stakeholders of Bukovinian identity, the Landsmannschaften. These communities had already lost considerable social and political weight and significance – as well as members – in their respective countries, after the main social, political and legal issues subsided and as the Cold War advanced. However, the attention paid to the region also gave these organizations renewed relevance and a chance to reorient and reinvent themselves. The Landsmannschaft in Israel took pride in the notoriety of the cultural figures it claimed as members of its community. The links between its members and people in West Germany and Austria became even closer than before. This was a time when Israelis and Jews elsewhere gained visibility and self-confidence in general, and Bukovinian Jews in particular positioned themselves as representatives of a bourgeois kind of Jewish Germanness linked to an idealized vision of the late Habsburg period – despite the fact that many of them had not even experienced this period. Developments among members of the Bukovinian German Landsmannschaft testify to a slow adaptation of their message to the new circumstances. Eventually, however, *their* Bukovina was also reframed as an ideal multicultural society, focusing on Bukovina's Habsburg incarnation, in which 'German culture' was believed to have been the agent of peaceful coexistence and interethnic cooperation. Reflecting a broader West German aspiration to carve out a positive role for itself in a divided Europe by the end of the Cold War, Bukovinian-German memory brokers summoned Bukovina for the sake of reconciliation in the present.

This reappraisal of Bukovina focusing on the Habsburg period and the experiences of both groups' elites produced unprecedented consensus and even resulted in a short-lived rapprochement between German and Jewish Bukovinians. However, it was symptomatic of the contemporary politics of appeasement, and ultimately, the simplified and fragmentary historical narratives of the late Cold War soon came up against their own limitations and contradictions. Indeed, up until 1989, changes in the relationship to and perception of Bukovina and its past remained largely constrained by political circumstances and marked by a general tendency to invent rather than explain the pre-world war past and the communist present. In particular, the protection of the Cold War status quo precluded any serious critical discussion of the interwar and wartime periods, ambivalences or what individual people had actually experienced. In other words, the idea of Bukovina as a site of German-Jewish symbiosis depended on these conditions, which stood in the way of a more critical and pluralist culture of memory, more fluid concepts of identity and more inclusive politics of belonging. Therefore, while this phase provided the ingredients for Bukovina's renewed idealization after 1989, it also underlay the urgent need for a fundamental re-evaluation and 'rediscovery' of what it meant to be Bukovinian, (West) German and Israeli as soon as the postwar period truly came to a close.

* * *

By tracing the discourse about Bukovina as both a historical space and as a screen of projection from 1945 to 1989, this book has revealed how German and Jewish Bukovinians – German 'resettlers' and Jewish survivors from the region – constructed belonging in new homelands, compensated for the violent past, and achieved both individual and collective biographical coherence against the backdrop of changing political circumstances. Hence, this study has offered a history of a group of 'expellees' and a group of 'Holocaust survivors', primarily in West Germany and Israel and examined their interactions with each other and with members of their wider societies during the Cold War. However, in so doing, this book has also looked more generally at German and Jewish postwar modes of identification, the means of establishing belonging and the entanglements of these processes after the Second World War; it therefore constitutes a broader contribution to both the social and cultural history of the postwar period and an exploration of the dynamics of cultural change in general.

Beyond the specific cases of Bukovina and Bukovinians, three dimensions and potentials of the approach adopted here deserve reiterating here. The first is the long-term perspective, which can help us rethink what, as well as how, political, social and cultural shifts occurred and were perceived, and identify new continuities and breaks. Indeed, this research has challenged or at least qualified the significance of the classic turning points of 1945, 1968, 1979 and 1989 by showing that change was sometimes quick, but often slow, varying across social groups (political groups but also generations) as well as space. Change itself depended on different, interrelated factors including policies, legislation and institutions, as well as the actions and initiatives of specific groups or individuals and events of various sorts (a trial, a film, the publication of a book). The long-term perspective made it possible to identify new moments, suggest new connections and areas of interest, and study their effects, such as the emotions and social trends to which historical actors might have contributed or responded. This, in turn, legitimized conceiving of Bukovinians' history in accordance to new chronologies and thematic arrangements.

In other words, the long-term approach made it possible to reconceptualize the idea of legacy or reverberations as something multifaceted and uneven, and in constant need of further differentiation. As some historians have already emphasized, it is useful to focus on continuities in discourse – that is, which ideas, terms and narratives endured and which did not – and to draw new lines of continuity, for instance, from the interwar or wartime period to the postwar and post-Cold War period.[9] As this research has shown, our attention should also be drawn to how the meaning of terms, such as 'German', 'Jewish' or 'European', inconspicuously changed while being continuously deployed. Furthermore, the long-term approach might encourage us to re-evaluate the role of different actors at different times and over time. For example, this study has brought attention to personnel continuities between Bukovinian leaders before and after the war and, more generally, to the role of Landsmannschaften in a period when many regarded them as irrelevant. As became apparent after 1989 and as Karl Schlögel had already noted in his 1986 book *Die Mitte liegt ostwärts* (*The Middle Lies Eastwards*), 'if pictures of Germans from Central Europe were no longer to be seen', it was simply because Germans were 'unsure whether they [were] allowed to take them out of the drawer in which they [were] hidden'.[10] This is therefore the drawer that needed to be opened. The scale of the 'rediscovery' of Bukovina as a 'Jewish space' after 1989 suggested that the same applied to Bukovinian Jews. Indeed, as others have pointed out and as this research has shown more extensively, German 'expellees' did not have the monopoly on nostalgia for the 'lost German East'.[11] In this sense, this study and its framework might serve as an impulse to revisit the political cultures of the Cold War and related perceptions of Eastern Europe in West Germany and Israel especially, both to make better sense of these Cold War societies and to better evaluate what happened after the Cold War ended.

Second, by offering an entangled history of German and Jewish Bukovinians, and those who identified as German 'resettlers' and Jewish survivors especially, this study has shed new light on the transnational dynamics that informed national narratives and circumstances already during the Cold War, while at the same time further specifying the particularity of each factor of the comparison. With this, it encourages us to revisit Dan Diner's famous notion of 'negative symbiosis' linking German and Jews after the Holocaust by showing, in line with more recent research, that the entanglement was not only on an abstract level, but also concerned the very real overlap of the institutions they dealt with, their aims and objects, their self-representation and public perception.[12] Indeed, after the Second World War, the German–Jewish relationship was shaped by both profound historical connections and diverse contemporary practical intersections as well as powerful inhibitions and lasting prejudices. In this sense, the relationship was both asymmetrical and hopelessly intertwined. For a long time, the debate about how to write a history of the Holocaust to satisfy both sides missed the point that the only correct history integrates the two.[13] Despite the challenge this represents, the same applies to the diverse attempts to engage with the violent past in the increasingly interconnected postwar world.

Indeed, looking at German and Jewish Bukovinians together has forced us to reflect on what 'German', 'Jewish' and 'Bukovinian' meant, but also proved these categories to be mutually constituted because of their entangled politics of memory, identity, history and belonging, which derived directly from experiences made in the war and their later interpretations. While these two communities were particularly suited to juxtaposition due to the shared language as well as their similar size and modes of organization, such an entangled history casts light on the potential of focusing on the wider, evolving and, to borrow from Michael Rothberg, 'multidirectional' character of postwar developments relating to the recent past in general.[14] This is why it has been useful to think of German and Jewish Bukovinians in terms of 'communities of experience' – resettlers and survivors – linked to different 'communities of connection and identification' that emerged later on. Such a framework makes it possible to analyse the very different but interwoven and parallel ways in which the same events affected the lives of two separate groups, without equating their experiences.[15]

Beyond this, the case of Bukovina and Bukovinians has illustrated that during the Cold War and especially in relation to German-Jewish history, particular events, spaces and narratives became invested with specific meanings and qualities, and served as platforms to play out larger debates and questions. Hence, focusing on concrete historical spaces and certain activities relating to the past also gave us an insight into the broader issues of memorialization, morality and transmission.[16] These dynamics became even more complicated and layered as a result of the post-1989 'memory boom' in a context where Eastern Europe as a whole was 'rediscovered', and many Europeans and their states turned to history – and especially the Holocaust – to define their values and face the future. In this context, German and Jewish identities became ever more explicitly and exclusively associated with the moral categories of 'perpetrator' and 'victim'. Exploring systematically what this meant for Bukovinians and for Bukovina as a prism and an idea after 1989 remains to be done.

Finally, then, while, on the one hand, this study has highlighted the significance of the meanings we give to the past – the stories we tell about the past – on the other hand, it has demonstrated the malleability, contingency and constant contestation of this information. This is why such an approach thus ultimately transcends any conventional and static concept of memory. This research has shown how experiences were mobilized for different purposes, how narratives changed and evolved, what gaps and limitations these narratives presented, as well as how they reflected and influenced personal and collective behaviours, beliefs and choices. Where Bukovinians placed the emphasis of the narrative – on experiences during the war, the interwar or the Habsburg period, friendly encounters or conflicts, times of happiness or suffering – was neither entirely incidental nor benign (the stories we tell never are), but it was not inevitable either. This dynamic between the past – via experience – and its mobilization and re-activation at a later point in time has been the focus here and deserves further attention and theorization.

In particular, focusing on narratives and the discourses underpinning them has reminded us that events in and of themselves have no meaning, that spaces are not places until they are claimed and that identities are always enacted and construed for the purposes of the present. These practices themselves are both informed by and contribute to sustaining specific ideologies and discourses; narratives are what turns a community of experience into a community of identification, which in turn narrates experience. This book has shown that this dialectic process is subject to continuous renegotiation in light of new knowledge as well as changing circumstances, beliefs, norms and power relations. It is this constant contestation, relating to the interpretation of a particular set of events and experiences, that needs to be studied and made explicit. As Deborah Eisenberg argued in her introduction to Rezzori's *Memoirs of an Anti-Semite*:

Once a great public cataclysm has occurred, it is nearly impossible for people to recall what it is they felt and how they behaved during it or just prior to it. Misery is a potent aid in obliterating memory, and shame in distorting it. The mind's mandate is to interpret, and even in the most routine course of things the mind confects a stand – codifies, retroactively, reactions and attitudes; interpretation springs instantaneously from experience, but interpretation is inherently inaccurate.[17]

This is why, although the experience of the war and the Holocaust made the process of identification and the politics of belonging of German and Jewish Bukovinians look especially unavoidable, it should in fact only make us all the more cautious and critical.

Notes

1. Adapted from the group interview with the author, Bitterfeld, December 2012.
2. See e.g. M. Rosenkranz, *Im Untergang: Ein Jahrhundertbuch* (Munich: Südostdeutsches Kulturwerk, 1986); H. Brenner, *Mein zwanzigstes Jahrhundert* (Brugg: Munda, 2006); C. Hirsch, *A Life in the Twentieth Century: A Memoir*, published online: http://www.ghostsofhome.com (retrieved 23 September 2019).
3. See e.g. Erhard Roy Wiehn's publication of many memoirs by Jews from Bukovina in the Schoàh & Judaica series of the Hartung Gorre Verlag. See also G. Coldewey et al. (eds), *Zwischen Pruth und Jordan: Lebenserinnerungen Czernowitzer Juden* (Cologne: Böhlau, 2003); G. Ranner, et al. (eds) *'… und das Herz wird mir schwer dabei' Czernowitzer Juden erinnern sich*, 3rd edn (Berlin: Kulturforum östliches Europa, 2009).
4. As one could read in E. Rückleben, *Heimatland Sprache: Leben und Zeugnisse bukowinische Dichter* (Innsbruck: Traditionsverb. Kath. Czernowitzer Pennäler, 2005), 15: 'the real people [*das eigentliche Volk*] of Bukovina were the Jews'. Similarly, Eric Hobsbawm argued that '"Middle Europeans" are only those that the twentieth century made homeless'; E. Hobsbawm, *Fractured Times: Culture and Society in the 20th Century* (London: Hachette Digital, 2013), 91.
5. G. von Rezzori, *Greisengemurmel: Ein Rechenschaftsbericht* (Munich: Bertelsmann, 1994), 57. He obtained Austrian citizenship in 1982. On Rezzori and this term, see C. Spinei, *Über die Zentralität des Peripheren: Auf den Spuren von Gregor von Rezzori* (Berlin: Frank und Timme, 2011), especially 25–28.
6. Though the term was first used in the 1970s, it only really caught on in his later, autobiographical works. See G. von Rezzori, *Der Tod meines Bruders Abel* (Munich: Goldmann Verlag, 1976), 35. See also von Rezzori, *Greisengemurmel*, 33, 49, 244; G. von Rezzori, *Mir auf der Spur* (Munich: Bertelsmann, 1997), 13.
7. See e.g. J. Hampel and O. Kotzian (eds), *Spurensuche in die Zukunft: Europas vergessene Region Bukowina* (Augsburg: Bukowina-Institut, 1991); H. Heppner (ed.), *Czernowitz: Die Geschichte einer ungewöhnlichen Stadt* (Cologne: Böhlau Verlag, 2000); A. Afsari (ed.), *Mythos Czernowitz: Eine Stadt im Spiegel ihrer Nationalitäten* (Potsdam: Deutsches Kulturforum östliches Europa, 2008).

8. M. Meng, *Shattered Spaces: Encountering Jewish Ruins in Post-war Germany and Poland* (Cambridge, MA: Harvard University Press, 2011), 263.
9. On this, see R. Moeller, 'Germans as Victims? Thoughts on a Post-Cold War History of World War II's Legacies', *History and Memory* 17(1–2) (2005), 147–94.
10. K. Schlögel, *Die Mitte liegt ostwärts: Die Deutschen, der verlorene Osten und Mitteleuropa* (Berlin: Siedler, 1986), 72.
11. E.g. A. Demshuk, '"Wehmut und Trauer": Jewish Travelers in Polish Silesia and the Foreignness of *Heimat*', *Jahrbuch des Simon-Dubnow-Instituts* (December 2007), 311–35.
12. See e.g. D. Diner, *Rituelle Distanz: Israels deutsche Frage* (Munich: Deutsche Verlags-Anstalt, 2015).
13. On this, see C. Maier, *The Unmasterable Past: History, Holocaust, and German National Identity* (Cambridge, MA: Harvard University Press, 1988); and O. Bartov, *Mirrors of Destruction: War Genocide and Modern Identity* (Oxford: Oxford University Press, 2000). For a model, integrated history of the Holocaust, see S. Friedländer, *Nazi Germany and the Jews: The Years of Persecution, 1933–1939* (New York: HarperCollins, 1998) and S. Friedländer, *Nazi Germany and the Jews, 1939–1945: The Years of Extermination* (New York: HarperCollins, 2007).
14. M. Rothberg, *Multidirectional Memory: Remembering the Holocaust in the Age of Decolonization* (Stanford: Stanford University Press, 2009).
15. On this, see D. LaCapra, *History in Transit: Experience, Identity, Critical Theory* (Ithaca, NY: Cornell University Press, 2004), 104, 113.
16. On this, see e.g. E. Lehrer and M. Meng (eds), *Jewish Space in Contemporary Poland* (Bloomington: Indiana University Press, 2015).
17. D. Eisenberg, 'Introduction', in G. von Rezzori, *Memoirs of an Anti-Semite: A Novel in Five Stories*, translated from German by J. Neugroschel (New York: New York Review of Books Classics, 2011), loc. 75.

BIBLIOGRAPHY

Archives

Archiv der Akademie der Künste, Berlin
Arhiva Centrului pentru Studiul Istorie Evreilor din România, Bucharest (ACSIER)
Arhivele Naționale Istorice Centrale (ANIC)
Archiv des Bukowina-Instituts, Augsburg (BI)
Brandenburgisches Landeshauptarchiv, Potsdam
Bundesarchiv, Bayreuth (BArch-LAA)
Bundesarchiv, Berlin (BArch-B)
Bundesarchiv, Koblenz (BArch-K)
Central Zionist Archives, Jerusalem (CZA)
Heinrich-Heine-Institut: Rheinisches Literaturarchiv (HHI)
Hessisches Staatsarchiv Darmstadt (Hess. StADA)
Institut für deutsche Kultur und Geschichte Südosteuropas an der LMU München (IKGS)
Institut für Volkskunde der Deutschen des östlichen Europa, Freiburg (IVDE)
Landesarchiv Baden-Württemberg – Hauptstaatsarchiv Stuttgart
Leo Baeck Institute, New York (LBI)
Muzeul Național al Literaturii Române, Bucharest (MLR)
Serviciul Județean al Arhivelor Nationale Suceava (SJAN-S)
Staatsarchiv, München
Stadtarchiv, Darmstadt
Stadtarchiv, Stuttgart
United States Holocaust Memorial Museum, Washington DC (USHMM)
Visual History Archive, University of Southern California Shoah Foundation (VHA)
Yad Vashem Archives, Jerusalem (YVA)

Periodicals

Brücke zum Westen
Buchenland
Bukowina Bulletin
Chug Olej Bukowina
Curierul Israelit
Czernowitzer Morgenblatt
Darmstädter Echo

Darmstädter Tagesblatt
Der Spiegel
Der Südostdeutsche
Der Tag
Die Stimme
Die Zeit
Filder-Zeitung
Frankfurter Allgemeine Zeitung (FAZ)
Kaindl-Archiv: Mitteilungen der Raimund Friedrich Kaindl Gesellschaft
Kölner Stadt-Anzeiger
Mântuirea
Neamul Evreesc
Neue Literatur
Neuer Weg
Neue Zürcher Zeitung (NZZ)
Raimund-Kaindl-Bund (Heft 1-2-3)
Renașterea,
Scânteia
Stuttgarter Nachrichten
Stuttgarter Zeitung
Südostecho
Viața Evreiască

Films

Der Klang der Worte. Deutsche Sprache in Jerusalem. Directed by Gerhard Schick. DVD. Jerusalem: Goethe Institut, 2008.
Die papierene Brücke. Directed by Ruth Beckermann. DVD. Austria: R. Beckermann, 1987.
Herr Zwilling und Frau Zuckermann. Directed by Volker Koepp. DVD. Berlin: Salzgeber and Co. Medien GmbH, 1999.

Published Primary and Secondary Material

Afsari, A. (ed.). *Mythos Czernowitz: Eine Stadt im Spiegel ihrer Nationalitäten*. Potsdam: Deutsches Kulturforum östliches Europa, 2008.
Ahonen, P. *After the Expulsion: West Germany and Eastern Europe 1945–1990*. Oxford: Oxford University Press, 2003.
———. *People on the Move: Forced Population Movements in Europe in the Second World War and its Aftermath*. Oxford: Berg, 2008.
———. 'On Forced Migrations: Transnational Realities and National Narratives in Post-1945 (West) Germany'. *German History* 32(4) (2014), 599–614.
Aleksiun, N. 'Returning from the Land of the Dead: Jews in Eastern Galicia in the Immediate Aftermath of the Holocaust'. *Kwartalnik Historii Żydów* 2 (2013), 257–71.
Alexandru, J. et al. (eds). *Martiriul Evreilor din România: 1940–1944: Documente și Mărturii*. Bucharest: Editura Hasefer, 1991.
Altshuler, M. 'The Soviet "Transfer" of Jews from Chernovtsy Province to Romania, 1945-1946'. *Jews in Eastern Europe* 36 (1998), 54–75.

Altskan, V. 'The Closing Chapter: Northern Bukovinian Jews, 1944–1946'. *Yad Vashem Studies* 43(1) (2015), 51–81.
Aly, G. *Endlösung: Völkerverschiebung und der Mord an den europäischen Juden*. Frankfurt am Main: Fischer, 1995.
Ancel, J. *Transnistria: The Romanian Mass Murder Campaigns*, 3 vols. Tel Aviv: Goldstein Goren Diaspora Research Center, 2003.
———. 'Statistik des Holocaust in Rumänien'. *Halbjahresschrift für Südosteuropäische Geschichte, Literatur und Politik* 17(2) (2005), 29–44.
———. *The History of the Holocaust in Romania*. Translated from Hebrew by Y. Murciano. Edited by Leon Volovici with the assistance of Miriam Caloianu. Lincoln, NE: University of Nebraska Press, 2011.
———. *Prelude to Mass Murder: The Pogrom in Iași, Romania, June 29, 1941 and Thereafter*. Translated from Hebrew by F. Seckbach. Jerusalem: Yad Vashem, 2013.
Angrick, A. *Besatzungspolitik und Massenmord: die Einsatzgruppe D in der südlichen Sowjetunion 1941–1943*. Hamburg: Hamburger Edition, 2003.
———. 'Power Games: The German Nationality Policy (Volkstumspolitik) in Czernowitz before and during the Barbarossa Campaign'. *Dapim: Studies on the Holocaust* 24(1) (2010), 89–135.
Appelfeld, A. *The Story of a Life: An Extraordinary Memoir of Survival*. Translated from Hebrew by A. Halter. London: Penguin, 2004.
Applegate, C. *A Nation of Provincials: The German Idea of Heimat*. Berkeley: University of California Press, 1990.
Arbeits- und Sozialminister NRW (ed.). *Das Auslandsdeutschtum in Osteuropa einst und jetzt*. Troisdorf: Wegweiserverlag, 1963.
Armbrüster, C. *Deutsch-Satulmare: Geschichte eines buchenländischen Pfälzerdorfes*. Karlsruhe: n.p., 1962.
Assmann, A. *Der lange Schatten der Vergangenheit: Erinnerungskultur und Geschichtspolitik*. Munich: C.H. Beck, 2006.
Assmann, A., and U. Frevert, *Geschichtsvergessenheit Geschichtsversessenheit: Vom Umgang mit deutschen Vergangenheiten nach 1945*. Stuttgart: Deutsche Verlags-Anstalt.
———. '1968 in Germany: A Generation with Two Phases and Faces'. *Eurozine*, 22 June 2018. Retrieved 24 September 2019 from https://www.eurozine.com/1968-germany-generation-two-phases-faces.
Assmann, J. *Das kulturelle Gedächtnis: Schrift, Erinnerung und politische Identität in frühen Hochkulturen*. Munich: C.H. Beck, 1992.
Ausländer, R. *Gesammelte Gedichte*. n.p., 1977.
Aust, S., and R. Augstein (eds). *Die Flucht: Über die Vertreibung der Deutschen aus dem Osten*. Augsburg: Weltbild, 2013.
Axmann, E. *Wege, Städte: Erinnerungen*. Aachen: Rimbaud Verlag, 2005.
———. *Die Kunststrickerin: Erinnerungssplitter*. Aachen: Rimbaud Verlag, 2010.
Ballinger, P. 'The Culture of Survivors: Post-Traumatic Stress Disorder and Traumatic Memory'. *History and Memory* 10(1) (1998), 99–132.
———. *History in Exile: Memory and Identity at the Borders of the Balkans*. Princeton: Princeton University Press, 2002.
———. 'Imperial Nostalgia: Mythologizing Habsburg Trieste'. *Journal of Modern Italian Studies* 97 (2003), 84–101.
Bankier, D. (ed.) *The Jews are Coming Back: The Return of the Jews to Their Countries of Origin after WWII*. New York: Berghahn Books; Jerusalem: Yad Vashem, 2005.
Bannasch, B., and M. Rupp (eds). *Rückkehrerzählungen: über die (Un-)Möglichkeit nach 1945 als Jude in Deutschland zu leben*. Göttingen: Vandenhoeck & Ruprecht Unipress, 2018.

Barkan, E. *The Guilt of Nations: Restitution and Negotiating Historical Injustices.* New York: Norton, 2000.
Barthes, R. *Mythologies.* Paris: Seuil, 1957.
Bartlett, R., and K. Schönwälder (eds). *The German Lands and Eastern Europe.* Basingstoke: St Martin's Press, 1999.
Bartov, O. *Mirrors of Destruction: War Genocide and Modern Identity.* Oxford: Oxford University Press, 2000.
Bartov, O., and Weitz, Eric (eds). *Shatterzones of Empires: Coexistence and Violence in the German, Habsburg, Russian and Ottoman Borderlands.* Bloomington: Indiana University Press: 2013.
Bechtel, D., and X. Balmiche (eds). *Les Villes Multiculturelles en Europe Centrale.* Paris: Belin, 2008.
Beck, E. *Bukowina: Land zwischen Orient und Okzident.* Freilassing: Pannonia-Verlag, 1963.
———. *Bibliographie zur Landeskunde der Bukowina: Literatur bis zum Jahre 1965.* Munich: Verlag des Südostdeutschen Kulturwerks, 1966.
———. *Bibliographie zur Kultur und Landeskunde: Literatur aus den Jahren 1965–1975.* Dortmund: Forschungsstelle Ostmitteleuropa, 1985.
———. *Bibliographie zur Kultur und Landeskunde: 1976–1990.* Wiesbaden: Harrassowitz, 1999–2003.
Beckermann, R., and C. Ransmayr (eds). *Im blinden Winkel: Nachrichten aus Mitteleuropa.* Vienna: Brandstätter: 1985.
Beer, M. 'Im Spannungsfeld von Politik und Zeitgeschichte: Das Großforschungsprojekt "Dokumentation der Vertreibung der Deutschen aus Ost-Mitteleuropa"'. *Vierteljahrshefte für Zeitgeschichte* 46(3) (1998), 345–89.
Beer, M., and G. Seewann (eds). *Südostforschung im Schatten des Dritten Reiches: Institutionen – Inhalte – Personen.* Munich: Oldenbourg, 2004.
———. *Flucht und Vertreibung der Deutschen: Voraussetzungen, Verlauf, Folgen.* Munich: C.H. Beck, 2011.
Beer, M., and S. Dyroff (eds). *Politische Strategien nationaler Minderheiten in der Zwischenkriegszeit.* Munich: Oldenbourg Verlag, 2013.
———. 'Die deutsche Südosteuropa-Forschung zwischen Nationalsozialismus und Bundesrepublik: Kontinuität-Bruch-Neubeginn'. *Südosteuropa Mitteilungen* 4 (2014), 28–45.
———. 'Zur Entstehung und Beharrlichkeit von Geschichtsbildern. Die Patenschaft des Landes Band-Württemberg über die "Volksgruppe der Donauschwaben"'. *Donauschwaben und andere. Tübinger Südosteuropaforschung* 61 (2015), 105–34.
Bendas-Ast, M. *Die Bukowina heute.* n.p., 1981.
Bensoussan, G. (ed.). *L'Horreur Oubliée: La Shoah Roumaine.* Paris: Mémorial de la Shoah, 2011.
Benz, W. *Die Vertreibung der Deutschen: Ursachen, Ereignisse, Folgen.* Frankfurt am Main: Fischer, 1985.
———. (ed.). *Holocaust an der Peripherie: Judenpolitik und Judenmord in Rumänien und Transnistrien 1940–1944.* Berlin: Metropol, 2009.
Bergen, D.L. 'The Nazi Concept of "Volksdeutsche" and the Exacerbation of Anti-Semitism in Eastern Europe, 1939–45'. *Journal of Contemporary History* 29(4) (1994), 569–82.
Berger, S., and B. Niven (eds). *Writing the History of Memory.* London: Bloomsbury, 2014.
Bernsand, N. 'Returning Chernivtsi to the Cultural Map of Europe'. *East European Politics and Societies* 33(1) (2019), 238–56.

Bessel, R. (ed.). *Life after Death: Approaches to a Cultural and Social History*. Cambridge: Cambridge University Press, 2003.
Bickle, P. *Heimat: A Critical Theory of the German Idea of Homeland*. Rochester, NY: Camden House, 2002.
Biess, F., and R.G. Moeller (eds). *Histories of the Aftermath: The Legacies of the Second World War in Europe*. New York: Berghahn Books, 2010.
Bird, S. *Comedy and Trauma in Germany and Austria after 1945: The Inner Side of Mourning*. Cambridge: Legenda, 2016.
Bird, S., M. Fulbrook, J. Wagner and C. Wienand (eds). *Reverberations of Nazi Violence in Germany and Beyond: Disturbing Pasts*. London: Bloomsbury Academic, 2016.
Blacker, U., and A. Etkind (eds). *Memory and Theory in Eastern Europe*. New York: Palgrave Macmillan, 2013.
Bodemann, M. *Jews, Germans, Memory: Reconstructions of Jewish life in Germany*. Ann Arbor: University of Michigan Press, 1996.
Bornemann, I. (ed.). *Bukowina: Landschaften – Bauten – Denkmäler*. Munich: Landsmannschaft der Buchenlanddeutschen, 1986.
———. (ed.) *Mit Fluchtgepäck die Heimat verlassen ... 50 Jahre seit der Umsiedlung der Buchenlanddeutschen*. Augsburg: Verlag 'Der Südostdeutsche', 1990.
Bornemann, I., P. Tiefenthaler and R. Wagner (eds). *Czernowitz: Eine Stadt im Wandel der Zeit: mit Berücksichtigung ihres deutschen kulturellen Lebens*. Munich: Bertsch, 1988.
Bornemann, J., and J. Peck, *Sojourners: The Return of German Jews and the Question of Identity*. Lincoln, NE: University of Nebraska Press, 1995.
Borutta, M., and J.C. Jansen. (eds). *Vertriebene and Pieds-Noirs in Postwar Germany and France: Comparative Perspectives*. Basingstoke: Palgrave Macmillan, 2016.
Boym, S. *The Future of Nostalgia*. New York: Basic Books, 2001.
Brandes, D., H. Sundhaussen and S. Troebst (eds). *Lexikon der Vertreibungen: Deportation, Zwangsaussiedlung und ethnische Säuberung im Europa des 20. Jahrhunderts*. Vienna: Böhlau, 2010.
Braun, H. (ed.). *Rose Ausländer: Materialen zu Leben und Werk*. Frankfurt am Main: Fischer, 1991.
———. (ed.). *Czernowitz: Die Geschichte einer untergegangenen Kulturmetropole*. Berlin: Links Verlag, 2005.
Braun, M. 'Paul Celan und die "Fremde der Heimat": Zum 90. Geburtstag und 40. Todestag des Dichters'. *Die Politische Meinung: Zeitschrift für Politik, Gesellschaft, Religion und Kultur* 492 (2010), 70–75.
Brenner, H. *Mein zwanzigstes Jahrhundert*. Brugg: Munda, 2006.
Brenner, M. (ed.). *Geschichte der Juden in Deutschland von 1945 bis zur Gegenwart: Politik, Kultur und Gesellschaft*. Munich: C.H. Beck, 2012.
———. *Geschichte des Zionismus*, 4th edn. Munich: C.H. Beck, 2016.
———. *Israel: Traum und Wirklichkeit des jüdischen Staates: von Theodor Herzl bis heute*. Munich: C.H. Beck, 2016.
Broszat, M. 'Von der Kulturnation zur Volksgruppe: Die nationale Stellung der Juden in der Bukowina im 19. und 20. Jahrhundert'. *Historische Zeitschrift* 200(3) (1965), 572–605.
———. *Nach Hitler: Der schwierige Umgang mit unserer Geschichte*. Munich: Deutscher Taschenbuch Verlag, 1988.
Brubaker, R. 'Migrations of Ethnic Unmixing in the "New Europe"'. *International Migration Review* 32(4) (1998), 1047–65.
———. *Ethnicity without Groups*. Cambridge, MA: Harvard University Press, 2004.

Brucker, J. *Und immer wieder Hoffnung: Buchenlandtrilogie*. Munich: Landsmannschaft der Buchenlanddeutschen, 1984.
Bundesministerium für Vertriebene, Flüchtlinge und Kriegsgeschädigte (ed.). *Dokumentation der Vertreibung der Deutschen aus Ost-Mitteleuropa*. 5 vols. Bonn: Bundesministerium für Vertriebene, Flüchtlinge und Kriegsgeschädigte, 1953–62 [reprint: Munich: Deutscher Taschenbuch Verlag, 1984].
———. *Das Schicksal der Deutschen in Rumänien*. Vol. 4. Bonn: Bundesministerium für Vertriebene, 1957.
Burke, P. *Varieties of Cultural History*. Ithaca, NY: Cornell University Press, 1997.
Carp, M. *Cartea Neagră: Suferinţele Evreilor din România, 1940–1944*, 3 vols. Bucharest: Editura Diogene, 1996 [1945–48].
Celan, P. *Gesammelte Werke in fünf Bänden*, 5 vols. Frankfurt am Main: Suhrkamp, 1992.
———. *Der Meridian: Endfassung, Entwürfe, Materialen*. Edited by B. Böschenstein and H. Schmull. Frankfurt am Main: Suhrkamp, 1999.
———. *Correspondance: 1951–1970 : Avec un Choix de Lettres de Paul à son Fils Eric*. Paris: Seuil, 2001.
———. *Die Gedichte: Kommentierte Gesamtausgabe*. Frankfurt am Main: Suhrkamp, 2005.
Cercel, C. *Romania and the Quest for European Identity: Philo-Germanism without Germans*. Abingdon: Routledge, 2019.
Cesarani, D., T. Kushner and M. Shain (eds). *Place and Displacement in Jewish History and Memory: zakor v'makor*. London: Vallentine Mitchell, 2007.
Cesarani, D. et al. (eds). *Survivors of Nazi Persecution in Europe after the Second World War*. Portland, OR: Vallentine Mitchell, 2010.
Cesarani, D., and E. Sundquist (eds). *After the Holocaust: Challenging the Myth of Silence*. London: Routledge, 2012.
Chalfen, I. *Paul Celan: Eine Biographie seiner Jugend*. Frankfurt am Main: Insel-Verl., 1979.
Chichopek-Gajraj, A. *Beyond Violence: Jewish Survivors in Poland and Slovakia, 1944–1948*. Cambridge: Cambridge University Press, 2014.
Ciuciura, T. 'Provincial Politics in the Habsburg Empire: The Case of Galicia and Bukovina'. *Nationalities Papers: The Journal of Nationalism and Ethnicity* 13(2) (1985), 247–73.
Cohen, B. *Israeli Holocaust Research: Birth and Evolution*. Abingdon: Routledge, 2013.
Cohen, G.D. *In War's Wake: Europe's Displaced Persons in the Postwar Order*. Oxford: Oxford University Press, 2011
Coldewey, G. et al. (eds). *Zwischen Pruth und Jordan: Lebenserinnerungen Czernowitzer Juden*. Cologne: Böhlau, 2003.
Colin, A., and A. Kittner (eds). *Versunkene Dichtung der Bukowina*. Munich: W. Fink, 1994.
———. *Paul Celan: Holograms of Darkness*. Bloomington: Indiana University Press, 1991.
Confino, A. 'Collective Memory and Cultural History: Problems of Method'. *American Historical Review* 102 (1997), 1386–403.
———. *The Nation as a Local Metaphor: Württemberg, Imperial Germany, and National Memory 1871–1918*. Chapel Hill: University of North Carolina Press, 1997.
Confino, A., and P. Fritzsche (eds). *The Work of Memory: New Directions in the Study of German Society and Culture*. Urbana: University of Illinois Press, 2002.
Connor, I. *Refugees and Expellees in Post-War Germany*. Manchester: Manchester University Press, 2007.
Corbea-Hoisie, A. (ed.). *Czernowitz: Jüdisches Städtebild*. Frankfurt am Main: jüdischer Verlag, 1998.
Corbea-Hoisie, A. *Czernowitzer Geschichten: Über eine städtische Kultur in Mittelosteuropa*. Vienna: Böhlau, 2003.

———. *La Bucovine: Eléments d'Histoire Politique et Culturelle*. Paris: Institut d'études slaves, 2004.

———. 'Bukarest als intellektuelle Hauptstadt der deutschsprachigen Bukowina: 1945–1947'. unpublished conference paper presented at the conference *Bukovina and Bukovinians after the Second World War: (Re)shaping and (Re)thinking a Region after Genocide and 'Ethnic Unmixing'*. University of Augsburg, 14–15 September 2016.

———. *Paul Celans 'unbequemes Zuhause': Sein erstes Jahrzehnt in Paris*. Aachen: Rimbaud Verlag, 2017.

Corbea-Hoisie, A., and M. Astner (eds). *Kulturlandschaft Bukowina: Studien zur deutschsprachigen Literatur des Buchenlandes nach 1918*. Iași: Ed. Univ. Alexandru Ioan Cuza, 1990.

Corbea-Hoisie, A., G. Guțu and M. Hainz (eds). *Stundenwechsel: Neue Perspektiven zu Alfred Margul-Sperber, Rose Ausländer, Paul Celan, Imanuel Weissglas*. Konstanz: Hartung-Gorre, 2002.

Cornis-Pope, M., and J. Neubauer (eds). *History of the Literary Cultures of East-Central Europe: Junctures and Disjunctures in the 19th and 20th Centuries*. Vol 1. Amsterdam: John Benjamins Publishing, 2004.

Csáky, M., A. Kury and U. Tragatschnig (eds). *Kultur – Identität – Differenz: Wien und Zentraleuropa in der Moderne*. Innsbruck: StudienVerlag, 2004.

Csáky, M., and E. Mannová (eds). *Collective Identities in Central Europe in Modern Times*. Translated from Czech by M. Styan. Bratislava: Academic Electronic Press, 1999.

Csáky, M., and P. Stachel (eds). *Die Verortung von Gedächtnis*. Vienna: Passagen Verlag, 2001.

Dácz, E. (ed.). *Räumliche Semantisierungen: Raumkonstruktionen in den deutschsprachigen Literaturen aus Zentral- und Südosteuropa im 20.–21. Jahrhundert*. Regensburg: Verlag Friedrich Pustet, 2018.

Davis, F. *Yearning for Yesterday: A Sociology of Nostalgia*. New York: Free Press, 1979.

Dawson, J. 'Finding Blanka: A Story of Sorrow and Strength in Post-war Romania'. *Holocaust. Studii și Cercetări* 6(1) (2013), 8–99.

De Berg, A. *'Nach Galizien': Entwicklung der Reiseliteratur am Beispiel der deutschsprachigen Reiseberichte vom 18. bis zum 21. Jahrhundert*. Frankfurt am Main: Peter Lang, 2010.

Dear, I., and M.R.D. Foot (eds). *The Oxford Companion to World War II*. Oxford: Oxford University Press, 2005.

Deletant, D. *Hitler's Forgotten Ally: Ion Antonescu and his Regime, Romania 1940–1944*. Basingstoke: Palgrave Macmillan: 2006.

Demshuk, A. 'Citizens in Name Only: The National Status of German Expellees, 1945–53'. *Ethnopolitics: Formerly Global Review of Ethnopolitics* 5(4) (2006), 383–97.

———. '"Wehmut und Trauer": Jewish Travelers in Polish Silesia and the Foreignness of Heimat.' *Jahrbuch des Simon-Dubnow-Instituts* (December 2007), 311–35.

———. 'What was the "Right to the Heimat"? West German Expellees and the Many Meanings of Heimkehr'. *Central European History* 45 (2012), 523–56.

———. *The Lost German East: Forced Migration and the Politics of Memory 1945–1970*. New York: Cambridge University Press, 2012.

———. 'Godfather Cities: West German *Patenschaften* and the Lost German East', *German History* 32(2) (2014), 224–55.

Demshuk, A., and T. Weger (eds). *Cultural Landscapes: Translatlantische Perspektiven auf Wirkungen und Auswirkungen deutscher Kultur und Geschichte im östlichen Europa*. Munich: De Gruyter Oldenbourg, 2015.

Diner, D. 'Negative Symbiose: Deutsche und Juden nach Auschwitz'. *Babylon* 1 (1986), 9–20.

———. 'On Guilt Discourse and Other Narratives'. *History and Memory* 9(1–2) (1997), 301–20.

———. *Beyond the Conceivable: Studies on Germany, Nazism, and the Holocaust*. Berkeley: University of California Press, 2000.

———. *Rituelle Distanz: Israels deutsche Frage*. Munich: Deutsche Verlags-Anstalt, 2015.

Douglas, R.M. *Orderly and Humane: The Expulsions of the Germans after the Second World War*. New Haven: Yale University Press, 2012.

Dressler, J.C. *Illischestie: Chronik der Bukowiner Landgemeinde*. Freilassing: Pannonia Verlag, 1960.

Drozdowski, G. *Damals in Czernowitz und rundum: Erinnerungen eines Altösterreichers*. Carinthia: Verlag der kleinen Zeitung, 1984.

Dumitru, D. *The State, Antisemitism, and Collaboration in the Holocaust: The Borderlands of Romania and the Soviet Union*. New York: Cambridge University Press, 2016.

Eigler, F., and J. Kugele (eds). *Heimat: At the Intersection of Memory and Space*. Berlin: De Gruyter Oldenbourg, 2012.

Elkins, C., and S. Pedersen (eds). *Settler Colonialism in the Twentieth Century: Projects, Practices, Legacies*. New York: Routledge, 2005.

Erll, A. *Memory in Culture*. Translated from German by S.B. Young. Basingstoke: Palgrave Macmillan, 2011.

Erll, A., A. Nünning and S. Young (eds). *Cultural Memory Studies: An International and Interdisciplinary Handbook*. Berlin: Walter de Gruyter, 2008.

Evans, R. *Austria, Hungary, and the Habsburgs: Essays on Central Europe, c. 1683–1867*. Oxford: Oxford University Press, 2006.

Faehndrich, J. *Eine endliche Geschichte: Die Heimatbücher der Deutschen Vertriebenen*. Cologne: Böhlau, 2011.

Faerber, M.M. (ed.). *Stimmen aus Israel: Eine Anthologie deutschsprachiger Literatur in Israel*. Gerlingen bei Stuttgart: Bleicher, 1979.

———. (ed.). *Auf dem Weg: Eine Anthologie deutschsprachiger Literatur in Israel*. Gerlingen: Bleicher, 1989.

Feichtinger, J., and G.B. Cohen (eds). *Understanding Multiculturalism: The Habsburg Central European Experience*. New York: Berghahn Books, 2014.

Feichtinger, J., and H. Uhl (eds). *Habsburg neu denken: Vielfalt und Ambivalenz in Zentraleuropa: 30 kulturwissenschaftliche Stichworte*. Vienna: Böhlau Verlag, 2016.

Felstiner, J. *Paul Celan: Poet, Survivor, Jew*. New Haven: Yale University Press, 1995.

Fendl, E. 'Reisen in die verlorene Vergangenheit – Überlegungen zum "Heimwehtourismus"'. *Jahrbuch für deutsche und osteuropäische Volkskunde* 41 (1998), 85–100.

———. (ed.). *Zur Ästhetik des Verlusts: Bilder von Heimat, Flucht und Vertreibung*. Münster: Waxmann, 2010.

Festschrift zur Feier des 25-jährigen Bestehens der Heimstättensiedlung Darmstadt Süd 1932–1957. Darmstadt: n.p., 1957.

Fichman, P. *Before Memories Fade*. New York: Pearl Fichman, 1989; 2005.

Filaretow, B. *Kontinuität und Wandel: Zur Integration der Deutsch-Balten in die Gesellschaft der BRD*. Baden-Baden: Nomos Geschichte, 1990.

Fischer, T., and M.N. Lorenz (eds). *Lexikon der 'Vergangenheitsbewältigung' in Deutschland: Debatten- und Diskursgeschichte des Nationalsozialismus nach 1945*. Bielefeld: Transcript, 2015.

Fisher, G. 'Between Liberation and Emigration: Jews from Bukovina in Romania after the Second World War'. *Leo Baeck Institute Year Book* 62(1) (2017), 115–32.

———. 'Heimat Heimstättensiedlung: Constructing Belonging in Postwar Germany'. *German History* 35(4) (2017), 568–87.

———. 'Looking Forwards through the Past: Bukovina's "Return to Europe" after 1989–1991'. *East European Politics and Societies* 33(1) (2019), 196–217.
Fisher, G., and M. Röger (eds). 'Bukovina and Bukovinians after the Second World War: (Re)shaping and (Re)thinking a Region after Genocide and "Ethnic Unmixing"'. *East European Politics and Societies* 33(1) (2019), special issue, 176–256.
———. 'Bukovina: A Borderland Region in (Trans-)national Historiographies after 1945 and 1989–1991,' *East European Politics and Societies* 33(1) (2019), special issue, 176–195.
Fisher, J. *Transnistria: The Forgotten Cemetery*. South Brunswick, NJ: T. Yosseloff, 1969.
François, E., and H. Schulze (eds). *Deutsche Erinnerungsorte*, 3 vols. Munich: Beck, 2001–2.
Franzos, K.E. *Vom Don zur Donau: Neue Kulturbilder aus 'Halb-Asien'*. Leipzig: Duncker und Humblot, 1877.
Franzos, K.E., and J. Strelka, *Erzählungen aus Galizien und der Bukowina*. Berlin: Nicolai, 1988.
Frei, N. *Adenauer's Germany and the Nazi Past: The Politics of Amnesty and Integration*. Translated from German by J. Gold. New York: Columbia University Press, 2002.
Frei, N., J. Brunner and C. Goschler (eds). *Die Praxis der Wiedergutmachung: Geschichte, Erfahrung und Wirkung in Deutschland und Israel*. Göttingen: Wallstein, 2009.
Friedländer, S. *Nazi Germany and the Jews: The Years of Persecution, 1933–1939*. New York: HarperCollins, 1998.
———. *Nazi Germany and the Jews, 1939–1945: The Years of Extermination*. New York: HarperCollins, 2007.
Friling, T., R. Ioanid and M. Ionescu (eds). *Final Report of the International Commission on the Holocaust in Romania*. Iași: Polirom, 2004.
Frunchak, S. 'The Making of Soviet Chernivtsi: National "Re-unification", World War II, and the Fate of Jewish Czernowitz in Post-war Ukraine'. D.Phil. thesis. University of Toronto, 2010.
———. 'Commemorating the Future in Post-War Chernivtsi'. *East European Politics and Societies* 24 (3) (2010), 435–63
———. 'Studying the Land, Contesting the Land: A Select Historiographic Guide to Modern Bukovina'. *The Carl Beck Papers in Russian and East European Studies* 2108, vol. 1 (Essay) and vol. 2 (Notes) (2011).
Fulbrook, M. *German National Identity after the Holocaust*. Cambridge: Polity Press, 1999.
———. *Reckonings: Legacies of Nazi Persecution and the Quest for Justice*. Oxford: Oxford University Press, 2018.
Gailing, L., and M. Leibenath. 'Von der Schwierigkeit, "Landschaft" oder "Kulturlandschaft" allgemeingültig zu definieren'. *Raumforschung und Raumordnung* 70(2) (2012), 95–106.
Gaschler, N. 'Die Umsiedlung der Buchenlanddeutschen im Spätherbst 1940 und ihre Folgen für die Katholiken und ihre Priester aus Bessarabien, der Bukowina und der Dobrudscha' [in two parts]. *Analele Bucovinei* XVII(1) (2010), 301–42 and XVII(2) (2010), 427–36.
Gatrell, P., and N. Baron. *Warlands: Population Resettlement and State Reconstruction in the Soviet-East European Borderlands, 1945–50*. Basingstoke: Palgrave Macmillan, 2009.
Gelber, Y. 'The Historical Role of the Central European Immigration to Israel'. *Leo Baeck Institute Year Book* 38 (1993), 323–39.
Geissbühler, S. *Blutiger Juli: Rumäniens Vernichtungskrieg und der vergessene Massenmord an den Juden 1941*. Paderborn; Munich: Ferdinand Schöningh, 2013.
———. (ed.). *Romania and the Holocaust: Events, Contexts, Aftermath*. Stuttgart: Ibidem, 2016.
Glajar, V. *The German Legacy in Central Europe as Recorded in Recent German Literature*. Rochester, NY: Camden House, 2004.

Glajar, V., and J. Teodorescu (eds). *Local History, Transnational Memory in the Romanian Holocaust*. New York: Palgrave Macmillan, 2011.
Glasberg-Gold, R. *Ruth's Journey: A Survivor's Memoir*. New York: iUniverse Inc., 2009 [1996].
Glass, H. *Zerbrochene Nachbarschaft: das deutsch-jüdische Verhältnis in Rumänien 1918–1938*. Munich: Oldenbourg, 1996.
———. *Minderheit zwischen zwei Diktaturen: zur Geschichte der Juden in Rumänien 1944–1949*. Munich: Oldenbourg, 2002.
———. *Deutschland und die Verfolgung der Juden im rumänischen Machtbereich, 1940–1944*. Munich: Oldenbourg, 2014.
Gold, H. (ed.). *Geschichte der Juden in der Bukowina: ein Sammelwerk*, 2 vols. Tel Aviv: Olamenu, 1958 and 1962.
Goltschnigg, D., A. Schwob and G. Fuchs (eds). *Die Bukowina: Studien zu einer versunkenen Literaturlandschaft*. Tübingen: Francke, 1990.
Goschler, C. '"Versöhnung" und "Viktimisierung": Die Vertriebenen und der deutsche Opferdiskurs'. *Zeitschrift für Geschichtswissenschaft* 53(10) (2005), 873–84.
———. *Schuld und Schulden: Die Politik der Wiedergutmachung für NS-Verfolgte seit 1945*. Göttingen: Wallstein, 2005.
Grill, T. (ed.). *Jews and Germans in Eastern Europe: Shared and Comparative Histories*. Berlin, Boston: De Gruyter Oldenbourg, 2018.
Gross, J.T. *Fear: Anti-Semitism in Poland after Auschwitz: An Essay in Historical Interpretation*. New York: Random House, 2006.
Grossmann, A. *Jews, Germans and Allies: Close Encounters in Occupied Germany*. Princeton: Princeton University Press, 2007.
Gruber, R.E. *Virtually Jewish: Reinventing Jewish Culture in Europe*. Berkeley: University of California Press, 2002.
Guggenberger, G. *Georg Drozdowski in literarischen Feldern zwischen Czernowitz und Berlin (1920–1945)*. Berlin: Frank and Timme, 2015.
Gutman, Y., and A. Saf (eds). *She'erit Hapletah 1944–1948: Rehabilitation and Political Struggle*. Jerusalem: Proceedings of the Sixth Yad Vashem International Historical Conference October 1985, 1990.
Guțu, G. 'Drinking the Milky Blackness, Romanian Journal of Artistic Creativity'. *Romanian Journal of Artistic Creativity* 1 (2013), 138–48.
Guțu, G., and P. Motzan (eds). *Die Buche: Eine Anthologie deutschsprachiger Judendichtung aus der Bukowina*. Aachen: Rimbaud Verlag, 2009.
Hacohen, D. 'The Law of Return as an Embodiment of the Link between Israel and the Jews of the Diaspora'. *Journal of Israeli History* 19(1) (1998), 61–89.
———. *Immigrants in Turmoil: Mass Immigration to Israel and its Repercussions in the 1950s and after*. New York: Syracuse University Press, 2003.
Hahn, H.H., and E. Hahn. *Die Vertreibung im deutschen Erinnern: Legenden, Mythos, Geschichte*. Paderborn: Ferdinand Schöningh, 2010.
Halbwachs, M. *On Collective Memory*. Translated from French by L.A. Coser. Chicago: University of Chicago Press, 1992.
Hann, C., and P. Robert Magocsi (eds). *Galicia: A Multicultured Land*. Toronto: University of Toronto Press, 2005.
Halperin, L. *Babel in Zion: Jews, Nationalism, and Language Diversity in Palestine, 1920–1948*. New Haven: Yale University Press, 2015.
Hampel, J., and O. Kotzian (eds). *Spurensuche in die Zukunft: Europas vergessene Region Bukowina*. Augsburg: Bukowina-Institut, 1991.

———. (eds). *Das Bukowina-Institut in Augsburg*. 2nd edn. Augsburg: Bukowina-Institut e. V., 1994 [1990].
Hartman, G. (ed.). *Holocaust Remembrance: The Shapes of Memory*. Oxford: Blackwell, 1994.
Haupt, A. *Meine Reise in die alte Heimat: Erinnerungen*. Eichwalde: Raku Verlag, 2007.
Hausleitner, M. *Die Rumänisierung der Bukowina: Die Durchsetzung des nationalstaatlichen Anspruchs Grossrumäniens 1918–1944*. Munich: Oldenbourg, 2001.
———. 'Rolul intelectualilor evrei în Europa est-centrală pornind de la exemplul Bucoviniei'. *Studia et Acta Historiae Iudaeorum Romaniae IX* (2005), 263–81.
———. 'Die Geschichte der Bukowina in der ersten Hälfte des 20. Jahrhunderts aus der Sicht von Deutschen, Juden und Rumänen'. *Die Bukowina: historische und ethnokulturelle Studien*. [Beiträge der IV. internationalen wissenschaftlichen Konferenz 'Kaindlische Lesungen'.] (Chernivtsi: Selena Bukowina, 2007), 122–35.
———. 'Die Deutschen in der Bukowina'. *Jahrbuch der Deutschen aus Bessarabien* 64 (2013), 93–101.
———. *'Viel Mischmasch mitgenommen': Die Umsiedlungen aus der Bukowina 1940*. Berlin: Verlag Walter de Gruyter, 2018.
Hausleitner, M., B. Mihok and J. Wetzel (eds). *Rumänien und der Holocaust: zu den Massenverbrechen in Transnistrien 1941–1944*. Berlin: Metropol, 2001.
Heinemann, I. 'Towards and "Ethnic Reconstruction of Occupied Europe": SS Plans and Racial Policies'. *Annali dell'Instituto storico-germano in Trento* XXVII (2001), 493–517.
———. *Rasse, Siedlung und deutsches Blut: Das Rasse- und Siedlungshauptamt der SS und die Rassenpolitische Neuordnung Europas*. Göttingen: Wallstein, 2003.
———. and P. Wagner (eds). *Wissenschaft, Planung, Vertreibung: Neuordnungskonzepte und Umsiedlungspolitik im 20. Jahrhundert*. Stuttgart: Steiner, 2006.
Heinen, A. *Rumänien, der Holocaust und die Logik der Gewalt*. Munich: Oldenbourg, 2007.
Helfrich, C. *Es ist ein Aschensommer in der Welt: Rose Ausländer: Biographie*. Weinheim: Quadriga, 1995.
Heppner, H. (ed.). *Czernowitz: Die Geschichte einer ungewöhnlichen Stadt*. Cologne: Böhlau Verlag, 2000.
Hestermann, J. *Inszenierte Versöhnung: Reisediplomatie und die deutsch-israelischen Beziehungen von 1957 bis 1984*. Frankfurt: Campus Verlag, 2016.
Heymann, F. *Le Crépuscule des Lieux: Identités Juives de Czernowitz*. Paris: Editions Stock, 2003.
———. 'Aspects of Jewish Life in Bukovina before the Holocaust'. *Holocaust and Modernity* 8(2) (2010), 37–46.
———. 'Voyage à Chernivtsi ou Retour à Czernowitz? Les Paradoxes de la Mémoire et de la Nostalgie'. *Teoros* 29(1) (2010), 17–30.
Hillgruber, A. *Zweierlei Untergang: Die Zerschlagung des Deutschen Reiches und das Ende des europäischen Judentums*. Berlin: Siedler, 1986.
Hirsch, M. *Family Frames: Photography Narrative and Postmemory*. Cambridge, MA: Harvard University Press, 1997.
———. *The Generation of Postmemory: Writing and Visual Culture after the Holocaust*. New York: Columbia University Press, 2012.
Hirsch, M., and N.K. Miller (eds). *Rites of Return: Diaspora Poetics and the Politics of Memory*. New York: Columbia University Press, 2011.
Hirsch, M., and L. Spitzer. *Ghosts of Home: The Afterlife of Czernowitz in Jewish Memory*. Berkeley: University of California Press, 2010.
Hobsbawm, E. *Fractured Times: Culture and Society in the 20th Century*. London: Hachette Digital, 2013.

Hockerts, H.G. 'Wiedergutmachung in Deutschland: Eine historische Bilanz 1945-2000'. *Vierteljahrshefte für Zeitgeschichte* 49(2) (2001), 167–214.
Hodgkin, K., and S. Radstone (eds). *Contested Pasts: The Politics of Memory*. London: Routledge, 2003.
Horn, M., and P. Rothermel. *Heimat in der Fremde: Dokumentation zur Geschichte der Vertriebenen in der Stadt Darmstadt und im Landkreis Darmstadt-Dieburg*. Darmstadt: Reba-Verlag, 1993.
Hughes, M. *Shouldering the Burdens of Defeat: West Germany and the Reconstruction of Social Justice*. Chapel Hill: University of North Carolina Press, 1999.
———. '"Through No Fault of Our Own": West Germans Remember Their War Losses'. *German History* 18(2) (2000), 193–213.
Iancu, C. *Les Juifs en Roumanie (1919–1938): De l'Emancipation à la Marginalisation*. Paris-Louvain: E. Peeters, 1996.
Ingrao, C., and F. Szabo (eds). *The Germans and the East*. West Lafayette, IN: Purdue University Press, 2008.
Ioanid, R. *The Holocaust in Romania: The Destruction of Jews and Gypsies under the Antonescu Regime, 1940–1944*. Chicago: Ivan R. Dee, 2000.
———. *The Ransom of the Jews: The Story of the Extraordinary Secret Bargain between Romania and Israel*. Chicago: Ivan R. Dee, 2005.
———. (ed.). *Securitatea și Vânzarea Evreilor: Istoria Acordurilor Secrete dintre România și Israel*. Bucharest: Editura Polirom, 2015.
Ionescu, S.C. *Jewish Resistance to 'Romanianization', 1940–44*. Basingstoke: Palgrave Macmillan, 2015.
Irwin-Zarecka, I. *Frames of Remembrance: The Dynamics of Collective Memory*. New Brunswick, NJ: Transaction, 1994.
Jachomowski, D. *Die Umsiedlung der Bessarabien-, Bukowina- und Dobrudschadeutschen: von der Volksgruppe in Rumänien zur 'Siedlungsbrücke' an der Reichsgrenze*. Munich: Oldenbourg, 1984.
Jaspers, K. *Die Schuldfrage*. Heidelberg: Schneider, 1946.
Judt, T. *Postwar: A History of Europe since 1945*. London: Heinemann, 2005.
Kaindl, R.F. *Geschichte der Bukowina von den ältesten Zeiten bis zur Gegenwart unter besonderer Berücksichtigung der Kulturverhältnisse*. Czernowitz: Verlag der k. k. Universitätsbuchhandlung H. Pardini 1895.
Kansteiner, Wulf. 'Finding Meaning in Memory: A Methodological Critique of Collective Memory Studies'. *History and Theory* 41 (2002), 179–97.
———. *In Pursuit of German Memory: History, Television, and Politics after Auschwitz*. Athens, OH: Ohio University Press, 2006.
Katz, Leo. *Totenjäger*. Aachen: Rimbaud Verlag, 2005.
Kauders, A. *Unmögliche Heimat: Eine deutsch-jüdische Geschichte der Bundesrepublik*. Munich: Deutsche Verlags-Anstalt, 2007.
———. 'West German Jewry: Guilt, Power and Pluralism'. *Quest. Issues in Contemporary History. Journal of Fondazione CDEC* 1 (2010), 17–33.
Keil, E.E. *Ostdeutsches Lesebuch. Vier Jahrhunderte deutscher Dichtung vom Baltikum bis zum Banat/2: Deutsche Dichtung der Jahrhundertmitte vom Baltikum bis zum Banat*. Bonn: Kulturstiftung d. Dt. Vertriebenen, 1984.
Kilcher, A., and E. Edelmann-Ohler. *Deutsche Sprachkultur in Palästina/Israel. Geschichte und Bibliographie*. Berlin: De Gruyter, 2017.
Kiraly, S. *Ludwig Metzger: Politiker aus christlicher Verantwortung*. Darmstadt: Historische Kommission für Hessen, 2004.

Kittner, A. *Hungermarsch und Stacheldraht: Verse von Trotz und Zuversicht*. Bucharest: ESPLA, 1956.
———. *Briefe/4: Briefe an Alfred Margul-Sperber 1932–1966*. Aachen: Rimbaud Verlag, 2015.
Kittner, A., W. Kirsten and R. Kiefer. *Briefe/3: Briefe an Wulf Kirsten: Ausgewählte Briefe*. Aachen: Rimbaud Verlag, 2010.
Kittner, A., and E. Silbermann. *Erinnerungen 1906–1991*. Aachen: Rimbaud Verlag, 1996.
Klein-Haparash, J. *... der vor dem Löwen flieht*. Stuttgart: Deutscher Bücherbund, 1961.
———. *He Who Flees the Lion*. Translated from German by C. Winston and R. Winston. New York: Atheneum, 1963.
Klug, A. (ed.). *Bukowiner deutsches Dichterbuch*. Stuttgart: E. Wahl, Stuttgarter Volksdeutsche Bücherei, 1939.
Kneightly, E., and D. Pickering. *The Mnemonic Imagination: Remembering as a Creative Practice*. Basingstoke: Palgrave Macmillan, 2012.
Kolf, B. 'Eine Gegend, in der Menschen und Bücher lebten. Die Bukowina als lyrische Landschaft'. *Akzente* 4 (1982), 336–83.
Komjathy, A., and R. Stockwell. *German Minorities and the Third Reich: Ethnic Germans of East Central Europe*. New York: Holmes and Meier, 1980.
Kosmala, B., and G. Verbeeck (eds). *Facing the Catastrophe: Jews and Non-Jews in Europe during World War II*. Oxford: Berg, 2011.
Kossert, A. *Kalte Heimat: Die Geschichte der deutschen Vertriebenen nach 1945*. Munich: Siedler, 2008.
Kotzian, O. *Die Umsiedler: die Deutschen aus West-Wolhynien, Galizien, die Bukowina, Bessarabien, der Dobrudscha und in der Karpatenukraine*. Munich: Langer Müller, 2005.
Koranyi, J. 'Between East and West: Romanian German Identities since 1945'. D.Phil. thesis. University of Exeter, 2008.
Koziura, K. 'The Spaces of Nostalgia(s) and the Politics of Belonging in Contemporary Chernivtsi, Western Ukraine'. *East European Politics and Societies* 33(1) (2019), 218–37.
Krauss, M. (ed.). *Integrationen: Vertriebene in den deutschen Ländern nach 1945*. Göttingen: Vandenhoeck & Ruprecht, 2008.
Kugelmass, J., and J. Boyarin (eds). *From a Ruined Garden: The Memorial Books of the Polish Jewry*. New York: Shocken Books, 1983.
Kührer-Wielach, F., and Konrad G. *Mutter: Land – Vater Staat: Loyalitätskonflikte, politische Neuorientierung im österreichich-russländischen Grenzraum*. Regensburg: Verlag Friedrich Pustet, 2017.
Kuzmany, B. 'Habsburg Austria: Experiments in Non-territorial Autonomy'. *Ethnopolitics* 15(1) (2016), 43–65.
Kuzmany, B., and R. Garstenauer. *Aufnahmeland Österreich: Über den umging mit Massenflucht seit dem 18. Jahrhundert*. Vienna: Mandelbaum Verlag, 2017.
LaCapra, D. *History in Transit: Experience, Identity, Critical Theory*. Ithaca, NY: Cornell University Press, 2004.
Landsberg, A. *Prosthetic Memory: The Transformation of American Remembrance in the Age of Mass Culture*. New York: Columbia University Press, 2004.
Lang, F. 'Sprache und Literatur der Deutschen in der Bukowina'. *Südostdeutsche Heimatblätter* 4 (1955), 192–219
———. (ed.). *Buchenland: hundertfünfzig Jahre Deutschtum in der Bukowina*. Munich: Verlag des Südostdeutschen Kulturwerks, 1961.
Langer, L. *Holocaust Testimonies: The Ruins of Memory*. New Haven: Yale University Press, 1991.
Lapierre, Nicole. *Le Silence de la Mémoire: A la Recherche des Juifs de Plock*. Paris: Plon, 1989.

Lappin, E., and A. Lichtblau (eds). *Die 'Wahrheit' der Erinnerung: Jüdische Lebensgeschichten*. Innsbruck: Studienverlag, 2008.
Last, S. *Die letzten Juden*. Rothenburg ob der Tauber: J.P. Peter, 1960.
Lazăr, N. 'Populaţia evreiasca din Rădăuţi în timpul Holocaustului şi imediat după'. Unpublished conference paper presented at the Conference of the Federation of Jewish Communities of Romania *Evreii din Rădăuţi*. 25 July 2012.
Lazăr, N., and L. Benjamin (eds). *American Jewish Joint Distribution Committee în România: Documente*. Bucharest: Hasefer, 2017.
Lehrer, E., and M. Meng (eds). *Jewish Space in Contemporary Poland*. Bloomington: Indiana University Press, 2015.
Lemberg, E. (ed.). *Die Vertriebenen in Westdeutschland*. Kiel: Ferdinand Hirt, 1959.
Leniger, M. *Nationalsozialistische 'Volkstumsarbeit' und Umsiedlungspolitik 1939–1945: von der Minderheitenbetreuung zur Siedlerauslese*. Berlin: Frank und Timme, 2006.
Le Rider, J. *La Mitteleuropa*. Paris: PUF, 1994.
———. 'Der österreichische Begriff von Zentraleuropa: Habsburgischer Mythos oder Realität?'. Ingeborg Bachmann Centre Lecture 2007. London: Institute of Germanic and Romance Studies, School of Advanced Study, University of London, 2008.
———. 'Mitteleuropa, Zentraleuropa, Mittelosteuropa: A Mental Map of Central Europe'. *European Journal of Social Theory* 11(2) (2008), 155–69.
Lissak, M. 'The Demographic Revolution in Israel in the 1950s: The Absorption of the Great Aliyah'. *Journal of Israeli History* 22(2) (2003), 1–31.
Livezeanu, I. *Cultural Politics in Greater Romania: Regionalism, Nation Building and Ethnic Struggle, 1918–1930*. Ithaca, NY: Cornell University Press, 1995.
Lorenz, W. *Der Zug der Volksdeutschen aus Bessarabien und dem Nord-Buchenland*. Berlin: Volk und Reich Verlag, 1942.
Lotz, C. *Die Deutung des Verlusts: Erinnerungspolitische Kontroversen im geteilten Deutschland um Flucht, Vertreibung und die Ostgebiete (1948–1972)*. Cologne: Böhlau, 2007.
Ludi, R. *Reparations for Nazi Victims in Post-war Europe*. Cambridge: Cambridge University Press, 2012.
Lumans, V.O. *Himmler's Auxiliaries: The Volksdeutsche Mittelstelle and the German National Minorities of Europe, 1939–1945*. Chapel Hill: University of North Carolina Press, 1993.
Luppes, J. 'The Commemorative Ceremonies of the Expellees: Tag der Heimat and Volkstrauertag'. *German Politics and Society* 30(2) (2012), 1–20.
Macdonald, S. *Memorylands: Heritage and Identity in Europe Today*. London: Routledge, 2013.
Maeder, P. *Forging a New Heimat: Expellees in Post-war West Germany and Canada*. Göttingen: Vandenhoeck & Ruprecht Unipress, 2011.
Magris, C. *Danube*. New York: Farrar, Straus and Giroux, 1989.
Maier, C. *The Unmasterable Past: History, Holocaust, and German National Identity*. Cambridge, MA: Harvard University Press, 1988.
Mandel, R. *Cosmopolitan Anxieties: Turkish Challenges to Citizenship and Belonging in Germany*. Durham, NC: Duke University Press, 2008.
Maner, H.C. *Parlamentarismus in Rumänien (1930–1940): Demokratie im autoritären Umfeld*. Munich: Oldenbourg, 1997.
Mankowitz, Z. *Life between Memory and Hope: The Survivors of the Holocaust in Occupied Germany*. Cambridge: Cambridge University Press, 2002.
Margalit, G. *Guilt, Suffering, and Memory: Germany Remembers its Dead of World War II*. Translated from Hebrew by H. Watzman. Bloomington: Indiana University Press, 2010.
Margul-Sperber, A. *Geheimnis und Verzicht: Das lyrische Werk in Auswahl*. Bucharest: Kriterion, 1975.

Marten-Finnis, S., and M. Bauer. 'Jüdische Konfliktkultur und urbane Öffentlichkeit in Czernowitz, 1908–1922'. *Internationales Archiv für Sozialgeschichte der deutschen Literatur* 32(2) (2007), 116–27.
Marten-Finnis, S., and W. Schmitz (eds). *'... zwischen dem Osten und dem Westen Europas': Deutschsprachige Presse in Czernowitz bis zum Zweiten Weltkrieg*. Dresden: Thelem, 2005.
Marten-Finnis, S., and M. Winkler. 'Location of Memory versus Space of Communication: Presses, Languages, and Education among Czernovitz Jews, 1918–1941'. *Central Europe* 7(1) (2009), 30–55.
Martin, H. 'Czernowitz/Bukowina als europäische Lektion'. *Kakanien Revisited* (17 August 2005), http://www.kakanien.ac.at/beitr/fallstudie/MHainz1.pdf (retrieved 24 September 2019).
———. 'Nostallergie: Die Czernowitzer Inkongruenzkompensationskompetenz'. *CAS Working Paper* 1 (2009), 1–23.
Massey, D. 'Places and Their Pasts'. *History Workshop Journal* 39 (1995), 182–92.
———. *For Space*. Los Angeles: Sage, 2005.
Massier, E., J. Talsky and B.C. Grigorowicz (eds). *Bukowina: Heimat von gestern*. Karlsruhe: Selbstverlag 'Arbeitskreis Bukowina Heimatbuch, 1956.
Massier, E. (ed.). *Fratautz und die Fratautzer: Vom Werden und Vergehen einer deutschen Dorfgemeinschaft in der Bukowina*. Pleutersbach: n. p., 1957.
Mazower, M. *Dark Continent: Europe's Twentieth Century*. New York: Random House, 1998.
———. (ed.). *Postwar Reconstruction in Europe: International Perspectives, 1945–1949*. Oxford: Oxford University Press, 2011.
Mendelsohn, E. *The Jews of East Central Europe between the World Wars*. Bloomington: Indiana University Press, 1983.
Meng, M. *Shattered Spaces: Encountering Jewish Ruins in Post-war Germany and Poland*. Cambridge, MA.: Harvard University Press, 2011.
Menninghaus, W. '"Czernowitz/Bukowina" als Topos deutsch-jüdischer Geschichte und Literatur'. *Merkur* 53(3–4) (1999), 345–57.
Messerschmidt, R. *Hessen und die Vertriebenen: Eine Bilanz 1945 bis zur Gegenwart*. Wiesbaden: Stiftung Vertriebene in Hessen, 2010.
Metzger, L. *In guten und in schlechten Tagen: Berichte, Gedanken und Erkenntnisse aus der politischen Arbeit eines aktiven Christen und Sozialisten*. Darmstadt: Reba Verlag, 1980.
Michman, D. (ed.). *Remembering the Holocaust in Germany, 1945–2000: German Strategies and Jewish Responses*. New York: Peter Lang, 2002.
Mircu, M. *Progromul de la Iași*. Bucharest: Editura Glob, 1944.
———. *Pogromurile din Bucovina și Dorohoi*. Bucharest: Editura Glob, 1945.
———. *Pogromurile din Basarabia și Transnistria*. Bucharest: Editura Glob, 1947.
Mittelmann, H. *Illustrierter Führer durch die Bukowina*. Edited by H. Kusdat. 1907–8; reprint: Vienna: Mandelbaum Verlag, 2001.
Mitscherlich, A., and M. Mitscherlich. *Die Unfähigkeit zu trauern*. Munich: Piper, 1968.
Moeller, R.G. *War Stories: The Search for a Usable Past in the Federal Republic of Germany*. Berkeley: University of California Press, 2001.
———. 'Germans as Victims? Thoughts on a Post-Cold War History of World War II's Legacies'. *History and Memory* 17(1–2) (2005), 145–94.
Motzan, P., and S. Sienerth (eds). *Wahrnehmung der deutsch(sprachig)en Literatur aus Ostmittel- und Südosteuropa – ein Paradigmenwechsel? Neue Lesearten und Fallbeispiele*. Munich: IKGS Verlag, 2009.
Mühle, E. (ed.). *Germany and the European East in the Twentieth Century*. Oxford: Berg, 2003.

Münz R., and R. Ohliger (eds). *Diasporas and Ethnic Migrants: Germany, Israel and Post-Soviet Successor States in Comparative Perspective*. London: Frank Cass, 2003.

Nachum, I. 'Reconstructing Life after the Holocaust: The Lastenausgleichsgesetz and the Jewish Struggle for Compensation'. *Leo Baeck Institute Year Book* 58 (2013), 53–67.

Nachum, I., and S. Schaefer. 'The Semantics of Political Integration: Public Debates about the Term "Expellees" in Post-War Western Germany'. *Contemporary European History* 27(1) (2018), 42–58.

Nargang, I. *Die Deutschen aus der Bukowina: Herkunft, Umsiedlung/Flucht, Neubeginn*. Vienna: Österreichische Landsmannschaft, 2013.

Narvselius, E. 'Tragic Past, Agreeable Heritage: Post-Soviet Intellectual Discussions on the Polish Legacy in Western Ukraine'. *The Carl Beck Papers in Russian and East European Studies* 2403 (2015).

Niven, B. *Facing the Nazi Past: United Germany and the Legacy of the Third Reich*. London: Routledge, 2002.

———. (ed.). *Germans as Victims: Remembering the Past in Contemporary Germany*. Basingstoke: Palgrave Macmillan, 2006.

———. 'On the Use of "Collective Memory"'. *German History* 26(3) (2008), 427–36.

Niven, B., and C. Paver (eds). *Memorialization in Germany since 1945*. Basingstoke: Palgrave Macmillan, 2010.

Nora, P. (ed.). *Les lieux de Mémoire*. 7 vols. Paris: Gallimard, 1984–92.

Novick, P. *The Holocaust and Collective Memory: The American Experience*. London: Bloomsbury, 2001.

Nowak, S. *Sicherheitsrisiko NS-Belastung: Personalüberprüfungen im Bundesnachrichtendienst in den 1960er Jahren*. Berlin: C.H. Links, 2016.

O'Donnell, K., R. Bridenthal and N. Reagin (eds). *The Heimat Abroad: The Boundaries of Germanness*. Ann Arbor: University of Michigan Press, 2005.

Ofer, D. 'Holocaust Survivors as Immigrants: The Case of Israel and the Cyprus Detainees'. *Modern Judaism* 16(1) (1998), 1–23.

Ofer, D., F.S. Ouzan, and J. Tydor Baumel-Schwartz (eds). *Holocaust Survivors: Resettlement, Memories, Identities*. New York: Berghahn Books, 2012.

Ohliger, R. 'Menschenrechtsverletzung oder Migration? Zum historischen Ort von Flucht und Vertreibung der Deutschen nach 1945'. *Zeithistorische Forschungen/Studies in Contemporary History* 2(3) (2005), 429–38.

Ohliger, R., K. Schönwälder and T. Triadafilopoulos (eds). *European Encounters: Migrants, Migration and European Societies since 1945*. London: Ashgate, 2003.

Olaru, M. 'Documente Rădăuțene IV'. *Analele Bucovinei* 1 (2011), 279–303.

Olick, J.K. *The Sins of the Fathers: Germany, Memory, Method*. Chicago: University of Chicago Press, 2016.

Ornstein, F. *Suferințele Deportaților în Transnistria: Gândiți-vă la tot ce s-a petrecut în Transnistria (1941–1944)*. Bucharest: Editura Asociației, 1945.

Panagiotidis, J. 'Laws of Return? Co-ethnic Immigration to West Germany and Israel (1948–1992)'. D.Phil. thesis. European University Institute, 2012.

———. '"The Oberkreisdirektor Decides Who is a German": Jewish Immigration, German Bureaucracy, and the Negotiation of National Belongings, 1953–1990'. *Geschichte und Gesellschaft* 38(3) (2012), 503–33.

———. 'A Policy for the Future: German-Jewish Remigrants, Their Children, and the Politics of Israeli Nation-Building'. *Leo Baeck Institute Year Book* 60 (2015), 191–206.

Patt, A. *Finding Home and Homeland: Jewish Youth and Homeland in the Aftermath of the Holocaust*. Detroit: Wayne State University Press, 2009.

Pinto, D. *Israel Has Moved*. Cambridge, MA: Harvard University Press, 2013.
Pollack, M. *Nach Galizien: Von Chassiden, Huzulen, Polen und Ruthenen: Eine imaginäre Reise durch die verschwundene Welt Ostgaliziens und der Bukowina*. Vienna: C. Brandstätter, 1984.
Popovici, V., W. Dahmen, and J. Kramer (eds). *Gelebte Multikulturalität: Czernowitz und die Bukowina*. Frankfurt am Main: P. Lang, 2010.
Porat, D. *Israeli Society, the Holocaust and its Survivors*. London: Vallentine Mitchell, 2008.
Prelitsch, H. (ed.). *10 Jahre Landsmannschaft der Buchenlanddeutschen 1949–1959: Gründung, Werdegang und Jubiläum*. Munich: Landsmannschaft der Buchenlanddeutschen, 1959.
———. *Student in Czernowitz: die Korporationen an der Czernowitzer Universität*. Munich: Landsmannschaft der Buchenlanddeutschen, 1961.
Prokopowitsch, E. *Das Ende der österreichischen Herrschaft in der Bukowina*. Munich: Oldenbourg, 1959.
———. *Die Entwicklung des Pressewesens in der Bukowina*. Vienna: n.p., 1962.
Pross, C. *Wiedergutmachung: Der Kleinkrieg gegen die Opfer*. Frankfurt am Main: Athenäum, 1988.
———. *Paying for the Past: The Struggle over Reparations for Victims of Nazi Terror*. Translated from German by B. Cooper. Baltimore: Johns Hopkins University Press, 1998.
Ranner, G. et al. (eds). *'... und das Herz wird mir schwer dabei': Czernowitzer Juden erinnern sich*, 3rd edn. Berlin: Kulturforum östliches Europa, 2009.
Rechter, D. 'Nationalism at the Edge: The Jüdische Volksrat of Habsburg Bukovina'. *ASCHKENAS – Zeitschrift für Geschichte und Kultur der Juden* 18/19(1) (2008–9), 59–89.
———. *Becoming Habsburg: The Jews of Austrian Bukovina, 1774–1918*. Portland: Littman Library of Jewish Civilization, 2013.
———. 'Habsburg Bukowina: Juden am Rande des Reiches'. *Grenzen: Jüdischer Almanach der Leo Baeck Institute* (2015), 84–94.
Reifer, M. *Massa Hamaweth*. Translated from Gerrman by J. Tulkes. Tel Aviv: Am Owed, 1945.
———. *Dr. Mayer Ebner: Ein jüdisches Leben*. Tel Aviv: Edition Olympia, 1948.
———. *Menschen und Ideen*. Tel Aviv: Edition Olympia, 1952.
Reinisch, J., and E. White (eds*). The Disentanglement of Populations: Migration, Expulsion and Displacement in Postwar Europe, 1944–1949*. Basingstoke: Palgrave Macmillan, 2011.
Retterath, H.W. (ed.). *Germanisierung im besetzten Ostoberschlesien während des Zweiten Weltkriegs*. Münster: Waxmann, 2018.
Richardson, T. *Kaleidoscopic Odessa: History and Place in Contemporary Ukraine*. Toronto: University of Toronto Press, 2008.
Ricœur, P. *Memory, History, Forgetting*. Translated from French by K. Blamey and D. Pellauer. Chicago: University of Chicago Press, 2004.
Rill, B. (ed.). *Deutschland und seine Partner im Osten: Gemeinsame Kulturarbeit im erweiterten Europa*. Munich: Hans Seidel Stiftung, 2004.
Röger, M. *Flucht, Vertreibung und Umsiedlung: Mediale Erinnerungen und Debatten in Deutschland und Polen seit 1989*. Marburg: Verlag Herder-Institut, 2011.
———. and R. Leiserowitz (eds). *Women and Men at War: A Gender Perspective on World War II and its Aftermath in Central and Eastern Europe*. Osnabrück: Fibre, 2012.
Rosenkranz, M. *Im Untergang: Ein Jahrhundertbuch*. Munich: Südostdeutsches Kulturwerk, 1986.
———. *Briefe an Alfred Margul-Sperber 1930–1963*. Edited by G. Guţu. Aachen: Rimbaud Verlag, 2015.
———. *Briefe an Kaspar Niklaus Wildberger 1978–1933*. Aachen: Rimbaud Verlag, 2016.

Rosensaft, M.Z. (ed.). *Life Reborn: Jewish Displaced Persons, 1945–1951*. Washington DC: U.S. Holocaust Memorial Museum, 2001.
Rosenthal, G., and A. Bogner (eds). *Ethnicity, Belonging and Biography: Ethnographical and Biographical Perspectives*. Berlin: Lit Verlag, 2009.
Rothberg, M. *Multidirectional Memory: Remembering the Holocaust in the Age of Decolonization*. Stanford: Stanford University Press, 2009.
Rotman, L. *History of the Jews in Romania*, vol. 5: *The Communist Era until 1965*. Tel Aviv: Tel Aviv University Press, 2004.
Rotman, L., and R. Vago (eds). *The History of the Jews in Romania*, vol. 3: *Between the Two World Wars*. Tel Aviv: Tel Aviv University Press, 2005.
Röskau-Rydel, I. (ed.). *Deutsche Geschichte im Osten Europas: Galizien, Bukowina, Moldau*. Berlin: Siedler, 2002.
Rozenblit, M. *Reconstructing a National Identity: The Jews of Habsburg Austria during World War I*. Oxford: Oxford University Press, 2001.
———. 'Jews, German Culture, and the Dilemma of National Identity: The Case of Moravia, 1848–1938'. *Jewish Social Studies: History, Culture, Society* 20(1) (2013), 77–120.
Rubinstein, M. *Der Jüdische Vatikan in Sadagora 1850—1950*, 2 vols. Tel Aviv: Olamenu, 1958.
Rückleben, E. *Heimatland Sprache: Leben und Zeugnisse bukowinische Dichter*. Innsbruck: Traditionsverb. Kath. Czernowitzer Pennäler, 2005.
Rudich, M. *La Brat cu Moartea: Vedenii din Transnistria*. Bucharest: Editura 'Hehaluţ', 1945.
Rudolph, R. *Evangelische Kirche und Vertriebene 1945 bis 1972*. Göttingen: Vandenhoeck & Ruprecht, 1985.
Schacter, D. (ed.). *Memory Distortion: How Minds, Brains, and Societies Reconstruct the Past*. Cambridge, MA: Harvard University Press, 1995.
Scharr, K. *'Die Landschaft Bukowina': Das Werden einer Region an der Peripherie 1774–1918*. Vienna: Böhlau Verlag, 2008.
Schippmann, S. '"Höchst unerwünschte Ausländer": The Fate of Ethnic German Expellees in Post-war Austria'. *Sprawy Narodowosciowe* 41 (2012), 7–21.
Schlögel, K. *Die Mitte liegt Ostwärts: die Deutschen, der verlorene Osten und Mitteleuropa*. Berlin: Siedler, 1986.
———. *In Räume lesen wir die Zeit: über Zivilisationsgeschichte und Geopolitik*. Munich: Hanser, 2003.
Schmidt, U. *Die Deutschen aus Bessarabien: Eine Minderheit aus Südosteuropa (1814 bis heute)*. Cologne: Böhlau, 2003.
Schmitt, C. (ed.). *Volkskundliche Großprojekte: Ihre Geschichte und Zukunft*. Münster: Waxmann, 2005.
Schmitt, O.J., and M. Metzeltin (eds). *Das Südosteuropa der Regionen*. Vienna: Verlag der österreichischen Akademie der Wissenschaften, 2015.
Schoeps, J., and Olaf G. (eds). *A Road to Nowhere? Jewish Experiences in a Unifying Europe*. Leiden: Brill, 2011.
Scholz, S. '"Opferdunst vernebelt die Verhältnisse" – religiöse Motive in bundesdeutschen Gedenkorten der Flucht und Vertreibung'. *Schweizerische Zeitschrift für Religions- und Kulturgeschichte* 102 (2008), 287–313.
Scholz, S., M. Röger and B. Niven (eds). *Die Erinnerung an Flucht und Vertreibung: Ein Handbuch der Medien und Praktiken*. Paderborn: Ferdinand Schöningh, 2015.
Schulze, R. 'Forgotten Victims or Beneficiaries of Plunder and Genocide? The Mass Resettlement of Ethnic Germans "heim ins Reich"'. *Annali dell'Instituto storico-germano in Trento* XXVII (2001), 533–64.

Schulze, R., with R. Rohde and R. Voß (eds). *Zwischen Heimat und Zuhause: Deutsche Flüchtlinge und Vertriebene in (West)Deutschland 1945–2000*. Osnabrück: Secolo Verlag, 2001.
Schwarz, M. *Die Umsiedlung und die Sowjets: Erlebnisse einer deutschen Frau*. Berlin-Leipzig: Nibelungen Verlag, 1942.
Schwarz-Gardos, A. (ed.). *Heimat ist anderswo: Deutsche Schriftsteller in Israel; Erzählungen und Gedichte*. Freiburg im Breisgau: Herder, 1983.
Schwartz, M. *Vertriebene und 'Umsiedlerpolitik' Integrationskonflikte in den deutschen Nachkriegs-Gesellschaften und die Assimilationsstrategien in der SBZ/DDR 1945–1961*. Munich: Oldenbourg, 2004.
———. 'Vertriebene im doppelten Deutschland. Integrations- und Erinnerungspolitik in der DDR und in der Bundesrepublik'. *Vierteljahrshefte für Zeitgeschichte* 56(1) (2008), 101–51.
Schwob, A. (ed.). *Die deutsche Literaturgeschichte Ostmittel- und Südosteuropas von der Mitte des 19. Jahrhunderts bis heute*. Munich: Verl. Südostdt. Kulturwerk, 1992.
Scribiac, S. 'Büsnau: Das Siedlungswerk der Buchenländer im Schwabenland'. *Südostdeutsche Vierteljahresblätter* 10 (1961), 17–21.
Segev, T. *The Seventh Million: The Israelis and the Holocaust*. Translated from Hebrew by H. Watzman. New York: Hill & Wang, 1993.
———. *1949: The First Israelis*. New York: Holt Paperbacks, 1998.
Siemens, D. 'Juristische Zeitgeschichte *avant la lettre*: Die Frankfurter Dissertation von Max Münz zur "Verantwortlichkeit für die Judenverfolgungen im Ausland" (1958)'. *Zeithistorische Forschungen/Studies in Contemporary History* 15(1) (2018), 184–92.
Shanes, J. *Diaspora Nationalism and Jewish Identity in Habsburg Galicia*. Cambridge: Cambridge University Press, 2012.
Shchyhlevska, N. *Verschränkungen: Leben und Werk von Autoren aus der Bukowina anhand von Briefen und Nachlässe*. Aachen: Rimbaud Verlag, 2011.
Slawinski, I., and J.P. Strelka (eds). *Die Bukowina, Vergangenheit und Gegenwart*. Bern: Lang, 1995.
Snyder, T. *Bloodlands: Europe between Hitler and Stalin*. New York: Basic Books, 2010.
Solomon, P. *Paul Celan: The Romanian Dimension*. Translated from Romanian by E. Tegla. Syracuse, NY: Syracuse University Press, 2019.
Solonari, V. *Purifying the Nation: Population Exchange and Ethnic Cleansing in Nazi-Allied Romania*. Baltimore: Johns Hopkins University Press, 2010.
Spielhaupter, W. *51 Jahre Heimatauskunftstelle Rumänien: 1953–2004*. Munich: Selbstverlag, 2005.
Spinei, C. *Über die Zentralität des Peripheren: Auf den Spuren von Gregor von Rezzori*. Berlin: Frank und Timme, 2011.
Stambrook, F. 'The Golden Age of the Jews of Bukovina, 1880–1914'. *Department of History University of Manitoba Working Paper* 3(2) (October 2003).
Stănescu, H. 'Der Dichter des "Nobiskruges", Immanuel Weissglas'. *German Life and Letters* 39(1) (1985), 1–20.
Steinhart, E. *The Holocaust and the Germanization of Ukraine*. New York: Cambridge University Press, 2015.
Steinweis, A., and D. Rogers (eds). *The Impact of Nazism: New Perspectives on the Third Reich and its Legacy*. Lincoln, NE: University of Nebraska Press, 2003.
Stenberg, P. *Journey to Oblivion: The End of the East European Yiddish and German Worlds in the Mirror of Literature*. Toronto: University of Toronto Press, 1991.
Stenzel, J. *Leo Sonntag: Ein jüdisches Emigrantenschicksal*. Essen: Verl. Die Blaue Eule, 1994.
Stern, F. *The Whitewashing of the Yellow Badge: Antisemitism and Philosemitism in Postwar Germany*. Oxford: Pergamon Press, 1992.

Sternberg, H. *Zur Geschichte der Juden in Czernowitz.* Tel Aviv: Olamenu, 1962.
Sternhell, Z. *The Founding Myths of Israel: Nationalism, Socialism, and the Making of the Jewish State.* Princeton: Princeton University Press, 1998.
Stickler, M. *'Ostdeutsch heißt Gesamtdeutsch': Organisation, Selbstverständnis und heimatpolitische Zielsetzung der deutschen Vertriebenenverbände 1949–1972.* Düsseldorf: Droste, 2004.
Stone, D. *Goodbye to All That?: The Story of Europe since 1945.* Oxford: Oxford University Press, 2014.
Süssner, H. 'Still Yearning for the Lost Heimat? Ethnic German Expellees and the Politics of Belonging'. *German Politics and Society* 22(2) (2004), 1–26.
Szejnmann, C.W., and M. Umbach (eds). *Heimat, Region, and Empire Spatial Identities under National Socialism.* Basingstoke: Palgrave Macmillan, 2012.
Taylor, C. et al. (eds). *Multiculturalism: Examining the Politics of Recognition.* Princeton: Princeton University Press, 1994.
Teich, M. *Für eine Revision der Luxembourger Verträge und der Wiedergutmachungs-Gesetze.* Tel Aviv: Selbstverlag, 1961.
Ther, P., and A. Siljak (eds). *Redrawing Nations: Ethnic Cleansing in East Central Europe 1944–1948.* Lanham, MD: Rowman & Littlefield, 2001.
Thum, G. (ed.). *Traumland Osten: Deutsche Bilder vom östlichen Europa im 20. Jahrhundert.* Göttingen: Vandenhoeck & Ruprecht, 2006.
Tiefenthaler, P. (ed.). *Festschrift zum 20-jährigen Jubiläums-Bundestreffen Pfingsten 1969; Zwanzig Jahre Landsmannschaft der Buchenlanddeutschen e. V. 1949–1969.* Planegg: Landsmannschaft der Buchenlanddeutschen 1969.
———. (ed.). *Festschrift zum 30-jährigen Jubiläums-Bundestreffen Pfingsten 1979: Dreißig Jahre Landsmannschaft der Buchenlanddeutschen e. V. 1949–1979.* Planegg: Landsmannschaft der Buchenlanddt., 1979.
Tuan, Y.F. *Space and Place: The Perspective of Experience.* Minneapolis: University of Minnesota Press, 2001.
Turczynski, E. *Geschichte der Bukowina in der Neuzeit: zur sozial- und Kulturgeschichte einer mitteleuropäisch geprägten Landschaft.* Wiesbaden: Harrassowitz, 1993.
Vago, R. 'The Unexpected Cosmopolitans: Romania's Jewry Facing the Communist System'. *European Review of History: Revue européenne d'histoire* 17(3) (2010), 491–504.
Van Drunen, J. *'A Sanguine Bunch': Regional Identification in Habsburg Bukovina, 1774–1919.* Amsterdam: Uitgeverij Pegasus, 2015.
Varga, B. 'Rise and Fall of an Austrian Identity in the Provincial Historiography of Bukovina'. *Austrian History Yearbook* 46 (2015), 183–202.
Verband deutschsprachige Schriftsteller in Israel (ed.). *Nicht das letzte Wort: Eine Dokumentation: 30 Jahre – 1975 bis 2005.* Berlin: Boesche, 2005.
Von Hirschhausen, B. et al. (eds). *Phantomgrenzen: Räume und Akteure in der Zeit neu denken.* Göttingen: Wallstein Verlag, 2015.
Von Moltke, J. *No Place Like Home: Locations of Heimat in German Cinema.* Berkeley: University of California Press, 2005.
Von Rezzori, G. *Maghrebinische Geschichten.* Hamburg: Rowohlt, 1953
———. *Oedipus siegt bei Stalingrad: Ein Kolportageroman.* Hamburg: Rowohlt, 1954.
———. *Ein Hermelin in Tschernopol: Ein maghrebinischer Roman.* Hamburg: Rowohlt, 1958.
———. *Tales of Maghrebinia.* Translated from German by C. Hutter. Harcourt, Brace and World, 1962.
———. *Der Tod meines Bruders Abel.* Munich: Goldmann Verlag, 1976.
———. *Memoiren eines Antisemiten: Roman.* Munich: Steinhausen, 1979.

———. *Blumen im Schnee: Portraitstudien zu einer Biographie, die ich nie schreiben werde*. Munich: Bertelsmann, 1989.

———. *The Snows of Yesteryear: Portraits for an Autobiography*. Translated from German by H.F. Broch de Rothermann. London: Penguin, 2010 [1989].

———. *Greisengemurmel: Ein Rechenschaftsbericht*. Munich: Bertelsmann, 1994.

———. *Mir auf der Spur*. Munich: Bertelsmann, 1997.

———. *Memoirs of an Anti-Semite: A Novel in Five Stories*. Translated from German by J. Neugroschel. New York: New York Review of Books Classics, 2011 [1969].

Vosskamp, S. *Katholische Kirche und Vertriebene in Westdeutschland: Integration, Identität und ostpolitischer Diskurs 1945–1972*. Stuttgart: W. Kohlhammer, 2007.

Voswinckel, K. *Paul Celan. Verweigerte Poetisierung der Welt: Versuch einer Deutung*. Heidelberg: Lothar Stiehm Verlag, 1974.

Wagner, R. 'Probleme zur Umsiedlung der Deutschen aus der Bukowina'. *Südost-Heimatblätter* 4 (1955), 168–74.

———. (ed.). *Alma Mater Francisco Josephina: Die deutschsprachige Nationalitäten Universität in Czernowitz: Festschrift zum 100. Jahrestag ihrer Eröffnung 1875*. Munich: Menschendörfer, 1979.

———. *Deutsches Kulturleben in der Bukowina*. Vienna: Schutzverein Österr. Landsmannschaft, 1981.

———. *Der Parlamentarismus und nationale Ausgleich in der ehemals österreichischen Bukowina*. Munich: Verlag 'Der Südostdeutsche', 1984.

———. *Das multinationale österreichische Schulwesen in der Bukowina*. Munich: Verlag 'Der Südostdeutsche', 1985–86.

———, A. Armbruster and P. Tiefenthaler (eds). *Vom Moldauwappen zum Doppeladdler: Ausgewählte Beiträge zur Geschichte der Bukowina. Festgabe zu seinem 80. Geburtstag*. Munich: Hofmann Verlag, 1991.

Wahl, D. *Lyris: deutschsprachige Dichterinnen und Dichter in Israel*. Frankfurt am Main: Beerenverlag, 2004.

Waldeck, R.G. *Athene Palace, Bucharest: Hitler's 'New Order' Comes to Romania*. London: Constable, 1943.

Wanner, C. 'The Return of Czernowitz: Urban Affect, Nostalgia, and the Politics of Place-Making in a European Borderland City'. *City and Society* 28(2) (2016), 198–221.

Warf, B., and S. Arias (eds). *The Spatial Turn: Interdisciplinary Perspectives*. London: Routledge, 2009.

Weber, H. *Die Bukowina im zweiten Weltkrieg: völkerrechtliche Aspekte der Lage der Bukowina im Spannungsfeld zwischen Rumänien, der Sowjetunion und Deutschland*. Hamburg: Metzner, 1972.

Weber, P. 'Regime Changes, Public Memory and the Pursuit of Justice: The Case of German-Speaking Jews in Bukovina 1920–1960'. D.Phil. thesis. University of Sussex, 2006.

Weczerka, H. 'Die Deutschen im Buchenland'. *Schriftenreihe der Göttinger Arbeitskreis* 51 (1955), 1–41.

———. 'Ethnien und öffentliches Leben in der Bukowina 1848–1914'. *Südostdeutsches Archiv* 42 & 43 (1999–2000), 23–40.

Weichers, B. *Der deutsche Osten in der Schule: Institutionalisierung und Konzeption der Ostkunde in der Bundesrepublik in den 1950er und 1960er Jahren*. Frankfurt: Peter Lang, 2013.

Welzer, H. (ed.). *Das soziale Gedächtnis: Geschichte, Erinnerung, Tradierung*. Hamburg: Hamburger Edition, 2001.

Wer sind die Buchenlanddeutschen? Augsburg: Landsmannschaft der Buchenlanddeutschen, 1996.

Werner, K. *Erfahrungsgeschichte und Zeugenschaft: Studien zur deutsch-jüdischen Literatur aus Galizien und der Bukowina*. Munich: IKGS Verlag, 2003.

Werner, M., and B. Zimmermann. 'Beyond Comparison: Histoire Croisée and the Challenge of Reflexivity'. *History and Theory* 45(1) (2006), 30–50.

Wichner, E. and H. Wiesner (eds). *In der Sprache der Mörder. Ausstellungsbuch: eine Literatur aus Czernowitz, Bukowina*. Berlin: Literaturhaus, 1993.

Wickham, C. *Constructing Heimat in Postwar Germany: Longing and Belonging*. Lewiston: Mellen, 1999.

Wieviorka, A., and I. Niborski. *Les Livres du Souvenir: Mémoriaux Juifs de Pologne*. Paris: Gallimard, 1983.

———. *The Era of the Witness*. Translated from French by J. Stark. Ithaca, NY: Cornell University Press, 2006.

Winkler, M., H. Bergel and R. Windish-Middendorf. *'Wir setzen das Gespräch fort…': Briefwechsel eines Juden aus der Bukowina mit einem Deutschen von Siebenbürgen*. Berlin: Frank und Timme, 2012.

Winkler, M. *Jüdische Identitäten im kommunikativen Raum: Presse, Sprache und Theater in Czernowitz bis 1923*. Bremen: Editions Lumières, 2007.

———. (ed.). *Presselandschaft in der Bukowina und der Nachbarregionen*. Munich: IKGS Verlag, 2011.

Wistrich, R., and D. Ohana (eds). *The Shaping of Israeli Identity, Myth, Memory and Trauma*. London: Frank Cass, 1995.

Wiszbiowski, F. *Radautz: die deutscheste Stadt des Buchenlandes*. Waiblingen: F. Wiszbiowski, 1966.

Wittlinger, R. *German National Identity in the Twenty-First Century: A Different Republic after All?* Basingstoke: Palgrave Macmillan, 2010.

Wolff, L. *The Idea of Galicia: History and Fantasy in Habsburg Political Culture*. Stanford: Stanford University Press, 2010.

Wolff, S., and D. Rock (eds). *Coming Home to Germany? The Integration of Ethnic Germans from Central and Eastern Europe in the Federal Republic*. New York: Berghahn Books, 2002.

Wollmann-Fiedler, C., and H. Brenner. *'Czernowitz ist meine Heimat': Gespräche mit der Zeitzeugin Hedwig Brenner*. Brugg: Munda, 2009.

Yablonka, H. *Holocaust Survivors: Israel after the War*. New York: New York University Press, 1999.

Young, J.E. *The Texture of Memory: Holocaust Memorials and Meanings*. New Haven: Yale University Press, 1993.

Yuval-Davis, N. 'Belonging and the Politics of Belonging'. *Patterns of Prejudice* 40(3) (2006), 197–214.

———. *The Politics of Belonging: Intersectional Contestations*. London: Sage, 2011.

Zahra, T. '"Prisoners of the Post-war": Expellees, Displaced Persons, and Jews in Austria after World War II'. *Austrian History Yearbook* 41 (2010), 191–215.

Zehfuss, M. *Wounds of Memory: The Politics of War in Germany*. Cambridge: Cambridge University Press, 2007.

Zertal, I. *From Catastrophe to Power: Holocaust Survivors and the Emergence of Israel*. Berkeley: University of California Press, 1998.

———. *Israel's Holocaust and the Politics of Nationhood*. Cambridge: Cambridge University Press, 2005.

INDEX

aliyah, 110, 119–23, 142
   and '*Great Aliyah*', 112, 132
   and *Aliyah Bet*, 110
Allies (the Allies, western Allies), 40, 48–49, 62, 64, 70, 75, 175
Alsace-Lorraine (Alsace and/or Lorraine), 45, 64–65, 97n14
Alt-Fratautz (Frătăuții Vechi), 97n14, 160, 162
America, 31, 119, 169, 232, 246n183
   Bukovina Society (of the Americas), 242n124
   North, 65, 121, 226
   South, 65, 121, 128, 217
Ancestral home/homeland (*Urheimat*), 17, 61–62, 65–66, 73–74, 76, 81, 106n172, 109, 131, 142, 251
antisemitism (antisemitic), 36–37, 39–43, 48–49, 92, 117, 129, 169, 172–73, 175, 182, 191, 206, 234, 246n196
Antonescu, Ion, 44, 46, 48, 117, 126, 155, 161
Arminia, 163, 220, 241n113
Appelfeld, Aharon, 138, 233
Armbrüster, Christian, 75, 80, 85
Association of Germans in Greater Romania. *See* Verband der Deutschen Großrumäniens
Augsburg, 19, 202, 230
Auschwitz, 114, 116, 129, 140, 150n175, 211, 251
   trials, 10
Ausländer, Rose, 6, 8, 174, 202, 204, 206–9, 211–14, 225–26, 232, 237nn29–30, 244n160, 255
Auslandsdeutsche, 42, 62, 70

Aussiedler (*Spätaussiedler*), 179, 181, 189, 190, 213, 229, 232
Austria (Austrian), 1–6, 20, 31–37, 39, 45, 55n97, 62, 64–65, 73–75, 78, 89, 91, 93, 96n10, 102n87, 113, 115, 128, 136–37, 155–56, 163, 165–69, 172, 182, 186–87, 203–7, 209, 212, 214, 217–21, 224–25, 230–31, 236n14, 238n42, 248, 250, 255, 260n5
   and Hungary (Austro-Hungarian), 32, 74, 87, 91, 93, 136, 167, 178, 248
Axis (Powers), 44, 46, 112
Axmann, Elisabeth, 210

Baden-Württemberg, 66, 68, 82, 242n128
Ball-Kaduri, Kurt Jakob, 139, 150n170
Baltic Germans, 66
Bavaria, 65, 67, 74, 91, 99n35, 102n93, 202, 220
Beck, Erich, 86, 105n142, 167–72, 203, 219
Beck, Oskar, 83, 85
Beckermann, Ruth, 241n101
Ben-Gurion, David, 132, 141
Bensch, Kurt, 67, 76, 97n15
Bergel, Hans, 210, 216, 227–28
Berlin, 11, 37, 65, 98n24, 102n93, 106n176, 166, 190
Bershad, 48, 113
Bessarabia (Bessarabian), 39, 43, 47–48, 54n90, 66, 115, 117
Birkner, Andreas, 210
Bitterfeld, 65, 260n1
Blaß, Peter, 102n95, 163, 199n155
Blass, Ottilie, 242n128
Blum, Klara, 215

Bohemia (Bohemian, *Böhmer*) 34, 52n49, 161
Bornemann, Irma, 219, 223, 227–28, 242n128
Brandt, Willy, 175, 221
Braun, Helmut, 246n196
Brucker, Johanna, 174, 219
Bucharest, 19, 46, 114–16, 119–22, 127, 145n38, 145n44, 147n71, 208–10, 213, 216, 228, 237n29
Buchenland (newspaper), 73, 75–77, 87, 91, 93
Buchenländer, 72, 155–56
Buchenlandheim, 220, 223
Buchenlandsiedlung. *See* Heimstättensiedlung
Buchenwald, 211
Bug (River), 48
'Bukovina myth', 5–8, 13, 32, 234
Bukowina-Institut (Bukovina-Institute), 19, 202, 230
Bukowinaer Provinzbote, 206
Bukowiner, 21n6, 31, 91, 155–56, 169, 217
Bukowinismus (Bukovinism), 49n1, 91
Bund der Heimatvertriebenen und Entrechteten (BHE), 78, 91
Bund der Vertriebenen (BdV), 173, 221, 227, 229
Bundesentschädigungsgesetz (BEG), 157, 177–81, 183, 185–86
Bundestreffen, 87, 187
Bundesvertriebenengesetz (BVFG) 86, 179, 184–85
Bundism, 37, 184, 206
Burdujeni, 47, 206
Büsnau, 68–69, 71–72, 82, 87, 93, 99n42, 100n49, 100n56, 167, 220

Caracas, 142, 159
Carinthia, 2, 224
Carp, Matatias, 118, 138, 150n168
Catholic, 33, 37, 52n49, 67, 76
  Caritas, 67
Celan, Paul, 6, 8, 156, 173–74, 202, 204, 207–9, 211–16, 225, 229, 232–35, 237nn29–30, 239nn75–76, 244n160, 246n183, 246nn190–91, 247n208, 255

'Central Europe' (Central European, *Mitteleuropa, Mitteleuropäer*) 5–7, 33, 62, 90, 111, 123, 129, 135, 204, 226, 257
Chalfen, Israel, 215
Chargaff, Erwin, 214, 218
Chernivtsi (Czernowitz, Cernăuți, Chernovtsy), 2, 5–6, 12, 20, 21n10, 31, 34, 37, 38, 40, 43, 45, 47–48, 51n25, 54n74, 55n96, 57n121, 84–85, 88–89, 97n24, 112–15, 120, 122, 127–29, 134, 136–37, 145n44, 159, 162–63, 165, 168–70, 173–74, 183, 189, 192n5, 197n112, 202, 207–8, 213, 215, 218–19, 222–24, 226, 229, 232, 235, 236n14, 248
  Language Conference, 37
  university, 34–35, 38, 41, 87, 168, 173, 202, 219, 230
Christian Social Party, 42, 172
Cisleithania, 32, 38
Cisek, Oskar Walter, 210
Cluj, 114
Colin, Amy, 230, 233, 246n183
Cuza, Alexandru C., 41
  and Goga, 43
Cyprus, 121, 127, 147n80
Czechoslovakia, 64, 66, 179, 229
Czernowitzer Deutsche Tagespost, 42, 172
Czernowitzer Morgenblatt, 126, 206

Daghani, Arnold, 138, 150n168
Darmstadt, 19, 61, 68–73, 87, 93, 95n1, 96n3, 98n30, 99n42, 107n182, 190, 220, 223
Das jüdische Echo, 36
denazification, 68, 173
Der Südostdeutsche, 7, 19, 86, 105n144, 159, 164–65, 171–75, 200n160, 221
deutscher Sprach- und Kulturkreis (DSK), 179–80, 184–88
Die Stimme, 7, 19, 126–28, 135–40, 158–59, 165, 170–71, 174–75, 183, 188–89, 211, 215–18, 224, 240n90
Dniester (River), 47
Displaced Persons (DPs), 11, 17, 25n37, 62, 66, 77, 119, 126
  camp, 124
Dorna Vatra (Vatra Dornei), 34, 47

Dressler, Johann Christian, 73, 105n141, 162–63
Dressler, Karl, 83
Drozdowski, Georg, 1–4, 21n4, 155–56, 165, 174, 176, 197nn110–11, 212, 214, 219–20, 224–25, 227, 237n30, 243n143
Düsseldorf, 217–18, 223, 229, 232

East Germany (GDR), 3, 62, 65, 74–75, 96n10, 101n66, 192n13, 221, 238n42, 238n51
Ebner, Mayer, 1, 36, 42, 51n34, 109, 131, 135–36, 141
Eichmann trial, 10, 175
Einsatzgruppe D, 57n122, 174
Einbürgerung, 66
Einheimische, 71, 73, 89
Engster, Adolf, 68, 70
Eretz Israel, 17, 120, 122, 126, 128–29, 135
Erneuerungsbewegung (Movement of National Renewal), 42, 54n84, 173
Evian, I.D., 182
Exodus, 109, 128, 130
'expellees' (*Heimatvertriebene, Vertriebene*), 4, 9–12, 17, 23nn25–26, 23n28, 24n34, 25n41, 27n60, 62–64, 70, 72–75 77–78, 80, 83–85, 90, 95, 107n192, 165, 175–83, 185–86, 188, 197n119, 221, 225, 228–29, 245n169, 252, 254, 256–57

Fălticeni, 121
Faerber, Meir Marcell, 216
Filderman, Wilhelm, 42
First World War, 22n14, 34, 37, 39–40, 51n25, 140, 170, 205, 213, 250
'flight and expulsion' (*Flucht und Vertreibung*, 'the expulsions'), 9–10, 24n28, 58n130, 62, 77–78, 82, 92, 96n7, 107n192, 179, 228–29, 245n173
Flondor, Iancu, 36
Franz Joseph (Emperor), 35
Franzos, Karl Emil, 6, 91, 173, 195n71, 202, 214, 225, 228

Galicia (Galician), 6, 21n10, 32, 34, 38, 97n24, 138, 180, 225–26

German-Jewish symbiosis (Jewish-German symbiosis), 6, 19, 36, 188, 204–5, 214–15, 218, 224, 231, 233–34, 254, 256
and negative, 258
Germanization, 32, 35, 45, 65, 84, 168
Germanness, 4, 10–11, 16, 18, 36, 46, 61, 63–64, 68, 72–74, 81, 85, 87–88, 95, 102n96, 135, 156–57, 163, 166, 179–82, 184–85, 187–88, 190–91, 212, 221, 224, 228, 231, 236n8, 253, 255
Gold, Hugo, 140–42, 160–61, 166, 187, 150n180, 193n24
Goldberg, David, 206
Gong, Alfred (Alfred Liquornik), 155–56, 174, 176, 197n111, 208, 214, 232, 237n29
Gross, Konrad, 83
Gura-Humorului (Gura Humora), 47, 85, 97n24

Habsburg (Empire), 1, 4–7, 16, 20, 22n14, 31–36, 38–39, 50n4, 50n6, 87, 105n142, 136, 161, 164, 167, 174, 190, 203, 205, 219, 224, 231, 233, 236n10, 253, 255–56, 259
Haifa, 121, 137, 165
Hasidism (Hasidic, Hasidim), 37, 52n45, 169, 225, 235
Hasmonaea, 36, 136, 160
Hebronia, 160, 183
Heimat, 1, 4, 15–16, 19, 27n60, 44, 71–73, 75–77, 80–81, 83–84, 86–87, 89–90, 93, 95, 107n185, 129, 137, 156, 158–60, 162–64, 167, 169–70, 172, 174–75, 181, 188, 192n5, 192n13, 203–4, 206, 215, 218–19, 221–222, 224, 229, 232, 241nn101, 241n112, 246n190, 248, 253–54
-*politisch*, 86, 91, 242n121
book, 159–60, 162, 172
old and, 1, 72, 84, 87, 89, 158–60, 215, 221, 229
Heimatkartei, 67
Heimatauskunftstelle (HASt), 80, 102n95, 181–82, 185, 189, 199n155
Heimstättensiedlung, 61, 68–69, 72, 99n42, 220

Hermann-Göring-Werke, 46, 65
Hesse (Hessen), 65, 68, 70, 73–74, 96n3, 102n93
Hilfskomitee, 67, 76
Hilsenrath, Edgar, 8, 164, 232
Holocaust, 2–4, 9–15, 17, 24n29, 31, 45–49, 56n109, 112–13, 124, 127–28, 131–32, 134, 138–40, 143, 143n4, 149n143, 150n171, 158, 162, 170, 174–75, 177, 204–5, 210–12, 218, 225–26, 228, 232–33, 250, 251, 253–55, 258–59, 261n13
  memory, 12, 16, 28n63, 21
  miniseries, 244n158, 245n173
  in Romania, 17, 47, 113, 138–40, 211
  survivor(s), 4–6, 9–12, 17, 111, 114, 124, 140, 149n143, 212, 217, 235, 250, 256
homo bucoviniensis, 31, 49n1, 91, 219
Hungary (Hungarian), 33, 39, 44, 52n49, 66, 86, 136, 169, 179, 181, 222
  and German, 72–73, 99n42
  -speaking, 161

Iași, 114
  pogrom, 46
Iorga, Nicolae, 36
Illischestie (Ilișești), 162
Institut für Zeitgeschichte (IfZ), 184
Iron Curtain, 158, 161, 209, 226, 250, 253, 255
Iron Guard. *See* Legion of the Archangel Michael
Israeli War of Independence, 130, 139
Itzcany (Ițcani), 47

Jaffa (Yafo, Yafa), 135, 141
Jelinek, Jakob, 75
Jerusalem, 5, 10, 19, 136, 215–16
Jewish Agency (Sochnut), 125–26
Jewish Democratic Committee (CDE), 118
Jewish Party of Romania (Partidul National Evreiesc), 42
Joint Distribution Committee (Joint), 116, 118, 146n46
Joseph II (Emperor), 33–34

Kaindl, Raimund Friedrich, 37, 52n42, 87, 89, 202, 207, 220, 236n10

Kaindl-Archiv, 219, 229
Katz, Leo, 196n101
Kimpolung (Câmpulung Moldovenesc), 34, 47
King Carol II, 43–44
Kipper, Heinrich, 73, 89, 174, 207, 212, 220, 225, 227, 230
Kittner, Alfred, 174, 206, 209–14, 227, 231–32, 237n30, 239n62, 255
Klein-Haparash, Jacob, 173, 196n102, 196n103, 213
Klett, Arnulf, 68, 70
Klug, Alfred, 207, 212, 227
Koalitionsverbot, 67
Kopecki, Franz, 55n96
Kotzian, Ortfried, 230, 245n177
Kulturnation, 36
Kundstadt, Lior, 217
Künzig, Johannes, 80–82, 102n97

Lachmund, Otto, 174
Lang, Franz, 88, 105n142, 163–66, 174, 196n99, 207, 212
Last, Siegmund, 173, 196n102
Lastenausgleichsgesetz (Equalisation of Burdens Act, LAG), 77–78, 157, 177–181, 183, 185–187
Law of Return, 132, 149n140
Legion of the Archangel Michael (the Legion, Iron Guard), 42–44, 106–7n176
Linz, 46, 65, 220, 241n113
Łodz (Litzmannstadt), 2
London, 123, 125, 142
Lublin, 116
Ludwar, Hans, 82–83
Lyriskreis, 216, 240n87

Maccabi, 136, 160
Majdanek, 116, 129
Manea, Norman, 233
Manger, Itzik, 211, 214
Margul-Sperber, Alfred, 18, 205–12, 216, 225, 227–29, 236n11, 236n15, 237n29, 238n42, 238n46, 238n51, 255
Mayer, Herbert, 42, 97n14, 219, 220, 241n109

Metzger, Ludwig, 69–71, 73–74, 98n32
Mircu, Marius, 118
Mogilev (Podolsk), 48, 113
Moldavia, 32, 34, 48, 114
Molotov–Ribbentrop Pact (Hitler-Stalin Pact), 43–44
Moravia, 34, 52n40, 216
multiculturalism (multicultural, multiculturality), 7, 12, 49, 195n82, 203–4, 214, 224, 230–31, 234, 248–49, 256
Munich, 75, 97–98n24, 124, 164, 174, 184, 220, 229, 239n75
Müller, Edgar, 67, 76
Müller, Herta, 229, 233

National Christian Defence League (LANC), 41–42
Neubauer, Ernst Rudolf, 206
New York (city), 142, 155, 160, 164, 183, 205, 208–9, 214, 217, 232, 237n29
northern Bukovina, 2, 17, 43–44, 55n99, 85, 114–15, 128, 130, 184
North Rhine-Westphalia (Rhineland-Westphalia), 65, 83, 85, 102n93, 173

olim (*oleh, olej*), 112, 123–26, 137, 149n140
Organization of Christian Germans. *See* Verein christlicher Deutscher
Orthodox
  Christian, 33, 169
  Church, 38
  Greek and, 33, 38, 50n12
  Judaism, 37, 150n180
Ost-Dokumentation (Documentation of the Expulsions), 85, 104n132, 107n192, 245n173
Ostjüdische Zeitung, 51n34, 183, 200n161
Ostpolitik, 83, 91, 221, 242n121

Pagis, Dan, 233
Palestine (Mandatory Palestine), 3, 17, 110–12, 116–17, 119–30, 132, 135, 137, 142, 250
Paris, 45, 97–98n24, 174, 205, 208, 215, 217, 235, 237n29
  and Peace Conference/Treaties, 39, 145n40

Pastior, Oskar Walter, 210
Patenschaft, 74, 100n61, 230
Pauker, Ana, 118
philosemitism (philosemitic), 169, 182, 204, 235n7
Plesch, Erhard, 182–83, 199n155
Poland, 32, 44, 55n97, 58n131, 64, 66, 82, 92, 115, 126, 140, 178, 229
Popovici, Traian, 47
Poppenberger, Fritz, 172, 196n96
Prelitsch, Hans, 67, 87–88, 91, 162, 172, 174, 203
Prokopowitsch, Erich, 172–73, 187, 196n99, 220
Protestant, 33, 37, 52n49, 67, 76
  and Church, 67
Prut (River), 5, 47

Radautz (Rădăuți), 34, 47, 68, 115, 128, 145n44, 160, 162, 167, 169, 172, 223
Raimund-Kaindl-Association (Raimund-Kaindl-Bund), 87, 90, 219
Rat der Südostdeutschen, 105n143
Recht auf die Heimat (right to (the) homeland), 77, 90, 221
Red Cross (International), 67, 115
Reichsgau Wartheland (Warthegau), 45, 70
Reifer, Manfred, 1–4, 21n5, 122–31, 134–36, 138–39, 150n169, 237n29
Rein, Kurt, 86, 105n142, 219, 230
Resettlement ('home to the Reich', *die Umsiedlung heim ins Reich*), 2, 44–46, 49, 55n94, 55n102, 56n107, 61–63, 66–67, 70, 74, 77, 80–85, 87, 90, 92, 97–98n24, 103nn120–21, 162–64, 179, 185, 190, 196n104, 214, 222, 229, 242n126, 243n141
Rhineland Palatinate (Palatinate), 65, 83, 97n14, 102n93
Romanian German, 209–210, 212, 226, 229, 233, 236n14
Romanianization, 46, 57n112
Romanization, 39–41, 168, 183, 205
Rosenkranz, Moses, 206, 208, 213, 232, 237n28, 238n46, 239n70, 239n76
Rosch (Roša), 189
Rubinstein, Mordechai, 160–61, 166
Rudel, Josef N., 216, 240n90
Russ-Schindelar, Rudolf, 82

Sadagora (Sadagura, Sadhora), 52n45, 160, 169, 235
Salzgitter (Salzgitter–Lebenstedt), 46, 65
Şaraga, Fred, 127
Satu Mare (Deutsch-Satulmare), 159, 163
Schellhorn, Fritz, 183, 187, 200n160, 200–1n176
Schlesak, Dieter, 174, 210, 244n161
Schmidt, Josef, 187
Schuster, Paul, 210
Schwaben (Swabia), 34, 52n49, 66, 70, 72, 168, 207, 231
  Banat and, 41, 209, 229, 233
  Danube and (*Donauschwaben*), 72
  district (*Bezirk*), 74, 230, 231, 242n128
Scribiac, Stefan, 72
Sereth (Siret), 34, 47
Shargorod, 48
shtetl, 37, 169, 225–26
Siberia, 2, 43, 90, 96–97n12, 114, 122–24, 127, 140, 148n105
Silbermann, Edith, 209, 229–30, 246n183
Simnacher, Georg, 230
Skrehunetz (Hillebrand), Bruno, 171–74, 196n96, 196n102
Sperber, Manès, 225–26, 243n149
Sochnut. *See* Jewish Agency
Solca, 47
Sonntag, Leo, 232, 237n29, 239n76
southern Bukovina, 44, 47, 55n94, 67, 113–14, 222
Soviet Union, 3, 43–44, 46–47, 58n130, 89–90, 110, 113–14, 117, 127, 142, 170, 178–79, 208, 218, 229, 238n42
Soviet zone, 62, 64, 65, 70
sprachdeutsch, 35
SS, 67–68, 84–85, 92, 97n24, 98n27, 174, 196n100, 196n104, 234
  and Waffen-, 42, 88, 210
Sternberg, Hermann, 159, 166
Storozynetz (Storozhynetsʻ), 205
Stuttgart, 19, 66, 68–71, 77, 107n182, 167, 241n112
Styria, 45
Suceava (Suczawa), 19, 32, 34, 47, 54n82, 121, 138, 146n51, 159, 168, 170, 206
Südostdeutsches Kulturwerk, 105n143, 244n160

Südostecho, 86
Südosteuropa Gesellschaft, 174

Teich, Meier, 54n82, 138, 170–71, 188, 215, 218
Tel Aviv, 1, 109, 112, 125, 137, 139, 150n180, 158, 160–61, 183
Tiefenthaler, Paula, 230, 242n128
Transnistria, 3, 17, 47–48, 57n118, 112–13, 115–17, 122, 126, 129, 138–40, 146n48, 146n51, 161, 164, 211, 243n141
Transylvania (Transylvanian), 32, 34, 39, 42, 44, 53n62, 86, 114–15, 210, 245n177
  Saxons, 41, 174, 182, 207, 209–10, 216, 227, 229, 231, 233
Turczynski, Emanuel, 86, 89, 95n1, 105n142, 195n82, 203, 219, 222

Uhrich, Hans, 67
Ukraine, 7, 25n42, 48, 142, 248
Umsiedlung (*heim ins Reich*). *See* Resettlement ('home to the Reich')
Union of Romanian Jews, 42
United Restitution Organisation (URO), 181
United States, 117, 194n47, 208, 232

Valjavec, Fritz, 105n143, 174, 196n98, 197n112
Vama, 47
Verband der Deutschen Großrumäniens (Association of Germans in Greater Romania), 41
Verein christlicher Deutscher (Association of Christian Germans), *also* Deutscher Kulturverein (German Cultural Association), 36, 88
Vienna, 2, 5, 34, 37, 40, 44, 121, 161, 165, 169, 172–73, 183, 202, 206, 208, 217, 232, 246n196
Vincent, Marianne, 174, 227
volksdeutsch (*Volksdeutscher*), 2, 35, 42, 62, 66, 70, 74, 79, 88, 93, 174, 179, 198–99n144, 231
Volksgemeinschaft, 78, 182
Volkszugehörigkeit (*Volkszughörige*), 179–81, 184–86, 189, 198n144

Von Rezzori, Gregor, 6, 8, 164–66, 174, 194n49, 194n61, 202, 213–14, 231, 249, 259, 260n5–6

Waffen–SS. *See* SS.
Wagner, Rudolf, 67, 75, 77, 83–85, 89, 91–92, 97–98n24, 103n121, 104nn131–32, 105n143 106n176, 173–74, 187, 193n16, 196n100, 219, 221, 228, 242n121, 242n123, 243n143
Wallachia, 48
Weczerka, Hugo, 86, 105n137, 105n142
Weinstein, Elias, 126, 129–30, 133–34, 137, 141, 151n182, 188, 237n29
Weisselberger, Salo, 51n25
Weissglas, Immanuel, 174, 209, 214, 237n30
Weizmann, Chaim, 125

Western zones, 62, 75
Winkler, Manfred, 215–16, 240n87
Wittstock, Erwin, 210
World Jewish Congress, 115–17
Wischnitz (Wizhnitz, Vyzhnytsia), 52n45

Yad Vashem, 19, 139–40
Yiddish, (Yiddishland, *Yiddishkeit*), 5, 36–37, 48, 116, 136–7, 182–84, 206, 226
Yishuv, 9, 119, 122–26, 133, 143, 250
Yugoslavia, 66, 121, 179
Zelgin, Max, 67
Zillich, Heinrich, 207
Zionism, 36–37, 110, 119, 122–26, 130, 132, 142–43, 172, 184, 187, 189, 206, 217
Zionist Jewish Party, 42
Zipser, 52n49

www.ingramcontent.com/pod-product-compliance
Lightning Source LLC
Chambersburg PA
CBHW071150070526
44584CB00019B/2740